Rebellious Nuns

Rebellious Nuns

The Troubled History of a Mexican Convent,
1752–1863

MARGARET CHOWNING

OXFORD

UNIVERSITY PRESS

2006

Oxford University Press, Inc., publishes works that further
Oxford University's objective of excellence
in research, scholarship, and education.

Oxford New York
Auckland   Cape Town   Dar es Salaam   Hong Kong   Karachi
Kuala Lumpur   Madrid   Melbourne   Mexico City   Nairobi
New Delhi   Shanghai   Taipei   Toronto

With offices in
Argentina   Austria   Brazil   Chile   Czech Republic   France   Greece
Guatemala   Hungary   Italy   Japan   Poland   Portugal   Singapore
South Korea   Switzerland   Thailand   Turkey   Ukraine   Vietnam

Copyright © 2006 by Oxford University Press, Inc.

Published by Oxford University Press, Inc.
198 Madison Avenue, New York, New York 10016

www.oup.com

Library of Congress Cataloging-in-Publication Data

Chowning, Margaret.
  Rebellious nuns : the troubled history of a Mexican convent, 1752–1863 / Margaret Chowning.
    p.   cm.
  Includes bibliographical references and index.
  ISBN-13 978-0-19-518221-7
  ISBN 0-19-518221-9
    1. Purísima Concepción (Convent : San Miguel el Grande, Guanajuato,
  Mexico)—History.   2. Convents—Mexico—Guanajuato—History.   I. Title.

BX4220.M4C46   2005
271'.97—dc22   2005040660

9 8 7 6 5 4 3 2 1
Printed in the United States of America
on acid-free paper

To Irv, Polly, and Sarah

Acknowledgments

First, many thanks to Sister María Lilia of the present-day community of the Order of the Immaculate Conception of San Miguel, whose story gave this book a much better ending than I could have hoped for. Sister María of the San José monastery of Conceptionists in Guadalajara, Spain, has also shown a keen interest in this book and helped out with technical questions about the order.

In Morelia, the staff of the archepiscopal archive has been warm and welcoming for many years, but was especially helpful on this book. Emelia Hernández Ramos, Sergio Monjaráz Martínez, and Hugo Sandino Bautista were always friendly and are now friends. Pat and Ben Warren have also been wonderful friends and hosts over many summers in Morelia.

Guillermo G. Engelbrecht of the Instituto Allende, housed in the summer home of María Josepha Lina de la Canal's family, went out of his way to photograph a lovely portrait of her that hangs in the chapel. Also in San Miguel, Helene Kahn made a valiant effort to track down artwork.

Andrew Paxman and Karen Melvin did legwork in Mexico City for me and willingly added my pile of photocopied documents to their own heavy paper burdens when they returned from field research. Karen also served as a research assistant in Morelia, culling the Santa Catarina documents for statistics on entrances and professions to that convent, and while the work that Nicole Von Germeten did during her research assistantship will mainly be used in another book, in a general way, it helped give shape to this one. Special thanks to Jessica Delgado, without whom this book would have had a blank space for a cover.

A number of colleagues, students, relatives, and friends have read all or part of the manuscript and have helped me to write a book that we all agreed should be accessible to general readers, but also adhere to high standards of scholarship—not always an easy balance to strike. William Taylor and Tom Brady read the manuscript twice, with their customary care and insight. Tulio Halperin-Donghi, Gene Brucker, and Randy Starn were also among the first to give me feedback on how to proceed, once the basic outlines of the narrative were in place. Stephanie Ballenger and Kristin Huffine made a number of suggestions for reading and revision on the section in Chapter 3 on the "mal," the strange affliction from which the nuns in Phelipa's faction suffered. Cynthia Read, my Oxford editor, helped me see ways to make the story of the mal, and other parts of the book as well, more compelling. Brian Connaughton's generous and close reading improved the manuscript and reinvigorated my enthusiasm for my original project on women, the church, and politics. At a later stage, Mark Healey, Yuri Slezkine, and Peggy Anderson offered suggestions, insights, and encouragement. My "lay readers" were my mother, Pat Chowning, who also helped tabulate some of the figures from the Santa Catarina convent, and Sue Kern, my college roommate and a better history major than I was. Martha Barber has always protected my best interests, and did so in the context of this book as well. Now that Sarah and Polly are in college and wading through many more books each week than they ever did in high school, they have been transformed into advocates for readability and brevity.

Most of all, though, my husband, Irv Scheiner, has been adviser, critic, and cheerleader from the very beginning. When I started coming back each evening from the archive with stories of what the rebellious nuns did "today," it was he, speaking as a fellow historian caught up in the excitement of the archival chase, who first said that I had a book (one that I hadn't intended to write). His good nature prevailed through spending our honeymoon in San Miguel, a town whose hills and cobblestones and narrow sidewalks give his knees fits, so that I could tie up a few "last" loose ends, and he kept his mouth mainly shut when I announced that I needed another trip back in the summer of 2004, to tie up the last of the last of the loose ends. Many thanks and much love.

Contents

Rebellious Nuns

Introduction

This book came about accidentally. In 1999, in the early stages of researching a project on women, the church, and politics in eighteenth- and nineteenth-century Mexico, I stumbled upon a bundle of letters, interviews, questionnaires, and commissioned reports in the archive of the bishopric of Michoacán, all concerning what the bishop called a "rebellion" in the convent of La Purísima Concepción in San Miguel el Grande, today San Miguel de Allende. The documents were misfiled with material from another convent also called "La Purísima Concepción," a Capuchin convent in Salvatierra.[1] It is not difficult to see how the filing error was made, but it meant that the unusually rich records on the San Miguel convent filed properly under "Concepcionistas" could not easily be married to the extraordinary documentation on the rebellion in the convent, mistakenly filed under "Capuchinas." It quickly became clear to me that this marriage should take place, and I put my original book on the back burner to focus on this one.

Although the long period of the rebellion (1759–1772), with its dramatic intensity and its remarkable cast of characters, is the centerpiece of the story, I have chosen to construct the book as a narrative of La Purísima's history during the whole period of its existence, from the decision in 1752 to found the convent to the forced eviction of the nuns in 1863. This organizational strategy was dictated in part by the abundance and importance of the material on the period after the rebellion—a body of documents that yielded its own vivid glimpses of convent life, story lines, and memorable characters—but mainly by my growing realization that what happened to the convent in the years after the rebellion quieted, not just in its immediate aftermath, but even decades later, remained connected to the crises of the 1760s and early 1770s. The rebellion, in other words, was of continuing relevance in the lives of the nuns of La Purísima. It shaped, or more precisely, it warped the entire experience of the convent, and it is fair to say that La Purísima never really recovered from it, right up to the moment that federal troops occupied the convent during the mid-nineteenth-century liberal reforms and turned the nuns out into the street.

What was the rebellion about? It began when some reform-minded nuns tried to impose a particularly strenuous regimen of prayer and a particularly demanding lifestyle on the others. These advocates of "strict observance" idealized a convent in which the nuns would live in full community (*vida común*), praying, cooking, eating, sleeping, recovering from illness, and working together—not, as was the rule among Mexican convents, leading essentially separate lives in convents that were more a collection of private households than a shared spiritual and social endeavor. They also wished to see the new convent adhere to a high standard of austerity, in rigorous interpretation of the vows of poverty and enclosure; this meant that at La Purísima there would be no personal servants (again, unlike most convents), and only a small number of community servants.

The "rebellious" nuns (*sublevadas*)—or, in another adjective deployed by the frustrated bishop, the "ungovernable" nuns (*díscolas*)—appear to have embraced these ideals in the glow of zealous enthusiasm that accompanied the foundation of the convent, but soon rejected them as too harsh and, in fact, antithetical to the spiritual goals of the convent. How could they serve God and their spouse Jesus Christ when they were hungry, exhausted, forced to do much of the work of servants, and deprived of the society of their family and friends? As one of them later put it, quoting St. Teresa, "where there is not abundance, there is not observance."[2] At least until the convent grew and there was a larger population of nuns to carry out necessary chores, they argued, it was crucial to tolerate a certain relaxation of the monastic Rule, to allow nuns to have personal servants, and to dispense with some of the more onerous aspects of the vida común. The rebellion began when these dissidents challenged the stubborn first abbess and then her successor, managing to force both of their resignations. Six years later, it evolved into a direct challenge by the rebellious nuns, now ensconced in leadership positions within the convent, to the bishop.

Many people, even many historians, have reacted to my short synopsis of the book with shock ("Rebellious nuns?"), but as anyone who has studied convents will attest, the battles fought, the issues debated, and the relationships tested in this convent were, in fact, commonplace. Periodic attempts on the part of authorities (both within and outside the convent) to impose greater austerity and discipline on nuns and resistance (sometimes very vigorous) to those attempts are almost certainly the rule rather than the exception, not just in New Spain, but in Europe and the rest of Latin America as well, and not just in the eighteenth and nineteenth centuries, but for centuries before. Internal dissension over what constituted proper observance of one's vows and prickly relationships between the convent and the bishop are, then, themes familiar to historians of female (and, for that matter, male) religious.

But it is rarely possible to develop such themes with much subtlety, since what went on behind the walls of convents was meant by the church to be mysterious. Especially great care was taken to prevent the "scandal" of factionalism in the nunneries from being widely broadcast. We know that other nuns in other convents rebelled against authority, but often we don't know how, or even why, to any satisfying degree; we don't get a well-rounded sense of the actors involved; we can't really fathom what was at stake for the nuns who resisted and for those who upheld the principles of reform. The documentation on this convent, however, gives us a rare view of the internal world of the convent and its interactions with church authorities, not just during the 12-year period of rebellion, but well beyond.[3] We have not only the voices, but also the personalities of the nuns and other actors, making it possible for us to empathize with all of them, to recognize the fragility of discipline and harmony in such a small community, and to understand the spiritual agonies that resulted when rhetoric about the convent as a garden of sublimely selfless virgins (which was certainly internalized by the nuns themselves) did not match reality—in short, to appreciate the complicated dynamics of having committed one's life not only to God, but also to one's community.

Besides allowing us to shine a light on the relatively common phenomenon of convent rebellion, the history of La Purísima contributes to several other areas of scholarly interest. A second major theme is the changing relationship between the convent and the larger world of the church, another subject that the surviving documentation rarely allows the historian to treat with much subtlety. Battles over the nature of the convent took place, first and foremost, among the nuns, whose experiences with and efforts to support or undermine reform drive the story, but the male ecclesiastical establishment was an ever-present factor in the outcome of these struggles. In the history of this convent, two figures were especially important: the convent's vicar, usually the parish priest of San Miguel, who did double duty as the liaison between the convent and the bishop, and the bishop himself, based in the diocesan capital of Valladolid (today Morelia), over 100 miles distant. The sometimes awkward "in-betweenness" of the vicar's position made for a complicated relationship between the vicar and the nuns and also between the vicar and the bishop. Some vicars were very much advocates and protectors of the nuns, while others saw themselves more as the bishop's local instrument of authority; some sided with the reformers among the nuns, while others (including the hapless vicar who served during the rebellion) saw reformism as a threat to peace in a community whose gender made it inherently combustible.

Equally complicated over the whole history of the convent was the relationship between the bishop and the nuns. During the periods of rebellion in the 1760s and early 1770s, the bishop was Pedro Anselmo Sánchez de Tagle, one of the great eighteenth-century prelates of New Spain. Sánchez de Tagle spent a great deal of time and energy dealing with the rebellion at La Purísima, supporting the reform-minded abbesses, maneuvering to depose the leader of the rebellion after she was elected to office in 1769, and writing long letters to all parties in an attempt to impose his will on the convent. The nuns on both sides of the rebellion deferred to him, of course, but they also tried to manipulate him, just as he was trying to manipulate them. In general, the nuns agreed with each other on the need to protect the right of the convent to govern itself, even when they disagreed on everything else, but at the same time, they tried to enlist the bishop for their own purposes and looked to him for solutions.

After the rebellion ended in 1772, the relationship between the bishops and the convent underwent a radical change, as both the bishops and the abbesses became less confrontational, more willing to compromise, and more mutually consultative. They cooperated in order to dilute the (excessive?) idealism and soften the hard-nosed government of their predecessors (both previous abbesses and previous bishops), and by so doing, to calm the passions aroused by the rebellion and prevent another crisis from erupting. After the wars for Mexican independence began in 1810, however, relations between the diocesan authorities and the convent entered yet a third phase, in which—to put it bluntly—the bishop's office seemed only tangentially interested in the female convents, including La Purísima, except insofar as their financial resources helped the church meet the demands put to it by the impoverished national government. This unresponsive attitude, which was frustrating to both the nuns and their increasingly protective vicars, led to ill-thought-out episcopal policies and actions that played a role in further undermining La Purísima.

The relationship between the convents and the larger ecclesiastical structures of authority is closely related to a third theme that this study allows us to explore: the changing intellectual and political life of the eighteenth and nineteenth centuries in Mexico. La Purísima's establishment in the mid-eighteenth century was not a random event, and its lack of success had much to do with the timing of its foundation. The convent was conceived and funded locally, but it was authorized by church and state officials in Valladolid, Mexico City, and Madrid, who wished to make a statement: From now on, they indicated with their approval of this reformed convent and others like it, Mexican convents would stand in answer to eighteenth-century "enlightened" critics, who called the monastic life decadent, wasteful, corrupt, ostentatious, and untrue to the precepts of "true" Christianity. This kind of convent would signal that the church was capable of reforming and renovating itself in accordance with the "enlightened" values of the "modern" world: simplicity, dignity, equality, and lack of pretense. In fact, after 1747, virtually the only new foundations of female convents that were authorized in Mexico were those that conformed to reformist principles (like La Purísima and a number of new Carmelite and Capuchin convents). La Purísima thus embodied the high hopes of local benefactors, but it also embodied the (different) high hopes of Catholic reformers and state reformers.

These expectations complicated the difficulties inherent in establishing a new convent. As a convent of Conceptionists, which was not an order with a reputation in Mexico for austerity or dedication to the vida común, La Purísima was assigned a particularly difficult role by the reformers. Girls and women contemplating entrance into Carmelite or Capuchin convents knew what to expect, but a reformed Conceptionist convent was an anomaly (as the first abbess indicated when she remembered the great joy and surprise she felt when it was determined that "there should be in this Kingdom a [strict observance convent] of the Purísima Concepción").[4] Understandably, entrants to La Purísima might be confused about what kind of lifestyle they could expect to lead—and they might be deeply unhappy under a system they had not anticipated. Thus, the particular intellectual climate of the mid-eighteenth century led Catholic and Bourbon reformers to favor an experiment in which a reformed convent would be founded with nuns from a notoriously unreformed order, the Conceptionists. This factor, I argue, played a role in the dissatisfaction of the younger nuns that led to the rebellion.

But the intellectual climate that was conducive to the creation of a reformed Conceptionist convent (and, indeed, in the late 1760s, favored extending the vida común to all Mexican convents) did not last long.[5] While within the convent, the reformist impulse remained strong after the rebellion faded— that is, many nuns continued to vigorously advocate the ideals of austerity and community as the truest path to Christian perfection—the commitment of church officials to those ideals waned with changing intellectual trends. By the 1780s, officials had begun to imbibe other ideas current in eighteenth-century Europe (rationalism, individualism, attention to the financial bottom line, competition as a positive good) which led to a decrease in their support for expensive, high-maintenance, community-oriented convents like La Purísima. In fact, in 1792, Bishop Fray Antonio de San Miguel and his right-hand man, Manuel Abad y Queipo, ordered the abolition of the vida común and its replacement with a system of individual monetary allowances, a highly controversial edict that was motivated, at least in part, I argue, by Abad's admiration for the individualism and market orientation of Adam Smith and other liberal thinkers and by his desire to rationalize not only convent finances, but also the financial practices of the bishopric in general.

The liberal ideas that influenced the abolition of the vida común remained below the surface at that time, but after Mexican independence, they came quickly to define the arena of political debate. Pamela Voekel has recently reminded us that we should not assume that liberals were antireligious or even necessarily anticlerical, but regarding one aspect of Mexican Catholicism—the male and female monasteries—they seem to have been unambiguously negative.[6] Discussions in the press, even before Mexican independence, swirled around the issues of the role of the monastic orders in society and the desirability of allowing, or forcing, friars to become secular priests and of permitting nuns to leave the convent if they chose.[7] The lack of free will (for male religious to leave the monastery and for nuns either to leave the convent or to avoid being sent there in the first place) was a central theme. Convents were antithetical to individualism and personal liberty, and for many Mexican liberals, nuns (and male religious) came to epitomize the ways that Catholicism stifled thought and freedom of action.

A fourth, related theme is the changing relationship between women and the church, as thinking about the Catholic feminine ideal and the role women should play in defending the faith shifted over time. La Purísima was founded in a last rush of full-throated enthusiasm for the cloistered nun as a model for women in general. Obedience, modesty, chastity, humility, passivity—these were characteristics that were seen as desirable in all women, and it was thought that they were modeled especially well in reformed convents like La Purísima. But even as the church hierarchy and the Bourbon state embraced the reformed convent after midcentury, they also indicated their approval of another new kind of convent: one dedicated primarily to teaching. (Most Mexican convents, including La Purísima, had a small teaching function, but it was ancillary to the convents' central function as a place of prayer and contemplation.) In 1753, just a year before La Purísima's foundation was approved, church and state officials invited the French Company of Mary, a teaching order, to establish a convent in Mexico City, and before the end of the colonial period, there were three such convents in New Spain. If the reformed convent met eighteenth-century criticisms of decadence, excessive luxury, and worldliness in the traditional convent, the teaching convent met the criticism of the convents as parasitical and socially useless. Support for both types of convent, then, was a product of the times.

But the two convent models carried very different implications for the church's relationship to women. The introduction of a teaching order into New Spain foreshadowed a new direction in the church's thinking about ideal Catholic womanhood, and slowly, over time, enshrinement of the passive, cloistered nun evolved into an embrace of the active, socially responsible nun, who operated in the world alongside the active laywoman, the Christian woman and mother, loyal to the church and vigilant in the defense of the faith. Teaching orders were joined, later in the nineteenth century, by charitable and nursing orders, and even before that, the church had begun first to tolerate and then to promote lay organizations of women that offered a channel for spiritual energies and socially useful activities to a much broader audience than that of the exclusive, cloistered, elite convent. In the wake of this fundamental change in the church's attitude toward women, and in light of the strapped financial situation of the church after independence, expensive-to-maintain convents like La Purísima became an anachronism, even within the thinking of the most conservative church intellectuals, and support for them wavered between non-existent and grudging.

Finally, this study allows us to explore the role of the convent in the urban world of the eighteenth and nineteenth centuries. We see the town of San Miguel el Grande—where today, tourists crowd the charming colonial streets and North American expatriates take art classes in the convent's common rooms—in a different light because of what we know about this convent. The aristocrats of San Miguel, whose well-preserved mansions contribute so much to the town's visual delights, enjoyed a self-image in the mid-1700s as leaders of an up-and-coming city, and why not? The town's proximity to the magnificent silver mines of northern New Spain had been exploited adroitly by these native-born entrepreneurs, who had invested in ranching and textiles to supply the mines and were thriving as a result. Such a town, they thought, deserved a female convent: A convent would be an architectural ornament to the town center; serve the daughters of the elite; lend its endowment to local property owners and thus operate as a kind of bank, whose funds could be used to maintain residential property and preserve and enhance the aspect of the town; symbolize the piety that was a major part of the town's identity; and put San Miguel in the same category as nearby, rival Querétaro and the diocesan capitals of Puebla, Oaxaca, Valladolid, and Guadalajara—provincial towns important enough to support large female convents. Furthermore, a convent would surely have been imagined by these town notables as standing in serene counterpoint to the grubby, dreary, amoral, contentious world of the textile factories, where many of them had made or invested their fortunes. The nuns—whom lengthy background checks had certified to be chaste and racially pure—would balance out, temper, and (perhaps most important) educate by example the heavily mulatto and mestizo population of exploited and, in the minds of the town's leaders, potentially dangerous factory and shop workers. San Miguel, then, had high hopes for the new convent and much invested—financially and otherwise—in its success.

But while the town enthusiastically embraced the *idea* of the convent, it failed to embrace it in actuality. When La Purísima faltered soon after its foundation (and the rebellion in the convent was surely well known outside its walls, despite the best efforts of the bishop and vicar to keep it secret), the town's elite turned on it in subtle ways. The anticipated flow of wealthy local girls into the convent, perhaps exaggerated under the best of circumstances (San Miguel was prosperous, but underpopulated compared with the other towns with large female convents), never materialized. With sluggish recruitment among the town's wealthiest citizens and, thus, sluggish growth of the endowment came financial problems, which, in turn, prevented La Purísima from anchoring the local credit system as boosters of the convent had expected it to do. Furthermore, the fact that La Purísima did not live up to high ideals of pacificity and community must, in some ways, have been interpreted as a betrayal of its intended social role as a model of stability and probably caused some embarrassment to those who had seen it as a symbol of piety and a source of civic pride. In retrospect, San Miguel was probably too small, its upper crust too thin, and the textile economy on which much of its wealth was based too fragile, too inelastic, and too vulnerable to outside competition to allow a grand convent like the one that was planned by its foundress and its benefactors to flourish. Everything would have had to go just right for this convent to thrive—there was no margin for error—and the rebellion ensured that this would not be the case. Thus, the convent failed the town, and the town failed the convent; if the timing of the foundation had much to do with its struggles, so, too, did the place.

The book takes up five themes of general scholarly interest, then: in telling the history of one convent, it sheds light on the relationship between female convents and the male ecclesiastical establishment, the impact of the worlds of ideas and politics on the female convent and on the church's policies toward the convent, the attitude of the church toward women, the interaction between the convent and the urban world, and of course, the ways that all of these changing influences and relationships affected the almost timeless tension within the convent between reform and relaxation.

By conceptualizing the history of La Purísima as bound up with the history of Mexico during this period, I have tried to avoid the trap of thinking about this convent as somehow having less to tell us about Mexican society or Mexican politics than the much more studied seventeenth- and early eighteenth-century convents, simply because it was neither as large nor as successful as the great, earlier foundations. But there is no question that the historiography on the convent in Latin America has been shaped, in large part, by an interest in the triumphant convent of the mature colonial period. Historians have underscored the deep social, economic, and spiritual relevance of the large convents during this period. Economic historians have pored through convent account books and gleaned important insights on colonial credit practices, urban property holding, and the tight relationship between the convent and the economic life of the colony, concluding that the convents were powerful players in credit and real estate markets. Social historians have opened up windows into the study of women and the family by utilizing the richly detailed records on entrances and professions into the large convents, pointing out the central importance of the convent as part of elite inheritance strategies, and demonstrating the ways that these wealthy convents insinuated themselves into the daily life of the colony through their sponsorship of processions and other religious functions, not to mention the ways that the baroque religiosity with which they were associated during this period provided a way for the colonial elite to celebrate and advertise their own wealth and position. Feminist and literary scholars have rediscovered Sor Juana Inés de la Cruz and other "writing nuns," who were especially prolific during the seventeenth and early eighteenth centuries, gleaning from their writings and the contexts in which they wrote important insights about the nature of female religiosity and spirituality among the larger population.

By contrast, although after the middle of the eighteenth century, new convents continued to be founded and women continued to enter these institutions, as well as the older religious communities, there were no new female monasteries that equaled in size, grandeur, and influence the great sixteenth- and seventeenth-century establishments (although it is clear that the backers of the San Miguel convent had hoped that La Purísima would be such an institution). As almost exclusively "reformed" institutions, the new foundations tended to be smaller, simpler, less economically powerful, and more isolated from the larger society than the older convents. Thus, in a sense, it is true that they were more marginal to the surrounding societies than the older convents, but while this may have caused historians to see them as less interesting, I hope to show that the foundational circumstances and fate of the kind of convent that was founded in the eighteenth century is at least as revealing of its time and place as historians have shown the great late sixteenth- and seventeenth-century convents to be of theirs.[8]

Another historiographical trap that I have tried to avoid is thinking about the convent as either a paradise or a hell for women, even though the presence of rebellious nuns at the center of my story may make it seem as if I have opted for the latter interpretation. Those who write about convents, with notable exceptions, have tended to align around either a kind of "pro-convent" or "anti-convent" axis. This is most easily seen, of course, in the large body of nonscholarly literature that has been generated about convents, much of which is quite polemical. The "pro-convent" school of popular writing tends to romanticize the convent, sanctify individual nuns, and downplay conflict within the community, almost as a matter of faith, and certainly as a matter of edification. Much of it is written by priests, nuns, or lay Catholics who are not trained historians. By contrast, the antagonistic school—for example, the nineteenth-century writers of the "María Monk" variety or Aldous Huxley's 1952 *The Devils at Loudon* (on which Ken Russell's scathing 1971 movie, *The Devils*, was based)—revels in conflict and dysfunctionality within the convent and tends to play it up.

For Spanish America, with a few exceptions (including Josefina Muriel's 1946 classic *Conventos de monjas*, which is still the single best overview and comparison of colonial convents), these varieties of nonscholarly or quasi-scholarly writing on the convent dominated until the late 1960s.[9] Beginning around that time, however, scholars began to pay serious attention to nuns and convents, led by historian Asunción Lavrin, whose many wide-ranging articles on Mexican convents have explored not only the religious aspirations and spirituality of the nuns, but also the social and economic roles of the convent.[10] Since then, there has been an explosion of academic interest in female religious and female convents.

Interestingly, despite its far greater theoretical sophistication and its rigorous scholarly apparatus, much of this newer writing on convents can be fit into roughly similar dichotomous categories as the nonscholarly literature (though it lacks that literature's polemical tone and freely borrows from, indeed, often depends—for background or context—on the work of scholars with different approaches).[11] For example, a variation on the essentially nonconflictual view of the convent is the depiction by many feminist scholars of the convent as a place where women could create fulfilling and productive communities with a minimum of male intervention and patriarchal influences, where girls (for the Hispanic world, most famously, Sor Juana Inés de la Cruz) with intellectual ambitions could avoid marriage to pursue scholarly or creative endeavors, and where all women were relatively free to express a distinctively feminine spirituality. In this literature, as in the popular proclerical literature, dissension among nuns tends to be downplayed, while gendered conflict between nuns and male authorities is given ample scope as scholars work to uncover the processes by which patriarchy and misogyny operated within the church. These authors do not ignore the existence of conflict within the convent community, but their emphasis is either on the potential for creating a female world independent of men, or alternatively, on the ways that conflict in the convent provided a context for the production of "spiritual autobiographies"— life narratives written by nuns at the insistence of their confessors—and other writing by nuns.[12] Typical is the following remark in Kathryn McKnight's fine work on Madre Castillo and her convent of Santa Clara, in Tunja, present-day Colombia: "This great mix of people, intentions, and activities inevitably led to conflicts and to a collective life less observant of the constitutions and rules of the order than some nuns and male clerics desired; but in the process, Santa Clara was home to a group of admirably strong women struggling to determine and guide their own lives."[13] McKnight expresses anxiety at having "hung out the historical laundry" of the convent by having acknowledged and detailed internal conflict, and she defends her treatment of the day-to-day realities of convent life as necessary in order to appreciate Madre Castillo's struggles as a female writer.[14]

Just as there is a scholarly counterpart to the nonconflictual convent model in the popular literature, there is also a counterpart to the convent-in-conflict model. Elaborated primarily by historians working with mundane texts, such as documents of profession and account books that were generated systematically over time in the convent (as opposed to the spiritual autobiographies upon which literary scholars have mainly relied), these writers have empha-

sized the social and economic functions of the convent. They point out, for
example, how it served the community as a lending institution, how it played
a prominent role in the inheritance strategies of wealthy families, or how the
phenomenon of the "involuntary nun" worked as a model for social control of
other women: beggars, women who had committed crimes, abused women,
immoral women.[15] In this historiography, convents (in many of which the nuns
themselves were the minority and servants and other laywomen the majority,
a point this literature tends to emphasize) are seen not only as an integral part
of the larger society, but also as a reflection of the "real world," complete with
status hierarchies, class and ethnic differences, and pettiness and obsession
with material concerns—in other words, places rife with conflict and potential
for conflict. Examples of this sort of writing on the convent are abundant for
Europe, but somewhat less so for Latin America, although influential works
have been produced by Susan Soeiro for Brazil; Asunción Lavrin, Rosalva Loreto López, and Kathleen Myers for Mexico; and Luis Martín and Kathryn Burns
for Peru.[16]

   In this book, I have tried to combine both approaches, a task that is made
easier by the fact that I have not only the mundane material used by most
historians, but also the extraordinary material on the rebellion.[17] I hope the
book reflects both my respect for and curiosity about the convent as a community of women, as well as my awareness of the convent as a place in which
conflict was not only unavoidable, but also natural and worthy of dissection for
what it can tell us about both the convent and the larger society. I see the
characters in this story, on both sides of the rebellion and, later, on both sides
of the vida común issue, as motivated by a sincere desire to make the convent
community work as a place of prayer and contemplation. Resistance against
extreme religiosity does not, or should not, imply antagonism toward religion,
and the rebellious nuns were, it seems to me, as pious as they were subversive.
Indeed, one of the heartbreaking facets of the rebellion was the distress that
the rebels obviously felt when they were accused of having a cavalier attitude
toward their spiritual obligations. They saw themselves as deeply committed
to prayer and life in religion; they just did not see how they could love and
honor God properly when they were so overscheduled, overworked, over-
stressed, harshly disciplined, and poorly nourished. As I argue in Chapter 3,
while it might be possible to explain the end of the rebellion in purely political
or sociological terms, a richer explanation takes into account the possibility
that the nuns chose to stop rebelling and to obey the bishop and abbess for
spiritual reasons having to do with their devotion to and desire to emulate and
honor the young woman who founded the convent, the saintly María Josepha
Lina de la Santísima Trinidad, after her untimely death.

   A word on María Josepha Lina and the other main characters in this book.
One of the bounties of the documentation is the extent to which full-bodied
personalities emerge from the raw archival material, and I hope that in the

course of translating their words into English, adding punctuation where, in the original, there was virtually none, and interrupting the narrative, from time to time, with scholarly contextualization (mainly comparisons to other convents in Mexico at the time, in order to give the reader a sense of how unusual or representative this particular convent was), I have not diminished them too much or forced them too much into the background. A common problem faced by narrative historians is that we are not always able to follow the main characters' life stories through to a satisfying conclusion. The bar for the study of nuns in New Spain has been set high because of the wonderfully dramatic life of Sor Juana Inés de la Cruz, whose words and feelings at her time of personal and spiritual crisis are relatively accessible and who died at a moment and in a fashion that a playwright could not have scripted with more pathos. Unfortunately, in this story, there are significant aspects of the lives of important characters that I have not been able to capture fully.

The biggest disappointment is the thin trail left by the foundress, María Josepha Lina, after the foundation itself. What she thought and how she reacted to the rebellion we mainly have to guess—we really have only one revealing document, her response to an episcopal interrogatory about the actions and behavior of the rebellious nuns. This is all the more frustrating because her death, in the middle of the second convent crisis, and arguably an important catalyst for the resolution of that crisis, *was* everything a cold-blooded historian interested in neat endings might ask for, in terms of its timeliness and potential significance. I am also not completely satisfied with my treatment of Phelipa de San Antonio, the enigmatic leader of the rebellious faction of nuns. Phelipa, like María Josepha Lina, did not leave us as many of her own words as we would like, and those she did leave are very difficult to interpret, so cloaked are they in pious artifice; however, she was so very much present in everyone else's words that careful inference can fill in many gaps. But unlike María Josepha Lina, she did not die at a dramatic moment. In fact, she lived 5 years beyond her departure from center stage, but the record reveals little of her postcrisis life. The best fleshed-out major personalities, in the sense that we can understand their motivations and can almost predict what they would do or say under certain circumstances, are the frustrated bishop during the rebellion, Sánchez de Tagle, and the uncompromising first abbess, María Antonia del Santísimo Sacramento, who both left us clear indications of their feelings and actions—and who both died at a dramatic moment in the narrative.

Still, even though some of the main characters leave us wanting more, I am grateful to have such complex and interesting characters to work with at all. Moreover, there are a number of minor characters whose personalities are quite vivid: María Joseph Lina's confessor, the indomitable and exuberant Luis Felipe Neri de Alfaro, whose vision of the convent came up against that of the foundress in ways that strongly contributed to the convent's failure to thrive; the fickle and weak second abbess, María Anna del Santísimo Sacramento;

Cayetana de las Llagas, an emotional and tormented ally of Phelipa; the self-centered vocalist, Josepha Ygnacia de San Luis Gonzaga (who takes center stage for a large part of Chapter 4); Juan de Villegas, the beleaguered parish priest and vicar of the convent, who found himself caught between the nuns and the bishop during the rebellion; Francisco de Uraga, another of the convent's vicars, who supported the nuns with his personal fortune after the wars for independence caused their income to shrink to a trickle, and who tried, in vain, to penetrate the church's calculated indifference toward the convent and save it from destruction; and Concepción de San Felipe Neri, a deeply unhappy nun who was the first of whom it was said (in a reflection of the church's changing attitude toward women in the nineteenth century) that she would have been better off a mother than a nun.

The archival material for this book comes primarily from the Archive of the Archbishopric of Michoacán, in Morelia, although I have also used some key documents from the Archivo General de la Nación, in Mexico City, and the Archive of the Cathedral Chapter of Michoacán, in Morelia. Most of the material on La Purísima in the archiepiscopal archive is found either with the documents on the "other" La Purísima Concepción, under "Capuchinas," or in the six large boxes of material on the Conceptionists, although there are very useful materials in the records of episcopal visitations (not only the reports on the convent itself, but also those on the town of San Miguel) and in the correspondence of the bishop and/or vicar general for convents with the religiosas, under "Correspondencia." Miscellaneous documents concerning La Purísima are also found in the boxes of materials on the Catarinas of Morelia, the Dominicas of Pátzcuaro, the Teresas of Morelia, and La Enseñanza of Irapuato (in fact, many of the documents on the entrance and profession of the San Miguel nuns are scattered throughout the boxes on other convents). More important than the fact that there is some misfiled information on La Purísima among these boxes, however, is the use I have made of the material that concerns these other convents in the bishopric, which I have developed in order to be able to evaluate the extent to which the sometimes striking events or trends at La Purísima were unique to this convent or generalized in the bishopric. The histories of Santa Catarina of Morelia and Nuestra Señora de la Salud of Pátzcuaro, the other elite convents that existed in the bishopric during the whole period of La Purísima's history, are particularly relevant.

Finally, about the tone and organization of the book: In this introduction, I have pointed out the ways that the book touches on a number of themes that are of broad interest to historians and scholars. I must warn the reader, however, that these themes are treated more explicitly in the introduction than they are in the body of the book, where I have deliberately chosen to let La Purísima's history emerge as naturally as possible. Inevitably, there are points along the way that demand contextualization, but I have tried not to let the context overwhelm the story, for with such rich material and such a strong narrative line, it seems to me that the interests of contributing to a richer understanding of large themes in Mexican or women's or church history are better served by allowing those themes to remain "embedded in the narrative" than by continually calling attention to them.[18]

Having said this, the first part of the book, which directly concerns the rebellion, is more narrative in tone and structure than the second part, which carries the convent's history forward in a loosely narrative fashion, but adopts a somewhat more traditionally academic, even (occasionally) social scientific mode of writing and analysis. Part I attempts to describe and analyze the rebellion as an unfolding drama, with Chapter 1 introducing the main characters, the town of San Miguel, and the details of the foundation of the convent; Chapter 2 devoted to the first convent crisis, 1759 to 1763; and Chapter 3 devoted to the second crisis, 1769 to 1772. Part II steps back from this very close look at the convent during its long decade of turmoil and focuses on analyzing the continuing repercussions of the rebellion from a somewhat more distant perch. There are interesting characters and plenty of enlivening detail about daily life in Part II, but there is also a different kind of analytical rigor, with more statistics and even some tables, and there is a greater emphasis on telling anecdotes than on sustained narrative. Chapter 4 analyzes the strategies used by both bishops and abbesses to preserve the reformed nature of the convent, but at the same time, avoid further turmoil. Chapter 5 concerns the ways those efforts were undermined not only by the lingering effects of the rebellion, but also by a financial crisis (itself connected to the rebellion) and the shattering abolition of the vida común in 1792. Chapter 6 deals with the institutional crisis brought on after independence by a one-two punch of state hostility and episcopal indifference toward convents. Finally, an epilogue sketches the post-1863 history of the convents in the bishopric, including La Purísima, and brings the story of a troubled convent to a surprising conclusion.

NOTES

1. The bundle can be found in AHAM, Diocesano, Gobierno, Religiosas, Capuchinas, caja 209 (XVIII), exp. 23. Quite a lot of additional material on the convent, including many documents of entrance and profession and most of the documents on the foundation of the convent, is also misfiled under Capuchinas, in boxes 208, 210, and 211.

2. Abbess María Augustina de la Santísima Encarnación to Vicar Ignacio Antonio Palacios, 1787, AHAM, Diocesano, Gobierno, Religiosas, Concepcionistas, caja 255 (XVIII), exp. 32.

3. It is the presence in the documentation of letters and testimonies written by the nuns themselves that distinguishes the account of rebellion in this book from the detailed accounts of convent rebellion in Luis Martín, *Daughters of the Conquistadores: Women of the Viceroyalty of Peru* (Albuquerque: University of New Mexico Press,

1983), chapter 9; and Asunción Lavrin, "Ecclesiastical Reform of Nunneries in New Spain in the Eighteenth Century," *The Americas* 22:2 (October, 1965).

4. Abbess María Antonia Theresa del Santísimo Sacramento to Bishop Pedro Anselmo Sánchez de Tagle, 31 July 1761, AHAM, Diocesano, Gobierno, Religiosas, Capuchinas, caja 209 (XVIII), exp. 23.

5. The colony-wide "vida común reforms" of the early 1770s are discussed briefly in Chapter 4.

6. Pamela Voekel, *Alone Before God: The Religious Origins of Modernity in Mexico* (Durham, N.C.: Duke University Press, 2003).

7. See the 3-year run of *El Pensador Mexicano*, edited by José Joaquín Fernández de Lizardi, from 1812 to 1815.

8. Naturally, there are exceptions to the rule: See many of the articles by Asunción Lavrin (for Lavrin's body of work, see note 10); Rosalva Loreto López, *Los conventos femeninos y el mundo urbano de la Puebla de los Angeles del siglo XVIII* (Mexico City: Colegio de México, 2000; Kathryn Burns, *Colonial Habits: Convents and the Spiritual Economy of Cuzco, Peru* (Durham, N.C.: Duke University Press, 1999); Ann Miriam Gallagher, "The Family Background of the Nuns of Two Monasterios in Colonial Mexico: Santa Clara, Querétaro; and Corpus Christi, Mexico City (1724–1822)" (Ph.D. diss., The Catholic University of America, 1972); Diana Romero Swain, "One Thousand Sisters: Religious Sensibility and Motivation in a Spanish American Convent, Santa María de Gracia, 1588–1863" (Ph.D. diss., University of California, San Diego, 1993). There is also a surprisingly slender historiography on the sixteenth-century convent in Mexico, though it is true that most foundations came so late in the sixteenth century that their focus is almost inevitably more seventeenth century. An excellent recent survey and analysis of sixteenth-century Mexico City convents is Jacqueline Heller, *Escogidas Plantas: Nuns and Beatas in Mexico City, 1531–1601* (Columbia University Press, electronic book, 2002).

9. Josefina Muriel, *Conventos de monjas en la Nueva España* (Mexico City: Editorial Santiago, 1946). Muriel's work is deeply archival, but at the same time it is so strongly sympathetic to the convent that it is almost polemical at the same time that it is scholarly.

10. Lavrin, "Ecclesiastical Reform," Asunción Lavrin, "The Role of the Nunneries in the Economy of New Spain," *Hispanic American Historical Review* 46:4 (November, 1966); Asunción Lavrin, "Problems and Policies in the Administration of Nunneries in Mexico, 1800–1835," *The Americas* 28:1 (1971); Asunción Lavrin, "Mexican Nunneries from 1835 to 1860: Their Administrative Policies and Relations with the State," *The Americas* 28:3 (1972); Asunción Lavrin, "Values and Meaning of Monastic Life for Nuns in Colonial Mexico," *Catholic Historical Review* 58:3 (October, 1972); Asunción Lavrin, "Women in Convents: Their Economic and Social Role in Mexico," in *Liberating Women's History*, ed. Bernice A. Carroll (Urbana, Ill.: University of Illinois Press, 1976); Asunción Lavrin, "Unlike Sor Juana? The Model Nun in the Religious Literature of Colonial Mexico," *University of Dayton Review* 16:2 (Spring, 1983); Asunción Lavrin, "El capital eclesiástico y las élites sociales en Nueva España a fines del siglo XVIII," *Mexican Studies/Estudios mexicanos* 1 (Winter, 1985); Asunción Lavrin, "La vida femenina como experiencia religiosa: Biografía y hagiografía en Hispanoamérica colonial," *Colonial Latin American Review* 2:1–2 (1993); Asunción Lavrin, "Espirituali-

dad en el claustro novohispano del siglo XVII," *Colonial Latin American Review* 4:2 (1995); Asunción Lavrin, "De su puño y letra: Epístolas conventuales," in *El monacato femenino en el imperio español: Monasterios, beaterios, recogimientos y colegios. Homenaje a Josefina Muriel,* ed. Manuel Ramos Medina (Mexico City: Condumex, 1995).

11. Much recent nonscholarly writing on the convent has also lost its polemical qualities. I have greatly profited, for example, by the nuanced treatments of convent life in two recent novels: Ron Hansen, *Mariette in Ecstasy* (New York: Edward Burlingame Books, 1991) and Mark Salzman, *Lying Awake* (New York: Knopf, 2000).

12. See, for example, Jean Franco, *Plotting Women: Gender and Representation in Mexico* (New York: Columbia University Press, 1989), chapter 1; Electa Arenal and Stacy Schlau, *Untold Sisters: Hispanic Nuns in their Own Words* (Albuquerque, N.M.: University of New Mexico Press, 1989); Kathryn Joy McKnight, *The Mystic of Tunja: The Writings of Madre Castillo, 1671–1742* (Amherst, Mass.: University of Massachusetts Press, 1997); Kristine Ibsen, *Women's Spiritual Autobiography in Colonial Spanish America* (Gainesville, Fla.: University Press of Florida, 1999); Elisa Sampson Vera Tudela, *Colonial Angels: Narratives of Gender and Spirituality in Mexico, 1580–1750* (Austin, Tex.: University of Texas Press, 2000); Kathleen Ann Myers, *Neither Saints Nor Sinners: Writing the Lives of Women in Spanish America* (New York: Oxford University Press, 2003).

13. McKnight, 100.

14. McKnight, 101.

15. Jutta Gisela Sperling, *Convents and the Body Politic in Late Renaissance Venice* (Chicago: University of Chicago Press, 1999), 4.

16. Susan Soeiro, "The Social and Economic Role of the Convent: Women and Nuns in Colonial Bahia, 1677–1800," *Hispanic American Historical Review* 54:2 (May, 1974); Lavrin, "Role of the Nunneries," "Women in Convents," "Problems and Policies," and "El capital eclesiástico"; Loreto López, *Los conventos*; Martín; Burns; Kathleen A. Myers, "A Glimpse of Family Life in Colonial Mexico: A Nun's Account," *Latin American Research Review* 28:2 (1993); Octavio Paz, *Sor Juana Inés de la Cruz, or The Traps of Faith* (Cambridge, Mass.: Harvard University Press, 1988); Fernando Benítez, *Los demonios en el convento: Sexo y religión en la Nueva España* (Mexico City: Editorial Era, 1985); *Místicas y descalzas: Fundaciones femeninas carmelitas en la Nueva España,* Manuel Ramos Medina, (Mexico City: Condumex, 1997). For Europe, see, for example, Sperling; Mary Laven, *Virgins of Venice: Enclosed Lives and Broken Vows in the Renaissance Convent* (London: Viking, 2002); P. Renée Baernstein, *A Convent Tale: A Century of Sisterhood in Spanish Milan* (New York, London: Routledge, 2002).

17. Two other historians who have taken a similar, multifaceted approach made possible by an extraordinary "find" are Craig Harline, *The Burdens of Sister Margaret: Private Lives in a Seventeenth-Century Convent* (New York: Doubleday, 1994) and Judith C. Brown, *Immodest Acts: The Life of a Lesbian Nun in Renaissance Italy* (New York: Oxford University Press, 1986).

18. The phrase is borrowed from Harline, xiii, whose success in employing such a strategy is exemplary.

PART I

Rebellion

I

An Ill-fated Convent for a Pious Town

No one, witnessing the joyous festivities that accompanied the foundation in 1756 of the convent of La Purísima Concepción in San Miguel el Grande, could have predicted the agonizing, even bizarre turns of event that would soon bring it to the verge of extinction. True, the funds used to construct and endow the convent came to young María Josepha Lina de la Canal under tragic circumstances: the death of both her parents within days of each other when she was just 12 years old. But the convent was not founded in grief-induced haste—the ponderous interventions of civil and ecclesiastical authorities made sure of that. Moreover, by using her inheritance to establish La Purísima, María Josepha Lina was, in a certain sense, merely following through on a project that her father had begun many years earlier.

María Josepha Lina's father, Manuel Tomás de la Canal, was already a wealthy man when he arrived in San Miguel from Mexico City around 1730. His own father was a Spaniard who had made a fortune as a wholesale merchant (originally specializing in the importation of peanuts), and Canal increased the value of his inheritance many times over first as a merchant in Mexico City, and then in San Miguel as a sheep rancher and wool merchant. One contemporary claimed that his arrival in the town was "inspired by God," referring to the 200,000 pesos that he is said to have spent on religious and civic building projects, roads, fountains, and other improvements to the town, including his mansion on the corner of the main square, remodeled in the late eighteenth century by his son to create the magnificent palace we see today (figure 1.1), and his "summer home," today the Instituto Allende.[1]

In 1736, the year that María Josepha Lina was born, Canal sponsored the construction of an opulent, gilt-walled chapel dedicated to the Virgin of Loreto, the Canal family's protectress, in the left transept of the church of the Oratory of San Felipe Neri, a duplicate of an earlier chapel to the Virgin that he had constructed in the church of Tepotzotlán, near Mexico City (figures 1.2 and 1.3).[2] Four years later, he petitioned royal and church officials for a license to establish a convent of Capuchin nuns attached to the chapel. To his dismay, this petition was turned down, because in order for the nuns to enjoy the direct access to the chapel that their cloistered state demanded, it would have been necessary to build the convent too close to the Oratory, which was a community of secular priests.[3] Only the Oratorians' church itself would have separated the living quarters of the nuns and the priests. In cases such as this, ecclesiastical authorities strained every nerve to maintain an unquestionable appearance of propriety: as the saying went, "entre santa y santo, pared de cal y canto" (roughly, "between saintly women and saintly men, walls of stone and mortar").[4] Despite the disappointing rejection of Don Manuel's proposed convent of Capuchins, however, the Canal family continued to be known for its piety and willingness to divert large parts of its vast fortune to support the church.[5] María Josepha Lina's decision to continue this tradition was no sudden impulse.

María Josepha Lina was not just the founder of the convent, however; she was to be its first novice (figure 1.4). Perhaps concerned that her youth and inexperience might have made life in a convent seem a sort of romantic escape from her worldly responsibilities as the oldest of the nine Canal orphans, her guardian—Francisco José de Landeta, the Count of Casa de Loja—insisted that she be closely interviewed by several "prudent, learned, and conscientious" persons, to be sure there was no doubt of her resolution.[6] One of these examiners was the Bishop of Michoacán, Martín de Elizacochea, who met with her—decked out in the fine clothing and jewels that her confessor, Father Luis Phelipe Neri de Alfaro, insisted she wear, against her innate sense of modesty—after summoning her to distant Valladolid, the seat of the bishopric, in March 1752. She was then 15.[7]

"Since her tender years," stated one of the testimonials solicited by the examiners, "María Josepha Lina has displayed extraordinary dignity and reserve, accompanied by such true virtue, that her parents used to say God had prepared her for some heroic enterprise . . . she has always inclined towards the religious life, and her vocation has continued to grow stronger and stronger each day to the present time. . . ." But, her interrogators wondered, did she understand "the austerity of the religious life, the seriousness of the three vows she must take—poverty, chastity, and obedience—the perpetual enclosure that she must observe for the rest of her life, the material comforts of which she

FIGURE I.I, *above*. Palace
of the Canal family.
(Francisco De la Maza.
San Miguel de Allende.
Mexico City: Instituto de
Investigaciones Estéticas,
Universidad Nacional
Autónoma de México,
1939.)

FIGURE I.2, *at right*. Chapel
of Loreto, María Josepha
Hervas and Manuel
Tomás de la Canal facing
one another. (Francisco
De la Maza. *San Miguel
de Allende*. Mexico City:
Instituto de Investigaciones
Estéticas, Universidad
Nacional Autónoma de
México, 1939.)

FIGURE I.3, *above*. Chapel of Loreto. (Francisco De la Maza. *San Miguel de Allende*. Mexico City: Instituto de Investigaciones Estéticas, Universidad Nacional Autónoma de México, 1939.)

FIGURE I.4, *at left*. Painting of María Josepha Lina de la Santísima Trinidad, anon. (Courtesy of the Instituto Allende.)

FIGURE 1.5, *at right.* Father Luis Phelipe Neri de Alfaro, from the frontispiece of his biography. (Juan Benito Díaz de Gamarra y Dávalos. *El sacerdote fiel, y según el Corazón de Dios. Elogio Funebre. . .a P. D. Luis Phelipe Neri de Alfaro.* Mexico City: Imprenta de la Biblioteca del Lic. D. Joseph de Jauregui, 1776.)

FIGURE 1.6, *below.* Father Alfaro as a penitent: painting on the wall of the Sanctuary of Atotonilco. (Julio Reza Díaz. *Atotonilco.* Zamora, Michoacán: Impresiones Laser del Valle de Zamora, 2002.)

FIGURE I.7, *at left*. Entrance to the Chapel of the Sepulcher at Atotonilco. (Julio Reza Díaz. *Atotonilco*. Zamora, Michoacán: Impresiones Laser del Valle de Zamora, 2002.)

FIGURE I.8, *below. Refectorio de Carmelitas Descalzas* (Refectory of Discalced Carmelites), anon. (Museo Nacional del Virreinato. Courtesy of CONACULTA.-INAH.-MEX.)

FIGURE I.9, *above*. Interior of a convent choir, anon. (Francisco De la Maza. *Arquitectura de los Coros de Monjas en México*. Mexico City: Instituto de Investigaciones Estéticas, Universidad Nacional Autónoma de México, 1956.)

FIGURE I.10, *below*. Oil painting of the villa of San Miguel el Grande, anon. The Sanctuary of Atotonilco appears in the foreground. The church, convent, and orchard of La Purísima are shown in the lower right portion of the town grid, almost hidden by the hill that the pilgrims are climbing to reach Atotonilco. The parish church (top) and the church and orchard of the Oratorians (lower left) are also prominent. The painting belongs to the parish church of Atotonilco. (Richard Kagen. *Urban Images of the Hispanic World, 1493-1793*. New Haven, Conn.: Yale University Press, 2000.)

FIGURES 1.11, *above*, and
1.12, *at right*. Religious
imagery on the streets of
San Miguel.

FIGURE 1.13, *above.* Main patio of La Purísima.

FIGURE 1.14, *below.* Fountain of the main patio of La Purísima.

FIGURE I.15, *above*. Catalog of the population of the convent of La Purísima
Concepción, 1765. (AHAM, Diocesano, Gobierno, Visitas, Informes, caja 504 [XVIII],
exp. 66.)

FIGURE I.16, *below*. *Traslación de las Monjas Catarinas* (Transfer of the Catharine
Nuns), anon. The painting depicts the nuns of Santa Catarina (Valladolid) being
transferred from their old convent to their new one in 1738. (Museo Regional de
Michoacán. Courtesy CONACULTA.-INAH.-MEX.)

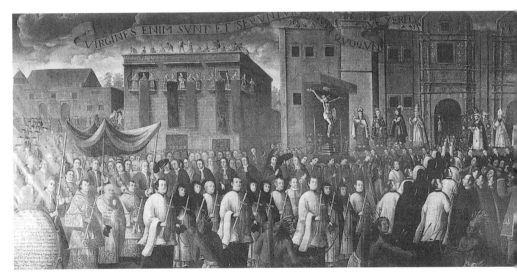

would be deprived, the total abnegation of the flesh, and the abandonment that her younger sisters would feel from the absence of the sister who had cared for them as a mother?" It appeared that she did. One examiner wrote that no dark possibility with which they confronted her "dissuaded her from her desire to fulfill her vocation and to benefit her Patria, the Villa of San Miguel el Grande. . . . I am convinced that her vocation is a true one, and that she has resolved spontaneously to make a donation of the majority of her inheritance" to build and maintain the convent.

Indeed, if even a small part of what her biographer wrote of María Josepha Lina's early commitment to the religious life is true, her interviewers could scarcely have determined otherwise. Father Juan Benito Díaz de Gamarra, working from her confessor's notes, claimed that from an early age she chose to live in a separate apartment within her parents' house, "as if she were a nun in her cell." To practice humility, she was said to have worked alongside the servants, helping them with household tasks and occasionally managing "with saintly ingenuity" to kiss their feet by pretending to drop something on the floor next to them. When her parents tried to tempt her to eat by offering her some delicacy from the table, she would decline, saying that such food made her sick to the stomach. She had such a full daily schedule of prayer and spiritual exercise that it took Díaz de Gamarra almost two full pages to recount. Naturally, she spurned suitors for her hand in marriage—she wanted only to marry Christ.[8]

The Inspiration for the Convent: The Foundress and Her Confessor

I have suggested that María Josepha Lina's decision to spend her inheritance on a convent was a way to honor her parents, whose own efforts to establish a convent had failed, and to institutionalize perpetual prayers for their souls. It is also possible that a bit of what her guardian feared was true, that is, that she saw the convent as an escape from worldly obligations. Indeed, the psychological burden of caring for and mothering her younger siblings must have seemed staggering to a young girl of such obvious intelligence, maturity, and seriousness. (How cruel, then, that her life as a nun proved in some ways to be much more trying and burdensome than her obligations to her siblings could ever have been!) But the "official" version of how her decision came about is provided by her biographer, Díaz de Gamarra.[9] In his narrative, María Josepha Lina's confessor, Father Alfaro, was the first to suggest that she might want to establish a female monastery in San Miguel. She is said to have replied, with characteristic humility, that she was unworthy of such an important enterprise. Alfaro, however, convinced her that her feelings of unworthiness were excellent proof of worthiness in the eyes of God, and he pushed on, presenting her with constitutions of various monasteries from which to choose a model for a convent in San Miguel. Again, she demurred, saying that she had no other will than that of her "director" (Alfaro) and that whichever he selected she would accept, knowing that the decision came from God. Upon receiving this response, Alfaro sent her, accompanied by a virtuous señora, to the sanctuary of Atotonilco, about 12 kilometers distant from San Miguel, for 8 days of retreat. She emerged resolved to found a convent of Conceptionist nuns, God's will presumably having been made clear to her during this period of intense prayer and spiritual exercise.[10]

It is entirely possible that the immediate inspiration for the foundation was indeed Alfaro, just as María Josepha Lina's biographer asserted: The confessor "directed" his apt young pupil with loving paternalism, and the girl obediently and modestly followed his direction. The best corroborating evidence of such a view of Alfaro's dominating influence is his own astonishingly energetic life (figure 1.5). Alfaro was not only a trusted and influential confidant of the Canal family, but also a commanding presence in San Miguel. He was something of a mystic, devoting over 25 years to the construction of the sanctuary of Atotonilco after a vision of Christ directed him to build a church near a hot spring in the middle of a barren, Jerusalem-like terrain, a place of worship that would be a "beautiful Paradise and an oasis of piety and sanctity" in a spot that was a gathering place for "those who sought the shadows in order to commit acts of iniquity" (the bathers at the hot spring).[11] Like many religious men and women (though not all, especially in the "enlightened" eighteenth century, when such practices began to be frowned upon by many, both inside and outside the church), Alfaro put penitence at the center of his devotions (see figure 1.6). Every Friday, he wore a hair shirt whose points were "so sharp you could not even touch them." On Good Friday, he re-enacted the Via Dolorosa by leading a procession from Atotonilco to San Miguel while wearing a crown of thorns that bathed his face in blood, carrying a heavy wooden cross, and (in a novel touch) paying a "robust young man" to hold him upside down by the feet and drive him head first into the ground every now and then, so that the crown of thorns would penetrate even more painfully.[12]

At the same time, Alfaro was practical and ambitious. He arranged for the purchase (it is not clear exactly how) of the hacienda of Atotonilco, whose revenues supported construction, maintenance, and the devotional exercises held at the sanctuary; this was a savvy way to guarantee an income without having to rely on alms or prompt service of interest on the part of borrowers.[13] A man who slept in a coffin to remind himself of his own mortality (and, as he joked, outlasted three of them: "ya se me han podrido tres chalupas"), Alfaro was also very much "of the world," often busy until late at night with some aspect of the building project or one of his other enterprises: founding the Sanctuary of Nuestra Señora de la Salud (using his own inheritance) in San Miguel; establishing the church of San Rafael (to which the nuns of La Purísima would be temporarily attached while their own church and convent were being built); or founding the Santa Escuela de Cristo, a kind of lay brotherhood, with an apostolic and charitable mission, to which many members of the San Miguel aristocracy belonged.[14]

David Brading calls Atotonilco, which was built over a period from 1740 to 1766, "among the most remarkable and personal creations of the Mexican baroque."[15] The main sanctuary and its collection of side chapels, some connected to the sanctuary by dark, low-ceilinged passageways, was crowded with images, statuary, altars, paintings, and most strikingly, was literally covered "from the vaults and cupolas and lantern niches all the way down to the very floor" with vibrant, multicolored murals painted by unschooled, but clearly enthusiastic, artists (figure 1.7).[16] The subjects of the murals were all dictated by Alfaro, who also penned the sonnets and mystical poems that informed them. Each year, thousands of the faithful came to Atotonilco to undergo spiritual exercises and cleanse their souls (and indeed, still do); they were housed in dormitories and fed in dining halls that were also part of the complex.[17]

The sanctuary at Atotonilco was not the only unusual feature of the religious landscape in and around San Miguel in which Alfaro had a hand, however. He was a member of the Oratory of San Felipe Neri, one of a small number of Oratories in New Spain and one of the earliest foundations outside of Mexico City (it was established in San Miguel in 1712, though not formally authorized until 1735). The Oratories required priests to live and work in common and to follow certain rules of community as they devoted themselves to intellectual, humanitarian, and spiritual pursuits. Dedicated to the idea of improving education for priests, it was natural for the Oratory in San Miguel to open a secondary school, the Colegio de San Francisco de Sales. Also founded in connection with the Oratory was the Beaterio de Santa Anna, in some ways a parallel female religious institution in the sense that, like the Oratorians, the *beatas* lived in community without taking solemn vows and devoted themselves to education.

Alfaro thus had direct or indirect connections to seven religious institutions in and around San Miguel: the sanctuary/religious retreat at Atotonilco, the Oratory of San Felipe Neri, the Beaterio de Santa Anna, the church of Nuestra Señora de la Salud, the church of San Rafael, the Colegio de San Francisco de Sales, and the Santa Escuela de Cristo. With these institutions already in place, it is not hard to imagine that he might have seen a female convent as an essential part of a larger project to allow San Miguel not only to fulfill its pious destiny, but also to enhance its civic pride, since the existence of a convent in a city was an index of its economic and cultural importance.[18]

With a female convent, San Miguel would be better equipped to compete with its rival in religiosity, the city of Querétaro.[19] Querétaro had a powerful spiritual reputation owing to its missionary tradition and its many churches and convents. There had been a sustained period of religious building and foundation in Querétaro from the mid-seventeenth century to the mid-eighteenth century, during which time 10 religious orders or churches were established, in addition to the five that already existed. Among these five was the flourishing convent of Santa Clara de Jesús, founded in 1607, which had some 100 nuns at midcentury, over half of whom came from Bajío towns that were at least as close as, if not closer to, San Miguel than to Querétaro.[20] It is likely that by establishing a convent in San Miguel, Alfaro and others thought to capture much of the "demand" for a convent for women that had been supplied, to date, by Santa Clara.

Díaz de Gamarra's version of the inspiration for the foundation of La Purísima, then, sees the zealous Alfaro, looking to elevate his adopted patria of San Miguel to new levels of Christian devotion, as the dominant, indeed domineering, force behind the foundation, with María Josepha Lina meekly following his lead. It is important, however, to remember the purpose of the biography in which the active-confessor, passive-founder version of the foundation appears: to provide an example for women, especially nuns, of obedience and submission to the direction of one's spiritual adviser, prized qualities in all women. The impression of María Josepha Lina that comes through the archival record, however, is rather less passive and yielding than the portrait of the deferential "exemplary nun" that Díaz de Gamarra paints or than is implied by Alfaro's indisputable energy and enthusiasm for new foundations. Sometime in her youth, sandwiched between a seemingly constant round of prayers and seclusion in her "cell" in her parents' house, she managed to receive a very good education, to judge by her elegant handwriting and unusually (for either sex) graceful and straightforward prose. In making decisions about the convent—how many nuns should be admitted, what the rules specific to her convent should be, and so on—she appears to have been quite capable and even assertive. There are several unusual features of the constitution of La Purísima (discussed below) that seem to have been included at her own insistence, some apparently against the advice of others, a fact that strongly encourages an interpretation of María Josepha Lina's role as active, perhaps even intransigent on certain subjects.

The most satisfying interpretation of the decision to found the convent makes room for a large role for Alfaro, but also acknowledges María Josepha Lina's own active participation and powerful motivations: not only her deep religiosity, but also her sense of obligation to her parents' memory and the closeness and loyalty to the town of San Miguel that she must have felt, deriving from her family's leading role in the town's society and recent history. I see María Josepha Lina acting as much in conscious imitation of Father Alfaro (by founding, as he had done several times, a new religious institution) as at his direction. The distinction is fine, but useful; it makes the relationship between María Josepha Lina and Father Alfaro that of relatively equal partners in the project to expand and enrich the religious life of the town of San Miguel rather than that of a seasoned priest–confessor and a naive rich girl.[21]

Much more important, however, than who had the idea to found the convent in the first place was the question of who determined what kind of convent it would be. With his ambition for high-profile religious projects, Alfaro may well have planted the idea of bringing the prestigious Conceptionists to San Miguel, as María Josepha Lina's biographer implies. It seems likely that he had personal connections at Regina Coeli, one of the eight Conceptionist convents in Mexico City.[22] Regina Coeli, in turn, had a reputation as a "founding convent," one active in sending out nuns to establish new convents. It is also possible that María Josepha Lina's tutor, the Count of Casa de Loja, was influential in the decision to select as a founding convent one of the oldest and most prominent of the Mexico City convents: The bishop of Michoacán, in a letter to the archbishop of Mexico (under whose jurisdiction were the Mexico City convents that were potential founding convents), stated that "Doña María Josepha Lina and her tutor have declared their preference for four Religiosas from the convent of Regina and one from the [also Conceptionist] convent of La Encarnación."[23]

But it seems to have been María Josepha Lina who insisted that if they were to be Conceptionists, they must nonetheless adhere to a certain way of life that was very much *not* associated with other Conceptionist convents in New Spain. Consistently, in the archival record, it is the young foundress who is depicted as insisting on strict observance and austerity, while others tried (subtly, of course) to moderate her dictates. She obviously had in mind a monastery like the one envisioned by her father when he sought to found a convent of Capuchins, rather than a convent of relaxed observance, as was the convent of Regina Coeli.[24] The difference was profound. If María Josepha Lina had been entirely independent of the influence of Alfaro, she might not have chosen to bring the Conceptionists to San Miguel in the first place, instead preferring the severe Capuchins or the rigorous Carmelites. But if she had not possessed a marked streak of independence, surely she would not have undertaken, at age 15, to impose a strict lifestyle on members of an order that had a history of laxity and luxury. As things turned out, this was a courageous, but fateful choice.

Licensing the Convent

María Josepha Lina's decision to found a convent was only the beginning of a long process that began with obtaining the necessary licenses—not a simple task, as is evident from the fact that the very wealthy and well-connected Manuel de la Canal had failed in his attempt to bring the Capuchins to San Miguel.

The first step was for local backers to put together a case to submit to various authorities, royal and ecclesiastical, regarding the need for a convent in their town. Often, they were required to provide funds in addition to those supplied by the founder, since even if the founder's donation was considered sufficient, a financial commitment from wealthy locals linked them to the new convent in a material way. It was not uncommon for 20 years to elapse between an initial attempt at a foundation and royal licensing, and after that, the arrangements for dispersal of the funds, building of the convent, and sending out of nuns from another convent to found the new one could take much longer.[25] In the bishopric of Michoacán, for example, the Capuchin convent at Salvatierra that was finally established in 1798 was first provided for in the 1766 will of Santiago Ginez de Parada, while the convent of La Enseñanza was proposed in 1759 (when it was planned for Celaya), but was not established (in Irapuato) until 1800.[26]

By these standards, La Purísima's foundation went extraordinarily smoothly. María Josepha Lina committed 58,000 pesos of her inheritance to the convent, and an impressive 200 residents of San Miguel pledged another 12,000 pesos, for a total of 70,000 pesos. In addition, 16,000 pesos had been provided by local benefactors for the dowries of the four founding nuns who would come from the Mexico City convent of Regina Coeli, and two more patrons had promised to pay 400 pesos a year for the maintenance of two other nuns who would enter right away.[27] These commitments were deemed ample to support the common expenses of the convent until its endowment could be built up and to build the church and cloister, whose cost they estimated at 39,623 pesos. This was a modest amount that the convent's backers must have assumed would raise eyebrows in Mexico City, because they went out of their way to justify it by pointing to the relatively low cost of building materials and labor in the region around San Miguel.[28]

But it was not enough simply to demonstrate that the money was there to support the convent. A strong case had to be made that a convent was necessary for the enlightenment and prosperity of the populace and for the material and spiritual well-being of young girls in the region.[29] (The more general justifications for female convents will be discussed in Chapter 2; here I will follow the framers of these supporting documents and I will focus on the specific reasons why the town of San Miguel needed a convent.) The argument began by situating the town in the geographic and economic landscape of New Spain:

> This Villa is located in the heart of the most populous part of the
> Diocese, known as the Chichimeca, where there are many large
> Cities and Villas in which commerce is conducted on a large and
> highly accredited scale, and in which commodity prices are usually
> high since it is the "throat" through which commerce from the
> north must pass. In addition, it is the site of a regional wool market.

The mines of Guanajuato, Guadalcazar, Comanja and Cerro de San Pedro are found in this part of the diocese, along with various woolens manufacturers . . . The prosperity and future growth of this Villa, which today boasts numerous residents with very large fortunes, are assured.

To hear its backers make the case, all the local economy lacked was a convent, which would cement the economic future of the town and the region. "A convent of religiosas, it is well known, causes [the town to grow] because many people from other regions move to be near the convent, either for the love of their daughters who take the habit, or to take advantage of the convent's need for services and supplies." Furthermore, the argument went, over time, a convent would come to be a species of lending house (*monte de piedad*), where residents could borrow money at a moderate rate of interest. This borrowed money, they said, would be used mainly for the building and maintenance of residences in the town, "preventing it from falling into ruin." Finally, there was a "certain prestige" that accrued to a town with a convent, attracting even more residents and further enriching the town and its environs. By contrast, the report went on, revealing particularly acutely the rivalry with nearby Querétaro, "without a convent, those [in this region] who can afford to do so send their daughters to the convent [of Santa Clara] in the city of Querétaro, in the Archbishopric of Mexico, and this means that they often leave their homes to move to Querétaro to be near their daughter, and as a result the Territory of Chichimecas experiences the stagnation of commerce and agriculture that results from the absence of so many honorable residents, along with their fortunes . . . to the detriment of the whole Diocese."

The argument, based on depositions from six clerics and six of the principal residents of the town, then shifted to the multiple benefits that a convent would bring to the pious young girls of the region. "For over 100 leagues from north to south and 40 leagues from east to west there is no other institution open to girls who want to dedicate themselves to the service of God, and who are not inclined to marriage. This leaves them without an Estate, exposed to the dangers of the world." There were only three convents in the bishopric at this time, two of which followed the same Rule (the Rule of St. Dominic) and were located close to each other, in Valladolid and Pátzcuaro, "and are therefore almost like one rather than two separate convents." The other, also in Valladolid, was a convent reserved for Indian girls who were descendants of caciques. As a result, "many girls who aspire to the religious life, because they do not wish to be so far away from their family, or because they do not have the funds to make the long trip to the convent of their choice, remain in the [outside] world, which would not happen if there were a convent in their Patria."

María Josepha Lina's Vision: La Purísima's Constitution

All convents of the Conceptionist order followed the same "Rule," a set of general precepts for the life in religion that had been given to their order by the Pope in 1511. Other female orders in New Spain followed different Rules (the Rule of St. Augustine, the Rule of St. Dominic, the Rule of St. Clare) that varied in terms of such things as their emphasis on certain vows and observances and the principles they followed for electing abbesses and other officers. But each individual convent also had a "constitution" that spelled out the "peculiar practices" that were to be followed. The constitution, then, was each convent's interpretation of how best to adhere to the Rule.

La Purísima's constitution did indeed contain several "peculiar" features. In composing it, María Josepha Lina worked with her confessor and family advisers, but it appears that she was the one to whom everyone else deferred.[30] Not only did the language that was used to describe the writing of the constitution invariably include the words "María Josepha Lina ordered . . ." or "The foundress decided . . . ," but on several occasions, it is clear that there was some debate about what should and should not be mandated, with the young foundress prevailing.

The constitution began by directing that the Virgin herself, the "Divine Queen, the Most Pure Empress of the Heavens and Earth, Holy Mary in the ineffable mystery of the Immaculate Conception," was to be the abbess of the convent, its "perpetual Prelate and Superior." In this assignment of a concrete earthly role to a heavenly creature, María Josepha Lina was perhaps influenced by her parents' wills, which had named the Virgin of Loreto as the guardian of their children. (The Count of Casa de Loja was not technically their guardian, then, but their tutor, and he acted as guardian in representation of the Virgin.) Here on earth, the nuns would only elect a "Vicaria Abadesa" (roughly, Vice-Abbess) who would stand in for the Virgin in the governance of the convent. (For ease of reference, and so as not to confuse the Vicaria Abadesa with the Vicaria de Casa, the second ranking officer in the convent, in this book, the Vicaria Abadesa will be referred to in English as the "abbess.")

The convent would have a maximum of 72 religiosas, 66 of whom would be choir nuns—nuns of the black veil—and 6 of whom would be *legas,* nuns who wore the white veil. Both would be fully professed, but the legas would have fewer prayer obligations and somewhat greater labor obligations (or at least more menial labor obligations) than the choir nuns.[31] The latter could occupy all positions within the convent, while the legas would not be admitted to the highest posts. Choir nuns were each to bring to their marriage to Christ a dowry of 3,000 pesos, a very substantial sum, roughly double or even triple the annual income necessary for a family to maintain an elite lifestyle, while the legas would bring dowries of 1,500 pesos, not an insignificant amount. There would also be an unspecified number of "honest and needful" women who would enter as *donadas,* a variety of unprofessed lay sister, and would perform most of the domestic service that the choir nuns and legas required. In a crucial decision, it was determined that there were to be no personal servants. Religiosas of all classes, including, ideally, the donadas (although this was not an ironclad rule), were to be free of "mala raza," that is, Jewish, Moorish, Indian, mulatto, mestizo, Negro, and other "bad blood."

There was an important and very unusual provision made for the donadas. In order to "give them hope of a prize," those of "quality and good blood" became eligible to take the habit and profess as legas (white veil nuns) after 10 years. If a donada with 10 years' service lacked the right social background to take the habit, she could not profess, but she would be protected from ever having to leave the convent, even if she became too sick or infirm to serve. The result of this provision—a swelling over time in the number of legas and permanent residents, as donadas finished their 10 years of service—was presumably unanticipated by anyone involved in advising María Josepha Lina, since no objections were raised. The policy toward donadas put a financial strain on the convent, which had to provide medical care and living expenses for these women, who had brought no dowries and had therefore made no contribution to the convent's endowment fund, from which most expenses had to be paid. But as we will see in later chapters, the special status of the donadas in this convent created problems beyond the merely financial: Not quite servants, they were resented by many of the nuns for their unwillingness to perform certain kinds of work, which in the absence of personal servants, the nuns themselves had to take on. It is also clear that the donadas themselves resented it when they were treated in servile fashion, especially after they had completed their 10 years' service.

The constitution of the convent firmly emphasized that a spirit of austerity was to prevail. For example, María Josepha Lina was determined to avoid the "excessive expenses that were abusively introduced into other, more lax convents under the name of gratuities (*propinas*) and other corruptions" in the ceremonies of entrance and profession. In some convents, it was customary to make a great celebration of a daughter's taking the habit as a novice and again when she professed after her year of probation. Magnificent feasts were held in the family home, friends and relatives were invited from miles around, there were fireworks and music, the girl herself (on the occasion of entering the convent) was bejeweled and dressed in "embarrassingly rich" clothing, and the family offered a sumptuous banquet within the convent, in addition to monetary and food gifts for all of the nuns—for example, little pastries with the names of the nuns written on them.[32] The cost was so considerable that, according to these documents, "some girls could not follow their vocations because their families could not support these expenses." María Josepha Lina did not want her convent to be a party to this waste. Instead, for her solemn entrance into La Purísima:

> The aspiring novice should be accompanied only by her godmother, or at most a small number of her relatives, and they should proceed without any pomp at all straight to the Church, and having heard Mass, she should enter to receive the habit, giving each of the religiosas a gift of a candle made of one-third of a pound of wax, with the exception of the Abbess, to whom she should give a candle weighing one-half pound, and no other thing, not then or later, not even under the pretext that the gifts are from her relatives or other persons. . . .

The girl's parents would be allowed to offer only a "modest refreshment" to the nuns. The same principle was to apply throughout her life in the convent: Relatives were not to bring in food or other objects that contravened this spirit of simplicity and dignity, and the expenses that the family was allowed to assume, especially for clothing, should be moderate and in keeping with the vow of poverty.

More fundamental to the functioning of the convent than the symbolic restrictions on excessive displays of wealth at the time of entrance or profession was another provision written into the constitution: The nuns of San Miguel would practice the *vida común*, or the life in community. We have already seen that there would be no personal servants and that the work necessary to sustain the convent would be performed by the nuns themselves and the common labor pool of donadas. Beyond sharing work and servants, the common life also required that the nuns eat together and that they eat food prepared for the whole community (instead of maintaining separate kitchens, as was the custom in more relaxed convents—see figure 1.8), that they receive medical treatment together in a common infirmary, and that they sleep together in six different dormitories, with 12 to a room, not in private cells. (There was considerable discussion on this point, and it appears that most nuns did eventually have private cells, although they were still required to sleep in the dormitories.) The dormitories were to be positioned so as to make it easy for the abbess to keep a watchful eye on them, a task made easier by the fact that the nuns were never to sleep in darkness, but rather were to burn candles all night long. These features of the vida común required that the convent be designed to accommodate this way of life: The architects would need to incorporate a large kitchen; storerooms for food, clothing, and supplies; a refectory; an infirmary; a common room in which to perform the small labors to which the nuns dedicated themselves each day, such as sewing and embroidery; and several dormitories.

Although the Conceptionist Rule, like other Rules followed by the contemplative orders, called for regular prayer around the clock, the constitution of the San Miguel convent, like that of most female convents, allowed Matins and Lauds (the middle-of-the-night prayers of the Divine Office) to be sung in the evening "by anticipation," to avoid the illnesses, it was said, that come from lack of sleep. Despite this modest relaxation of the Rule, however, the spirit of the constitution that María Josepha Lina had devised was clearly reformist in that it encouraged close adherence to the vows of poverty, chastity, obedience, and enclosure and required the nuns to follow the vida común. Like all constitutions (not just convent constitutions), however, it could be interpreted more or less strictly, largely depending on the abbess, who had much leeway in this regard. It was she who would determine the exact schedule of work, prayer, and recreation that the nuns would follow. A gentle and moderate abbess could ease the burdens on the nuns in a variety of ways, but a reform-minded abbess would interpret the reform-minded constitution closely. In the latter case, which is, of course, the one that obtained in the early history of this convent, the result was a very unusual phenomenon: a reformed, elite (dowry-requiring) convent. Very few convents in Mexico combined these two qualities.

Most of the other elite convents in Mexico had less strict constitutions to begin with and over the years had developed customs and practices in interpretation of these constitutions that enhanced relaxation of the Rule. In particular, the vows of poverty and enclosure were often breached, and personal servants, luxuries, and a wide range of activities to which the nuns were accustomed in their worldly lives were permitted within convent walls. The convent of Santa Clara in Querétaro, for example, was described as a "miniature city," with interior streets connecting the cloisters and the nuns' houses with plazas, gardens, chapels, hermitages, and cemeteries. Not only was the number of personal servants very large, but the nuns were also allowed to keep birds and animals in the cloister and to sing and dance to profane songs played by the musically talented among them.[33] In some Mexico City convents, nuns' cells were designed by famous architects, such as the elegant "palace-cell" created by Manuel Tolsá for the Marquesa of Selva Nevada in the convent of Regina Coeli, the very convent that Father Alfaro had suggested as the founding convent for La Purísima.[34] Many "cells" consisted of two or even three rooms, with a sunroof and a patio. Nuns might have their habits and underclothing specially made from fine fabrics, and they might adorn them with jewels and other luxuries. In these relaxed convents, an educated daughter from a prominent family would expect to hold high office, or she might spend her days writing poetry or music. While the vow of enclosure, strictly interpreted, would mean that a nun would never show her face, rarely receive visitors, and converse only at certain limited times of the day with a restricted number of people (primarily other nuns) and on restricted topics, in convents with relaxed observance, nuns would regularly receive family and friends in the convent's parlors (admittedly from behind a grille) and might even put on theatrical productions for their enjoyment (again, from behind a grille). Their households would probably include not only servants, but also children and adult women who had come to live with them for one reason or another.[35]

Of the 48 female convents in Mexico at the time of the foundation of La Purísima, 37 practiced this relaxed observance, while only 11 both prohibited personal servants and were devoted to the common life. These convents included the four convents of Capuchins—the order that María Josepha Lina's father had tried to bring to San Miguel; the four Carmelite convents; the two convents of Poor Clares who followed the original Rule of St. Clare (as opposed to the Urban Clares, like the nuns of Santa Clara, who followed a mitigated rule introduced by Pope Urban IV in the thirteenth century), and one convent of Bridgettines.[36] Of these, the four Carmelite convents and the Bridgettine convent were the only others besides La Purísima that required a dowry.[37] Thus, La Purísima was in a category (reformed, dowry-requiring convents) that included only six convents in all of Mexico. Perhaps even more to the point, it was the only reformed convent of Conceptionists (out of 13 Conceptionist convents). While young women from privileged backgrounds who entered Capuchin or Carmelite monasteries knew what to expect because these orders were strongly associated in the public mind with austerity and strict observance, since the Conceptionists were not noted as a reformed order, it is far from clear that the girls who entered La Purísima were psychologically prepared for the demanding, difficult life they found behind the convent's walls.

The Arrival of the Nuns

On February 1, 1756, after their carefully managed journey from Mexico City (the logistics required to preserve cloister while the nuns were in transit were quite staggering), the four founding nuns from the convent of Regina Coeli in Mexico City arrived in San Miguel.[38] While their new convent was being constructed, the nuns would live in the former home of the parish priest, now known as their Hospicio, which had been rehabilitated for them so that they could continue to observe cloister. Outside doors and windows were closed off, a refectory and an infirmary were fashioned out of rooms in the house, and a turnstile (torno) was constructed so that letters and small objects could be passed back and forth without the nuns who supervised the torna coming into physical or eye contact with those on the other side. The cost of new construction, furnishings, and ornamentation of the Hospicio came to a substantial 11,166 pesos.[39] Detailed reports as to the layout of the house and the furniture and goods with which it had been supplied were submitted to the bishop for his approval.[40]

The entrance of the founding nuns into San Miguel on February 1, 1756, was both festive and solemn. The nuns were met by Bishop Elizacochea on the hill overlooking the town, and his entourage combined with that of the nuns for the short trip to the Beaterio de Santa Anna, where they were served lunch. From there began a procession that was viewed by the entire town and included the bishop; the newly arrived nuns; a young woman who had accompanied them from Regina Coeli and would formally enter the convent in a matter of days; a girl from the Beaterio who would also enter within the week; the fathers of the Oratory of San Felipe Neri; the secular clergy, in their most splendid clerical garb; the 12 religious brotherhoods, in their own habits; and the dignitaries of the city government. The first stop was at the chapel of Nuestra Señora de Loreto (the chapel that María Josepha Lina's father had built), where María Josepha Lina was waiting. The bishop presented the novice's habit to her, and once she had been dressed in it, she joined the procession, which snaked down several streets—profusely adorned with flowers, arches, and banners—until it arrived in the center of town.

Sharing an atrium with the parish church (before its pseudo-Gothic nineteenth-century makeover), in front of the main square, was the church of San Rafael, which was to serve as the nuns' church until their own church and convent were completed. The four founding nuns, the new novice (María Josepha Lina), and the two soon-to-be novices entered the church and disappeared behind the grille that allowed them to listen to the mass without being seen. (In a convent church, the grille would separate the church from the choir, the large room or rooms at the back of the nave where the nuns prayed, sang the Divine Office, participated in the mass, and took communion—in short, their church within the church [figure 1.9].) After the mass, they made their way to their Hospicio through a special entrance that had been constructed to connect their living quarters to the church. The next day there began an 8-day series of masses and sermons to solemnize the foundation, accompanied by almost constant festivities: expensive fireworks every night; a program of theatrical comedies; bullfights every afternoon, with the best bulls brought in from the finest ranches in the region; and allegorical floats paraded through the streets.[41] According to one account, "the jubilation of the inhabitants of San Miguel el Grande was indescribable."[42]

The Convent and the Town

Who were the residents of this town? What kind of environment did San Miguel provide for the much-anticipated convent? Today, San Miguel is known as a haven for North American expatriates, a shopper's delight, and a quaint, preserved-in-amber colonial town. What was it like in the second half of the eighteenth century? We may begin with one brief report written in October 1756—the same year the convent was founded—by an episcopal inspector (vis-

itador) who spent several months in what is now the state of Guanajuato. José Ignacio Goyeneche called San Miguel:

> one of the principal cities of this bishopric, in that it has advanced so far in so little time, and also in that its residents are so well-versed in Christian doctrine. Because of this they are an uncommonly virtuous people. They are well-governed by the leaders of the town (*los Republicanos*), and they are very industrious, many of them working as weavers, since there are numerous large textile mills in the vicinity. There is no idleness among the populace.[43]

There are two points in Goyeneche's report that bear closer examination. The first is the suggestion that San Miguel was an exceptionally Christian town. The second is that it was a town with an unusual economic base and labor structure.

In 1756, the villa of San Miguel itself probably had a population of about 12,000 to 15,000, and the parish of San Miguel, which included surrounding villages and ranches, had as many as 25,000 inhabitants, making it one of the more populous parishes in the bishopric (figure 1.10).[44] Although there are no early eighteenth-century censuses by which to judge the growth of the town and its hinterland, it is safe to assume that this was a considerably larger population than at the beginning of the century. It was certainly a wealthier population, since by the time of the convent's foundation, San Miguel was one of the eight richest cities in the bishopric of Michoacán.[45] By the 1750s, 60% of the agricultural/pastoral production of the tithe district came from crops, as opposed to wool and livestock, compared with 20% in the 1720s. Clearly, in the short span of 30 years, many of the herds had been moved farther north and more profitable grains had taken over.[46] By the end of the eighteenth century, the 50 or so "prosperous" ranches and haciendas in the San Miguel tithe district harvested between 80,000 and 100,000 *fanegas* (120,000–150,000 bushels) of corn a year, a bountiful harvest that put the district among the most productive in the colony.[47]

The town's prosperity did not come exclusively from grains or livestock, however. Trade employed many and made several fortunes. As relatively isolated as it seems today, in the eighteenth century, San Miguel stood at the crossroads of several important trade routes, as the convent's boosters had been careful to point out. Roads to Querétaro, Celaya, Guanajuato, Zacatecas, San Luis Potosí, and Dolores, where Canal and several other wealthy residents of San Miguel owned haciendas, all radiated from San Miguel, as did access roads to the mines of Xichú and Atarjea. But even more important for our purposes, in the eighteenth century, San Miguel, along with nearby Querétaro, became an eighteenth-century version of an industrial city, specializing in the manufacture of leather goods, weapons, tools, and especially, woolen textiles and finished woolen goods (sarapes, blankets, rugs, etc.) that found markets primarily in the mining and ranching districts of the Bajío and the near north.[48]

The expansion of woolen textile factories, or *obrajes,* was a relatively recent phenomenon at the time of the founding of La Purísima. In 1744, there had been only two obrajes in the town. But the 1750s saw much increase in competition, and by the end of the eighteenth century, there were 18 large-scale textile operations in San Miguel. These factories coexisted with some 350 small shops, operated mainly by Indians, mestizos, and mulattos.[49] There was something of an unequal symbiosis between the two scales of weaving operations: The owners of the larger mills often contracted out work, particularly to Indian weavers, advancing them raw materials in exchange for exclusive control over their products.[50] Indian women also embroidered the beautiful quilts, bedcovers, and rugs that were produced in San Miguel and that one observer called "as tasteful as any produced in Europe."[51]

If Indians did most of the contract work, those who labored inside the obrajes tended to be mulattos or other castas (people of mixed racial background). Richard Salvucci, who has studied one particularly bitter court case occasioned by the murder of five mill workers within the span of 2 years, sees the case as exposing submerged socioethnic conflicts that had been sharpened by the growth of the textile industry. Specifically, one owner had tried to deal with growing competition from new mills by lowering wages and introducing a harsher labor regimen, giving rise to labor unrest and ethnic antagonisms. The case revealed not only the rift between white mill owners and casta workers, but also a split within the San Miguel elite, as one faction sided with the accused owner, who was the only peninsular Spaniard obraje owner, and another faction, made up of wealthy creoles, lined up against him.[52]

Contract workers and mill workers were not the only producers of woolen products, however. There were numerous artisans—Spaniards and creoles, but mostly mestizos and mulattos—who fashioned sarapes, ponchos, blankets, hats, and other clothing and household goods. These artisans were usually organized into guilds, as were the numerous artisans in the leather industry who cleaned, tanned, and processed hides into goods such as shoes or the saddles for which San Miguel was especially noted, and those who manufactured shotguns, pistols, machetes, knives, and swords, an industry related to the continuing presence of unconquered Indians to the north.[53] San Miguel's artisans occupied an ambiguous social position: Their ethnic profile was most like that of the mill workers, but their self-image—as pillars of the community and defenders of political order and church institutions—expressed through their guilds and the religious brotherhoods organized through and around those guilds, was closer to that of the town's creole aristocracy.

Thus, within San Miguel and its near environs, a variety of ethnic and social groups had relatively recently been thrust into closer contact than ever before, by virtue of the emerging importance of industrial and artisanal enterprises. Indian contract workers and weavers, mulatto and mestizo factory workers, casta and creole and Spanish artisans, and both creole and Spanish mill owners and ranchers—all were essential parts of the changing economic picture. That picture was one of industry and industriousness, as the episcopal inspector observed; but the class tensions and ethnic rivalries of the period also indicate significant, frightening social fissures. While the backers of the convent did not make specific reference to growing fears of disorder in the town when they justified the establishment of the convent, it is not hard to imagine that such fears could have been an added incentive to bring a convent to San Miguel. A convent could serve as an edifying example of an orderly and peaceful religious community; at the same time, the nuns could help to address the town's social problems by praying for the town and its sinners. The idea of the convent and its inhabitants serving as both example and mediators, then, may have had particular appeal in this volatile social landscape.[54]

The presence of large numbers of artisans helps to explain another comment made by the inspector: that San Miguel was an unusually Christian town. Although guilds slowly diminished in importance over the second half of the eighteenth century (as they did elsewhere in Mexico), they continued to strongly influence the religious character of the city. This was because many guild members were also members of confraternities, or brotherhoods devoted to a certain saint, usually the patron saint of their craft or profession. The confraternities took responsibility for upkeep of the altar on which the image of the saint rested during the year, and dressed in the garb and insignia of the confraternity, they carried the image through the streets on special occasions. The connection between guilds and confraternities meant that a town like San Miguel, with a large number of artisans, typically had an especially rich religious life, and indeed, the "excessive" number of religious celebrations in San Miguel brought about an order from the intendant in 1789 to eliminate some of them as wasteful and unseemly. But, according to one sympathetic historian, "the very Catholic city council protested," insisting that they be allowed to continue to worship as they chose, and the intendant was forced to back down.[55] A strong connection between the unusual industrial/artisanal character of the city, the development of religious institutions, and the city's sense of itself as an especially "Catholic" polity, is suggested by the fact that the city had almost as many confraternities (13) as Valladolid (15), the capital of the bishopric, and Guanajuato (17), a much larger city.[56]

Religion was also connected to San Miguel's social and economic organization in another way. San Miguel was a town with an unusually high ratio of creoles to Spaniards among the elite. Only two Peninsula-born Spaniards figured among the city's small aristocracy: Antonio de Lanzagorta and Balthasar de Sauto, and the former was very well connected by marriage to prominent creole families: Canal, Landeta, Unzaga, Allende, and Malo. Most of the wealth of the town, then, was creole wealth, and much of it was second- or even third-generation wealth, based on sheep and cattle ranching and the industries that finished those raw materials. The Canal family was typical—María Josepha Lina and her sisters and brothers belonged to at least the third generation of creoles on both their father's and their mother's sides, and their wealth derived from the profitable connections between their haciendas and their textile mills. Although they did not hold a title of nobility, the Canal family wealth was entailed in 1743, and a noble title was apparently in the works when, in 1810, Coronel Narciso María Loreto de la Canal, one of María Josepha Lina's nephews, was brought to trial for his role in the independence wars, and the title was never confirmed. The Canal children's guardian, Francisco de Landeta, however, held a title (the Count of Casa de Loja), and there were several other members of the titled nobility and/or holders of *mayorazgos* who owned houses in San Miguel. Today, San Miguel owes much of its charm to the residences built by this creole aristocracy: The number of ornate, unrestrainedly luxurious eighteenth-century palaces in San Miguel is extraordinary for the size of the town.

Manuel de la Canal and Luis Phelipe Neri de Alfaro were not the only wealthy creoles to view the church as a natural and essential part of their lives and to act on that conviction by supporting the church financially and by wearing their religiosity on their figurative sleeves. Indeed, there was a special connection between creoles and the church, forged by close economic, social, ideological, and educational ties. Most of the "distinguished señores" of San Miguel belonged to the Santa Escuela de Cristo, which Alfaro had organized as a permanent apostolate in the sanctuary of Atotonilco. Its members imitated Alfaro in his ascetic life, his penitence, and his apostolic vision, joining him on the famous procession from Atotonilco to San Miguel on Good Friday, for which they were memorialized in one of the paintings in the sanctuary.[57] Alfaro founded other Escuelas, but the one in San Miguel remained the most important. Other visible signs of the religiosity of wealthy creoles in San Miguel endure today, including stone crosses or religious images and symbols carved into niches on street corners or into the decorative space above magnificent wooden portals (figures 1.11 and 1.12). One whole district of the town, the "ciudad religiosa," was completely dominated by church architecture, much of which was funded by local contributors: the church and convent of San Francisco, the Oratory of San Felipe Neri, the Casa de Loreto (Manuel de la Canal's construction), the church of Nuestra Señora de la Salud, the Colegio de San Francisco de Sales, the church of the Third Order of Franciscans, and the church and Beaterio de Santa Anna, all situated within three blocks of one another.

On the same side of the town as these edifices, three or four blocks south, on a large site known as the "house of the orange trees" that formerly belonged to the conqueror and original founder of the villa, Juan González de la Cruz, in the barrio of "El Cerrito," workers were busy from 1755 to December 1765 building the church and convent of La Purísima.[58] The convent's property included about four times as much space as the present-day structures cover, forming an uneven quadrangle that measured between 380 and 440 feet on each side. The church, cemetery, and main patio of the convent were situated in the corner of the site, two blocks from the central plaza, but on its western side, away from the center of town, the property extended all the way to the Arroyo de la Fábrica, the stream used by one of the obrajes. On the northern side of the site were open space and the road to the Sanctuary of Atotonilco. Convents needed both a central location and space for gardens and orchards, which could be used to supplement the supplies purchased by the convent's business manager (*mayordomo*). These spatial demands placed some restrictions on a late-arriving convent like La Purísima, and in this case, they meant that parts of the convent were not quite in the "best" part of the town. Some of the convent's neighbors were not the sort of families that placed their daughters in nunneries. The *plaza de gallos*, where cockfights were held, was right across the street (probably on the lower part of Canal Street, near the stream), and it was said that:

> especially on Sundays there is music and women singing and there is never silence . . . and if there is a fight over the cocks or over bets that are made, there is not only inquietude but fear and confusion on the part of the timid religiosas . . . and on the part of the ladies of distinction who visit them . . . ; in a place they ought to be able to consider the height of security, their honor is offended and threatened by the drunken vagabonds that attend these fights.[59]

The construction project dragged on for almost 10 years, in part because of the ambitious designs of both church and cloister. The estimated cost of some 40,000 pesos when the foundation was approved quickly proved to be insufficient, and once the foundress's 58,000 pesos had been consumed, the money to finish the project was slow to come in. The huge church was never an architectural success—it was too large, poorly proportioned, heavy, and cold—and when the nuns finally occupied the convent in 1765, it was no more than half finished. Intended to be a "perfect cross," there was yet no transept, only a nave; its altar was temporary and propped up against an adobe wall; and it had neither dome nor tower, both of which were added much later, in the nineteenth century. There were complaints about "low-lifes" (*gentes de mal vivir*) taking advantage of the unfinished walls of the church to climb onto the roof of the convent, and from there, to spy on the nuns.[60]

The cloister was also unfinished when the nuns moved in, although it showed greater architectural promise.[61] Where the church was cavernous, the main patio of the convent was spacious and solid, qualities said to be unusual in convents of *recoletas*, or nuns living the life of strict observance.[62] The patio would eventually be surrounded by what the architect envisioned as "two flights of dancing arches," although it appears that only two, or possibly three, of the four sides of the upper cloister had been completed by 1765. (The record is somewhat unclear on this point.) The main entrance boasted a graceful vault with an elaborately carved wooden ceiling, modeled after one at the Colegio de Santa Rosa Viterbo in Querétaro. There was a lovely neoclassical fountain with a lamb at the center, in a design similar to that of the lamb in the chapel dedicated by the Canal family to the Virgin of Loreto (figures 1.13 and 1.14).

It was said later that the nuns' decision to move into their new convent in 1765 was made in part to spur the much-delayed construction project, and it did succeed in hastening the conclusion of the necessary offices (e.g., the refectory) and 12 cells, sufficient for the nuns to move out of their Hospicio and into their new convent.[63] But the decision was also made, no doubt, because the nuns had begun to outgrow their Hospicio (by this time, the population of the convent had grown to 31 choir nuns and legas). It is also possible—although there is no direct evidence to support this speculation—that the authorities both within and outside the convent felt that some of the terrible conflicts that had afflicted the nuns since at least 1759 were due to the fact that they continued to live in "temporary" quarters. Maybe all would be well once the nuns were ensconced in their own beautiful, if unfinished, convent.

The Convent Population in the 1760s

The documents that were generated at the time of the nuns' entrance into the convent and the time of their profession, a year later—baptismal records, testimonials by witnesses who knew the nuns' families and who attested to their "clean blood" going back several generations, documents associated with the liens placed on property to secure a dowry, and pro forma interviews with the nuns at the time of both entrance and profession—are scattered throughout the boxes of material on all five convents in the bishopric of Michoacán, but few have been lost altogether. These documents make it possible to construct a profile of the convent population in 1760, the year that profound discontent seems to have metamorphosed into outright defiance (the bishop's "rebellion") and again in the mid-1760s, at the time of the move into the new convent. Profiling the nuns in the middle of the decade captures the convent population at a midpoint between the two phases of the rebellion and allows us to make use of a 1766 "catalog" of the "Señoras Religiosas" of the convent that was prepared in connection with the visitation (inspection) of the convent by a high-ranking representative of the bishop.[64] This document is a marvelous example of the imperfect extent to which rationalist, scientific ideas of the Enlightenment had seeped into Mexico by the middle of the eighteenth century. As figure 1.15 shows, the document was arranged in an orderly, tabular fashion, as if it were a collection of statistics or a presentation of other short, factual information. Indeed, some of the information given was in the nature of the factual: the nuns' ages, the offices they held, the number of years professed. But there were also columns for more subjective qualities: their health, their specific talents (e.g., reading, writing, music, making artificial flowers, embroidery), their personalities and characters (humble, modest, impetuous, kind), and the extent to which they were "obedient."

During its first decade in existence, the convent population had several notable features. First, when the rivalries and personality conflicts that would plague the convent began to surface in the late 1750s, the age structure in the convent was very unbalanced. Of course, it was very difficult to avoid this kind of imbalance in any new convent, since novices and recently professed nuns, almost invariably young, formed the large majority of the convent populations. La Purísima was no exception—although the archbishop of Mexico, in selecting the four founding nuns, appears to have taken steps to mitigate generational imbalance. The abbess, María Antonia del Santísimo Sacramento, was in her late 50s when she arrived in San Miguel in 1756.[65] The founding nun who would become the second abbess, María Anna del Santísimo Sacramento, at 47, was about 10 years younger. The third founding nun, Gertrudis de San Raphael, in a story that will be told at the beginning of Chapter 2, returned to her home convent of Regina Coeli in Mexico City in 1759. As a result, no documents were generated in San Miguel that give her age, but we can guess that she was in her late 30s, since the fourth founding nun, Phelipa de San Antonio, was 29 when she arrived in San Miguel, leading us to suspect that the archbishop tried to include nuns who were about a decade apart in age. The youngest founding nun, Phelipa, was obviously meant to bridge the gap between the young nuns who would soon be entering the convent and the founding group. Indeed, since Phelipa ended up leading the rebellion to which many of these younger nuns would subscribe, it appears that the archbishop succeeded all too well in his effort to name a founding nun with whom the novices and newly professed nuns could identify. In the first years of the convent's existence, Phelipa was closer to the ages of the women in this younger group than to the ages of her fellow founders, but she was old enough for the new nuns to look up to her, especially given her position as one of the founding nuns and a member of the advisory council, the Definitorio.

By 1760, 4 years after the arrival of the founding nuns in San Miguel in February 1756, there were 19 new nuns, in addition to the 3 remaining founding nuns, and the age structure in the convent looked like this:[66]

60s   1 nun
50s   1 nun
40s   1 nun
30s   3 nuns

20s   9 nuns
10s   7 nuns

Six years later, in 1766, the age structure in the convent was not much more balanced:

50s   1 nun
40s   2 nuns
30s   8 nuns
20s   12 nuns
10s   4 nuns

What is the significance of generational imbalance? It seems plausible that a kind of camaraderie—the "special friendships" that all convents forbid—is more likely to develop among nuns who entered at roughly the same time at roughly the same age in a convent lacking older role models than in a convent with a balanced age structure and a large number of older nuns who could socialize the younger ones into the ways of this particular convent. La Purísima, of course, had no "ways," no traditions, no customs yet, because it had not had time to develop them, and it also had an unusually small number of older nuns—only the two older founding nuns fit this category. All of the comparable convents in the bishopric had more founding nuns than the four women (reduced to three in 1759) who were sent out to found La Purísima: Nuestra Señora de la Salud of Pátzcuaro had six founding nuns, who came from the nearby convent of Santa Catarina in Valladolid; the Capuchin convent at Salvatierra that was founded in 1798 had seven founding nuns; La Enseñanza of Irapuato in 1804 also had seven; and the Carmelites of Valladolid had five in 1824.[67]

Another telling characteristic of the convent population at La Purísima is that many of the women had entered the convent at a very young age. The median age at entrance between 1756 and 1766 was 18.5 (in other words, half of those who entered were 18 or younger), and nine girls were 16 or under when they entered the convent.[68] Significantly, the rival factions that developed in the convent correlated along lines of age at entrance: The women who were less mature when they entered the convent tended to be more rebellious, while those who were older when they entered the convent were less so. This pattern makes logical psychological sense; we would expect that older girls and women (on balance) might have made the decision to enter a convent on the basis of more mature consideration and a truer vocation than the younger girls and therefore might have been better prepared to make the sacrifices that were asked of them—more tolerant of what the younger women might consider excessive demands. The median age at entrance of the 12 members of the rebellious faction for whom we have information was 17 years old. Two of the rebellious nuns were 14 when they entered, three were 15, two were 17, one was 18, and one was 19; only three were over 20. We do not know the ages of Phelipa de San Antonio or María Anna del Santísimo Sacramento at entrance because these documents were kept in Mexico City, where they appear to have been lost. Among the eight nonrebellious, or "obedient," nuns, by contrast, only two were under 20 when they entered the convent, one of whom was the foundress, María Josepha Lina. (For biographical sketches of the rebellious and obedient nuns, see table 1.1. Biographical material on all of the other nuns who entered the convent from its foundation through 1854 can be accessed at http://history.berkeley.edu/faculty/Chowning/rebelliousnuns).

A third significant feature of the convent population was that it contained a large number of girls who had lost one or both parents. In itself, this was not unusual. One of the social functions of convents, after all, was to provide security for girls who had lost parental protection. Guardians of orphaned children felt that they could always do right by female charges by placing them in a convent. Widows who had lost their husbands' earning power saw the convent as offering a secure future to their daughters, and in some cases (not La Purísima, but many others), convents allowed widowed mothers to join their daughters in the convent if the need arose. Widowers might feel that they could not raise daughters on their own, and for widowed men or women, a second marriage might be made more attractive by the fact that a daughter from a first marriage who became a nun would make no claim on the surviving parent's property.

In its early years, however, the San Miguel convent seems to have attracted an unusually large number of orphaned girls: Between 1756 and 1765, only 15% of the entrants into the convent had both biological parents living, compared with 47% of the women who entered the convent of Santa Catarina (Valladolid) and 36% who entered the other new convent in the bishopric, Nuestra Señora de la Salud in Pátzcuaro, during the second half of the eighteenth century.[69] Almost two thirds (61%) of the entrants into La Purísima during its first decade had no living parents at all, whether adoptive or biological, compared with 27% for Santa Catarina in the 1750s and 1760s and 30% for Nuestra Señora de la Salud from 1750 to 1799.

Orphanhood may well influence attitudes and daily routines, and when it is as common as it was at the San Miguel convent, it may have extended its influence even beyond the orphaned girls themselves. One of the interesting justifications for the establishment of a convent in San Miguel was that families wanted to be able to visit their daughters in the convent and would even move to the convent city in order to be able to do so. The large number of orphans at La Purísima may have meant that there was less connection, via these family visits, to the outside world than was true at a convent like Santa Catarina, where many of the nuns came from prominent local families and visitors were a frequent (too frequent, many church officials thought) event. An argument could be made that the nuns at La Purísima were not as well integrated into

TABLE 1.1. Profiles of Rebellious and Obedient Nuns

The Rebellious Nuns

Phelipa de San Antonio

Age/date of entrance into convent: Unknown
Circumstances of birth: Unknown

The youngest of the founding nuns, Phelipa was 29 years old when she arrived in San Miguel. Perhaps significantly, she had only been a nun for some 5 or 6 years when she came to San Miguel, which meant that she was 23 or 24 when she professed and 22 or 23 when she entered the convent of Regina Coeli. In other words, she was relatively mature and formed when she entered the religious life. Although the catalog called her "obedient" (significantly, not "very obedient" or "blindly obedient," as was the case with some of the nuns) and "sweet-tempered, agreeable" (*dulce*), it also called her impetuous or excitable, literally, "fiery" (*fogoso*). As for her talents, it was noted that she knew how to read and write, and indeed, her letters indicate not only that she had mastered these skills, but also that she had some familiarity with the writings of church fathers and authorities. Phelipa had a strong will, but was not confrontational, preferring the oblique to the direct. She was an excellent politician and inspired devotion among her followers (no doubt the "kind" part of her personality).

Josepha Ygnacia de San Luis Gonzaga

Age/date of entrance into convent: 18 (1756)
Circumstances of birth: Natural child; adoptive parents deceased

Born in Querétaro, the natural child of parents without impediment to marriage. She and her brother were raised by their aunt, Da. Juana de Texeda y Parra. Her parents were attested by all witnesses to have been of noble Spanish blood. Always inclined to the religious life, she had no money for a dowry, so she dedicated herself to music in early childhood, hoping to be endowed by the convent, and indeed she was admitted on a scholarship as a vocalist (*a título de cántora*). Her aunt also raised another future nun, who entered the convent at the same time as Josepha Ygnacia: María de San Miguel. Though María was 22 years older than Josepha Ygnacia, the two women remained close friends and allies throughout their long lives. Both lived at least another 27 years, although they were described in 1766 as having "broken" health. Although a member of the "rebellious" faction, Josepha Ygnacia was nonetheless described as obedient, calm, and pleasant (*apacible*).

María de San Miguel

Age/date of entrance into convent: 39 (1756)
Circumstances of birth: Natural or abandoned child; adoptive parents deceased

According to the catalog, María de San Miguel entered the convent in 1756 at the advanced age of 39, although there are no entrance or profession documents to confirm this, and usually nuns over the age of 35 had to be exempted from age restrictions on such late entrance. Born in Querétaro, before she was admitted to La Purísima, she had lived for 7 years in the Beaterio of Santa Anna in San Miguel, "without leaving it except to come to this convent." Like Josepha Ygnacia de San Luis Gonzaga, she had been raised since infancy in the house of D. Bartolomé Fernández de Ortega y Mejía and Da. Juana de Texeda y Parra, both deceased. Also like Josepha Ygnacia, María de San Miguel was a vocalist. Witnesses repeated rumors that she was the niece of D. Bartolomé, but her baptismal record (not included in the record, but referred to by others) indicated that her parents were unknown. María's 3,000-peso dowry was imposed on a ranch in Celaya. She was obviously a difficult character from the point of view of the author of the catalog: she was described as very impetuous/excitable (*mui fogoso*) and willful/passionate (*vivo*).

(*continued*)

TABLE 1.1. Profiles of Rebellious and Obedient Nuns (*continued*)

The Rebellious Nuns

María Anna del Santísimo Sacramento

Age/date of entrance into convent: Unknown

Circumstances of birth: Unknown

> One of the founding nuns and at first an opponent, then a defender of the first abbess against the rebels during the first phase of the rebellion. She fought with the rebels herself when she succeeded the first abbess, and then changed her position again and came to be considered among the rebels during the second phase of the rebellion. At the time of the foundation, she was named to occupy the second highest office in the convent, the Vicaria de Casa. She was described as highly obedient, but also very willful/passionate (*mui vivo*). To judge by her own testimony and the testimony of her actions, she was somewhat weak-willed and fickle, with a cruel streak. She was said to know how to do "everything," which for a nun meant that she was able to read, write, sing, and perform all of the feminine tasks, such as sewing and embroidery.

Josepha Ygnacia de Santa Gertrudis

Age/date of entrance into convent: 19 (1757)

Circumstances of birth: Abandoned; adoptive parents deceased

> Born in León, in the province of Guanajuato, but quite distant from San Miguel. Brought a dowry of 1,500 pesos; the other 1,500 pesos needed for her to become a choir nun was granted in a music scholarship (*a título de música*). She was described as willful/passionate, but also modest or shy (*vivo y vergonsoso*), very obedient, healthy, and apt in all areas.

Cayetana de las Llagas

Age/date of entrance into convent: 17 (1758)

Circumstances of birth: Abandoned; adoptive parents deceased

> Born in Mexico City to unknown parents and abandoned on the doorstep of the Marquesa of Valle de la Colina, who is said to have greatly esteemed the child, keeping her at her side from the time she could walk. Witnesses stated that it was clear from an early age that she had "good blood," which was confirmed by her aspect as she grew older. After the death of the Marquesa, her son, the Marqués of Valle de la Colina (D. Pablo Maderazo, a nephew of Manuel de la Canal) and his wife brought Cayetana to San Miguel, where they placed her in the school of the Beaterio de Santa Anna. She left the school after a few years because of illness, and lived in the house of "a woman who later professed to La Purísima." Several men asked her to marry while she was still a schoolgirl, but she chose the religious life. The author of the catalog called her very willful/passionate (*mui vivo*), but obedient if treated with kindness, and talented in music and singing. Although reading and writing were not mentioned among her aptitudes, she must have been something of a student of the written word, since her own correspondence has a particular style (very baroque and emotive) and she obviously enjoyed writing.

Augustina de la Encarnación

Age/date of entrance into convent: 14 (1758)

Circumstances of birth: Both parents deceased

> One of the notorious Urbina sisters (when asked to name the rebellious nuns, almost all of the nuns interviewed placed "las Urbinas" at the top of the list), Augustina was 14 years, 11 months old when she entered the convent. She was born in the large mining city of Guanajuato; both of her parents, D. Joseph Urbina and Da. María Anna Mexía de Solis, were deceased. She and her sister were related to the prominent Martínez de Lejarza family. Augustina was described in 1766 as willful/passionate and pensive (*vivo y de reflexa*), readily obedient, healthy, and apt in most areas.

TABLE I.I. *(continued)*

The Rebellious Nuns

Xaviera de la Sangre de Christo

Age/date of entrance into convent: 17 (1758)
Circumstances of birth: Abandoned or orphaned; adoptive parents deceased

Born in Mexico City, Xaviera had been living in the Beaterio de Santa Anna in San Miguel since age 9 or 10. One document states that she was the legitimate daughter of D. Roque de Abila and Da. María Monzón and says nothing about either of them being deceased, but another says that she was the "huerfanita" (little orphan) of the Marquesa of Valle de Colina and that she was raised as an abandoned child, a designation that should not have been assigned if she was a legitimate child of known parents. This information is attested to by a witness who says that he heard it from the mouth of the Marquesa and Marqués. The Marquesa had also raised Cayetana de las Llagas as an *expuesta*. The two girls were exactly the same age, both were born in Mexico City, both were placed in the Beaterio of Santa Anna after the Marquesa's death; and both entered the convent in the same year. Xaviera was described as willful/passionate, but without malice (*vivo sin malicia*), with a talent for fashioning artificial flowers and needlework.

Vicenta del Corazón de Jesús

Age/date of entrance into convent: 15 (1758)
Circumstances of birth: Natural child; mother deceased

Born in the Villa de San Felipe (another town in Guanajuato), she was the natural child of D. Vicente García Puente, a Spaniard and notable (*vecino Republicano*) of San Felipe. There was no impediment to marriage. He always recognized her as his daughter, and he provided her dowry. Her mother, Angela Margarita de Salazar, was deceased. She was described as "humble and gentle" (*humilde y suave*), very obedient, and apt in feminine tasks.

Antonia de Señor San Joseph

Age/date of entrance into convent: 23 (1759)
Circumstances of birth: Both parents deceased

Born in Valle de Santiago (Guanajuato); she entered the convent on a music scholarship. She played the violin, cello, and organ. She was described as willful/passionate and delicate (*vivo y delicado*) and always obedient.

Gertrudis de San Joachín

Age/date of entrance into convent: 26 (1760)
Circumstances of birth: Both parents deceased

Born in Apaseo, a small town in Guanajuato, both of her parents were deceased. She was granted the dowry that had been occupied by Anna Gertrudis de San Raphael, one of the founding nuns, who in 1759 returned to the Regina Coeli convent in Mexico City. A competition was held for the dowry, with kinship to the Count of Casa de Loja, who had originally provided the dowry, the main criterion for success. She was described as very docile (*mui docil*) and highly obedient, with talents in the arts of sewing and making flowers.

Josepha del Rosario

Age/date of entrance into convent: 15 (1762)
Circumstances of birth: Both parents deceased

Although her sister Augustina had entered the convent in 1758 as a choir nun, Josepha chose to be a lega (white veil nun), against the wishes of her father, D. Joseph Urbina, who was willing to pay the higher dowry, but according to him, "the child did not want [the black veil]."

(continued)

TABLE I.I. Profiles of Rebellious and Obedient Nuns (*continued*)

The Rebellious Nuns

It is not easy to account for this decision—the black veil carried more prestige and traditionally a lighter workload, although this was not the way the overworked choir nuns at La Purísima saw things. One is tempted to suppose that Josepha's sister, who preceded her in the convent by 4 years, had warned her that the life of a choir nun was onerous, since choir nuns had to hold down multiple jobs and also carry the burden of a much stricter prayer schedule than that of the legas. She is described as very willful/passionate (*mui vivo*) and obedient, with the ability to read and write.

Anna María de los Dolores

Age/date of entrance into convent: 15 (1763)
Circumstances of birth: Mother deceased
> Entered the convent in 1763 as a lega (white veil nun). Born in León. Her sister, Ygnacia de Señor San Juan Nepomuceno, would enter the convent 2 years later. Like the Urbina sisters, one of these sisters, whose last name was Obregón, took the white veil, and the other was a choir nun: Anna María's sister would take the black veil 2 years later. Also like the Urbina sisters, "las Obregonas" were notorious rebels. Anna María was described as modest or shy (*vergonsoso*) and highly obedient, with an aptitude for sewing.

Ygnacia de Señor San Juan Nepomuceno

Age/date of entrance into convent: 14 (1765)
Circumstances of birth: Mother deceased
> Followed the footsteps of her sister Anna María de los Dolores, both into the convent and into the rebellion. She was simple-minded (*sencillo*), obedient, and capable of learning any task to which she applied herself.

The Obedient, or Well-Adjusted, Nuns (Nonrebels)

María Antonia del Santísimo Sacramento

Age/date of entrance into convent: Unknown
Circumstances of birth: Unknown
> "Presidenta" of the convent of Regina Coeli in Mexico City before being selected as a founding nun and the first abbess of La Purísima. We do not know how old she was when she arrived in San Miguel in 1756, since she died in 1763, before the preparation of the catalog that contains all the ages of the nuns. One study, however, names her parents and gives her date of profession as 1717.* If she were 19 to 22 when she professed (an average range), she would have been 55 to 58 when she arrived. María Antonia had a strong, deeply pious personality, but she was also blunt, driven, and peremptory, well-suited to demanding and exemplifying rigor in the observance of the rule and the constitution, but perhaps not well-suited to leadership. Since she died in 1763, she was not a part of the second phase of the rebellion.

María Josepha Lina de la Santísima Trinidad

Age/date of entrance into convent: 18 (1756)
Circumstances of birth: Both parents deceased
> The convent's foundress was 18 when she became its first novice in 1756. Described as very mild-mannered and calm (*apacible*), extremely gentle and kind (*suave suave*), and blindly obedient, by 1766, when the catalog was prepared, her health was already very poor. She died at age 32. She was deeply devout and respectful of male authority, but with a mind of her own. It is possible to see her as the most powerful personality in the convent, not so much by virtue of her family's social status and her position as foundress, and even less because she was "political" (like Phelipa), but because of her patent unwillingness to use status or position to

TABLE I.I. *(continued)*

The Obedient, or Well-Adjusted, Nuns (Nonrebels)

her own advantage. By exemplifying nunlike selflessness, she commanded the admiration and love of all members of the community, from the male authorities to the nuns of both factions.

Anna María Josepha de los Dolores

Age/date of entrance into convent: 32 (1756)
Circumstances of birth: Unknown

Accompanied the founding nuns to San Miguel after living for years in the Mexico City convent of Regina Coeli, hoping to amass the funds for a dowry. Offered a dowry by one of the convent's benefactors before she left Mexico City, she took the habit within a week of her arrival. Eventually, she became the third abbess; she presided over a brief period of relative calm between the two periods of rebellion, until she had to resign due to blindness and migraine headaches. She was described as very kind, gentle and sweet-natured (*mui suave y dulce*).

Manuela de la Santísima Trinidad

Age/date of entrance into convent: 22 (1756)
Circumstances of birth: Father deceased

According to the catalog, she entered the convent in 1756 at age 22, but this is unconfirmed by entrance or profession document. For reasons that are unknown, she did not profess until 1759. Sometimes a profession was delayed because of problems accumulating a dowry, but that was probably not the case here. Born in Salamanca, another small town in what is now the state of Guanajuato, her father, D. Juan Martínez Conejo, was a Regidor of the city and probably a man of some means. Manuela was described as willful/passionate (*mui vivo*), and indeed, she was one of the earliest and most vehement critics of the changes in the convent introduced in the late 1760s under the regime of Phelipa de San Antonio. She was also characterized as very obedient, another quality that corresponds to her later actions. She knew how to read and write, and it was noted that "there is not a single feminine skill that she has not mastered."

Gertrudis de San Joseph

Age/date of entrance into convent: 29 (1760)
Circumstances of birth: Both deceased

Born in Querétaro, Gertrudis had four sisters who were nuns and four uncles who were priests, and her father was the nephew of two priests. She was described as very willful and passionate (*mui vivo*), but also modest, with somewhat broken health and a consistent willingness to obey.

Theresa de la Luz

Age/date of entrance into convent: 16 (1760)
Circumstances of birth: Mother deceased

Born in León. Her father, Agustín de Septién y Montero, was a wealthy Guanajuato merchant who married an heiress, Da. María Anna de Austri, making María Theresa one of the few truly wealthy girls in the convent besides the Canal sisters. Her father first put her in the convent to protect her against a marriage entanglement after her mother died, but once she came to the convent, she abandoned all desire to marry and embraced the religious life. She was sent back to her home for a time, but she chose to return to San Miguel. She was described as very sweet-tempered and pleasant (*mui dulce y apacible*), very obedient, and apt in all things. Her answers to an interrogatory submitted to her by the bishop in 1769 suggest great intelligence and subtlety, as well as a good education.

(continued)

TABLE 1.1. Profiles of Rebellious and Obedient Nuns (*continued*)

The Obedient, or Well-Adjusted, Nuns (Nonrebels)

María de Jesús

Age/date of entrance into convent: 23 (1764)
Circumstances of birth: Father deceased; mother unknown
  Born in Querétaro. Her half-sister Gertrudis de San Joseph had professed in 1760. Their brother Manuel paid her dowry. Described as very timid (*mui encojido*) and obedient, she could sew and make artifical flowers.

Rita de la Santísima Trinidad

Age/date of entrance into convent: 29 (1768)
Circumstances of birth: Both parents living
  Born in Aguascalientes. A great-uncle was a prebendary in the Valladolid cathedral; Rita also had two uncles who were priests. She had childish and inexpert handwriting and seems to have been barely literate.

---

* María Concepción Amerlinck de Corsi, and Manuel Ramos Medina, *Conventos de monjas: fundaciones en el México virreinal* (Mexico City: Condumex, 1995), p. 225.

Sources: Documents concerning admission and profession scattered throughout AHAM, Diocesano, Gobierno, Religiosas; "Cathálogo de las Señoras religiosas de Choro, y Velo Negro, y de Velo Blanco . . . ," de AHAM, Diocesano, Gobierno, Visitas, Informes, caja 504 (XVIII), exp. 66.

local society and cared less about the mores of local society and what that society thought of them than would be true in a very well-connected, well-visited, long-established convent, such as Santa Catarina.

Exacerbating this relative lack of connection between the convent and the town was the fact that until 1774, the only nuns whose families lived in or near San Miguel were María Josepha Lina de la Canal and her two sisters, whereas in the Santa Catarina convent, over the course of the eighteenth century, one third of the nuns came from Valladolid itself and another 24% came from towns within a day's travel. In the convent of Nuestra Señora de la Salud, 52% came from Pátzcuaro and another 18% came from nearby towns; and in the convent of Santa Clara in Querétaro, half of the nuns came from the city of Querétaro itself.[70]

In addition, more of the San Miguel nuns were abandoned or natural children (daughters of parents who had not married despite the fact that there was no impediment to marriage) than the nuns of Santa Clara, Santa Catarina, or Nuestra Señora de la Salud. Six out of the 25 girls and women who professed between 1756 and 1765 (24%) fell into these categories, compared with 9 out of the 56 girls and women who professed to Santa Clara between 1750 and 1769 (16%), 5 out of 30 (17%) who professed to Santa Catarina during the same period, and 7 out of the 65 (11%) who professed to Nuestra Señora de la Salud in the period 1750 to 1799.[71] Indeed, quite a few of the young nuns at La Purísima were doubly orphaned—abandoned, not acknowledged, or insufficiently acknowledged by one or both of their parents, and then orphaned again with the death of the adoptive parents. These women, even more than those who had been orphaned, but might have sisters or brothers or aunts and uncles to support them, were cut off from the "outside" world. In some cases, they may also have harbored some resentment against their parents, whose identities were often quite well known to them, even when their birth record indicated that they were the children of "unknown" parents. Josepha de San Luis Gonzaga, for example, was a natural child whose parents were well known to have been "noble" Spaniards. Vicenta del Corazón de Jesús was another natural child whose father and mother were named by all witnesses; her father (who did recognize her) was a prominent citizen in the villa of San Felipe, where she was born. María de San Miguel's official record states that her parents were unknown, but there were rumors of a blood relationship with her adoptive father (he may have been her uncle); this rumor was cited as evidence of her Spanish blood. María Cayetana de las Llagas was born in Mexico City to supposedly unknown parents and abandoned, but rumors swirled around her birth, too, with public opinion clearly accepting that her parents were "noble." All told, 6 of the first 12 girls and women who entered the convent (between 1756 and 1758) were not only orphans, but also had some question marks in their baptismal record, and all 6 figured among the 14 "rebellious" nuns, along with 4 other orphans and 2 sisters who had lost their mothers.

In short, the social backgrounds of the San Miguel nuns, compared with those of nuns in the well-established convents of Santa Catarina, Nuestra Señora de la Salud, and Santa Clara, suggests that La Purísima was a place where discipline might be difficult to establish due to the extreme youth of its population, the unbalanced age structure, the fact that so few of them had families living nearby, and the large numbers of orphans and/or girls of illegitimate birth. As we will see in Chapter 2, these factors are by no means the only explanations for the rebelliousness of the convent, but they may well have contributed.

Occupying Their Convent

Although the convent had already been through one phase of the rebellion by 1765 (still unresolved and soon to resurface), this did not prevent the staging of a costly celebration in conjunction with the transfer of the nuns from their Hospicio, where they had lived for 9 years, to their new convent, just a few blocks away. The bishop sent a visitor general, Dr. Gerónimo López Llergo, to preside over the most "solemn, stately, and glorious celebration possible in this part of the world." Citizens of all social classes were called upon to weave palm fronds together in order to completely block the sun from the streets through which the nuns and the rest of the procession would pass (figure 1.16). "Ple-

beians as well as Nobles" were urged to adorn themselves and their homes "to
the extent possible and appropriate. . . . Every doorway should have luminaries,
there should be torches on the balconies and bonfires on the rooftops . . . and
to make sure that everyone complies, there will be announcements posted on
the doors of all the churches."[72] The visitor general ordered that a complete
record of the proceedings be kept, so that the villa of San Miguel would always
be able to remember this singularly important day in its history. This written
record began:

> On Saturday the 28th day of December of the year 1765, the Most
> Reverend Conceptionist Mothers were brought from their Hospicio
> to their Royal Convent: thus were the finest flowers and most fra-
> grant lilies [of New Spain] transplanted to their beautiful new Gar-
> den. . . . The day began with a solemn procession that departed from
> the parish church and moved at a suitably measured pace toward
> the new sanctuary. The seven blocks it traversed were canopied with
> woven branches decorated with tapestries, costly hangings, and
> shining mirrors, and equal attention was paid to the ground beneath
> as to the sky above: iron bars and grates leveled out any imperfec-
> tions in the streets, and sand was brought in to smooth the surfaces
> throughout. For significant stretches of the route, at the personal ex-
> pense of a Gentleman Ecclesiastic, the street was paved with
> wooden beams for the processants to walk upon. . . . Residences
> along the way were adorned profusely, and the musical warbling of a
> multitude of songbirds was accompanied by sweet choirs of expert
> musicians.
>
> The procession was led by the twelve sacred standards of the confra-
> ternities, each attended by twelve members, all carrying torches;
> they were followed by the members of the Venerable Third Order of
> Penitents, and in their midst, on the shoulders of four Clerics, was
> the image of the Most Holy Patriarch Señor San José, who as the
> patron of the procession carried in his hands the keys to the new
> Temple. The Third Order was followed by the sons of the Paduan
> Thaumaturge [San Antonio] carrying on their shoulders an image of
> the saint that was so beautiful and so exquisitely staged that it com-
> manded the attention of all. Then came the great Patriarch San Fe-
> lipe Neri on the shoulders of his sons [the Oratorians]. . . .

His image was followed by those of Santo Domingo (carried by the Franciscan padres), Santa Anna (accompanied by "her daughters" from the Beaterio
de Santa Anna and carried by four priests; the visitor reported that the image
was so richly dressed and interestingly adorned that she occasioned applause
all along the route), María de la Purísima Concepción (the "true and legitimate

Abbess and Prelate" of the new convent), and Señor Ecce Homo (this "Man God and God Man who has worked such prodigious miracles here and in all of America"). Detailed descriptions of each of the images were included: how they were dressed, what they carried in their hands, how they were positioned on the platform that was carried through the streets.

After the procession of images came the "Reverend Community of Virgins, daughters of María Purísima and brides of Christ. Each one carried her husband on her chest, in an image of the holy child, lit by a candle that she carried in her right hand." Then followed the Eucharist, "that Divine sun that carries out eternal Justice, draped in white and . . . transported in a canopied throne by the Visitor General, Dr. D. Gerónimo López Llergo." Finally came the representatives of civil authority, the venerable city council, "dressed in their finest robes, as befits such a magnificent, costly, and splendid occasion." "The crowds of onlookers hid the streets from view; to find a spot of earth to stand on was impossible, so precious was space along the route of the procession. To be squeezed from all sides was considered the height of comfort. . . ."

After various churches had been visited and the nuns deposited in their new convent, Vespers commenced, followed by the general illumination of the streets, towers, and rooftops, and a brilliant fireworks display; these observances were continued for 3 nights, and every day there were more celebrations and church functions, until on the fourth day, the procession reversed itself, and all of the images were returned to their churches, leaving behind the nuns of La Purísima. No doubt it was the hope of their abbess, Anna María de los Dolores, that the move to the new convent would prove to be a new start for a community that was deeply troubled. It was not to be the case.

NOTES

1. Francisco de la Maza, *San Miguel de Allende* (Mexico City: Instituto de Investigaciones estéticas, Universidad Nacional Autónoma de México, 1939), 56; Richard Salvucci, "Aspectos de un conflicto empresarial: El obraje de Balthasar de Sauto y la historia social de San Miguel el Grande, 1756–1771," *Anuario de Estudios Americanos* 36 (1979), 418. Salvucci quotes one contemporary of Manuel de la Canal, who estimated his wealth at over half a million pesos. See also Esteban Sánchez de Tagle, *Por un regimiento, el regimen: Política y sociedad. La formación del Regimiento de Dragones de la Reina en San Miguel el Grande, 1774* (Mexico City: Instituto Nacional de Antropología e Historia, 1982), 66.

2. De la Maza, *San Miguel de Allende,* 56; José Guadalupe Romero, *Noticias para formar la historia y la estadística del Obispado de Michoacán* (Guanajuato: Gobierno del Estado de Guanajuato, 1992 [1860]), 113; Leobino Zavala, *Tradiciones y leyendas sanmiguelenses* (Mexico City: M.E. Zavalo de Campos, 1990), 63. Among the many costly ornaments of the chapel were statues of Manuel de la Canal and his wife, María de Hervas y Flores, depicted adoring the Holy Sacrament and holding in their hands lamps with eternal flames.

3. Power of attorney from Manuel de la Canal to Francisco de la Vega, May 12, 1740, AHAM, Diocesano, Gobierno, Religiosas, Capuchinas, caja 208 (XVIII), exp. 5; De la Maza, *San Miguel de Allende*, 76–77.

4. De la Maza, *San Miguel de Allende*, 76. Today, the chapel is open to the public on certain days of the week and is well worth a visit.

5. De la Maza, *San Miguel de Allende*, 56; David Brading, *Church and State in Bourbon Mexico: The Diocese of Michoacán, 1749–1810* (Cambridge, England: Cambridge University Press, 1994), 42.

6. Since the reforms of the Council of Trent, the church itself, as a matter of standard procedure, interviewed prospective novices to be sure of their true vocation. But María Josepha Lina's guardian went beyond this practice, no doubt because she was not simply entering a convent, but spending her inheritance to found one. "Informes hechos a su Magestad y su Excelencia en orden a la impetración de licencia para la fundación de un convento de Religiosas en la Villa de San Miguel el Grande," 1752, AHAM, Diocesano, Gobierno, Religiosas, Capuchinas, caja 208 (XVIII), exp. 11.

7. Juan Benito Díaz de Gamarra y Dávalos, *Ejemplar de Religiosas, Vida de la muy reverenda madre Sor María Josefa Lino* [sic] *de la Santísima Trinidad, fundadora del convento de la Purísima Concepción, en la ciudad de San Miguel de Allende, Obispado de Michoacán* (Mexico City: Imprenta Alejandro Valdés, 1831), 15–16.

8. Díaz de Gamarra, *Ejemplar*, 7–10. This particular biography-hagiography was typical of the genre and of its cousin, the spiritual autobiography, in many respects: After a short discussion of a childhood that demonstrated an extraordinarily early religious vocation and a maturity well beyond the child's years, the biography abandoned chronological narrative and was organized according to the virtues displayed by the subject (e.g., humility, obedience). For comparisons to tropes in spiritual autobiographies, see McKnight, 132; Ibsen, 67.

9. Díaz de Gamarra was an important figure in the late eighteenth-century church in his own right.

10. Díaz de Gamarra, *Ejemplar*, 11–13. The Conceptionist order was founded in Spain in the late fifteenth century by a holy woman named Beatriz de Silva, who was a lady of honor to the Portuguese princess Isabel before being banished because of Isabel's jealousy of her beauty (so the story goes) to a convent in Toledo, where she was visited frequently by Queen Isabella of Castile. Isabella eventually used her influence with Pope Innocent VIII to approve the new order; she also donated a palace for the convent and a church for the use of the nuns. The Conceptionist order was the first female order to be established in Mexico. Muriel, *Conventos de monjas*, 16–17, 47–48; Pilar Gonzalbo Aizpuru, *Las mujeres en la Nueva España: Educación y vida cotidiana* (Mexico City: El Colegio de México, 1987), 243; Abbess María Antonia Theresa del Santísimo Sacramento to Bishop Pedro Anselmo Sánchez de Tagle, July 31, 1761, AHAM, Diocesano, Gobierno, Religiosas, Capuchinas, caja 209 (XVIII), exp. 23.

11. Juan Benito Díaz de Gamarra y Dávalos, *El sacerdote fiel, y según el Corazón de Dios. Elogio Funebre . . . a P. D. Luis Phelipe Neri de Alfaro* (Mexico City: Imprenta de la Biblioteca del Lic. D. Joseph de Jauregui, 1776), ii; Jorge F. Hernández, *La soledad del silencio. Microhistoria del Santuario de Atotonilco* (Mexico City: Fondo de Cultura Económica, 1991), 55.

12. Díaz de Gamarra, *El sacerdote fiel*, 23.

13. Brading says that he used 20,000 pesos of his inheritance to purchase Ato-tonilco; Bravo Ugarte mentions D. Ignacio García, whom Alfaro allegedly persuaded to purchase the hacienda. Brading's account is more specific (and therefore more credible), including a description of the material improvements, among others, a dam that was made to make the hacienda more profitable, but his source is unclear. Brad-ing, *Church and State*, 43; José Bravo Ugarte, *Luis Phelipe Neri de Alfaro. Vida, escritos, fundaciones, favores divinos* (Mexico City: Editorial Jus, 1966), 34.

14. Díaz de Gamarra, *El sacerdote fiel*, 25. Sleeping in a coffin was either rela-tively common among particularly pious men, or it was common for those who eulo-gized them to claim that they did.

15. Brading, *Church and State*, 43.

16. De la Maza, *San Miguel de Allende*, 210.

17. On the design of Atotonilco, see also Díaz de Gamarra, *El sacerdote fiel*, ii–iv; Bravo Ugarte, 16, 34–37; Hernández, 112; José Mercadillo Miranda, *La pintura mural del Santuario de Atotonilco* (Mexico City: Editorial Jus, 1950), 9.

18. Loreto López, *Los conventos*, 15; Heller, especially the introduction and chap-ter 3.

19. Querétaro was also San Miguel's rival in the economic sphere, since it was the other large textile-producing city in the Bajío region.

20. Gallagher, 84, 109; Cecilia Landa Fonseca, ed., *Querétaro: Textos de su histo-ria* (Querétaro: Instituto Mora, 1988), 47; John C. Super, *La vida en Querétaro durante la colonia, 1531–1810* (Mexico City: Fondo de Cultura Económica, 1983), 14–15; Marta Eugenia García Ugarte, *Breve historia de Querétaro* (Mexico City: Colegio de México, 1999), 86.

21. On the subject of reciprocity between male confessors and female penitents, see Jodi Bilinkoff, "Confessors, Penitents, and the Construction of Identities in Early Modern Avila," in *Culture and Identity in Early Modern Europe (1500–1800)*, ed. Bar-bara B. Diefendorf and Carla Hesse (Ann Arbor: University of Michigan Press, 1993), 83.

22. In a letter quoted at length in Chapter 2, the first abbess of the convent re-fers to Father Alfaro as having come to the convent of Regina Coeli several times to select the founding nuns, and the tone of the letter suggests that he was a familiar figure at the convent.

23. Bishop Martín de Elizacochea of Michoacán to Archbishop Manuel Joseph de Rubio y Salinas of Mexico, 27 October 1755, AHAM, Diocesano, Gobierno, Religiosas, Capuchinas, caja 208 (XVIII), exp. 12.

24. Muriel, *Conventos de monjas*, 51.

25. José Ignacio Paulino Dávila y Garibi, *Diligencias generalmente observadas en la Nueva Galicia para la fundación de conventos de monjas de vida contemplativa* (Mexico City: Editorial Cultura, 1959), 8.

26. "Sobre fundación de un convento de religiosas capuchinas en la Ciudad de Salvatierra," Año de 1800, AHAM, Diocesano, Gobierno, Religiosas, Capuchinas, caja 210 (XVIII), exp. 30. Various documents on the foundation of the convent of La En-señanza, AHAM, Diocesano, Gobierno, Religiosas, Concepcionistas/De la Enseñanza, caja 256 (XVIII), exp. 1.

27. "Informes hechos a su Magestad," 1752, AHAM, Diocesano, Gobierno, Religiosas, Capuchinas, caja 208 (XVIII), exp. 11.

28. In fact, the construction and related expenses ended up costing almost twice that amount, some 74,845 pesos, and the costs of housing the nuns for almost 10 years until the convent was ready, transporting them from Mexico City, and other miscellaneous charges eventually added over 20,000 pesos to the total. "Cuenta de los gastos erogados en la fábrica material del Rl. Convento de la Purísima Concepción de la Villa de S. Miguel el Grande, presentada por el Albacea del Sr. Conde de Casa de Loxa, a cuyo cargo corrió dicha obra," Valladolid, 1805, AGN, Templos y Conventos, vol. 26, exp. 2.

29. "Informes hechos a su Magestad," 1752, AHAM, Diocesano, Gobierno, Religiosas, Capuchinas, caja 208 (XVIII), exp. 11. The material in the remainder of this section is drawn from this folder.

30. "Autos hechos para la fundación del Convento que . . . ha de fundar en la Villa de San Miguel el Grande," and "Calidades y condiciones que se han de observar en el Convento Real de Señoras Religiosas Concepcionistas . . . ," October 15, 1755, AHAM, Diocesano, Gobierno, Religiosas, Capuchinas, caja 208 (XVIII), exp. 12. The rest of this section is drawn from material in these documents, unless otherwise indicated.

31. Among female convents in Latin America there was a great deal of variety in the roles of the legas. "Lega" is sometimes translated as "lay sister," which would mean that they were not professed nuns, but this was not the case at La Purísima. Legas who were lay sisters were more like servants than the white veil nuns at La Purísima. McKnight, for example (84), describes the legas at Tunja as "serving women," who did not take the vow of enclosure; Loreto López, *Los conventos*, describing the work performed by legas in Puebla convents, also makes them seem much more like servants than professed nuns.

32. Report of Lic. Vicente Antonio de los Ríos and Lic. Miguel José de Moche, 1781, AHAM, Diocesano, Gobierno, Religiosas, Catarinas, caja 242 (XVIII), exp. 335.

33. Gallagher, 83; Francisco de la Maza, *Arquitectura de los coros de monjas en Puebla* (Puebla: Gobierno del Estado, 1990), 12.

34. De la Maza, *Arquitectura de los coros de monjas en Puebla*, 12.

35. Ramos Medina, *Místicas y descalzas*, 116; Luisa Zahino Peñafort, *Iglesia y sociedad en México, 1765–1800. Tradición, reforma y reacciones* (Mexico City: UNAM, 1996), 155. For a description of the seemingly even more extravagant and worldly Lima convents, see Martín, 174–176, 206–230.

36. Several of the five Augustinian convents extant at midcentury also followed a version of the common life, but permitted personal servants, according to Muriel (253–256, 311). According to Gallagher, a few Dominican and Conceptionist convents had been "reformed," although Muriel's study of Mexico City convents describes seven of the eight Conceptionist convents in that city as unreformed. The eighth, Jesús María, was said to have followed the vida común, after a series of seventeenth-century reforms, only "to a certain degree" (65). She describes the Dominicans as "very austere," but notes that they followed only a limited version of the common life and had many servants (327). Gallagher's definition of "reform" seems to have meant adoption of some aspects of the vida común and not necessarily to have included a prohibition

on personal servants. My conclusion that, besides La Purísima, there were only five dowry-requiring convents that both prohibited servants and followed the common life is offered with these caveats. Gallagher, 57, 210–221.

37. By contrast, the Capuchins and Poor Clares did not require dowries (depending instead on alms for the funds to support the convent) and so tended to attract women from less privileged backgrounds than those who came to San Miguel; this was especially the case with the Poor Clares, whose convents were restricted to daughters of Indian caciques.

38. Archbishop Manuel Joseph de Rubio y Salinas to Bishop Martín de Elizacochea, 2 December 1755, AHAM, Diocesano, Gobierno, Religiosas, Capuchinas, caja 208 (XVIII), exp. 12.

39. "Cuenta de los gastos erogados en la fábrica material del Rl. Convento de la Purísima Concepción de la Villa de S. Miguel el Grande," Quaderno 2, Valladolid, 1805, AGN, Templos y Conventos, vol. 26, exp. 2.

40. Dr. Pedro de Jaurrieta to Bishop Martín de Elizacochea, 31 January 1756, AHAM, Diocesano, Gobierno, Religiosas, Capuchinas, caja 208 (XVIII), exp. 12.

41. Count of Casa de Loja to Bishop Martín de Elizacochea, 31 January 1756, AHAM, Diocesano, Gobierno, Religiosas, Capuchinas, caja 208 (XVIII), exp. 12.

42. Nicolás Rangel, *Historia del Toreo en México,* quoted in De la Maza, *San Miguel de Allende,* 89.

43. Lic. Joseph Ygnacio de Goyeneche to Bishop Martín de Elizacochea, 8 October 1756, AHAM, Diocesano, Gobierno, Religiosas, Capuchinas, caja 208, exp. 13.

44. Peter Gerhard, *México en 1742* (Mexico City: Porrúa, 1962), 25, using Villaseñor y Sánchez, put the population of San Miguel in 1742 at 18,150 "almas," and estimated the population of the alcaldía mayor of San Miguel (the civil jurisdiction, not just the town) to have been 23,800. Salvucci, 408, also basing his estimate on Villaseñor y Sánchez, agrees that the population of the villa in 1750 was between 15,000 and 20,000. Isabel González Sánchez, in her study of the relaciones geográficas for the bishopric of Michoacán, provides a census of the population of San Miguel that puts its population in 1756 at 25,218, including 6,802 Indians: *El Obispado de Michoacán en 1765* (Morelia: Gobierno del Estado, 1985), 298. She is clearly referring to the parish as a whole, and not just to the villa. An ecclesiastical census in 1791 (AHAM, Diocesano, Gobierno, Visitas, Informes, caja 509 (XVIII), exp. 103) gives a similar number as the other sources for the parish (25,549), but puts the population of the villa itself at 11,090 ("those who lived within the walls of the villa"). This suggests that Villaseñor y Sánchez's figures might be a bit high, and I have thus chosen the low end of Salvucci's estimate as the high end of my own.

45. Oscar Mazín, *Entre dos majestades* (Zamora, Mexico: Colegio de Michoacán, 1987), 55.

46. John Tutino, *From Insurrection to Revolution: Social Bases of Agrarian Violence, 1750–1940* (Princeton, N.J.: Princeton University Press, 1986), 65.

47. "Estado que manifiesta las Haciendas, Ranchos, Labores y Estancias que contiene la Jurisdicción de esta Villa de San Miguel el Grande . . . 1819," ACCM, Ramo Administración, Leg. 135; *Relación del siglo XVIII relativa a San Miguel el Grande* (Mexico City: Vargas Rea, 1950), 22.

48. Salvucci, 407–408, 415.

49. Salvucci, 422–424; Claudia Burr, Claudia Canales, Rosalía Aguilar, *Perfil de una villa criolla: San Miguel el Grande, 1555–1810* (Mexico City: Instituto Nacional de Antropología e Historia, 1986), 25.

50. Salvucci, 409.

51. Francisco de Ajofrín, *Diario del viaje que hicimos a México fray Francisco de Ajofrín y fray Fermín de Olite, capuchinos* (Mexico City: Secretaría de Educación Pública, 1986), 364.

52. Details of the case can be found in Salvucci; there is also a summary in De la Maza, *San Miguel de Allende*, 45. There was in fact a slight connection between the obraje crisis and the convent crisis. The beleaguered obraje owner, Balthasar de Sauto, lashed out against the construction of La Purísima, which was, of course, sponsored by the Count of Casa de Loja, as executor of the wills of María Josepha Lina's father and mother and as her guardian. Casa de Loja was the leader of the anti-Sauto faction. Sauto complained that the new convent would block one of the access roads to the villa, devaluing the properties in the neighborhood, many of which belonged to Sauto himself. Salvucci, 426.

53. Burr et al., 25–27.

54. Ramos Medina, *Místicas y descalzas*, 117.

55. De la Maza, *San Miguel de Allende*, 58.

56. Brading, *Church and State*, 135. Querétaro, San Miguel's rival in the economic arena as in the spiritual arena, also had a particularly rich religious/confraternal life, arguably, as I have suggested for San Miguel, because of the number of guilds in the other leading industrial city of the Bajío. On casta/mulatto confraternities in New Spain, see Nicole Von Germeten, "Corporate salvation in a colonial society: Confraternities and social mobility for Africans and their descendants in New Spain" (Ph.D. diss., University of California at Berkeley, 2003).

57. Bravo Ugarte, 17; Hernández, 50.

58. Bishop Elizacochea tour of building site, 18 March 1756, AHAM, Diocesano, Gobierno, Religiosas, Capuchinas, caja 208, exp. 12; Miguel J. Malo and F. León de Vivero, *Guía del turista en San Miguel de Allende, GTO* (Mexico City: N.d., n.p), 29. The dimensions of the site were 438 feet from east to west along what is now Canal Street, the side with the church and the cemetery; about 380 feet along Hernández Macías; about 425 feet on the west side, along the stream; and about 410 feet on the north side, from east to west.

59. Father Manuel Ramírez de la Concepción to Bishop Sánchez de Tagle, 1769, AHAM, Diocesano, Gobierno, Religiosas, Capuchinas, caja 210 (XVIII), exp. 35.

60. Vicar Ignacio Antonio Palacios to Bishop Fray Antonio de San Miguel, 8 July 1801, AGN, Templos y Conventos, vol. 6, exp. 1.

61. Vicar Ignacio Antonio Palacios to Bishop Fray Antonio de San Miguel, 8 July 1801, AGN, Templos y Conventos, vol. 6, exp. 1.

62. De la Maza, *San Miguel de Allende*, 93; Count of Casa de Loja to Intendant Juan Antonio de Riaño, 5 June 1801, and Vicar Ignacio Antonio Palacios to Bishop Fray Antonio de San Miguel, 8 July 1801, AGN, Templos y Conventos, vol. 6, exp. 1.

63. Vicar Ignacio Antonio Palacios to Bishop Fray Antonio de San Miguel, 8 July 1801, AGN, Templos y Conventos, vol. 6, exp. 1.

64. "Cathálogo de las Señoras religiosas de Choro, y Velo Negro, y de Velo

Blanco . . . de el Real Convento de Na. Sa. de la Concepción, de esta mui ilustre Villa de San Miguel el Grande, sus Virtudes, habilidades, Circunstancias, expresadas en la manera, y forma siguiente . . . ," AHAM, Diocesano, Gobierno, Visitas, Informes, caja 504 (XVIII), exp. 66.

65. See Table 1.1.

66. Two other girls had entered the convent, but had not professed; they are counted in statistics on entrances into the convent, but do not appear here because they had left the convent by 1760.

67. "Autos sobre la fundación del Convento de Religiosas Dominicas, en el Santuario de Nra Sra de la Salud de la Ciudad de Patzquaro," AHAM, Diocesano, Gobierno, Religiosas, Dominicas, caja 257 (XVIII), exp. 3; "Sobre fundación de un convento de religiosas capuchinas en la Ciudad de Salvatierra. Año de 1800. Lista de las Religiosas que del Convento de Sr. S. Jose de Gracia y Pobres Capuchinas de Querétaro ha nombrado su Excelencia el Arzobispo," AHAM, Diocesano, Gobierno, Religiosas, Capuchinas, caja 210 (XVIII), exp. 30; "Valladolid, 1804. Sobre que en el colegio de Educandas, que se construyó en Yrapuato en execución de la última voluntad del B.D. Ramon Barreto de Tabora, se funde por las Religiosas de la Enseñanza de la Corte de Mexico otro Convento de su Ynstituto," AHAM, Diocesano, Gobierno, Colegios, Varios, caja 4 (XIX), exp. 1 (La Enseñanza); "Sobre fundación del convento de Religiosas de Santa Tereza de esta Capital. Dr. y Mtro. Joaquín de Oteyra to Dean y Cabildo Sede vacante, 20 Nov. 1824," AHAM, Diocesano, Gobierno, Religiosas, Teresianas, caja 395 (XIX), exp. 1.

68. Between 1756 and 1760, the median age was 19.

69. Data concerning Santa Catarina and Nuestra Señora de la Salud here and in the following paragraphs is drawn from scattered expedientes in the following boxes and from other miscellaneous boxes that contain misfiled documents on these two convents. AHAM, Diocesano, Gobierno, Religiosas, Catarinas, cajas 215–254 (XVIII); AHAM, Diocesano, Gobierno, Religiosas, Dominicas, cajas 257–267 (XVIII).

70. Gallagher, 109.

71. Gallagher, 248–252.

72. "Año de 1765. Testimonio de los autos formados por el Sr. Visitador General . . . sobre la Translación de Religiosas del título de la Purísima Concepción . . . de su Convento viejo y real al nuevo, que se dedicó el 29 de Diciembre de este presente año en esta Villa de San Miguel el Grande," AHAM, Diocesano, Gobierno, Religiosas, Capuchinas, caja 209 (XVIII), exp. 28. The descriptions in the next several paragraphs all come from this expediente.

2

The First Crisis in the Convent (1756–1762)

Reforming Abbesses and Rebellious Nuns

Hints of internal turmoil that went beyond the ordinary and predict-able first leaked into the archival record in a document from late 1759, just over 3½ years after the foundation of the convent. It was a petition submitted by Gertrudis de San Raphael, one of the found-ing nuns, requesting that she be allowed to return to her home con-vent of Regina Coeli in Mexico City.[1] Afflicted with multiple infirmi-ties since she arrived in San Miguel, she wrote, she had suffered in silence as long as the convent population was still small, but now that the number of nuns had increased, her absence would not be so much missed. A doctor's report was appended, certifying that Gertrudis suffered from "grave headaches and indigestion, made worse by the hot and dry climate of San Miguel and by the fact that she has an abundance of melancholy humor. . . ." Detailed plans were made for her travel arrangements and submitted to the bishop, Pedro Anselmo Sánchez de Tagle, for approval.

But it is clear that Gertrudis de San Raphael's illnesses were not the real reason she wished to leave La Purísima. The confused and exasperated vicar of the convent, Juan de Villegas (the local priest who served as the liaison between the convent and the bishop), wrote to the bishop in October 1759 to report that he had met not only with Gertrudis, but also with María Anna del Santísimo Sacra-mento and Phelipa de San Antonio about returning to Regina—in other words, with three of the four founding nuns. It was obvious that all three were miserably unhappy and that the problem had to do with the strictness of the abbess, María Antonia del Santísimo Sacramento, but the vicar still came away from the meeting not knowing what to think or do. "Sir, they are women, and nuns . . . each one would tell me something different from the others . . . and I left feeling little enlightened. . . ."

(Here it seems appropriate to call the attention of the reader to the fact that two of the key personalities in this section share very similar names: María *Antonia* del Santísimo Sacramento was the first abbess, and María *Anna* del Santísimo Sacramento would become the second abbess. To reduce the confusion caused by the fact that virtually all of the nuns took "María" as their first name, I have followed their own custom in casual writing of eliminating the "María" for most of the nuns. Thus, María Antonia becomes simply Antonia, María Cayetana becomes Cayetana, and so on. María Anna, however, was never "Anna," and María Josepha Lina was always referred to by her full name, but in the cases of the others, it will be easier for the reader to drop the María altogether.)

The abbess, however, entertained no such ambivalence. She offered her discontented cofounders three stark choices: "either I leave, or you leave, or you submit to me." Villegas was of the opinion that she was entirely capable of enforcing this "trilema." In another exchange of letters, he and the bishop agreed that if the dissident nuns were "truly religious," they would follow the third path, that of submission—and indeed by November, Phelipa de San Antonio had already agreed to stay and submit. But since the other two were apparently not willing to do so, Villegas recommended that they be allowed to leave for the sake of peace and unity in the community, and Sánchez de Tagle concurred: "I suppose this is the better course if we are to preserve the Peace and direct the novices, in whose hearts it is important to sow the seed of obedience, which is so essential to the disposition of Doctrine."

In fact, there was no small hint of disappointment on the part of the bishop when María Anna had a last minute change of heart and also decided to stay. In an abject letter to him, she begged his forgiveness "a thousand times over" for the trouble she had caused, but she wrote in her own defense, "no one but my Lord and spouse Jesus Christ knows why I wished to return [to Regina]. . . ." Now, however, she withdrew the petition. With her confessor and others "close to her heart," she said, she had decided that she might as well die in one place as another. In the face of this decidedly unenthusiastic choice to remain at La Purísima, the bishop and vicar were backed into a corner—they had supported the ultimatum proposed by Mother Antonia, whereby the nuns would choose to leave or submit, but their preference was for María Anna to leave, as Gertrudis had already done: "we find ourselves with a great dilemma: how can we maneuver so that without a hint that we are trying to get rid of her or remove her by force, she departs, leaving in spiritual peace these tender plants in the vineyard of the Lord?" But they did not find a way to do so. In the end, Gertrudis was the only nun to return to Mexico City.

Although both Vicar Villegas and Bishop Sánchez de Tagle were disturbed by the defiance of the three founding nuns, the vicar had already concluded that there was some justification for their discontent: what he considered to be excessive demands placed upon them by the abbess, Mother Antonia, whose ideas regarding the purposes the convent should serve and how it should be administered in order to serve those purposes differed strikingly from those of her cofounders. This conflict of vision as to the proper meaning and function of the new convent, reflected in the differing attitudes of the four founding nuns, eventually spread to the new nuns, creating the crisis that is the main subject of this chapter and the one that follows.

Before we turn to the beginning of the rebellion, however, there is one other set of factors (besides the demographics of the convent population, discussed in Chapter 1) that we need to consider in order to understand how this convent, founded with such high expectations, came so quickly to the brink of disaster. To a certain extent, the issue over which the nuns of La Purísima divided—strict observance versus a relaxed interpretation of the Rule—was inherently troublesome, and virtually all convents, not only in Mexico, but also in Europe for centuries past, struggled with it. In order to appreciate the ways that this issue played out in this particular convent, we must place the convent's experience within a broad historical context.

The Spiritual and Social Roles of the Convent

The convent tradition in Europe, brought to Mexico shortly after the conquest, was a strong one, but it was by no means unchanging or unambiguous: Over the centuries, female monasteries had come to serve multiple purposes, some of which contradicted or at least undermined others.[2] This multiplicity of roles for the convent, in turn, implies a multiplicity of motivations for entering the convent, a fact that has historically created problems in unifying and governing convent communities. La Purísima was no exception.

In the spiritual realm, the convent represented "the triumph of celestial marriage over human sexuality," and it was a symbol of Christian perfectibility, since retreat from the world and rejection of worldly things and values—carried to its ultimate extreme in the convent—was understood to be the surest and happiest way to approach God.[3] As women who were closer to God than laypeople were, nuns could also intercede on behalf of the sinful or needy, and thus, the convent served an important function as a spiritual mediator. In addition, the convent was thought to have a positive influence on laypeople's religious habits and even their characters. It stood as a reminder of the role that daily prayer, self-examination, penitence, and contemplation should serve in people's lives, and beyond this, it acted as a "fortress standing against moral lapses and worldly perversity," a place where character traits that were treasured not only in the church, but also in the secular world—humility, modesty, austerity, chastity, self-abnegation, obedience, and respect for authority—were modeled by the nuns. In short, it was "a community whose zealous observance of their Rule [would] cause general edification among the public."[4] The populace was meant to imagine that, behind the convent walls, the very highest levels of Christian charity, community, and observance were being practiced on a daily basis. This could only inspire the town's far less perfect residents to try to follow the nuns' mysterious example.

But besides these spiritual purposes, convents also served important social roles. At an abstract level, they molded and showcased a unified elite identity, as girls from many different kinds of elite backgrounds came together and—in theory—created a harmonious community with no social distinctions, where hierarchies were determined by seniority and office, not background or degree of wealth. This was a role that was particularly crucial, of course, in the newly formed societies of sixteenth-century New Spain, but it retained importance in the eighteenth century as the daughters of Spanish immigrants and the daughters of old creole families—groups that were increasingly rivals in the outside world—entered the convents on equal footing with one another, adopted new names in religion (thus, obliterating their family names), wore the same habit, and called one another "Sister." The rules and customs of the convent, thus—again, in theory—worked to build a homogenized identity among the nuns that would be projected to the outside world, showing the elite an idealized image of itself.[5]

At a more concrete level, another social role of the convents, as we have seen, was to absorb orphaned or illegitimate daughters of the elite, providing a sort of social safety net for such girls. In an extension of this role, the convent also educated many daughters of the elite in convent schools, including orphaned or illegitimate girls, preparing them either for the nunnery or for marriage by teaching them the rudiments of reading and writing along with the other "feminine" skills, such as embroidery and sewing. Beyond this, convents allowed families whose daughters were unmarriageable for one reason or another to be placed in a respected institution, where their honor and the honor of the family would be served. In fact, successful estate planning strategies might well depend upon placing a daughter in a convent, where she would be removed from the inheritance equation, thus allowing the parents' estate to avoid excessive fractionalization.[6] Such a family might not even be fully aware, in a world that greatly esteemed the convent and saw it as the highest expression of female religiosity, that they were "placing" a daughter in a nunnery; rather, they, and probably the daughter, too, likely saw this as an honorable and attractive choice made by the girl herself. But a family that encouraged their daughter to enter the convent, whether they did so consciously or not, chose carefully. Certain convents had more social prestige than others (generally, the more relaxed convents), while others had more spiritual prestige (generally, the more rigorous ones), and which convent one's daughter entered spoke volumes about her and her family to a society that was as highly attuned to the nuances of convent selection as prominent or aspiring families today might be attuned to the nuances of prep school or college selection. Thus, while one of the purposes of the convent, in theory, was to break down and conceal social distinctions, and all convent constitutions employed the language of community and egalitarianism, other purposes of the convent, in practice, were to exhibit differences and to reproduce, admittedly in muted form, the lifestyle, hierarchies, and relationships of dependence existing in the outside world and to communicate to the society at large the family's social position, values, and aspirations.

Motivations for Entering the Convent

Just as the convent had many meanings and purposes, so also were there different reasons why individual women might choose to enter a convent. For some, the convent provided an opportunity to express their piety and devotion to God without worldly distraction. Behind its walls, they could escape the "seductive temptations of the Common Enemy" and the outside world and nurture their vocation in peace.[7] It was, then, a place of spiritual opportunity and refuge. But for other women, there were equally compelling, nonspiritual attractions of life in a nunnery: avoidance of marriage, a state in which women's subordinate status was ingrained in a strongly patriarchal system; avoidance of the burdens of childbearing; the opportunity to exercise the mind (since reading, writing, and creative activities were not incompatible with the contemplative life of the nunnery); and the opportunity to exercise power and authority within the religious community and even, to a point, outside convent walls, a quasi-public role that was absolutely denied to women in the secular sphere. Indeed, convents were frequently seen as places where women had too much power and were insufficiently submissive.

In the mid-sixteenth century, at the famous Council of Trent (1545–1563), a number of reforms of the female convents were introduced, including the requirement that prospective nuns must be interviewed to determine if they were choosing the religious life entirely of their own free will, or if their families were pressuring them to enter the convent. The goal was to reshape the convents into places where enclosure and strict adherence to the monastic rule were not just tolerated, but desired, by girls with a "true vocation." But these interviews seem quickly to have become pro forma, and it is certain that many girls who were not strongly or solely motivated by vocation were entering Mexican convents, pressed by their families, desirous of protection, seeking power and prestige, wishing to avoid marriage and childbirth, or to advance their education—all of the extraspiritual reasons why some women had traditionally chosen the religious life. At the same time, as always, there is no doubt that many nuns were deeply devout and did possess a burning desire to grow closer to God through the means made available only in the convents.

In Europe and in large cities in New Spain, the diversity of convent types—some very strict and some very relaxed—made it possible for women to choose one whose unique personality meshed with their own goals and motivations. But there were far fewer convents in New Spain than in Europe, and for many girls, there was only one convent that was located within a reasonable distance of their home. If they did not live in Mexico City or Puebla, or to a lesser extent, Querétaro or Guadalajara, their choices were very limited. Thus, in most Mexican convents, including La Purísima, deeply pious and zealous nuns, committed first and foremost to a life of strict observance, lived alongside nuns who were there for reasons that had only partially to do with their spirituality. It was the difficult job of the abbesses of these convents with diverse populations to balance and manage the needs of all of the nuns.

Motivations of the Founding Nuns at La Purísima

Father Alfaro chose as abbess for the new convent a woman who came to La Purísima with a mission to establish a shining model of strict observance, and she was prepared to be quite uncompromising in pursuit of this goal. Mother Antonia del Santísimo Sacramento was disdainful of laxities and lapses at Regina Coeli, and she saw the new foundation as a chance to build a more perfect community. She was fully in accord with the vision of the young foundress of the convent, María Josepha Lina, that this should be a reformed convent, the first reformed Conceptionist convent in Mexico, and indeed, was prepared to go beyond the spirit of simplicity and communality embodied in the constitution that María Josepha Lina and her advisers had formulated.

Her cofounders' motives for coming, however, are less transparent. There is no reason to question the sincerity of their desire to serve God—indeed, the decision to take part in a new foundation was meant and taken as a sign of unusual devotion. To leave one's home convent was understood as a supreme act of self-sacrifice: Temporarily, the nun's prayerful routines, made possible by enclosure, would be broken, and she would be forced to give up permanently the presumed comforts and consolations of her old convent and to separate herself from her sisters in religion, her family, her patrons, and her patria. Thus, since the time of the Council of Trent, when enclosure was elevated to a position of centrality in the convent ideal, the idea of leaving the convent, even for such a magnificent undertaking as to found another, was invested with great symbolic meaning, and the nuns who carried out the foundations were seen—and saw themselves—as spiritual heroines.

There was another possible motivation for leaving a home convent, however—one that was not so heroic and was not openly acknowledged by the church. A new foundation may have been seen by nuns who were not entirely content in their home convents as an opportunity for a fresh start. Any hint that the ecclesiastical authorities had sent an unhappy nun to found a new convent would have been very embarrassing, of course. In the first place, there were not, according to the idealized version of the convent, supposed to be any unhappy nuns; and in the second place, if there were, these were not the women who should be founding new convents. Nonetheless, officials must have been tempted to do just this—by removing a discontented nun, they might be able to solve her problems and also the problems that she caused or might eventually cause in her home convent. And in fact, one remark made by the new abbess of La Purísima about Phelipa de San Antonio (see her letter later in this chapter) does suggest that the archbishop of Mexico had initially opposed sending her as a founding nun, and there was some implication that it was because she was either miserable or disruptive at Regina Coeli. In any event, their unhappiness at La Purísima strongly suggests that the motives of Gertrudis, María Anna, and Phelipa were very different from those of Antonia, even though only Gertrudis ended up returning to Regina Coeli.

We are now ready to begin the story of the first convent crisis. In Chapter 1, we saw that a number of factors made for a potentially volatile community at La Purísima: the youth of the convent's population; the age gap between the younger nuns, who formed the large majority in the convent, and three of the four founding nuns; the social distance that may have separated the orphaned and illegitimate girls from the supportive society of San Miguel; and the fact that the convent belonged to an order that did not have a reputation for strict observance, but rather for laxity, which may have given mixed signals as to the lifestyle that novices would find within. In this chapter, we have added background of a different sort, situating this particular Mexican convent in a history of convents and convent reform and emphasizing the inherently awkward coexistence in the convent community of women with very different motivations for having joined the community in the first place. As we will see in the following pages, however, the personalities of the various actors in this drama were also important factors in the ways that the crisis emerged and evolved.

Mother Antonia's Story

"Although everyone esteems her religiosity, she is an overbearing women, very formal in her demeanor," the vicar wrote of the abbess, Antonia del Santísimo Sacramento, at the time of the return-to-Regina crisis. Later, in September 1761, he repeated the sentiment: "I have always venerated her great virtue, but I cannot deny her violent temperament, which occasions great fear and apprehension among all the nuns."[8] The vicar's view of Antonia's character—that she was admirable, but too zealous by half—makes her seem somewhat one-dimensional. Her own words, in numerous letters to the bishop and the vicar (one of which is quoted at length later) help us to complicate and deepen this perception of her as little more than a crusading fanatic of reform. Before we turn to Antonia's own words, however, we should outline the facts on which all parties agreed, since this will make her narrative and all of the others easier to follow.

One of the first things that Antonia did upon arrival in San Miguel was to put into place a rigorous "distribution," a daily schedule of prayers, masses, and observances. In addition to the recitation of the Divine Office, mandated in the Rule, Antonia required an unusually large number of optional devotions, examinations of conscience, and other "acts of community." On a typical week- day, the nuns rose at 4:30 A.M. in summer and 5:00 A.M. in winter and were expected in the choir half an hour later, where they prayed for 30 minutes before Prime, after which they prayed for another half hour. Around 7:00 A.M., they would be permitted to eat breakfast. If anyone had fallen asleep in choir, no one would get breakfast at all. The rest of the day was scheduled in a similarly demanding fashion, and the regimen was sufficiently harsh and un- accustomed that the dissident nuns privately branded Antonia's distribution not an interpretation of the Rule, but a new Rule altogether. (See table 2.1 for a typical daily schedule, with comments by Cayetana de las Llagas, one of Antonia's enemies.)

The burden of prayer and community acts was exacerbated by the fact that one of the reforms of the Council of Trent regarding the female convents had been to expand the number of officeholders in the convents. Thanks to these reforms and to La Purísima's constitution, which forbade personal servants, the nuns had many other responsibilities besides attending choir. In 1759, Gertrudis de San Raphael, for example, held six positions in convent gover- nance: She was one of four members of the Definitorio, the consulting body of the convent; she was the secretary and accountant of convent finances; she was in charge of the vocalists (*vicaria del choro del canto*); she was the head nurse and dispenser of medicines; she was a *seladora del silencio,* which meant that she had to take turns, along with the other four members of the Defini- torio, ensuring that silence was observed in the cloister; and she was an *escucha de las rexas,* which required her to monitor the visits that nuns were allowed to receive at the grille during specified hours.[9] Phelipa de San Antonio held five positions, and most of the first generation of new nuns held at least three each (table 2.2). The need for overlapping offices was a predictable problem in a new convent, but that did not prevent the nuns from feeling that some re- laxation of the Rule should apply until the convent population grew enough to diminish the day-to-day labor demands on each of them. But in general, An- tonia's view was that, if there was an interpretive space in the Rule and con- stitution for looser or stricter observance, she favored the stricter choice.

TABLE 2.1. 1761 Daily Distribution*

4:30	Arise
5:00	Half hour of prayer in Choir, Prime, another half hour of prayer
6:30	Breakfast (". . . if the poor nun did not leave the room in a sea of tears, because the Abbess had either reprimanded her or someone else for not raising her voice in singing the Divine Office, or because she nodded off and hit her head against the table in the Choir")†
7:30	Mass and recitation of the three lesser hours, Terce, None, Sext
9:15	Chocolate
9:30	Workroom with spiritual lesson and, on Thursdays, doctrine
11:00	Examination of conscience
11:30	Refectory with spiritual lesson (except days of recreation), prayer of thanks in Choir
1:00	Rest
2:00	Vespers, Magnificat, Salve Regina, Rosary of five mysteries, three Our Fathers and Hail Marys
4:00	Workroom
5:00	Rest
6:00	Compline, Matins, Magnificat, quarter hour of prayer, quarter hour of examination of conscience
8:00	Refectory with spiritual lesson, prayer of thanks
9:00	Blessing of the Abbess, one Our Father and ten Hail Marys, recitation of the Creed ("and thanks to God that it was nighttime, to rest")

* Summer schedule; in winter, everything occurred a half hour later.
† Parenthetical comments by Cayetana de las Llagas.

Sources: Sister María Josepha Cayetana de las Llagas to Sanchez de Tagle, 7 November 1769, AHAM, Diocesano, Gobierno, Religiosas, Capuchinas, Caja 209 (XVIII), exp. 23; "Visita a el Convento de las Monjas Concepcionistas de la Villa de San Miguel el Grande . . . 1775," AHAM, Diocesano, Gobierno, Religiosas, Capuchinas, Caja 211 (XVIII), exp. 44. The distribution summarized in Cayetana's letter refers to the special distribution that Mother Antonia created for Lent, but Cayetana's comments were meant to apply to the ordinary daily schedule as well. The 1775 visita documents include a copy of the distribution authorized by Bishop Elizacochea in 1761, with one exception: In an effort to reconstruct Mother Antonia's distribution, table 2.1 includes two half-hour periods of prayer in the morning, which we know that Elizacochea reduced to one half-hour period and one quarter-hour period. Other changes that Elizacochea might have made to modify Antonia del Santísimo Sacramento's distribution cannot be known, but Antonia herself said that this was the major change.

Soon Antonia's three cofounders, accustomed to a very different style of life in their home convent of Regina Coeli, rebelled against her regime: All three petitioned to return to Regina Coeli. As we saw at the beginning of the chapter, one of them (Gertrudis) did, in fact, leave the convent, but the other two (María Anna del Santísimo Sacramento and Phelipa de San Antonio) decided—in María Anna's case, reluctantly—to remain. After the return-to-Regina crisis, however, it was Phelipa de San Antonio who emerged as the leader of a group of nuns who opposed Antonia's strict regime. The opposition mounted by Phelipa's faction finally made things so difficult for the abbess that she was toppled from power in May 1761, when the bishop decided to accept her resignation as abbess, after he had twice rejected it in an effort to save her. The new abbess, named by the bishop at the suggestion of the vicar, was María Anna del Santísimo Sacramento, the other cofounder besides Phe-

TABLE 2.2. Offices Held by Nuns, 1759*

Vicaria Abadesa	Antonia del Santísimo Sacramento (1)
Vicaria de Casa	María Anna del Santísimo Sacramento (2)
Definidoras	Gertrudis de San Raphael (6)
	María Josepha Lina de la Santísima Trinidad (3)
	Anna María de los Dolores (3)
	Phelipa de San Antonio (5)
Porteras y torneras	María Anna del Santísimo Sacramento (mayor)
	Phelipa de San Antonio (segunda)
	Josepha de San Luis Gonzaga (tercera) (1)
Maestra de Novicias	María Josepha Lina de la Santísima Trinidad
Sacristanas	Juana María de San Phelipe Neri (mayor) (3)
	Rita de Jesús (segunda) (1)
	Josepha Ygnacia de Santa Gertrudis (tercera) (3)
Secretaria y contadora	Gertrudis de San Raphael
Mayordoma	Josepha Ygnacia de Santa Gertrudis
Vicaria del Choro del Canto	Gertrudis de San Raphael
Vicaria del Choro del Reso	Manuela de la Santísima Trinidad (2)
	Josepha Ygnacia de Santa Gertrudis
	Cayetana de las Llagas (3)
Maestra de Niñas	Anna María de los Dolores
Provisora	María de San Miguel (1)
Ropera	Manuela de la Santísima Trinidad
Enfermeras y Boticaria	Gertrudis de San Raphael (Mayor)
	Phelipa de San Antonio (segunda)
	Juana María de San Phelipe Neri (tercera)
Seladoras del Silencio	Gertrudis de San Raphael
	María Josepha Lina de la Santísima Trinidad
	Anna María de los Dolores
	Phelipa de San Antonio
Escucha de las Rexas	Gertrudis de San Raphael
	Phelipa de San Antonio
Corredora del Choro Baxo	Cayetana de las Llagas
Corredora del Padre Capellan	Juana María de San Phelipe Neri
Recoletera	Cayetana de las Llagas
Obrera	Anna Rosa de Nuestra Señora de Guadalupe (1)

* Numbers in parentheses represent number of offices held by each individual.

Source: "Tabla de los Oficios que ande exercer las Religiosas en este Trienio, 10 March 1759," AHAM, Diocesano, Gobierno, Religiosas, Capuchinas, caja 208 (XVIII), exp. 19.

lipa who had originally wanted to return to Regina Coeli and had changed her mind. María Anna was destined to have a short term in office—and one that was even more disastrous than Antonia's.

Antonia tells her side of this story in a letter written to Bishop Sánchez de Tagle in July 1761, after she had resigned as abbess. It was indisputably written in her own words and hand, both of which were very distinctive.[10] In this letter, she demonstrates not only the "violent temperament" singled out by Vicar Villegas, but also considerable strength of character, enough to stand up to powerful secular figures, as well as to the relatively ineffectual vicar, and a strong sense of her duty to protect the convent's independence, its principles of self-government, and the physical well-being of its population. She did not like backing down, and when she was forced to do so, she did not give up, but rather waited for another opportunity to press her own agenda. She saw herself as the martyr/heroine of the story she was telling, a quality present in many spiritual autobiographies, but in other ways, her writing differed significantly from that well-known genre of female religious writing. Far from the timeless, circular quality that characterizes these autobiographies, this letter shows a genuine flair for narrative, telling her story in dramatic, but orderly and logical fashion.[11] She could be witty and sarcastic, and she abjured the flowery and deferential language adopted by so many relatively well-educated nuns; instead, she plunged ahead in a very straightforward fashion, almost completely without punctuation or paragraphs (not an unusual trait, but one that she carried further than many of her contemporaries), and she always included at least one postscript, as if she had built up such a head of steam in her writing that she could not quite bring herself to stop. In sum, her prose, like her handwriting and her character itself, was far from elegant or polished, but all three had verve, strength, and authority.

Antonia begins her version of the events sketched above when she, as a middle-aged nun living in the convent of Regina Coeli, heard that a new convent was to be founded in San Miguel. Falsely modest about her own chances to be named as abbess (extreme humility was a typical pose adopted in spiritual autobiographies), she established herself as a firm advocate of reform, against the laxity of the "convents of Mexico City":

> When I heard of the Canal daughter's decision to found in this Villa a convent of *descalzas* [discalced, literally "barefoot," meaning strict-observance nuns] of the Purísima Concepción I could not contain myself: that which my soul so greatly desired, that there should be in this Kingdom such a convent, was to come to pass. I begged Father Alfaro [María Josepha Lina's confessor and her agent in the recruitment of the convent's founding nuns] to persuade those chosen as founders to take me along, as their cook if need be. But instead they chose me to be the first abbess. I told the Archbishop, my beloved father, that as long as the convent was to be comprised of *descalzas* who would observe the Rule as it is written, then I would come with great pleasure, but that if it was to be like the convent of Regina and the rest of the convents of Mexico [City] then I did not want to go. . . . Father Luis Phelipe Neri de Alfaro assured me forcefully and repeatedly that it would be as I hoped.

In the early part of the letter, she also demonstrates a practical regard, expressed with considerable feistiness, for the material welfare of the convent. She was concerned about the possibility that the nuns would not have a pension or an allowance of their own with which to satisfy their material needs (such an allowance would have been quite common at Regina Coeli). Characteristically, her solution was to pray day and night in order to find God's answer:

> And so I determined to come, but when I realized that the nuns were not to be given in common everything they needed, nor was there to be a pension provided for them so that they could arrange to buy clothing and other necessary items, I asked God and my confessor to guide me in how to go about correcting this situation, and I decided to make a distribution [schedule of prayers and other acts of community] for every hour of the day, because this is the way that the brides of Christ must consult with His Divine Majesty.

In the next paragraphs, she begins to lay out the divisions between herself and her cofounders, in which her central argument is that they agreed to come to a reformed convent, well knowing what they were doing:

> As soon as the religiosas who came with me heard that I had been asked to be a founder, they begged me to bring them with me. I told them how strictly the convent was to follow the Rule, and that silence would be observed to the full extent of the Rule, and that there was to be no disagreement or bickering, but only much union and peace, and I read them the distribution that I had made and that was when they showed the most pleasure, and the youngest of those who came [Phelipa] demonstrated great contentment that there was to be an hour of prayer in community and all three told me that that was what they wanted, that that was why they came, because this is the way it should be, and they promised me all of this, and the Archbishop allowed them to come.

Things began to go badly almost from the beginning. As her cofounders grew more restless under her regime, they even went so far as to pressure a secular figure, the Count of Casa de Loja (the guardian of the Canal children) to intervene—one pictures secretive meetings between the unhappy nuns and the convent's patron, the count, at the parlor grille. The count's intrusion into convent affairs was intolerable, from Antonia's point of view, and here she shows her willingness to use sarcasm as a rhetorical tool to undermine his authority:

> Finally came the day of departure and during the journey I began to sense the change in them, though I attributed it to the rigors of the road . . . I had a thousand anxieties about how to put [the Rule] into practice, but my companions did not feel the same because they began immediately to complain about the amount of prayer. Priests and seculars alike came to tell me many things, asking why did I

burden the nuns with so much prayer, and I could not believe that these complaints came from my sisters, and I was confused. Father Alfaro asked me for a copy of the distribution, because my beloved prelate Sr. D. Martín de Elizacochea [the bishop of Michoacán], may he rest in peace, wanted to see it, and he reviewed it and only removed half an hour of prayer in the morning and he left the other half an hour and everything else just as it was. Then my sisters turned to the Conde de Casa de Laxa [sic], may he rest in peace, to ask him to make the distribution because they did not want to follow mine, and they told him to remove all of the religious observances that I had included except the Mass, and when he had completed it he called me to tell me that the nuns would be happy with his distribution, and I could not suffer this . . . I told him that I had never realized that seculars governed the convents, and that if the nuns did not want my distribution I did not want his, and we would have neither one nor the other. I sent for my confessor prepared to return to Regina but with great prudence he calmed me. . . .

At this point, Antonia's confrontation with the dissident nuns began to turn against her. Although she painted Bishop Elizacochea's alteration of her distribution as a victory, since he changed less than the others wanted, the truth is that she had not yet been able to find a single male figure—whether her confessor, the bishop, the count, or the vicar—who did not insist that she moderate her demands. She did, however, in a very important conquest, shame María Anna, who would soon succeed her as abbess, into accepting her direction. The other founding nun, Phelipa de San Antonio, however, grew bolder and more defiant:

I called a meeting of the Definitorio in which I reprimanded their effrontery and their lack of constancy in the many promises they had made to the Archbishop and to me, and I told them that now things would be as in Regina, with no distribution at all, at which Mother María Anna del Santísimo Sacramento, who is now our abbess, fell to her knees and with clasped hands begged me not to take away the distribution. I put to her this question: if the Conde's distribution was intolerable and if they did not want my distribution, what was to be done? She suggested that my confessor write one, and I consulted with him, and he told me that I should write it, and then I should give it to him and he would transcribe it in his own handwriting, and so I did. When he saw that mine still contained an hour of prayer in the morning he consulted many learned friars and he moderated it so that it only called for a half hour of prayer and a quarter of an hour of examination of conscience in the morning and another half hour of prayer at night and nothing else. This is the

distribution that has been observed from then until now though the
gainsaying and opposition of my companions has never ceased. . . .

Defeated, Antonia bided her time, waiting until the time was right to reintro-
duce the more rigorous distribution that she had devised before she even arrived in San Miguel:

> My confessor ordered me to be quiet and suffer this until there were
> enough new nuns, and when there were enough [I brought back my
> distribution] and this is when my companions wanted to return [to
> Regina], and one of them did leave. The second, Mother María
> Anna, changed her mind and decided to stay, asking my pardon and
> making me many promises never to depart from what I ordered her
> to do, and this she has done, setting a very good example for the
> others. The third [Phelipa] told me that she had come with me and
> that she would obey me and do whatever I wanted her to do, in
> which she has not only failed, but she has put herself at the head of
> a faction (*bando*) that she has organized, and may God give me
> strength to tell you what has now happened to this poor convent.

At some point during late 1760 and early 1761, then, according to Antonia,
the rebellion that began with the three cofounders became more organized and
extended to new nuns, who could not, of course, demand a return to their
home convent. Phelipa de San Antonio became ever more clearly their "cau-
dillo" (to use the bishop's word), a term more frequently associated with
nineteenth-century strongmen. When the bishop, no doubt advised by the vicar
to do so, finally accepted Antonia's third resignation and replaced her with
María Anna del Santísimo Sacramento in late May 1761, Phelipa and her followers transferred their opposition to the weaker and more vulnerable new
abbess.

One of the methods that Phelipa used, whether consciously or uncon-
sciously, to challenge the authority of both abbesses had to do with an illness
that many, though not all, thought she was feigning: what was referred to as
the "salto" (literally, jumping sickness, an affliction that the bishop described
as "dancing, gesturing, and disordered words"). When she was suffering from
this affliction, she stayed in her cell, where she was visited frequently by her
confessor, a young priest named Pedro de Rubí, and as the bishop pointed out,
the more she suffered from it, the more often she needed to confess.[12] Her
relationship with Rubí was seen as suspicious, to say the least. Antonia's account:

> [Soon after our arrival, Sister Phelipa de San Antonio] was overcome
> by an illness that can best be described as an invention of the Devil,
> because it consisted of dancing and bobbing about and finding a
> thousand excuses to confess with the R. P. Prepósito of the Oratorio

de San Phelipe Neri. Every time she was afflicted with the dancing
sickness she wanted her confessor to come and he finally could not
suffer this, and seeing that he did not want to confess her as often
as she wished, she dismissed him and took up as her confessor Br.
Pedro Rubí, who is a very young boy who had only been a priest for
one year when we came here [Rubí was 27 years old at the time of
the convent's foundation].[13] He was named by Father Alfaro as his
substitute chaplain, since Father Alfaro is very busy at the sanctu-
ario of Atotonilco, and ever since we arrived this has given me some
frightening nightmares.

Rubí's visits grew more frequent, and it was as if Phelipa drew strength and
courage from her relationship with him; meanwhile, the number of adherents
to her faction grew:

Having chosen him as her confessor, Sister Phelipa was soon calling
him every day . . . and sometimes he was there all morning and all
afternoon, and I would pass by and hear guffaws of laughter from the
Father and the sick nuns and I heard nothing of a confession. So I
asked one of the sick, a timid and fearful girl, when the confessions
took place, and she said that she did not know but that the nun who
had left [Gertrudis] and another sick nun had assured her that it was
nothing more than a game. I immediately called our Vicar and he
told me to talk to my own confessor . . . meanwhile Sister Phelipa
continued to enjoy her affliction, and she would not hear Mass or
leave her cell for anything, and so I denied entry to Father Rubí,
whereupon she left her cell and spent the whole afternoon with him
in the *tornita* [little turnstile] of the sacristy. . . . I was disconsolate
but what most chills my heart is . . . the disdain with which they
treat the poor abbess [María Anna] ever since I barred Father Rubí
from entering the cloister. . . . They refuse to say "good day" to me
in front of other people and once [Phelipa] grabbed a door handle
from me which I was opening for her and pushed ahead of me and
this too was seen by many people. . . . At that time I was still able to
walk and if they saw me coming they would run away and hide. . . .

Clearly, there was a range of issues that disturbed Antonia. She was upset
by the breaking of cloister (the abuse of the turnstile and the constant confessions in her cell demanded by Phelipa); by the fact that Phelipa used her illness
as an excuse to avoid attending choir, therefore undermining the life in community and the devotion to prayers; and by petty insults directed both at her
and at her protégé María Anna, which she took very seriously as breaches of
the principles of obedience and respect for one's superiors. But Antonia was
also fighting a larger battle against Phelipa's wholly different vision of what

the convent should be, a vision clearly in conflict with its austere constitution and the wishes of its foundress, María Josepha Lina. Phelipa was promoting an agenda that involved not just a more liberal interpretation of the convent's constitution, but also major changes in it—indeed, a reversion to the model of the "unreformed" convent. As Antonia continues, we get a sense of what changes Phelipa and her allies desired to make, as well as the frustration they felt with Antonia's regime:

> Four more have joined her band, and she has been attracting them by telling them that once she is abbess she will remove all of my inventions, and she will also get rid of the donadas [the lay sisters who did most of the manual labor in the convent] and instead each nun will have her own servant, and she will give them money for their own food so that they can eat whatever they want.

Phelipa, in other words, according to Antonia, was promising an end to the vida común. Things came to a head in spring of 1761, when Phelipa confronted Antonia directly in her cell:

> On the night of Palm Saturday I was preparing myself to take communion the next day and she [Phelipa] entered my cell as if she were my Mistress and from seven o'clock to eight o'clock she lectured me with great anger and gestures so extreme I thought she might strike me, telling me that I had never learned to be a good Mother, that I had not allowed her the consolation of confession with her Father, that she and all the nuns were in despair over me, that they were suffocating, and asking who had told me that I could order all the inventions that I have put in place, and saying that she would remove them, that she would write to Your Excellency telling you many things. . . . I asked her, had she not read the distribution before we even left Regina, did she not praise it and tell me that it was just what she wanted . . . and she told me that then she was blind and now she saw the light, and at last her fury was vented and I stood there, listening until she left, and I did not reprimand her nor punish her as she deserved because my confessor was sick and I wanted to consult with him about her penance, and it got back to Father Rubí that I was [going to punish Phelipa] and was just waiting for my confessor and he caused a great scandal not only in the convent but also in the Villa of San Miguel and the convent of San Francisco. Finally my father confessor, still sick, came to the turnstile of the sacristy to tell me that later that day, on Easter Sunday, I should resign the office of Prelada and so I did. . . .
>
> My Lord, since that night when Sister Phelipa came to tell me so many things, taking such liberties, I became very dismayed be-

cause they despaired of me even when I have loved them and tried to please them, and my nights were spent lying awake with hardness in my heart and belly and the next week I fell ill with all the ailments that are tormenting me to this day, for which Sister Phelipa and her confessor have all the blame. They will be the death of me. . . . This convent is transformed into a hell of lies and factions. . . . I cannot bear it that a girl I brought with me when she had only been a nun for five years, and whom the Archbishop vigorously opposed, should wipe away everything that we her elders have accomplished.

After this emotional climax, Antonia resumed her usual straightforward style, offering specific recommendations to resolve the crisis, even though the letter was written after she had been forced to resign. Why did she not trust the new abbess, María Anna, to find solutions to the problem? She knew her cofounder well, and she knew María Anna would be too weak to apply what she considered to be the necessary punishments in order to accomplish the goals of both smoothing the dissent and preserving the principle of reform. So she turned to the bishop. Only he could dismiss Father Alfaro as chaplain of the convent, a position that he had ignored as he became more and more preoccupied with the magnificent building project at Atotonilco, and only he could revoke Father Rubí's license to confess nuns, which she hoped would cause Phelipa to be willing to return to Regina Coeli. Moreover, the bishop had more power to punish at his disposal than did the abbess, and Antonia clearly thought that penances imposed by the bishop would carry more weight than those imposed by María Anna:

Our Mother [María Anna, the new abbess] was the one who wanted to write to you, but she started two letters and could not find the will to go on, and so she asked me if I would write, telling me that God would give me strength. The first remedy for our problems is that you must rid us of the substitute chaplain [Father Rubí] by ordering Father Alfaro to resign his title of chaplain and giving us a new chaplain chosen by you and our Vicar, and you must not only rid us of him as substitute chaplain but also as a confessor of nuns, because if he confesses them, who knows what he will order them to do? And the second remedy is for Sister Phelipa to return to Regina, which she should be willing to do if she is denied her confessor; and the third remedy is for Your Excellency to punish the nuns who joined her Band for not submitting to the Preladas and for treating them with such disdain, so that they will know they can and will be punished and in the future they will know that they must submit and not tell tales and spread gossip which so greatly prejudices the community. All these remedies Our Mother the Vicaria Abadesa and I ask of you, prostrated at your feet, by the blood of our sweet Redeemer . . . and also that you console us with a personal visit.

P.S. And what Sister Phelipa says about getting rid of the donadas and giving money to each Religiosa, this has nothing to do with anything I have done, since it is written in the particular observances of the convent approved by Dr. D. Martín de Elisacochea; the only complaint of theirs for which I bear responsibility is the half hour of prayer and the two quarters of examination of conscience.

María Anna's Story

Five days later, apparently asked by the bishop to give her version of the affairs in the convent, Antonia's replacement as abbess, María Anna, gathered herself to respond.[14] She would rather be buried alive, she wrote, than comply with his order to recount the recent sorrowful events, but "stimulated by my conscience as well as by my desire to obey," she must tell him that in this "recently planted community, the Enemy that never sleeps is about, and clever as he is, he has raised a Faction (*Bando o Bandera*) . . . and only three or four nuns have not surrendered to it." She went on to say that she was very grateful to Antonia for writing to him when she could not bear to do so. Antonia was in a better position than she to write such a letter, given her "great spiritual strength combined with much experience," while:

> as for me it could be doubted whether the two letters I started to write would benefit you, and I did not have the will to continue them partly because I have only occupied this position such a short time, and partly because it might be thought that I was going beyond my jurisdiction, and I thought it sufficient that you be made aware [by Antonia] of what is going on, and how this small flock of my beloved Jesus, is being made into something that breaks the heart. . . .

Aside from blaming the Devil rather than Phelipa (as Antonia, the more instinctively political of the two, had done), María Anna's perspective does not differ much from Antonia's, but it is worth underscoring the extent to which the new abbess deferred to her predecessor, whom she had originally defied. She had made an abrupt turnabout from wishing to return to Regina Coeli to begging Antonia to let her stay, and even more astonishingly, later in the decade, she became at least loosely associated with the rebels. She was the least literate of the eighteenth-century abbesses—her handwriting was very awkward and childish, and she wrote almost completely phonetically: In a wonderful phonetic mistake, she once addressed Bishop Sánchez de Tagle as "San

Chisdetagle." María Anna seems to have been an insecure woman with a mean streak (as we will see), and because of her weakness of character and perhaps because of her semiliteracy, it appears that she lacked the authority that Antonia, even at her most despised, nonetheless commanded.[15] For all of these reasons, she was not a good choice to replace Antonia, although with the departure of Gertrudis, there was really no alternative—the foundress, María Josepha Lina, was too young and too recently professed, and Phelipa was, of course, out of the question.

Phelipa's Story

Unlike Antonia and María Anna, Phelipa did not offer her own version of the unfolding of the rebellion. We have to infer her point of view and her motivations primarily from the words that her nemesis, Antonia, wrote about her, and that is a dangerous endeavor for a historian.[16] Still, some speculation seems warranted, even required, because of her central role in the events related to this point and those to come.

One question is whether Phelipa was ever committed to Antonia's vision of the convent or whether she was duplicitous from the start, saying that she embraced this vision in order to escape from Regina Coeli and Mexico City (for reasons we cannot possibly know). Both interpretations are plausible, but perhaps even more satisfactory is a third possibility that borrows elements of the other two: that she had deluded herself into thinking that a change of convent would solve whatever problems she had at Regina Coeli, and that she later regretted the move. This would account for her seemingly genuine enthusiasm about coming to a very different kind of convent from the one she had professed five years earlier. Perhaps more rigor and a deeper commitment to the spiritual life would provide a solution to her unhappiness at Regina Coeli. Thus, true to the religious spirit of the age, Phelipa had initially sought relief from her problems in a closer relationship to God and in a more deeply spiritual and self-abnegating community. But she soon found this new kind of convent to be not a solution at all: Instead of resolving her problems, the strictness of the regimen became stifling, "suffocating" (to use the word that Antonia attributed to her), and deeply frustrating. Significantly, her cofounders also found it extremely difficult to adjust to the kind of convent that Antonia was trying to create, suggesting that Antonia had crossed the line between seriously reformist and obsessively reformist. It was not, in other words, just Phelipa who could not tolerate her regime, a point made repeatedly by Vicar Villegas.

One of Phelipa's cofounders became ill with the effort of carrying on, and she eventually left the convent to go back to Mexico City. Phelipa herself, by the accounts of both Antonia and the vicar, went back and forth on the question of whether to stay or go—surely, we can infer that she was deeply conflicted over this decision, since the bishop offered her the opportunity to return to Regina and, indeed, seems to have preferred that she do so. Yet, ultimately, she decided to stay and obey. The fact that she soon found obedience impossible Antonia interpreted as willfulness and duplicity, but what we know of the facts suggests otherwise. Frantically, she sought counsel with her confessor; indeed, according to Antonia, Phelipa wanted to see him so often that he became exasperated with her and told her that he would not come as often as she wished, at which point, she turned to a different confessor, the young priest Father Rubí. With Rubí, she obviously found some solace; indeed, Antonia writes of hearing "guffaws of laughter" from her cell when Rubí visited her sickbed. This was probably an exaggeration, but still, it can surely be read as an indication of a congenial relationship. When a suspicious, or vindictive, Antonia told Phelipa that she could no longer confess with him, Phelipa was, predictably, distraught. Although it is certainly possible, we need not assume a romantic or sexual relationship between Phelipa and Father Rubí in order to see this separation as devastating—the confessor–penitent relationship is often extremely close and fraught with complicated emotion, and this is especially so between nuns and their spiritual directors.[17] In any event, Phelipa became so desperate that eventually, like Gertrudis, her distress became manifested in physical symptoms: in her case, the strange affliction, the "salto."

Thus, it was only after agonizing about whether to stay or go, only after turning in despair to one confessor who rejected her because of her excessive demands and to another who was turned away by Antonia, and only after having her anxiety translate into strange physical afflictions that Phelipa seems to have blamed the abbesses and the nature of the convent community itself and to have determined to change them. It is important to recognize the possibility that she was not trying to undermine the spirituality of the convent, but rather to find a way for God to be more present in this community. To her, the insistence on blind obedience to an abbess who had a willful disregard for the extreme physical demands of the daily schedule that she had devised was not the way toward the establishment of a successful community. That this brought her into direct conflict with the abbess was not something desirable, but at the same time, it was clearly not something from which she was willing to turn away.

Phelipa seems, then, to have undergone a transformation during this period of the first convent crisis, emerging as a strong leader within the convent, with an alternate vision of what the convent should be. We cannot know to whom we should attribute the cliché in both Spanish and English—Phelipa herself, or Antonia's paraphrase—but it effectively captures this profound change in Phelipa's attitude: Antonia reported that when she had asked Phelipa, during their heated confrontation in her cell, whether Phelipa had not praised the strict distribution and told Antonia "that it was just what she wanted . . . she told me that then she was blind and now she saw the light."

The Vicar and the Bishop

The Conceptionist order, since its beginnings in the late fifteenth century, had always been under the direct supervision of the bishop, and so during the rebellion, the bishop and his local representative, the vicar, were necessarily involved in the rebellion. Even if they had wanted to stay out of the conflict (and it is not at all clear that they did), the nuns themselves forced their hands; in fact, the nuns' unsolicited letters to the bishop are a key source for understanding their attitudes and beliefs, the ways they interacted with each other, and the ways they both relied on and tried to manipulate the bishop and the vicar. The documentation also, however, includes many exchanges between the bishop and the vicar, in which their own differing views of the rebels and their own attempts to manipulate the situation come through clearly. The vicar tended to sympathize with the nuns, who had to live under their abbess's uncompromising gaze, perhaps because he himself had to live under the same gaze. The bishop, however, from his distant palace in Valladolid, was thunderingly impatient with the rebellious nuns and remained sympathetic to Antonia and, later, her successor, María Anna, if not personally, then, to the idea of the abbess as guardian of the highest values in convent culture: self-abnegation, religious virtue, and especially obedience.

Although the factions in the convent had developed and come out into the open by February or March 1761, at the latest, Bishop Sánchez de Tagle appears not to have been made fully aware of the dissension in the convent until August. He had accepted Antonia's resignation in May, he later wrote, because he believed her when she said that her health was not good enough to continue as abbess; it was only after she had resigned that she wrote the long letter (quoted extensively earlier) to explain what had really happened, possibly at his request (since we know that he requested a letter of explanation from María Anna at roughly the same time). On August 14, he wrote an angry letter to the vicar, in which he criticized Villegas for not telling him sooner about the rebellion.[18] At this point, he was not even sure of Phelipa's name in religion, and he was still prepared to put most of the blame on Father Rubí, her confessor, as if Phelipa herself would not have been capable of conceiving the rebellion (he was later disabused of this notion):

> From a chance traveler I have come to know of the lamentable state
> in which this tender plantation of virgins that is under your care
> finds itself. Thus I have just found out that Mother Phelipa, whose

second name I do not know, but I think it may be San Antonio,
along with the better part of the community composed of the spiritual daughters of Father Pedro Rubí, have denied, in the most igno-
minious fashion, obedience to the past Abbess and the present one
... Although three or four who are not directed by Father Rubí have
joined the congregation of ungovernable nuns, from his position as
substitute chaplain [for Father Alfaro], he exercises the power to fo-
ment discord through the person of Mother Phelipa, who heads the
Rebellion. They have sown the Doctrine that the abbesses have no
larger role in the Monasteries than the Housekeeper (*Ama de llaves*)
in private households ...

Why had Villegas not apprised Sánchez de Tagle of the rebellion? When
María Anna asked for the bishop's support, in her letter of August 4, she
implied that she needed it because the vicar had sided with the dissidents
(presumably, this is the reason that both she and Antonia had written the
bishop without permission from Villegas). Sure enough, the vicar did put a
very different spin on the affairs related by Antonia and María Anna; he saw
it as a minor spat among women, frankly, somewhat justified, in light of Antonia's excessive zeal. At this stage in the crisis, he displayed relatively little
concern for the breaking of cloister, the lapses in attendance at choir, and even
the challenge that Phelipa had apparently mounted to the authority of the
abbess; instead, he was primarily concerned with how to avoid scandal in the
San Miguel community. This led him to downplay the importance of the whole
series of troubling events.

Writing to the bishop in late August 1761, Villegas was embarrassed that
the two senior nuns had written to the bishop without consulting him.[19] He
had been about to leave for Querétaro, where his niece was to take the veil at
the convent of Santa Clara, when the urgent August 14 letter from the bishop
caught up with him. We cannot know for sure whether he had dismissed the
rebellion as unimportant, had not thought it threatening enough to involve the
bishop, or had thought that it reflected poorly on him and therefore had kept
it quiet, but now that Sánchez de Tagle was in the know, he had to appear to
take it as seriously as the bishop obviously did. Calling the rebellion "a grave
matter," he said that he decided to visit Brother Miguel de Figueroa, María
Anna's confessor and a provincial secondary in the convent of San Francisco,
and his brother, also a Franciscan, Brother Carlos de Figueroa, who confessed
Antonia. "I described my affliction and my fears of scandal, and they both
advised me to consult with you about the best way to get rid of the chaplain
Father Pedro Rubí." The problem was that it was not easy to do that without
causing waves. "Much of what you have been told about the events in the
convent has indeed occurred," Villegas wrote to Sánchez de Tagle, "but it is
also true that the convent is not in such bad shape as you have been led to

believe because nothing that has gone on inside the cloister has escaped its walls. . . . In the Villa, there is not the slightest scandal . . . which leads me to judge that if I dismiss Father Rubí outright . . . [it will look suspicious] and the hidden will be revealed." His plan was to remove Rubí by having the bishop offer him a promotion to another town, and he even had one in mind: There was an opening in the distant (and not very desirable) parish of Los Pozos.

Having agreed that Rubí, a sharp and "naturally petulant" person, should be removed, the vicar nonetheless had some things to say in defense of the substitute chaplain. It was true that Rubí entered the cell of Sister Phelipa when she was ill, but that was because she was very sick indeed; in fact, the doctor thought once that she had died in the throes of one of her spells of "extraordinary movement." There were always *escuchas* (listeners) present when Rubí was in her cell, and much of the communication between Phelipa and Rubí, including the episode recounted with horror by Antonia, in which they spoke through the turnstile of the sacristy, occurred because Rubí had studied a bit of medicine and could talk to her about her illness, according to Villegas. Some of the nuns thought the illness was not real, but the doctor had testified that it was genuine, and he, Villegas, was also convinced by her general aspect of its authenticity. As for the other problems in the convent, he did not think that the dissident nuns were refusing to obey the abbess out of willfulness or malice. He had met with five of them at the grille, and they denied lacking obedience and treating the abbess with disdain. They pleaded with him to convince María Anna not to chastise them so much in choir and to correct their faults with love and not with harsh words, and he repeated this request to the bishop. In other words, he laid considerable blame at the feet of Antonia and now María Anna; at least, he thought, the bishop should suspend judgment.

Sánchez de Tagle, however, was not mollified.[20] How could he not be concerned about "rebellious nuns (*religiosas sublevadas*) who resist the observance of their constitutions, who deny obedience to their past and present Abbesses, and who are enlisted in a Band under the leadership of Sister Phelipa de San Antonio? If she is allowed to carry out her projects and to develop them under the protection of Father Pedro Rubí, we cannot expect any less than an explosive scandal in the Villa and its surrounding areas and even in the whole bishopric." He was dubious that the nuns could keep all this a secret, inside convent walls: "already there may be people who are not openly discussing the problems of the convent, but are secretly censuring them." He agreed that it was necessary to take away Rubí's license to confess nuns and to move him to some place where there were no convents. If Villegas' ploy to get him away from San Miguel by luring him to Valladolid for an interview with the bishop about the opening at Los Pozos did not work, then Villegas must find some other way.

Meanwhile, the bishop also wrote to María Anna to reassure her that he had taken steps to remedy the problems in the convent and calm the dissidents.[21] But he also had some advice for her: He urged her to "hold onto the leash, but not always to pull so tightly on it, correcting the nuns with temperate words (and if possible in private), full of charity, so that they know that these words have their origin in your holy desire to serve your office of Abbess, and not in any other source." She should be lenient about hours of prayer and other distributions that are optional in the Rule, because "by this gentle means you will tame the wills of the rebels . . . and they will embrace the Cross of Religion for the edification of those inside and out of the cloister. . . . And you and Mother Antonia will set examples that will speak to the souls of those who are cold [to religion], and even more so if their spiritual Fathers fan the flames of their hearts to engender in them the love of their divine Spouse."

Less than a month after his first letter to the bishop suggesting a scheme to get rid of Rubí, and after frustrating meetings with a number of nuns on both sides of the rebellion, Villegas began having second thoughts.[22] To this point, he had accepted the idea that Rubí's relationship with Phelipa had to end, although he clearly wanted to end it in a manner that preserved Rubí's career and every appearance of propriety. Now, however, his impatience with all of the nuns began to come through more clearly. Put bluntly, if the nuns were as irrational as they had shown themselves to be, then Rubí's blame in the whole matter necessarily lessened. Already, in his previous letter, Villegas had defended Rubí's relationship with Phelipa. Now, perhaps because of pressure from the townspeople, the vicar mounted an even stronger defense of Rubí and painted a more gloomy picture of what would happen if he, Villegas, tried to remove him. "Father Rubí is well thought of in the Villa," he wrote, and, he added meaningfully, at least one of the novices owed her vocation to him: the daughter of the extremely wealthy silver miner Agustín Septién y Montero, Theresa de la Luz (who was *not* a member of Phelipa's faction). If we remove Rubí now, "who will dare to serve the nuns?"

Meanwhile, Villegas had tried to make further investigations into the state of the convent, meeting separately with María Josepha Lina and Phelipa. María Josepha Lina (now the novice mistress) told him that "most days she and her novices were the only ones to attend prayer before Prime." Phelipa, however, claimed that there were no lapses in observance. "Every instant I became more confused listening to the two of them," Villegas complained. "If you were to interview each of the nuns in this convent," he said, "they all are rational. [But] what one says, and even swears to be true, another one denies. I have to dissemble in my answers to them, because if I did not, they would begin to imagine things." As an example of the nuns' contrariness, he pointed out that, in her letter, Antonia asserted that her cofounders had agreed to her distribution before leaving Regina, while they told him that they had not consented. "These contradictions are encountered at every turn," he lamented. Like Ignacio de Loyola, he would rather govern the whole Company of Jesuits than three nuns. Still, he said, returning to his theme of caution in the matter of dismissing Rubí with too much haste, "it is true that there is childish behavior and bad feelings among the religiosas, but I repeat that the convent is not in such bad shape as you have been led to believe."

Sánchez de Tagle, however, was not pleased with this backsliding on the part of his vicar.[23] No less patronizing toward the nuns, in his way, than Villegas, he fully accepted that they were behaving childishly and irrationally, but he did not believe that these "female" qualities that Villegas invoked in order to explain what was going on were the real problem, since those behaviors were to be expected in a community of women. Instead, it was the problem of lack of obedience, lack of order, and lack of attention to the principle of hierarchy within the convent that was of most concern. As a bishop who took seriously the church's eighteenth-century project of tightening ecclesiastical administration and bringing the regular orders under the jurisdiction of the bishop, Sánchez de Tagle was deeply concerned about the lack of obedience.[24] In his view, it was important for women in the convents, no less than rural priests or friars, to bow to authority, and the authority of the abbess, no matter how ill-received or ill-conceived her actions might be, must be defended, for through her flowed the authority of the bishop himself:

> You write me that you have conferred with both Sister Lina and Sister Phelipa and that Sister Lina told you that the distribution was not being observed, and that Sister Phelipa told you it was. . . . The report that I judge to be true is that of Sister Lina, which means that the voices I hear . . . telling of disorder in the convent are also true. You say that these are just childish things, sentimentalities among the Religiosas, so I suppose that the lack of obedience does not seem to you to be a grave matter. But I am persuaded that without obedience, all is chaos and confusion; the fundamental principle of good government of any community is that all of its subjects pay heed to the voice of the Prelate, and that they execute precisely his commandments although they might concern matters of small moment, because if he is not obeyed in the small matters, how is he to be obeyed in large ones?[25]

Since Villegas seemed to have the ear of the dissident religiosas, Sánchez de Tagle continued, he should take advantage of this fact to impress upon them the obligations of their estate. "I have read the Rule and any married Woman, managing at the same time her own family and attending to her Husband so that he lacks for nothing, could observe it, which leads me to believe that it cannot be that hard for the Religiosas of this monastery to comply."

In this exchange, the bishop rages against both Villegas (who, he believed, was not taking the problems seriously enough) and the nuns (except for María Josepha Lina). But in other letters, Sánchez de Tagle demonstrates a more moderate sensibility, a sincere desire to find a middle ground. He followed the intemperate letter to Villegas with a much gentler one to Antonia, assuring her that he had taken measures to change the style of Vicar Villegas (about whom Antonia had complained), apologizing for the vicar's "harsh treatment" of María Anna, and reassuring her that he was serious about getting rid of Rubí.[26] He also enlisted her in the effort to get María Anna to follow his advice and to ease up on her demands on the other nuns, so that the vicar would see that she was acting in good faith. Here, the matter of the crisis in the convent was put to a tenuous rest for 4 months, at least so far as the documentary record is concerned, but in spring of 1762, it not only resurfaced, but also reached new heights.

The Crisis Escalates

On March 24, 1762, Vicar Villegas wrote once again to Bishop Sánchez de Tagle, with more urgency than ever before. "All of the nuns, all I repeat, are mortified by the present Vicaria Abadesa. . . ."[27] He had collected testimonies from many of them that supported this claim, and he forwarded them to the bishop. Even two respected members of the "obedient" faction, María Josepha Lina and Anna María de los Dolores, were concerned because the less effective and more hated was Mother María Anna, the more Phelipa succeeded in winning converts to her cause. Villegas worried that the decision made by one of María Josepha Lina's sisters to leave the convent (before she had professed) was influenced by the behavior of Mother María Anna; he concluded to the bishop that he thought it was not related, but the fact that he brought it up at all suggests that he had not entirely convinced himself.

Four days later, an incident occurred that confirmed his worst fears and forced the bishop to act. On March 28, 1762, Cayetana de las Llagas, the former protégé of the Marquesa of Valle de Colina and among the first generation of new nuns to enter the convent, tried, apparently without great resolve, to hang herself in the garden. We have two accounts of this episode: that of María Anna, the distraught abbess, and that of Cayetana herself, recorded 7 years later in a 15-page letter to Sánchez de Tagle. Let us begin with María Anna's account, which presents the attempted suicide as another in a long string of efforts to persecute her:

> My tribulations are many since there are more conspirators every
> day and the Religiosas never cease their agitations . . . on the day of
> Nuestra Señora de la Encarnación at the foot of a tree in one of the
> patios I found a Religiosa . . . who was hanging herself with a belt
> tied around her neck. She appeared moribund [but then she] began
> to scream and shout and cause great scandal in the whole convent,
> and the only thing she would say was that she wanted to be "an-

other Judas."[28] The cause of this was that the day before, tired of tol-
erating her mocking faces and her uncontrolled behavior and seeing
that she was so impertinent with me, I took her to the novitiate and
I told the Father Vicar what had happened although I did not hope
for much consolation from him, and after awhile I went in person
to release her, and knowing how bellicose she is I approached her
with much affection but she was still furious, and she went alone to
Mass. . . . I implore you for the love of God and Purest Mary that
you intervene, that you put aside the many burdens of your office
and come to visit us . . .[29]

Cayetana's version of the story emphasized María Anna's cruel streak and
her willingness to humiliate the nuns under her command. Since Phelipa
wrote often, but unrevealingly, Cayetana's volubility gives us one of the more
intimate glimpses of the desperation of the rebellious nuns, though her letter
will serve us better in Chapter 3, since, having been written in 1769, it belongs
in time to the period of the second convent crisis. Note the contrast between
Cayetana's attitude toward María Anna and her attitude toward María Josepha
Lina, even though the latter was not a member of Phelipa's group:

In the days when María Anna del Santísimo Sacramento was Prelada (which you will remember, as I do, though I do not wish to), I
was punished by her . . . with the most shameful punishment possible for a Profesa (professed nun) and office holder, which is to be
sent back to the Novitiate. . . . Sir, I did not quietly accept this punishment, although all I did was to express my pain in lamentations
and weeping. I did not even spend the whole day in the Novitiate,
because the Novice Mistress, who had also been my Mistress when I
was a novice, that Angel incarnate Sister María Josepha Lina de la
Santísima Trinidad, could not bear to see me in such a state. . . . On
that night of the 28th of March I went to the cell of Mother María
Anna and there I overheard her recounting my tragic story with
great relish . . . I went out into the garden and found a tree from
which to hang myself; I stayed there long enough for them to miss
me; I was bruised and hurt, and I caused great commotion in the
whole convent . . .[30]

Sánchez de Tagle did not specifically mention this incident in a flurry of
letters and decrees he sent in early April 1762 (among them, his decision to
accept the resignation of María Anna as abbess), but it seems likely that the
suicide attempt triggered his actions.[31] The first of the letters was to Villegas,
on whom he had to depend to execute his commands, although he did not
entirely trust him since he considered him "soft" on the rebels. Much of the
letter was devoted to spelling out exactly how Villegas should handle the deli-

cate situation; for example, he baldly advises Villegas to use duplicity in dealing with the nuns, observing that sometimes that was the only way to handle women. The letter echoes many of his earlier preoccupations; he remained deeply concerned about the lack of obedience and hierarchy in the convent and about the threat of scandal in the outside world. He also continued to express his frustration and impatience with the convent's problems, which, he complained, were taking time away from other important business, including a "difficult" problem with the Augustinians.[32] But for the first time, he demonstrates a concern that the rebellious nuns not only failed to follow the Rule, not only failed to observe cloister, not only failed to obey, but also displayed an unacceptable spirit of independence. It is as if he was finally beginning to understand the depth of the challenge that Phelipa and her allies were mounting. This was no longer a rebellion against a too strict or too vindictive abbess, no longer the malevolent influence of Father Rubí, but rather a rebellion against the whole way of life represented by the reformed convent, a point that had been, for the most part, lost on both Villegas and Sánchez de Tagle, to date, in their fixation on avoiding scandal and enforcing obedience.[33] The dissident nuns, he writes, succinctly summarizing his increasingly subtle view of the situation, simply cannot be allowed to think that they are "free to do as they please"; they must abandon the "depraved illusion that they can live according to their own free will, as if they were mistresses of their own actions."

> In your letter of 24 March, you tell of the mortification that all of the Religiosas feel toward the Vicaria Abadesa; but she is no less mortified by them, and especially by Sister Phelipa de San Antonio, head of the Band of disobedient nuns . . . and this excuses [Mother María Anna] for her lack of moderation in the execution of her duties as Vicaria Abadesa, a position from which she has several times asked me to release her . . . which request I have decided to grant, naming in her place Sister Anna María de los Dolores. [In this packet] I include a letter directed toward the whole community, by way of pastoral exhortation, the writing of which took time away from my handling of the difficult business of the Augustinians among other important matters of concern in the bishopric. I worry about these other matters, but what preoccupies me the most are the Religiosas of that convent who have not submitted to the distribution that you formed with their consent and which I approved, so that it could serve as the instrument of their spiritual improvement and reduction to obedience, which they resist so much, wishing instead to be free to do as they please. Their unwillingness to abide by the vows they professed makes this situation a labyrinth, even a hell, as in any congregation where there is neither order nor hierarchy.[34]

He tells Villegas that he is writing to Phelipa, and he wants Villegas to read the letter first, so that he knows what the bishop has told her:

> I also write to Sister Phelipa, in which letter I privately admonish her and I tell her the punishment that I had considered imposing on her and that I will yet impose if she does not change her ways. Read it yourself and when you are finished give it to her, sealed and in private, and tell her that you have read it and that I have enjoined you to be vigilant that she complies with this correction, which is the only one I will make in this fashion; advise her that she must change her life completely and be an example for good rather than for bad. . . .

Also, he tells Villegas, in the packet of letters is one to Anna María de los Dolores, the new abbess, the third that the convent has had in its brief 6 years of existence. In it, he says, he reiterates that he wants the distribution to be strictly observed, no matter that the rebellious nuns are resisting it. Privately he tells Villegas that if the disasters of her two predecessors are to be avoided, Villegas must help her put an end to the subversive meetings that take place in Phelipa's cell:

> I also write to the new Vicaria Abadesa. I do not specify the changes that she needs to make, because it would be impossible to reform everything at once, but to you I will say that you must aid her in extirpating the abuses and transgressions of the Rule and assuring that the admirable customs in the distribution are upheld. . . . The rumors that are spread in the cell of Sister Phelipa, where [the diso-bedient nuns] convene to censure the every movement of the Pre-lada . . . must cease.[35]

Determined to shut down news coming into or out of the convent, Sánchez de Tagle prescribes a rigorous enforcement of the principle of enclosure: His concern is the very real problem that scandals associated with the convent will deter young women from entering it. The doctor and chaplain must be reined in and made aware of their violations of enclosure, and the nuns in charge of comings and goings in the convent must be the most trustworthy and cautious. Thus he continues in his long letter to Villegas:

> [We must guard against] the convent losing such public credit that not a single Person would want to enter his daughter in it. For this reason it is important for you to meet with the doctor to alert him that under no circumstances may he agree to deliver messages, let-ters, or papers to anyone outside the convent, even if they are meant for the confessors of the nuns, even if they are meant for you . . .

and to be even more sure that this practice does not continue or in-crease, you will apply the punishment of major excommunion if he makes an excuse secretly to linger and speak with any Religiosa on any subject that does not have to do with her infirmities; and I also charge you with making sure that the chaplain does not succumb to the same transgression because of a deception on the part of a Reli-giosa; and I also charge you to be sure that the *sacristanas,* who by exercise of their office monitor the common rooms, the main doors, and the choir grille, do not consent to these excesses. . . . I also name as monitor of the main door Sister Juana María Dolores de San Phelipe Neri, who is to exercise great vigilance that enclosure is observed in every respect; she will be as wary as Argos that papers and letters never leave the convent without the permission of the Vi-caria Abadesa. These measures, undertaken with all possible pru-dence, should accomplish our purposes . . .[36]

Sánchez de Tagle also wants to see the vida común reinvigorated, but it appears that his goal here was not specifically to uphold the convent's constitution, but to enforce this principle because it allowed him to replace Phelipa as vice-abbess (Vicaria de Casa), since her illnesses did not allow her to attend religious functions, meals, and sermons:

Care must also be taken that everyone attends all the acts of com-munity, including meals and sermons as well as prayers, unless they have a true excuse, and not a pretext, such as the pretext of illness that Sister Phelipa uses so that she will not have to attend choir. For this reason I have decided that it is necessary to remove Sister Phe-lipa from her position as Vicaria de Casa, and to name in her place Sister Lina, who will fill this position without giving up that of Nov-ice Mistress. I am certain she will serve in exemplary fashion, and she will help the Vicaria Abadesa to carry the Cross of Government in this convent. . . .[37]

Finally, Sánchez de Tagle advises Villegas on how to conduct himself in order to deceive the rebellious nuns, or at least to avoid giving rise to their suspicions that he is in collusion with the new abbess, although that is exactly what the bishop has admonished him to do. "After all," he writes, "they are Women, and it is necessary to use some deception from time to time in dealing with them."

I expect you will be pleased at my choice of Sister Anna María de los Dolores as Vicaria Abadesa, since it is to be hoped that with this measure the abuses and disobedience in the convent will be extin-guished, and to be sure of this it is very important that you not lend your ear to any of the nuns, nor that you conduct private meetings with the Vicaria Abadesa at the grille, even though she may request such a meeting, and that you be seen as deferring to her dispositions. In this way if there is any problem that requires remedy you can see it and advise on what is to be done, while allowing the community to believe that it comes from the Vicaria Abadesa alone, although it really comes from you . . . thus she will have more courage and authority to correct the faults of her children, and they will have less room to maneuver and manipulate in their attempts to disobey, [which is important] because the slightest cause, even imaginary, is excuse for them to refuse to pay heed to their Prelada. After all, they are Women, and it is necessary to use some deception from time to time in dealing with them, and when it is necessary to confront them, the individual case should determine whether that confrontation should be gentle or rigorous. You do not have the experience in the government of Religiosas that you have in other areas and matters of greater seriousness, and for this reason I have thought it convenient to spell out the steps we must take so that you can proceed with the tact that we desire.[38]

Following this candid—indeed, scheming—letter from Sánchez de Tagle to Villegas are the other letters he mentioned, beginning with the letter to the whole community. Much more formal and stern in tone than his other letters—in fact, more like a sermon than a letter—here, Sánchez de Tagle shows little of the candor that he demonstrated in the Villegas letter, though one common element is his frustration with the nuns' stubbornness and refusal to obey:

The first prophets that existed in the world began by announcing peace, in the coming of Our Redeemer. They called him the Lamb, the gentle King, the Angel of Peace. . . . Christians who sow discord, within whatever guild or corporation, create by their actions a true Hell out of what should be a delicious Heaven. . . . And in such a community, amidst so much harm, prejudice, and confusion caused by the malignant spirits allied with Satan, the only way that good can come is by means of obedience to their Prince or superior . . . Do the Religiosas of the Convent of the Villa of San Miguel el Grande obey their Superiors, their Preladas, who govern them in the name of God? Shamefully, they do not, in any way. . . . They despise their Abadesa who is the organ through which the commands of the Lord are made known . . . ; just as their Spouse is docile, gentle, humble, poor, obedient, chaste, pure, and patient, so ought his wives to be . . . but the Religiosas of San Miguel are many leagues distant from these qualities, according to reports I have received over-the last eight months. Because of disunion among them and lack of respect for their superiors, they are on the verge of losing their souls.[39]

Sánchez de Tagle then used this letter to tell his side of the story. He began with the reason why he accepted the resignation of Antonia, the chosen first abbess:

> Mother Antonia resigned her position as Vicaria Abadesa several times under pretext of illness, so as no longer to have to endure the insults, contempt, and disrespect of her subjects, whom she was not able to reduce to compliance with their Institute, with the admirable customs in which they have been raised and educated, not even with those that were introduced by common consent of the Founders. . . . These motives I did not recognize when I accepted her resignation, thinking only that she was too ill to shoulder the burden of her position . . . I named Mother María Anna del Santísimo Sacramento in her place, and as is the custom her subjects pledged to obey her, but it seems that this pledge came only from their mouths, and not from their hearts. . . .

He then went on to justify his decision now to accept María Anna's resignation, which had to be made to seem as if it did not defer to the wishes of Phelipa's disobedient faction.

> To remedy these faults the vicar of this convent devised the formation of various rules, in consultation with the leading and exemplary Religiosas, and when all consented to them, promising to abide by them unquestioningly, and they were signed by the members of this Definitorio, I believed that having accepted them, they would also be observed, and I approved them, believing that they would calm the troubled spirits including those who have formed a Band to which they attract the innocent with the depraved illusion that they can live according to their own free will, as if they were mistresses of their own actions. The hopes that I had for the success of this remedy began to fade with the reports that I started receiving soon after, and now that the vicar has given me full proof of the turmoil in this convent provoked by the worst possible influences, I am forced to accede to the wishes of the present Prelada, who has many times begged me by the entrails of Jesus Christ to relieve her of her position . . . I hope and expect that the community of this Convent, well understanding my holy wishes, will unite so that all aspire to the perfection to which they are obligated by their estate . . . The sure path to perfection is observance of the vows that they professed, and of these the most important is that of obedience, because without it

everything is confusion, and if this is true in the households of the outside world, how much more true it is in the houses of Religion. . . .[40]

At this point, the bishop's letter to the whole community continued for several pages on the subject of obedience.

This was, predictably, the same theme that he took up in his private letter to Phelipa, which was angry in tone, but surprisingly restrained in substance.[41] As outside observers would note when they reviewed the files 7 years later, the bishop was less than clear about exactly what punishments further rebellion on Phelipa's part would bring about, and he failed to impose some of the punishments that might already be justified by the circumstances. The delicacy with which the bishop felt he must handle Phelipa and the other rebellious nuns would be an even more prevalent theme in the second stage of the rebellion, which would begin in 1769:

> Sister Phelipa. . . . There is nothing hidden that is not revealed, as the Holy Spirit says, and so . . . the deplorable state in which this convent finds itself, and your irregular actions which have caused it, have become known to me, beginning with your exquisite infirmities of the physical body, and continuing with those of the Spirit, which are so contagious that they have afflicted other Innocents, who instead of finding in this place of retirement their own salvation have been put in danger of losing it by not complying with the obligations they accepted upon professing as religiosas, disdaining the principal of these, which is blind obedience to the precepts of the Prelada, which come from her mouth via the hand of God. . . .

> The accounting that you must make for the bad example you have set and for encouraging some of your sisters, whose caudillo you are, not to behave as daughters of Mary, is tremendous, and frightening even to contemplate. . . . At times I have regretted not acting as a surgeon to cut off the putrid limb so that the whole body does not perish, separating you from this community and transplanting you to the convent [of Santa Catarina in Valladolid] so that being closer to me, I could apply the cautery. . . .

> We are in a critical stage, for every day you and your allies grow more incorrigible and move farther away from mending your errors, but for now I decline to cure these errors with the punishments established by your Rule and in the sacred canons, instead trusting that by this private admonition you will come to your senses, and take responsibility for the damage that has been done to this sainted community by the fomenting of secret conspiracies against the Preladas and against those who obey them.[42]

Phelipa's response to the bishop's letter to her, written in her usual fine hand and displaying her usual cool intelligence, is included in the documentation.[43] Like most of her letters, it is quite self-consciously bland. All of the other nuns who wrote to the bishop and other authorities revealed more of themselves than did Phelipa, whose studied reserve contrasts sharply with their heated and passionate pleas. Phelipa's main weapon in her battle with the bishop was superficial compliance—she did not accept that the charges against her were true, but did not complain or issue specific denials, either. This was as good a tactic as she could possibly have devised to protect herself and go about promoting her project of building alliances that would ultimately allow her to reinvent the convent, at least to judge by the reactions of the bishop himself and of his advisors, who reviewed the files later in the decade. They were never sure whether Phelipa was actually defiant or was simply misguided and weak—and thus, they could never formulate a plan to bring her down that would accomplish that goal while protecting their consciences against the fearsome possibility of destroying a nun who was not "incorrigible." This was a word that the bishop had used in his letter to Phelipa, with all of its specific doctrinal meaning, but it was not an accusation to be made lightly (as we will see in more detail in Chapter 3). Here, then, is Phelipa's reply, contrite, but not abject, and not willing to concede guilt:

> I receive your Paternal correction, which was motivated by reports of my harmful behavior and irreligiosity and bad example, but by the infinite grace of God I cannot think what wrongs I might have done; I must assume that because of my grave past sins His Divine Majesty wants now to do me the great good of allowing me to be accused of such terrible faults when I am blameless. I say nothing more nor do I answer your letter point by point because this would try your patience and in any event I leave the matter in the hands of God, who will make the truth known to you, since no matter how much I might say my word would not stand up against the many reports that you have collected. I well know that my silence may imply that I am guilty but I do not open my lips to say more. This is the fruit of God's bringing me here as a Founder in the company of my beloved sisters. The only thing I desire is a visit from you; as my father I ask you to ask God to give me strength in the future; whatever you command I will obey. . . .[44]

The Crisis Diminishes

Did the measures taken by the bishop (the acceptance of María Anna's resignation as abbess and the naming of a replacement, the letter to the community, and the letters to Villegas and Phelipa) temporarily resolve the crisis? Or was it the moderate demeanor and behavior of the new abbess, Anna María de los Dolores? Or perhaps the move from relatively cramped quarters in their Hospicio to their spacious new convent in 1765? We do not know much about the internal affairs of the convent during the mid-1760s; aside from the ordinary correspondence between the bishop and the abbess and the documents generated by the entrances of novices and professions of nuns, from this period, we have only the sanitized description of the religiosas as models of piety during the procession that brought them to the new convent. All we really know is that the situation improved enough to prevent the "obedient" nuns from continuing to complain in writing to the vicar or the bishop, since the trail of anguished correspondence ends with Anna María de los Dolores' installation as abbess in 1762.

We do know of one change recommended by the new abbess that was designed to address the convent's factionalism. In a 1764 letter to the bishop noting that, in a month, one of the novices would have completed her year of probation, Anna María advised that he grant her license to profess, since her "sweet character and innocent qualities," as well as the fact that her father had come up with her dowry, qualified her to join the community.[45] She added, however, that she had heard a rumor that this novice was going to ask the bishop to exempt her from the "jovenado," the period (in this convent, 8 years) after their profession during which young nuns were not allowed to vote or hold office. In the early years of the San Miguel convent, it was commonplace to dispense with the jovenado, for obvious reasons: With such a small convent population, it was crucial for newly professed nuns to serve offices as soon as possible. Holding office conferred prestige (the reader may recall how insulted Cayetana de las Llagas felt when María Anna punished her by sending her, a "professed nun and office holder," to the novitiate), but it was also a burden that fell heavily on the senior nuns, and the sooner those burdens could be spread around, the better.

As Anna María de los Dolores implied in her letter to the bishop in 1764, however, there were also good reasons for easing young nuns slowly into the structure of power in the convent: The jovenado gave the newly professed a chance to learn the ways and customs of the convent before they were allowed to participate in its governance. Without the period of the jovenado, young nuns were given power before they had a chance to acquire an instinct for how to exercise that power without disrupting the bonds of community. Regarding this particular novice's likely request for an exemption, and recommending against it, Anna María wrote: "she is still a girl," adding darkly that, "as we have learned, this dispensation [from the jovenado] can be the principal cause of disorder and anxiety in the community."[46]

Although we may infer from the absence of evidence to the contrary that Anna María de los Dolores was able to smooth at least the surface of the turmoil within La Purísima, it is clear that, during her tenure, the factionalism in the convent did not disappear. In 1769, a new election to fill convent offices was held. Anna María had served two 3-year terms, and her health was not good (she had an unspecified problem with her eyesight and suffered from migraines), and she removed her name from consideration for reelection. There were 19 nuns present at the solemn ceremony; 2 others were sick, and their ballots were collected separately. The election was conducted by the vicar, with full ceremony, according to the Rule. When the ballots were counted, María Anna del Santísimo Sacramento received 2 votes for the position of abbess, María Josepha Lina received 7 votes, and no doubt to the horror of Bishop Sánchez de Tagle, Phelipa de San Antonio received 12 votes, the required majority.

A letter from Phelipa to Sánchez de Tagle, written just after her election, was a model of modesty and obedience: "I prostrate myself at the feet of Your Excellency . . . humbly submitting for your paternal eyes the honor that this Pious Community, in its great misjudgment, has seen fit to bestow on me, electing me its unworthy Prelada, although before the Election I renounced my right to vote in recognition of my uselessness, and despite this the Holy Community chose me . . . as your humble servant."[47] But rumors would soon swirl that she had plotted and politicked for election to the position of abbess for years. Her ascension to power marked the beginning of the second—and even more heated—phase of rebellion at La Purísima, a phase in which she made every possible effort to put her own vision of the purpose and nature of the convent into place.

NOTES

1. "Diligencias que se hicieron en orden de la translación o regreso de la R. M. Anna Gertrudis de San Raphael, una de las fundadoras del Real Convento de la Purísima Concepción . . . a su primitivo Convento de Regina de la Ciudad de México . . . ," AHAM, Diocesano, Gobierno, Religiosas, Capuchinas, caja 209 (XVIII), exp. 20. All material on the return of Gertrudis comes from this bundle of documents.

2. This discussion of the meaning of the convent in Catholic society is drawn from many sources, but particularly helpful have been: Heller; Brading, *Church and State*, chapter 5; Ramos Medina; McKnight; Lavrin, "Vida femenina"; Sperling; Loreto López, *Los conventos*; Gonzalbo Aizpuru, *Las mujeres*, especially chapter 9; Rosalva Loreto López, "La fundación del convento de la Concepción: Identidad y familias en la sociedad poblana (1593–1643)," in *Familias novohispanas, siglos XVI al XIX*, ed. Pilar Gonzalbo Aizpuru (Mexico City, Colegio de México, 1991); Francois Giraud, "Mujeres y familia en Nueva España," in *Presencia y transparencia: La mujer en la historia de México*, ed. Carmen Ramos Escandón et al. (Mexico City: Colegio de México, 1987).

3. R. Po-Chia Hsia, *The World of Catholic Renewal, 1540–1770* (Cambridge, England: Cambridge University Press, 1998), 140.

4. "Solicitud que hacen las monjas del convento de Carmelitas Descalzas de la ciudad de Querétaro para fundar . . . ," 1817, AHMM, XIX, caja 7, exp. 39.

5. For a particularly interesting discussion of this role of the convent in the New World, see Burns, chapter 1; this point is also emphasized in Loreto López, *Los conventos*; and Heller, chapter 3.

6. Spanish law provided for partible inheritance, that is to say, equal shares for all children.

7. "Solicitud que hacen las monjas del convento de Carmelitas Descalzas de la ciudad de Querétaro para fundar . . . ," 1817, AHMM, XIX, caja 7, exp. 39.

8. Vicar Juan de Villegas to Bishop Sánchez de Tagle, 25 September 1761, AHAM, Diocesano, Gobierno, Religiosas, Capuchinas, caja 209 (XVIII), exp. 23.

9. "Tabla de los Oficios que ande exercer las Religiosas en este Trienio," 10 March 1759, AHAM, Diocesano, Gobierno, Religiosas, Capuchinas, caja 208 (XVIII), exp. 19.

10. Abbess María Antonia Theresa del Santísimo Sacramento to Bishop Pedro Anselmo Sánchez de Tagle, 31 July 1761, AHAM, Diocesano, Gobierno, Religiosas, Capuchinas, caja 209 (XVIII), exp. 23. The original Spanish text of the letter can be accessed at http://history.berkeley.edu/faculty/Chowning/rebelliousnuns.

11. McKnight, 55. Most of the well-studied spiritual autobiographies have come from earlier periods, before the rise of the fictional narrative and before the eighteenth-century emphasis on linear thinking, so it might be predicted that a nun's story from the eighteenth century would be more "straightforward" than a spiritual autobiography, although the absence of linear narrative structure continued to pervade the biographical/hagiographical literature (e.g., the biography of María Josepha Lina that was used in Chapter 1) well into the nineteenth century.

12. Bishop Pedro Anselmo Sánchez de Tagle to Vicar Juan de Villegas, 14 August 1761, AHAM, Diocesano, Gobierno, Religiosas, Capuchinas, caja 23 (XVIII), exp. 23.

13. "Visita general . . . 1791," AHAM, Diocesano, Gobierno, Visitas, Informes, caja 509 (XVIII), exp. 103, gives Rubí's age as 62 in 1791. He was then the head sacristan in Dolores.

14. Abbess María Anna del Santísimo Sacramento to Bishop Pedro Anselmo Sánchez de Tagle, 4 August 1761, AHAM, Diocesano, Gobierno, Religiosas, Capuchinas, caja 209 (XVIII), exp. 23.

15. Abbess María Anna del Santísimo Sacramento to Bishop Pedro Anselmo Sánchez de Tagle, 28 March 1762, AHAM, Diocesano, Gobierno, Religiosas, Capuchinas, caja 209 (XVIII), exp. 23. Like the absence of punctuation in Antonia's prose, this phonetic spelling was not unusual, but was carried by María Anna to an exaggerated degree.

16. Abbess María Antonia Theresa del Santísimo Sacramento to Bishop Pedro Anselmo Sánchez de Tagle, 31 July 1761," AHAM, Diocesano, Gobierno, Religiosas, Capuchinas, caja 209 (XVIII), exp. 23.

17. Only a small minority of priests was licensed to confess nuns, and there were constant complaints from the nuns at the convents in small towns (San Miguel, Irapuato, and Salvatierra) because of a dearth of confessors, due to this restriction.

18. Bishop Pedro Anselmo Sánchez de Tagle to Vicar Juan de Villegas, 14 August 1761; Bishop Pedro Anselmo Sánchez de Tagle to Religiosas, 6 April 1762, AHAM, Diocesano, Gobierno, Religiosas, Capuchinas, caja 209 (XVIII), exp. 23.

19. Vicar Juan de Villegas to Bishop Pedro Anselmo Sánchez de Tagle, 25 August 1761, AHAM, Diocesano, Gobierno, Religiosas, Capuchinas, caja 209 (XVIII), exp. 23.

20. Bishop Pedro Anselmo Sánchez de Tagle to Vicar Juan de Villegas, 28 August 1761, AHAM, Diocesano, Gobierno, Religiosas, Capuchinas, caja 209 (XVIII), exp. 23.

21. Bishop Pedro Anselmo Sánchez de Tagle to Abbess María Anna del Santísimo Sacramento, 19 September 1761, AHAM, Diocesano, Gobierno, Religiosas, Capuchinas, caja 209 (XVIII), exp. 23.

22. Vicar Juan de Villegas to Bishop Pedro Anselmo Sánchez de Tagle, 25 September 1761, AHAM, Diocesano, Gobierno, Religiosas, Capuchinas, caja 209 (XVIII), exp. 23.

23. Bishop Pedro Anselmo Sánchez de Tagle to Vicar Juan de Villegas, 10 October 1761, AHAM, Diocesano, Gobierno, Religiosas, Capuchinas, caja 209 (XVIII), exp. 23.

24. On Sánchez de Tagle's battles with the Augustinians in Michoacán, see Mazín.

25. Bishop Pedro Anselmo Sánchez de Tagle to Vicar Juan de Villegas, 10 October 1761, AHAM, Diocesano, Gobierno, Religiosas, Capuchinas, caja 209 (XVIII), exp. 23.

26. Bishop Pedro Anselmo Sánchez de Tagle to Abbess María Antonia del Santísimo Sacramento, 14 November 1761, AHAM, Diocesano, Gobierno, Religiosas, Capuchinas, caja 209 (XVIII), exp. 23.

27. Vicar Juan de Villegas to Bishop Pedro Anselmo Sánchez de Tagle, 24 March 1762, AHAM, Diocesano, Gobierno, Religiosas, Capuchinas, caja 209 (XVIII), exp. 23.

28. This is a puzzling remark; it is not at all clear what Cayetana might have meant if María Anna is reporting her words correctly. Judas, full of guilt, did commit suicide by hanging himself; why Cayetana felt sufficiently guilty to emulate Judas, however, is a mystery. Perhaps she refers only to the method of suicide she chose.

29. Abbess María Anna del Santísimo Sacramento to Bishop Pedro Anselmo Sánchez de Tagle, 28 March 1762, AHAM, Diocesano, Gobierno, Religiosas, Capuchinas, caja 209 (XVIII), exp. 23.

30. Sister María Josepha Cayetana de las Llagas to Bishop Pedro Anselmo Sánchez de Tagle, 7 November 1769, AHAM, Diocesano, Gobierno, Religiosas, Capuchinas, caja 209 (XVIII), exp. 23.

31. Bishop Pedro Anselmo Sánchez de Tagle to Vicar Juan de Villegas, 2 April 1762; Bishop Pedro Anselmo Sánchez de Tagle to Abbess Anna María de los Dolores, 6 April 1762; Bishop Pedro Anselmo Sánchez de Tagle to Sister Phelipa de San Antonio, 6 April 1762; AHAM, Diocesano, Gobierno, Religiosas, Capuchinas, caja 209 (XVIII), exp. 23; "Nombramiento de Vicaria Abadesa y Vicaria de Casas, 6 April 1762," AHAM, Diocesano, Gobierno, Religiosas, Catarinas, Clarisas, Concepcionistas, caja 254 (XVIII), exp. 2.

32. In fairness to Sánchez de Tagle, the problem with the Augustinians was not insignificant: Royal authorities had undermined the bishop's efforts to secularize the convent at Yuriría, and the friars were attempting in April 1762 to regain their church and their rental properties; there was even some violence associated with the episode. See Mazín, 60–67.

33. It appears that by this time Rubí had been transferred to another parish.

34. Bishop Pedro Anselmo Sánchez de Tagle to Vicar Juan de Villegas, 2 April 1762, AHAM, Diocesano, Gobierno, Religiosas, Capuchinas, caja 209 (XVIII), exp. 23.

35. Bishop Pedro Anselmo Sánchez de Tagle to Vicar Juan de Villegas, 2 April 1762, AHAM, Diocesano, Gobierno, Religiosas, Capuchinas, caja 209 (XVIII), exp. 23.

36. Bishop Pedro Anselmo Sánchez de Tagle to Vicar Juan de Villegas, 2 April 1762, AHAM, Diocesano, Gobierno, Religiosas, Capuchinas, caja 209 (XVIII), exp. 23.

37. Bishop Pedro Anselmo Sánchez de Tagle to Vicar Juan de Villegas, 2 April 1762, AHAM, Diocesano, Gobierno, Religiosas, Capuchinas, caja 209 (XVIII), exp. 23.

38. Bishop Pedro Anselmo Sánchez de Tagle to Vicar Juan de Villegas, 2 April 1762, AHAM, Diocesano, Gobierno, Religiosas, Capuchinas, caja 209 (XVIII), exp. 23.

39. Bishop Pedro Anselmo Sánchez de Tagle to Religiosas del Convento de la Villa de S. Miguel el Grande, 6 April 1762, AHAM, Diocesano, Gobierno, Religiosas, Capuchinas, caja 209 (XVIII), exp. 23.

40. Bishop Pedro Anselmo Sánchez de Tagle to Religiosas del Convento de la Villa de S. Miguel el Grande, 6 April 1762, AHAM, Diocesano, Gobierno, Religiosas, Capuchinas, caja 209 (XVIII), exp. 23.

41. Bishop Pedro Anselmo Sánchez de Tagle to Sister Phelipa de San Antonio, 6 April 1762, AHAM, Diocesano, Gobierno, Religiosas, Capuchinas, caja 209 (XVIII), exp. 23.

42. Bishop Pedro Anselmo Sánchez de Tagle to Sister Phelipa de San Antonio, 6 April 1762, AHAM, Diocesano, Gobierno, Religiosas, Capuchinas, caja 209 (XVIII), exp. 23.

43. Sister Phelipa de San Antonio to Bishop Pedro Anselmo Sánchez de Tagle, 23 April 1762, AHAM, Diocesano, Gobierno, Religiosas, Capuchinas, caja 209, exp. 23.

44. Sister Phelipa de San Antonio to Bishop Pedro Anselmo Sánchez de Tagle, 23 April 1762, AHAM, Diocesano, Gobierno, Religiosas, Capuchinas, caja 209, exp. 23.

45. Abbess Anna María Josepha de los Dolores to Bishop Pedro Anselmo Sánchez de Tagle, 20 October 1764, AHAM, Diocesano, Gobierno, Correspondencia, Religiosas, caja 39, exp. 10.

46. Abbess Anna María Josepha de los Dolores to Bishop Pedro Anselmo Sánchez de Tagle, 20 October 1764, AHAM, Diocesano, Gobierno, Correspondencia, Religiosas, caja 39, exp. 10.

47. Capítulo y elección de Prelada y demas officios del Real Convento de la Concepción . . . 1769, AHAM, Diocesano, Gobierno, Religiosas, Capuchinas, caja 210, exp. 33.

3

"Seminary of Discord"

La Purísima under Phelipa de San Antonio,
1769–1772

The reemergence of open factionalism and scandalous behavior at
La Purísima was first reported by Manuela de la Santísima Trinidad,
who broke a 7-year epistolary silence on the part of the so-called
obedient nuns with a long letter in 1769 to her confessor, Licenciado Agustín de Agüera, the sacristan of the parish of San Miguel.
She began with a surprising observation: Vicar Villegas and the new
abbess, Phelipa de San Antonio, were "at constant odds with one another."[1] During the convent's earlier crisis (1761–1762), the vicar had
repeatedly defended Phelipa's behavior to the bishop. The fact that,
so early in her regime, she felt that she could afford to alienate the
previously sympathetic Villegas is an indication of how far Phelipa
had already come in her effort to remake the convent, and by so doing, to challenge the authority of the bishop himself. The speed with
which she had begun to impose her will on the convent clearly
prompted Manuela's letter, setting in motion a series of actions and
reactions on the part of the bishop and the nuns. This chapter tells
the story of the second stage of the convent crisis.

"Something of Her Own Creation"

After beginning her letter to the bishop by describing the deteriora-
tion of the abbess–vicar relationship, Manuela went on to describe
an incident that had caused great distress among some of the nuns.
It seems that during the celebration of La Purísima, the Franciscans
of San Miguel and elsewhere were invited to participate. A friar

came from Querétaro to give the sermon; the guardian of the convent of San Francisco in San Miguel sent over all of his silver for the celebration of the mass; still other friars came from Celaya. The donadas were commanded to ring the church bells constantly from the time that the Franciscans left their convent until their arrival at the church of La Purísima, about four blocks away. As they entered the church, fireworks were set off. After the services, the visitors were feted with a delicious and expensive meal.

All of this was seen as unseemly and excessive by some of the nuns, including Manuela, who pointedly observed that they had taken vows of poverty upon profession. But to her, the most scandalous parts of the incident were, first, that during the Franciscans' visit, the grille was removed from the sacristy so that the nuns, including the novices, could talk to and be seen by the friars, in clear violation of the principle of enclosure; and second, that the nuns in Phelipa's faction turned a cold shoulder to the vicar when he entered the church, in stark contrast to their fawning treatment of the Franciscans. "They treated him like a *carbonero* (charcoal carrier)," Manuela complained. This was not the first time that Phelipa and her principal allies had snubbed the vicar. In fact, to hear Manuela tell it, Phelipa had embarked on a furious campaign to discredit him: "she goes from cell to cell, teaching even the girls in the school . . . that the Vicar is a simpleton, that he cannot even find his own face, that he persecutes her . . . that he is an ignoramus who knows nothing of convent governance. . . ."

The renewed factionalism and turmoil in the convent was confirmed by Cayetana de las Llagas—one of the nuns named by Manuela as a key ally of Phelipa (also the nun who had tried to commit suicide in 1762)—in a 15-page letter to the bishop about 2 months after Manuela's letter to Agüera.[2] Carefully composed in Cayetana's emotional and apologetic style, it began: "Most Benign Father, Shepherd, and Lord: if it were possible for tears to penetrate walls, or for sighs to travel the distance between this Villa and your Palace . . . you would already know of the grave tribulations that in my eleven years as a Religiosa I have buried deep inside my chest. . . ." Cayetana then went on to acknowledge problems in the convent, but most of her letter, despite her constant insistence that she was by no means trying to justify her actions, was devoted to giving the bishop an explanation for the behavior of the rebellious nuns. This was not the first time that Cayetana had taken it upon herself to offer the rebels' point of view to the bishop. In fact, since Phelipa's strategy in dealing directly with the bishop was to strike a tone of deference and humility, and not to defend herself, Cayetana became a sort of spokesperson for her, and it is probably safe to assume that her letters can be taken as generally representative not only of her own feelings, but also of those of Phelipa and her other allies:

The time has come for Your Excellency to know the purpose to which these poor scratchings aspire; the time has come for me to

delay no longer in baring my soul, because I can bear it no longer
... I confess that you have one thousand reasons to have looked
with I cannot imagine what species of despair on this your poor
Convent. You have one thousand reasons! But alas, poor me! Most
Illustrious Señor, ay de Mí! And alas this poor Convent! This poor
convent that had so many [people] against her, and never has had
even one in her favor! For my part, I pardon with all my heart, so
that God may pardon me, I pardon that person that caused you so
much anguish and caused me (and this poor community) so much
pain and travail: there was an Abbess who was willing to inform you
of how badly her daughters were behaving, but [until now] there has
not been a daughter who was willing to inform you of how badly the
Abbesses have behaved!

As the last line indicates, Cayetana's defense of the rebellious nuns rested
on blaming the first two abbesses for the convent's distress. María Anna, in
particular, could be cruel, she wrote, citing her laughter in the face of Cayetana's humiliation on the day of her attempted suicide, her harsh punishments
when the nuns fell asleep in choir, and her refusal to give Cayetana "an old
tunic to cover her nudity" once when she was sick. She was telling the bishop
all this, she wrote, "not to lower his opinion of any person," but merely to show
him the imprudence of the government of the first two abbesses. "Although I
do not deny that they have been exemplary Religiosas," she wrote, displaying
a mostly hidden sarcastic streak, "neither the one from her grave [Antonia died
in 1763] nor the other in all the days of her life has performed any miracles,
and from this I conclude that they are not quite ready for canonization."
   But while her strategy was to emphasize the failings of the abbesses themselves, implicit in her remarks about their "imprudence" was a challenge to
the whole idea of the reformed convent. The convent's problems, she wrote,
stemmed from the fact that most of the founding nuns who came to San
Miguel "were near the end of their years, very old." Having lived most of their
lives in the convent of Regina Coeli, they had seen a chance to come to San
Miguel as reformers, and the result for the newly professed nuns was "disastrous." She explained that, in other convents, the custom was for "the nuns
who hold office to tell the servants what to do . . . whereas in this convent, we
ourselves have to do the work . . . and we often serve several offices at one time,
some of which are incompatible with each other."[3] This was a complaint that
had less to do with whether or not the abbesses were excessive in their demands
or overbearing in their demeanor than with whether the convent would be a
reformed convent or not, since La Purísima's constitution specifically prohibited the introduction of personal servants and required that the nuns themselves perform the work associated with their offices. As we have seen, the
small size of the convent population made this requirement extremely bur-

densome, and it is true that Antonia's rigorous daily schedule and María Anna's arbitrary manner exacerbated its effects, but neither of these abbesses invented it. By suggesting that the introduction of servants would go far toward resolving the crisis, then, Cayetana, and by extension, Phelipa, hoped to persuade the bishop to tolerate fundamental changes in way that those who governed the San Miguel convent interpreted its constitution.

The bishop, however, did not look kindly on Cayetana's attempt to wrap her plea for counterreform in criticism of long-gone abbesses. Slow to recognize the seriousness of the challenge to the principle of reform in the earlier crisis, he responded quickly to this new threat. In February 1770, he wrote a strong and angry letter to Agüera, obviously concerned that the convent was verging on chaos.[4] No longer was the problem "merely" scandal in the villa or disobedience and laxity within the convent. The most fearsome development was that Phelipa's affliction, the salto, had become an epidemic, and he believed that she was actively spreading the "mal," just as she spread confusion and discontent among the more vulnerable nuns. The convent, he feared, threatened to spin out of control as Phelipa worked to transform it into "something of her own creation" and to break down the very foundation on which it rested—its constitution:

> With great pain and bitterness in our heart, we have learned of the lamentable state and grievous decadence of the Royal Convent of La Purísima Concepción . . . ever since the election as Vicaria Abadesa of the Reverend Mother, Sister Phelipa de San Antonio, because of the despotism with which she has altered the Rule observed by her predecessors . . . , transforming the Convent into something of her own creation; she has refused to recognize or obey the Vicar of that Convent Licenciado D. Juan Manuel de Villegas, censuring his determinations with little fear of God; along with her partisans, she mistreats the well-adapted Religiosas, even her predecessor [Anna María de los Dolores] and the Mother Vicaria de Casa [María Josepha Lina], whom she ought to respect because of the offices they hold and because of their virtue and religiosity; she sets a bad example for the new nuns and allows them to do the same; she fractures the peace of the convent, fomenting factions, converting into a Seminary of Discord that which ought to be a Garden of Virtue; she feigns strange infirmities in order to take to her bed, so that all those who applaud her caprice have an excuse to visit her in her cell, and, perhaps in order to please her, to mimic these infirmities, in whose symptoms and movements she has instructed them. With all this, disorder in the community has arrived at such an extreme that there is no one to serve the offices, and no one to clean and maintain the Sacristy.

The bishop concluded this tirade by ordering the sacristan, Agüera, to submit the religiosas in the obedient faction to questioning on the subject of disorder in the convent, and he gave him the precise interrogatory that he should put to them, one that was seemingly designed to elicit answers that would confirm what Sánchez de Tagle already believed to be true.[5] The questions had to do with the changes that Phelipa, as abbess, had made in the daily schedule; her relationship to the vicar; the existence of a faction whose primary allegiance was to Phelipa; and the strange sickness from which many of the nuns were suffering.

The tone of the responses to this interrogatory is desperate and despairing. The "obedient" nuns seemed genuinely to fear for the future of the convent and for their own souls, and they did not have great faith that a remedy could be found. The bending and breaking of the Rule deeply upset and angered them, but the most frightening issue was the illness that the majority of Phelipa's faction had contracted. Since the nuns, as well as the bishop and the three advisers he asked to analyze the convent's situation (their reports will be examined in detail later), took this illness very seriously, let us pause, before we turn to the nuns' testimonials, to examine it more closely.

The "Mal"

While it is clear that the "mal" was very much a concern of the bishop, his three advisers, and the nuns who were interrogated at his command, unfortunately, their testimonies and reports provide relatively little descriptive detail that might help us to interpret what was for them (as well as for us) a strange and mysterious illness. Most frustrating is the absence of any concrete sense of how often the attacks occurred; how long the nuns had been suffering from them (the implication is that it had been a matter of years, since we know that Phelipa herself had been afflicted as early as 1761, but in fact, it is not certain when the other nuns first began to display the symptoms); whether they occurred in a cluster, affecting all or several nuns at the same time, or separately; and whether there were any common triggers. What we do know is this: The affliction came on the suffering nuns suddenly and was characterized by deeply unsettling and unnatural behavior. "Those who are afflicted," wrote Gertrudis de San José, "act dazed and hurt themselves with their movements but what is most frightening is that when they talk they are shameless in their utterances, speaking whatever comes into their heads, talking like little girls and making childish faces." Others also described jerky, awkward movements, a trancelike state, and loss of self-control.

There were several labels attached to this condition by the various observers. "Salto" (literally, "jump," or "leap") was the colloquial term used in connection with Phelipa's illness during the first convent crisis, but by the late

1760s, the word most frequently used by the nuns to refer to the sickness was a more general and more ominous one: the "mal," implying something between malady and evil. The physician who attended the convent population wrote that the 10 afflicted nuns, as well as an unspecified number of donadas and niñas, suffered from "suffocation and uterine vapors, from which proceed other pernicious and disquieting symptoms."[6] One of the bishop's advisers called it "hysteria," while another referred to it as "epilepsy."[7]

To readers without some knowledge of premodern medical parlance, these terms are confusing. "Suffocation of the uterus" and "uterine vapors" convey almost no meaning at all to us, while "hysteria," which denotes a range of psychosomatic illnesses, and "epilepsy," which we know as a neurological condition, seem to have little to do with each other. But in fact, the use of these labels reflects something of a convergence of contemporary opinion as to what was afflicting the nuns. The Greek root for "hysteria" means "womb," and a hysterical illness was one thought to originate in a disturbance or dysfunction of the uterus. When the uterus migrated, or moved around, as it was thought to do, it could produce "vapors" and an uncomfortable "suffocation" of other organs. Many illnesses suffered by women were diagnosed as some sort of uterine disorder: The physician Thomas Willis wrote in 1684 that "when at any time a sickness happens in a Woman's Body, of an unusual manner . . . we declare it to be something Hysterical," that is, related to the uterus.[8] Furthermore, before the late nineteenth century, hysteria and epilepsy were considered by physicians to be closely related conditions. Common symptoms of hysteria included convulsions and bodily contortions—similar to epileptic seizures.[9] Even today, there is a large literature devoted to the sometimes difficult distinction between epileptic events (with a physiological cause) and nonepileptic events (with a psychological cause).[10]

Mid-eighteenth-century opinion offered four possible causes for hysteria and epilepsy (the terms appear to have been used interchangeably, although "epilepsy" occurs most frequently in the documents concerning convents). Only two of them were invoked by the nuns and advisers in the case of La Purísima in order to explain the "mal," but the explanations that were *not* employed are nonetheless worth summarizing, for both of them tell us something about how contemporaries viewed the La Purísima epidemic.

Natural causes of epilepsy among nuns were acknowledged by contemporaries, though not at La Purísima. There were two reasons why it was thought that nuns were naturally susceptible to disease in general, and to epilepsy in particular, more so than the population at large. First, it was to be expected that nuns would have a high incidence of illness because of the arduous practices of fasting, self-mortification, and continual prayer. Prospective nuns were required to attest that they were in good health, since only the robust would be able to endure the hardships of living in a convent, but illness was endemic, despite this modest attempt at screening the novices: The correspondence and other records of Mexican convents are full of sorrowful references to the large number of ailing nuns at any given time. To some extent, this is an epistolary trope—it was expected that the abbess, in her letters to authorities, would name the sick so that their spiritual fathers could pray for them. Reports on the high incidence of illness may also have been a subtle way to signal that the nuns were taking their spiritual duties very seriously, since great piety required physical sacrifice. Thus, general ill health in a convent was expected. But there was another natural reason why nuns would particularly suffer from hysteria/epilepsy, according to contemporary opinion: their abstinence from sexual activity. Since Galen, the idea that sexual deprivation might do harm to the uterus and cause or contribute to hysteria had led to a special association between nuns and hysteria/epilepsy.

Natural causes were frequently invoked to account for individual cases of epilepsy—it would surprise no one, for example, for the especially pious nun who engaged in practices of self-mortification and extreme fasting to contract the disease—but it was much harder to stretch the explanation to include epidemics. In surveying the literature on convents and the smattering of published spiritual autobiographies in Mexico and South America, I have come across a number of references to epilepsy: It is mentioned as having afflicted nuns in the convents of San José de Gracia in Mexico City, Nuestra Señora de la Soledad in Oaxaca, Santa Clara in Querétaro, the Carmelite convent in Puebla, and a Carmelite convent in Guatemala City; no doubt a search of the many unpublished spiritual autobiographies would yield many more such references.[11] But in all but one of these cases the disease struck a single nun; in other words, they were not cases of mass contagion.

The one other case, however, of an epidemic of epilepsy is especially important for our purposes because it involved nuns of the convent of San Jerónimo in Puebla less than a decade before the disease broke out in San Miguel. There, between 1750 and 1754, epilepsy spread to 14 of the 77 nuns in the convent. The specific symptoms at the Puebla convent were different from those suffered by the nuns at La Purísima, though there were some general similarities. The best description of these symptoms comes from the testimony of a nun who began to experience them in 1753 (some 3 years after the epidemic began), soon after an earthquake hit the city. The disease, she wrote, "struck me with great force, with intervals of blows and suspensions, and no amount of prayer helped . . . thus I continued for nine months and seventeen days, most of which I passed in great and arduous pain, and there was one occasion that my chest closed up so much that I couldn't hear what I was saying . . . my jaws locked so I couldn't eat. . . ."[12] The abbess commissioned an investigation into the epidemic, which resulted in a fascinating volume published in 1763, entitled *Informe Médico-Moral de la Peñosíssima y Rigorosa Enfermedad de la Epilepsia*, written by a physician, Pedro de Horta.[13]

Horta, to whose work we will return later, explored the possibility that natural causes accounted for the epidemic—rehearsing the arguments given above, that is, that the physical demands of the convent could have caused the illness. But in the end, he concluded that it was extremely unlikely that an epidemic would be caused by forces of nature alone. And if the Puebla case could not be explained by natural causes, it was even less logical to do so at La Purísima, since it was not only a mass outbreak, but it affected only the nuns on one side of the political divide in the convent—that is, the nuns in Phelipa's faction. As one of the bishop's advisers pointed out, the disease was not only confined to the convent and did not infect anyone else in the villa of San Miguel, but it also did not spread to the obedient nuns. (It did, however, according to the doctor, strike at least a few donadas and niñas. No one else commented on this; all of the other observers stated or implied that it was the rebellious nuns alone who were afflicted, perhaps because it was the nuns who were the main object of the bishop's inquiry, although this is another area about which we would clearly like to know more than the documents tell us.) Thus, although contemporaries were prepared to accept natural explanations for what they called epilepsy, the particular circumstances at La Purísima did not seem, in their judgment, to warrant such an interpretation.

The second explanation that was *not* invoked at La Purísima was divine interference, the idea that God had visited the disease on the nuns. Epilepsy, of course, has a unique history among diseases as a "sacred" illness. Famously, Hippocrates wrote "On the Sacred Disease" in 400 B.C., refuting its divine origins, but it was not until the second half of the nineteenth century that Hippocrates' idea that epilepsy was a brain disorder translated into the investigation of the disease by neurologists. Even today, as Anne Fadiman has found among the Hmong peoples of northern Laos, there is cultural persistence of the idea that epileptic seizures leave sufferers more open to prophetic visions and capable of receiving sacred knowledge.[14] In early modern times, as spiritual specialists, the bishop's advisers would have been well aware of the historical association between epilepsy and supernaturally caused states of ectasy.[15]

But just as Horta reasoned that natural causes were unlikely to have caused an epidemic, as opposed to a single case of epilepsy, so also was God unlikely to have caused an epidemic. God might test or visit a state of ectasy on one nun, he wrote, but not on so many of them all at once. Furthermore, and perhaps most important of all, it was impossible for either the obedient nuns or the bishop's advisers to imagine that God would have chosen Phelipa or her faction to test, for this would imply divine favor and interest—and surely God did not favor the disobedient nuns over the obedient ones. As a result, no one in the case of La Purísima suggested that the illness had divine origins, except in the frequently used expression referring to "the disease that God has seen fit to send us," an illness cliché common to the era.

A third explanation offered by contemporaries, and one of the two that was invoked at La Purísima, was that the sickness was the devil's work. Dia-

bolical interference was strongly insinuated by three of the nuns in their answers to the bishop's interrogatory (María de Jesús, Gertrudis de San José, and
Anna María de los Dolores) and somewhat more tepidly by one of the bishop's
advisers, Miguel Joseph de Moche. The reasoning was simple: Clearly, the devil
would wish to prevent this (and any other) convent from thriving, since the
convent represented the surest path to Christian perfection and inspired the
piety of the citizenry at large. He must be active at La Purísima, since what
other explanation could there be for the profound disobedience of Phelipa
(through whom he had presumably been working since the time of the first
convent crisis) and for her ability to gain converts to a cause that undermined
the purpose and success of the convent? Historically, symptoms generally similar to those experienced by the nuns at La Purísima were typical of both epilepsy and hysteria, but also of possession by demons or the devil, especially
convulsions, fits, and insensibility.[16] The demonic possession explanation had
the advantage that it accounted much more successfully than natural causes
or divine intervention for the spread of the disease and for the fact that only
one faction (the one that was trying to undermine the reformed convent) was
afflicted.

While, for reasons that are beyond the scope of this narrative, it seems
clear that the role of the devil in eighteenth-century Spanish America was being
de-emphasized by many churchmen, and certainly by many lay thinkers, diabolical involvement still remained a powerful tool for understanding the mysterious.[17] It was, in fact, the explanation that the physician Horta gave for the
epidemic at Puebla, which he blamed on "transnatural causes," by which he
meant mainly diabolical forces, although these causes could also include tormented souls in purgatory. Despite the precedent of this explanation for the
Puebla outbreak, however, and despite its logical utility in explaining what was
happening at La Purísima, the case for the devil having caused the illness there
was not articulated by anyone with much passion, conviction, or specificity.

The nuns who blamed the convent's general malaise and the epidemic of
epilepsy, in particular, on the "infernal enemy" were extremely vague about his
role—as one of the advisers summarized their view, "some of them say they
do not understand [the disease], but they believe it must be a thing of the Devil."
It is not clear whether they thought that the disease was a manifestation of
some sort of pact that each of the nuns had made with the devil, a sign that
the devil was trying to possess them and that they were battling him, or a
means to an end, and if so, what end (debilitation? demoralization? terror?).
In short, the role that they assigned to the devil is ambiguous, and this seems
to be more of a default explanation than something of which they were truly
convinced.

The bishop's advisers were also uncommitted, to say the least, to a diabolical explanation. One (Joachín de Cuevas) did not mention the devil at all.
Another (Ricardo Gutiérrez Coronel) did not specifically name the devil or

diabolical forces, though he did suggest that the nuns might try taking the Virgin of Guadalupe as their patron, since this action seemed to have greatly ameliorated the severity of the disease among the Hieronymite nuns in Puebla (this had been Horta's recommendation to the abbess of the convent in his treatise on the epidemic, following his diagnosis that diabolical forces explained the epidemic). Still, this was a suggestion that Gutiérrez Coronel included almost as an afterthought, at the end of his lengthy report, and it was very much presented as something that would not do any harm, rather than as something in which he had great faith. The one adviser (Miguel de Moche) who agreed that, at bottom, the devil must have been responsible for the nuns' behavior, did so in a very vague and perfunctory fashion, and his report concentrated on other aspects of the case. None of the afflicted nuns was seen by any of the advisers as doing the work of the devil in any but the most general way (that is to say, undermining the stability of the convent); it was not claimed that the devil was speaking through them, nor were any of the more dramatic and clear-cut signs of demonic possession present (displaying horror and revulsion in the presence of sacred things; floating in the air, which was one of the symptoms described by the Puebla nun quoted earlier; expelling grotesque foreign objects; speaking blasphemies; stomping on the host, scourging the crucifix, and other behaviors triggered by coming into contact with religious objects or priests; speaking in foreign tongues; exhibiting superhuman strength; and demonstrating clairvoyance).[18] Perhaps most tellingly, no one ever suggested the obvious recourse where diabolical involvement is suspected: exorcism.

If the nuns and the bishop's advisers did not suggest natural causes, divine intervention, or diabolical forces as compelling explanations for the disease, how did they account for it? Simply put, they thought that the nuns were faking it. Just as the history of epilepsy is full of references to the sacred, the disease has a long association with the "difficult problem of fraud."[19] In England, "chucking a dummy," or feigning epilepsy, was a relatively common method of escaping military duty or gaining a transfer to a less strenuous job while in jail.[20] Fraud was widely understood by both skeptical doctors and skeptical churchmen as a distinct possibility whenever they were confronted by a complex of symptoms such as those occurring at La Purísima. It should not surprise us that fraud surfaced as an explanation for a "mal" that was so threatening to the established authorities.

According to this view, Phelipa was fully aware of what she was doing (and so, probably, were her fellow sufferers), which was to disrupt the purposes to which the convent was dedicated and install a wholly new regime—as Sánchez de Tagle put it, "something of her own creation." Even those inclined to make room for the devil in instigating or spreading the "mal" were much more specific and detailed about Phelipa's role than they were about his. Whether she was pictured as shrewdly manipulative, vindictive and cruel, or weak and lacking in leadership skills, they held her, and not forces beyond her own control, primarily responsible for the rebellion and the epidemic of illness. This explanation was advanced forcefully by the bishop, two of his advisers, and two of the nuns, and given credence by most of the other nuns as well.

Manuela de la Santísima Trinidad was very clear that Phelipa was instructing her cohorts in the symptoms of her affliction and that they, in turn, instructed others. One of the other obedient nuns, she wrote, had told her that one of the nuns who suffered from the disease had offered to teach her its movements, but she had declined. Manuela reported this exchange with great confidence in the trustworthiness of her confidante, and although it is true that she does not name this person, two of the other obedient nuns, in their testimony, also referred to Phelipa and other afflicted nuns offering to teach its symptoms. She also described what we would call Phelipa's use of the power of suggestion: She would tell healthy nuns "that they had a propensity for [the disease] because of their temperaments (*complexiones*), and that they would probably catch it from her, and sure enough they contracted it soon after."

In the beginning of her written testimony, Gertrudis de San José was slightly more cautious than Manuela about asserting that Phelipa was feigning the disease. "I have a thousand questions about it," she wrote, "because I cannot say with surety that it is feigned, but it appears to be a thing of the Devil, who has brought us so many evils." But in the rest of her answer to the question in the interrogatory about the disease, she made it clear that she believed that Phelipa knew what she was doing and consciously manipulated the other nuns. The Mother Abbess, she asserted, "is the originator of this mal . . . and in her hands it is so powerful that before the election the Urbina sisters were not part of her faction, but then she gave the mal to María Josepha [Urbina] and from that time on she was completely at her command."

Another nun, Theresa de la Luz, had a more subtle interpretation of Phelipa's role in spreading the disease. "I do not know," she wrote, "nor have I seen that our Mother and the others infected with the mal teach it to others who do not have it . . . but I am persuaded . . . that to please our Mother they allow themselves to be carried away by the affliction." To Manuela's insight about the power of suggestion, Theresa thus adds the notion that the afflicted nuns wanted to please Phelipa, and so they "allowed" themselves to catch it. Then she went on to make a very interesting comment: "I do not believe that on the first occasion they are feigning it but once they already have it malice enters." In other words, she makes a distinction between the first experience with the disease, which she sees as genuine, and subsequent experiences. This seems to imply that the experience of the attack was, in some way, positive, something that the nuns might wish to reenact, though she does not say for what reason this might be so.

Here, Theresa seems to be very close to an explanation of the disease that would occur to modern readers: that the spells or fits were motivated by a

complicated group dynamic that gave the sufferers attention, a sense of belonging, a kind of validation of their individual selves within the group context,
and even a kind of strange excitement—not necessarily pleasant, certainly not
ecstatic, but something in which they were caught up and pulled along, and
having made it through the experience, something in which they might even
take a certain pride.[21]

Anna María de los Dolores describes a sister who was terrified of "catch-
ing" the disease and had to be reassured that she was suffering from something
very different; from this, it seems that the healthy nuns looked upon the disease
with trembling. But, she continued, afterward, "those who were injured by the
accident loved Phelipa very much, whereas before they had not done so." In
other words, they had been transformed by the experience of having been
chosen by Phelipa and made a part of a select and illicit group (special friendships were expressly forbidden in convents, because they were held to undermine the sense of community and sisterhood). Manuela de la Santísima Trinidad seems to confirm this characterization of a transformative experience.
Qualifying her testimony that Phelipa was able to suggest the disease upon
her followers, she corrected herself: "I said that all of her partisans became ill
with this mal but I did not explain myself well; of the fourteen in her faction,
five do not have it and she says that is because they are too old." The implication
is that those in her faction who did *not* become ill were almost disappointed,
or at least required an explanation as to why the expected had not occurred.
Another indication that the shared experience of the affliction provided a kind
of positive group identity is that, as one of the bishop's advisers pointed out,
the symptoms were especially acute when they were within the group: "when
they are among their own," he wrote, "it worsens, and in the presence of those
who are not in their faction, it subsides."[22] The experience of the attack itself
might or might not be remembered by the nuns (this is never made clear), but
its aftermath would have found them still, as John Demos put it in his description of a demoniac in seventeenth-century New England, on "center stage."
Exhibitionism, for him, was one of the underlying characteristics of the possessed accusers of the witches he studied, whose behavior during their spells
was not unlike that of the afflicted nuns. Another was an inclination toward
dependency on a person with a strong personality, a characteristic that fits with
the central role assigned to Phelipa in virtually every version of the spread of
the epidemic.[23] There is ample indication in the nuns' reports, as well as those
of the bishop's advisers, that the women in her faction were deeply devoted to
her, even revered her (a point not lost on the bishop or his advisers, as we will
see, and one that caused them to move against her extremely cautiously).

Phelipa, thus, in this interpretation, becomes a charismatic personality
with the power to gain adherents because she offered them an experience that
not only made them feel chosen, but also had other positive reverberations:
attention, belonging, and excitement. The origins of her magnetism may have

been purely personal, of course, but we should take into account the strong belief in Catholicism in general, and in the convent in particular, that suffering brings one closer to God. Phelipa was the first to suffer from the "mal," or the "salto." Her affliction did not necessarily make the other nuns believe that Phelipa had been *chosen* by God, but they may have believed that she was closer to God than were the nonsuffering nuns. If this was so, then emulation of her symptoms would bring her supporters closer to God themselves. In obvious ways, this increased her power and authority in the convent.

What of the personalities of the followers, though? Can we make any generalizations about whether the nuns in Phelipa's faction were more emotionally needy, more insecure, and possibly, more susceptible to the opportunity to become part of a select group within the convent than were the nuns who did not join her? As we saw in Chapter 1, there were, in fact, some personal characteristics that were more common among the rebellious nuns than among the obedient ones. First, the rebellious nuns tended to be younger when they entered the convent: The median age at entrance of the 12 rebellious nuns whose age at first entrance into the convent we know was 17 years, compared with 23 years for the obedient nuns (see table 1.1). Second, we do not know which of the 14 rebellious nuns were the 9 who were afflicted with the disease, but as we have seen, Phelipa had told some nuns that they were too old to catch it, and from this, perhaps we can assume that the afflicted nuns were also younger, on average, at the height of the epidemic than the obedient nuns. Third, the rebellious nuns, as a group, tended to come from less settled family backgrounds than the obedient nuns. Six of them were either illegitimate or born to "unknown parents," and their adoptive parent or parents had also died. Four others were orphans, and two more had lost their mothers. (The other two were Phelipa and María Anna, whose family backgrounds are not known since they were founding nuns and their records remained in Mexico City.) If we combine early entrance into the convent with these circumstances of birth, we can probably infer that the rebellious nuns were likely to fall into the category of girls who were placed in the convent rather than powerfully drawn to the convent for reasons of vocation. Beyond that, even more speculatively, a certain emotional vulnerability, a desire not only to "fit in," but also to "stand out," would not be unexpected among a group with these characteristics of youth upon entrance and orphanhood. Two of the rebellious nuns we have already seen in other contexts have shown themselves to be weak and insecure (María Anna del Santísimo Sacramento, the second abbess) or emotionally unstable (Cayetana de las Llagas, who tried half-heartedly to commit suicide in 1762).

So, one explanation that occurs to modern readers revolves around the powerful figure of Phelipa, the unusually large number of women in this convent with weak ties to outside society and unstable family backgrounds, and the complicated group dynamics that might result when these actors come together in a tightly closed community. A slightly different explanation also begins with the proposition that a closed community might give rise to intensified group dynamics and interrelationships and adds to that the notion that a religious community might be an especially fertile ground for epidemics of psychological dysfunction. Here, the emphasis is less on the idea that religious women might admire a sufferer and express solidarity with her by emulating her than on the extreme stressfulness of convent life. There was not just the claustrophobia of this small, enclosed, single-gender world, but also the extra anxiety produced by a nun's lifetime commitment to God and her spouse Jesus Christ. H. Erik Midelfort reminds us that "the profoundly ascetic, penitential, religious atmosphere of the monastery," and "the awe-filled sense that one can never sufficiently humble oneself before God," may "create and structure" madness.[24] In other words, the very effort to live up to one's own expectations of service to God could be deeply stressful. That this Promethean effort might have physical manifestations—like the fits and spells suffered by the afflicted nuns—does not surprise us. Indeed, we are well familiar with the idea that some kinds of seemingly irrational behaviors can serve a "rational" medical purpose. Speaking in voices that were not their own and saying things that they would not have said in their right minds (one of the nuns noted that "those to whom this accident has befallen do whatever they wish and they show no respect at all for the others, using the accident as their excuse") can be seen as ways that the rebellious nuns gained emotional relief because these behaviors allowed them to step outside their everyday routines and roles, a point that is often made in historical studies of demonic possession.[25] As one historian puts it, "religious women inscribed their psychic struggles on their own bodies."[26]

Beyond these challenges that are common to all convents, however, the situation at La Purísima presented unusual emotional land mines. It must have been very difficult for the nuns to reconcile their divisiveness with the fact that the idealized convent *has* no factions. Conflict here had gone well beyond the petty bickering and quarrels of community life; the rebellious nuns found themselves in more or less organized combat with women who were supposed to be their sisters. In addition, the rebellious nuns may have suffered considerable internal emotional conflict as a result of the impugning of their piety by the abbesses and others in the obedient faction. No matter what the circumstances of their entrance into the convent—whether they had always had a clear religious vocation or were placed in the convent by their families or guardians because there was nowhere else for them to go—they surely had come to think of themselves as pious women and models of piety for the outside world. In other words, to a considerable extent, they must have internalized the values of the religious life. Indeed, part of the "rivalry" that Solange Alberro refers to as "fundamental" in a convent was a rivalry over who was most devout.[27] Certainly, the language of the rebels, where we have it (mainly in the letters of

Cayetana de las Llagas and Phelipa), suggests that they continued to see themselves not only as very pious, but also as better daughters of the bishop than the reforming abbesses—the tyrannical Antonia and the heartless María Anna (see Cayetana's letter, quoted at the beginning of this chapter, and also later). How difficult it must have been, then, to be accused by them and by self-righteous nuns, like Manuela, of impiety.

It is tempting to dismiss the eighteenth-century explanations as illogical (the natural causes explanation), irrational (the demonic and divine intervention explanations), or mean-spirited, cynical, and even misogynist (the feigned disease explanation), in favor of some version of these modern interpretations, which are informed by over a century of psychological and anthropological research and theories. However, with the important caveat that no questionnaires were distributed to the rebellious nuns, whose points of view are therefore much more elusive than those of the obedient nuns and the male authorities, I am inclined to give considerable weight to the opinions of the bishop and the others who believed that, at least by the time of the second convent crisis, Phelipa and her cohorts were consciously manufacturing symptoms of illness.

This does not mean that the factors of emotional vulnerability and complicated group psychology, combined with tremendous stress experienced in a closed religious community, were not important in producing or focusing symptoms, nor does it mean that the illness was not "real" at some level or at some point in time, perhaps early on in its manifestations in each sufferer. In fact, I think we have to assume that the nuns were indeed suffering. How else is it possible to understand how the nuns could convince witnesses that they were experiencing an uncontrollable attack? Even the obedient nuns, who lived closely with the suffering nuns and observed them daily, were not entirely sure when these were genuine attacks and when they were performances. Here, I think the insight of Theresa de la Luz is especially important—that when her sisters were first afflicted, there was no fraud involved, and that it was only later that they learned to "stage" the fits.

Unfortunately, we have only one case in which we have a fairly clear sense of the trajectory of the affliction over time, that of Phelipa herself; but hers fits the pattern suggested by Theresa. It seems extremely likely that when Phelipa was first afflicted by the "salto," in 1761 and 1762 (whose symptoms, as described by the bishop, resembled those of the later "mal"—"dancing, gesturing, and disordered words"), she was not faking her symptoms (although, even then, she was accused of doing so, as we saw in Chapter 2).[28] Either she suffered from a disease with somatic origins that could produce symptoms such as abnormal body movements and disordered speech under conditions of extreme stress, or stress alone had caused an emotional breakdown that brought with it physical manifestations.

There is no question that in these early years Phelipa was under considerable stress. On top of the crisis in the convent that had already led to one of the founding nuns returning to her home convent in Mexico City, she had her own personal crisis: Antonia's opposition to her confessional practices and choices of confessors and the abbess's eventually successful effort to separate her from her second (and favorite) confessor, Father Rubí. As her psychological distress took a physical toll, Phelipa was confined to her cell and treated as an invalid—in the process, gaining certain privileges that may very well have been unanticipated, but that provided emotional and practical relief from over-whelmingly difficult circumstances. At least at first, her illness allowed her to see her confessor more often than she would have been able to see him oth-erwise. It also meant that she ate better food, since, in most convents with a common kitchen, the sick enjoyed special meal privileges, such as a larger ration of meat or chocolate. Most important, it excused her from choir, refec-tory, and other community activities, allowing her to stay in her cell rather than struggle through the motions of her daily routine.[29]

Over time, however, the nuns' testimonies suggest that the onset of Phe-lipa's symptoms became more conscious. She fell ill at opportune moments; the relief she sought for the illness looked suspiciously like relaxation of the Rule, and even recreation; and most damning of all, the disease began to spread—but only to her allies. In the years after the first convent crisis, during which, according to several of the nuns' testimonies, she was maneuvering to become abbess, she must have realized that she could recruit followers by, in effect, making them sick—thus allowing them, too, to partake of the significant practical and psychological benefits of illness in a convent. The privileges that Phelipa herself had enjoyed and the attention that she had received were almost like political capital that she could bestow on others by "infecting" them. Once she became abbess, these benefits were even easier to dispense because she could not only offer sick nuns personal care and attention, better food, and release from choir and official duties, but she could also invent new perquisites: for example, bringing horses into the convent so that the sick nuns, but not the well ones, could ride.[30] As one of the bishop's advisers later put it, "illness came to be a privilege that distinguished [the nuns who had it] and excused them from standards of behavior that were demanded of everyone else."[31]

Although in Phelipa's case, the possibility of a disease with a somatic origin exists, it seems certain that the affliction was psychosomatic in her fol-lowers. Emotional need, suggestibility, exhibitionism, the desire to belong, the desire to grow closer to God, as they felt Phelipa had done, extreme stress—all could account for the other nuns' initial susceptibility to the disease. The first attacks, we might surmise, were quite genuine, and for this reason, very convincing. Perhaps even the second and third attacks (we don't really know how many the nuns suffered) were also powerful emotional experiences—not feigned. But what if the attacks or fits did not appear as often or in as timely a fashion as the sufferers might wish or expect? What if a nun suffered only

one or two spells? Might she worry about endangering her newly special relationship to Phelipa? Might she miss the attention and concern that accompanied the spell? Might she feel excluded from the group? Might she find it
difficult to resist exaggerating her symptoms a little? And if that worked, perhaps to exaggerate them a little more the next time? In other words, by the
time the bishop issued the interrogatory, the nuns responded to it, and the
advisers responded to those responses, is it possible that many of the attacks
were what the bishop suspected: largely feigned? It seems to me that this is
the best way not only to understand the conviction with which many of the
nuns and the bishop (advised by the vicar, as well as his three appointed advisers) believed that the symptoms were manufactured, but also to understand
how it was that so many women could carry off complicated and demanding
performances that *did* convince, compel, and frighten others sufficiently to get
the bishop involved in the first place.

If, then, by the mid-1760s, Phelipa was able, at least to a considerable
extent, to manipulate her illness and suggest it to others, what purpose did it
serve in her projects and program? First, it offered her and her allies a way to
continue to test the authority of the vicar and bishop without direct confrontation, to keep them off balance, and to prevent them, to a certain extent, from
interfering with her agenda. These male authorities may have believed that the
disease was willfully feigned by the rebellious nuns, in blatant disregard of the
principle of obedience—the bishop certainly did—but they still would have
had trouble insisting that nuns with such pronounced symptoms of affliction
be denied access to nursing care or extra rations of especially palatable food,
or that they be forced to attend choir when they were ill or recovering from an
attack. Beyond this, while they, themselves, may not have believed that the
devil was involved, several of the nuns apparently did, which meant that they
had to act carefully. Even the remote possibility of demonic influence raised
doubt about how to handle the situation and made it even more difficult simply
to crack down on the afflicted nuns. So illness protected Phelipa's efforts to
remake the convent in the sense that the male authorities did not know quite
how to intervene. As we will see, the bishop's advisers urged caution and
proposed only modest measures to address the situation.

Second, spreading the disease had very practical repercussions in this still-
underpopulated convent and helped to advance Phelipa's project of loosening
adherence to—and eventually, even amending—the convent's constitution.
Several of the nuns, remarking on lapses in the care of the sacristy and the
instruments of mass, and on poor attendance at choir and other acts of community, support the comment of one of the bishop's advisers that the disease
"prevented the healthy from carrying out their offices for the need to attend to
the sick."[32] Since one of Phelipa's primary goals in remaking the convent was
to get around the prohibition against personal servants, she may have hoped
that a disease that, in effect, paralyzed the convent's religious functions by

occupying all of the healthy nuns with the care of the sick would result in the bishop allowing outside servants to enter. The constitution did allow for this possibility in the case of an "epidemic." There is no evidence that this was ever permitted, but that does not preclude it as a possible motivation for Phelipa to "spread" her illness.

The salto/mal was the most dramatic feature of Phelipa's tenure as abbess, but it was not the only disturbing thing about her regime. In fact, while all of the nuns wrote about it (they were, after all, required to do so by the questionnaire), and all three of the bishop's advisers saw it as one of the most intractable problems that faced the ecclesiastical authorities who were trying to control the convent, it was only one of the disturbing changes that occurred since Phelipa had become abbess. For others, let us turn to the responses of the "obedient" nuns to the bishop's questionnaire.

The Interrogatory

The questions that the bishop ordered the sacristan to put to the obedient faction of nuns were the following:

1. Has Mother Phelipa altered or changed the Rule and distribution set out in the constitution?
2. Has she failed to obey the Vicar?
3. Has she spread rumors against him?
4. If there are Parties in the convent, who belongs to them?
5. Has Mother Phelipa abused and insulted the well-adapted nuns?
6. Does she feign illness?
7. Is the sacristy kept clean? In the sacristy, is there communication with outsiders?
8. Does Mother Phelipa fail to appear at Choir, prayer, and other distributions?
9. Were the grilles in the sacristy removed, so that from the interior of the Church the friars of San Francisco could see and speak to the novices, scandalizing the other Religiosas?
10. Has Mother Phelipa taught other nuns to feign illnesses?
11. Have Mother Phelipa and her party taken over the convent to the extent that they are the ones who run it, mistreating some of the other Religiosas and the donadas?
12. Was there undue celebration when the Franciscans came to visit?

The responses were extraordinary. Most of the seven nuns whose testimonies are contained in the documentation volunteered long and detailed answers to the questions, which they presumably wrote in secrecy over what must have been a period of many days. Five of them, asked if there was anything that they would like to add, did so—in some cases, laboriously penning page upon page of additional commentary on the problems and scandals in the convent. Their complaints ran the gamut from the trivial to the profound and back again, and they were often presented in an almost stream of conscious-ness manner—though, it should be noted the order of questions in the inter-rogatory itself was quite illogical, so to a considerable extent, the fact that the nuns' responses jump abruptly from one topic to another was dictated by the format of questioning put to them by the bishop. For example, the question about Phelipa feigning illness was followed by a question about whether the sacristy was kept clean, and a follow-up on whether Phelipa taught others the symptoms of her illness did not come until three questions later.

By far, the most temperate of the responses, and indeed, the only one that did not thoroughly condemn Phelipa's actions, but rather sought to understand and explain them, was that of María Josepha Lina. As we saw in Chapter 1, Mother Lina's biographer painted a picture of a young girl almost too pious to be believed; in fact, one is tempted to dismiss it as exactly the sort of portrait in words one would expect to be commissioned by the descendants of the foundress of a convent. Unfortunately, we do not have much else to go on. María Josepha Lina did not express her thoughts on the rebellion in letters to the bishop or vicar, as some of the other nuns did. The only document she produced, other than a few unrevealing letters on uncontroversial subjects, is this one, and it was written only because the bishop commanded her response. The personality that comes through, however, is surprisingly like that of the "exemplary nun" characterized in her biography: gentle, forgiving, almost saintly. Clearly pained by the extent to which Phelipa and her allies had un-dermined the original vision of the convent (her own) and the rules and prac-tices devised by the first abbess in order to carry out that vision, she was, nonetheless, unwilling to contribute any more than necessary to the atmo-sphere of divisiveness. She went out of her way to see the nuns on both sides as trying their best to serve the best interests of the convent. She was the only nun who did not seem angry at Phelipa, even though, given her position as foundress, she was the one with the best reason to feel betrayed; indeed, she pleaded with the bishop to treat Phelipa kindly and gently.

The picture that she painted of the convent's situation, however, was not positive. She confirmed that Phelipa had changed every element of the daily distribution that Antonia, the first abbess, had set up, removing some parts of it altogether. It was also true, she admitted, that Phelipa failed to obey the vicar, saying that it was not his business to manage the internal affairs of the convent. Once, when María Josepha Lina chided Phelipa for this behavior, Phelipa harshly responded that the foundress could obey the vicar if she wished, but in that case, she, Phelipa, was not Mother Lina's abbess, because she (Mother Lina) would be governed by the vicar instead. Phelipa, she continued, had indeed clashed with the "well-adjusted" nuns, and she had heard her say that their ways made her laugh and that they would be better off emulating her faction and not adhering to their "precious and ridiculous" customs. Regarding Phelipa's affliction, María Josepha Lina was not sure whether she was pretending to be sick—all she knew was that the doctors were unsure what the disease was and what might be its cure—and she also did not know whether Phelipa was teaching its symptoms to the others, only that the others certainly displayed those symptoms, whether to please Phelipa or not, she could not say. Because so many were sick, it was true that the sacristy was not cleaned as regularly as before. She had heard about the grille being removed from the sacristy, but she had not actually seen it herself. She had also heard that the religiosas in Phelipa's faction mistreated the donadas, but she had only witnessed this on one occasion, when they threatened to throw one of the donadas off the tower because they had ordered her to ring the church bells and she said that she could not because she had to take care of a sick nun.

Having thus answered all of the set questions, María Josepha Lina volunteered a number of examples of laxity in the observance of enclosure. The doctor came every day, sometimes unnecessarily. Frequently, there was not a listener at the grille in the parlor (when she mentioned this to Phelipa, she responded that she allowed this because there might be something that a religiosa wanted to say to her parents or siblings that she did not want the escucha to hear, but still, the Rule was very clear that an escucha must be present at all times). Those who entered the cloister from the outside were not always accompanied by one of the senior nuns, as the Rule dictated; and when those who were in charge of the main door and the turnstile could not fulfill these duties, often someone else of inadequate seniority was named to fill in. Finally, Phelipa had allowed horses in the cloister so that the nuns could ride them, justifying this by saying that those who were sick needed to get some exercise. This new custom, María Josepha Lina said, particularly appalled her. She concluded by reiterating her distress that "all of the practices that were observed since the time of our Mother Antonia have been removed."

But in Phelipa's defense, María Josepha Lina noted that the total number of hours spent in choir remained the same; it was just the scheduling of the singing of the Divine Office that had been changed. Furthermore, although she was the only one to do so, María Josepha Lina raised the possibility that Phelipa genuinely had the best interests of the convent at heart, that she sincerely believed that a relaxation of the rigor with which the Rule had been interpreted was necessary, given the small number of nuns, the great amount of work, and especially, the pervasive illness. "I understand that everything that our Mother does, she does to see if by these means she can ease the burdens on all of the sick, because she has told me that that is her intention when she removes or alters any of our observances," she explained. She concluded with the fervent hope that Sánchez de Tagle would remedy that which he considered needful of correction, but "for the love of God I beg that it be with the gentlest means possible."

María Josepha Lina's generosity of spirit with regard to Phelipa was absent in all of the other testimony. Phelipa's predecessor as abbess, Anna María de los Dolores, gave a very detailed answer to question 1, regarding the various alterations in the distribution and customs of the convent introduced by Phelipa, essentially agreeing with María Josepha Lina that "everything" had been changed. In her responses to questions 2 and 3, she affirmed that the nuns in Phelipa's faction disobeyed the vicar and spread rumors about him. Question 4—essentially, who were the members of Phelipa's faction?—she answered by noting that she had much to say on this subject, which she considered to be the principal problem of the convent. She named:

> Mother Josepha Ygnacia who from the first has shown herself to be very partial to Phelipa; the two vocalists Mothers María de San Miguel and Josepha de Sr. San Luis; the two urbinas [their surname was Urbina] Mothers Augustina and Josepha; the Reverend Mother María Anna del Santísimo who in the last few days has shown herself to be a partisan; Mothers María Cayetana de las Llagas; Xaviera de la Sangre de Christo; Vicenta del Corazón de Jesús; María Antonia de San Joseph; María Gertrudis de S. Joachín; the two obregonas [surname Obregón] María Ygnacia de S. Juan Nepomuceno and Anna María de los Dolores—all of them dispose, all of them govern, all of them command and all of them chastise those who are not partial to the Mother Abbess. . . .

One of the things that bothered Anna María the most was that Phelipa "goes about giving those whom she loves anything they fancy." Desperate for Phelipa's removal from office, she felt bound by a pledge she had made to Antonia, the first abbess of the convent, never to allow changes in the practices of the convent. She herself had served as long as she could in her capacity as abbess, until her eyes became too weak (she apologized for her poor handwriting, blaming it on her failing eyesight), knowing all the while that Phelipa was operating behind her back and doing great damage to the community. "For the love of God [we must be given] a remedy and may it be sooner rather than later, because in delay lies the greatest danger."[33]

On the subject of the mal, Anna María de los Dolores was among those who saw the influence of the devil. "I cannot say whether the disease is true or feigned," she wrote, "but it is beyond understanding, and many ills have come and are coming of it, and it seems that the Devil has much part in it because those to whom this accident has befallen do whatever they wish and they show no respect at all for the others, using the accident as their excuse." While some of the other nuns portray Phelipa as offering to teach the symptoms of the mal to those who joined her, Anna María de los Dolores focused on how frightening the prospect of the disease could be for those who did not want to catch it:

> Just now there is a poor Religiosa who is sick with a very different illness and she is afraid that it is the mal . . . and the doctor has told another religiosa that it is necessary to purge her, but her fear was great that if she took [the purgative] that it would give her the mal . . . and this poor patient was so indisposed that she sent for me to ask me if she should take the purgative and I told her that she should not take it, and afterwards, seeing her so full of apprehension, I arranged to have her bled telling her that this would not give her the mal.

But if they did catch it, afterward, "those who were injured by the accident loved Phelipa very much, whereas before they had not done so," another sign of the devil at work.

The testimonies of María de Jesús and Rita de la Santísima Trinidad contributed some detail, but for the most part, reiterated what the others said. María de Jesús did include a long "additional comments" section, but it tended toward petty complaint, and Rita not only added little beyond the required response, but also had quite childish and awkward handwriting and obviously found the task of writing to be rather overwhelming. Theresa de la Luz's response was elegantly penned and very literate, but she added little that was new and stuck to the questions that were asked. As we have already seen, she did have an interesting view on the question of whether or not Phelipa was teaching the mal to others:

> I do not know if our Mother feigns illness so that the other sisters come to visit her, nor if these visits are used to discuss the governance of the Convent; although I have seen that they go to see her and they meet in her cell . . . and these meetings have been going on since before the election [of 1769] and so too have the parties and factions in the convent. I do not know nor have I seen that our Mother and the others infected with the mal teach it to others that do not have it . . . but I am persuaded . . . that to please our Mother they allow themselves to be carried away by the affliction, although I do not believe that on the first occasion they are feigning it but once they already have it malice enters and they use it for the motives I have already insinuated.

If these three testimonies failed to venture much beyond the questions posed by the bishop, two others are rich mines for insight into the state of the convent under Phelipa's regime and the attitudes not only of the obedient nuns, but also of the rebels. Gertrudis de San José and Manuela de la Santísima

Trinidad produced indignant, opinionated, self-confident, passionate reports of what they saw as the travesties occurring under Phelipa's stewardship of the convent. Together, they confirm the picture of the convent that began to emerge in María Josepha Lina's declaration, of a place where the lines between the secular and the religious were being intentionally blurred, and where the demanding standards of behavior and religious virtue, written into the constitution and adopted by the first three abbesses, were being ignored, even ridiculed. From their testimonies, in combination with the others, it is clear that, after years of emphasis on silence, rigid enclosure, common life, constant prayer, self-discipline, and self-denial, asceticism was no longer the rule, or even the ideal, at La Purísima. The timeless tug of war between rigor and relaxation, then—played out, at least to a certain extent, in most convents—was now being won, in this particular convent, by the advocates of relaxation, whom these two angry and distressed nuns characterize as self-indulgent, even childish.

But the testimonies of Gertrudis and Manuela also give us a fascinating glimpse of other changes introduced by Phelipa, changes that show that Phelipa had more on her mind than finding ways for the nuns to avoid prayer and work and to make their lives in the convent more like their lives outside the convent. For one thing, Phelipa—influenced, perhaps, by eighteenth-century ideas of social equality—aimed to restructure relationships among the nuns, and between the convent and the male religious authorities, along more egalitarian lines. Within the convent, she presided over an almost revolutionary undermining of the principle of hierarchy, collapsing three levels of seniority and status distinction among the nuns into one, a radical change that requires some reading between the lines to interpret: Either she saw this as a way to defuse tensions among the nuns by putting them on a more equal basis with one another, or she was shrewdly maneuvering to garner support among the nuns with less seniority and lower status by treating them the same as their elders and betters. In either case, however, she was using the "modern" idea that equality was a good thing to serve her ends.

Besides treating the nuns in a more egalitarian fashion, Phelipa also gave them much more freedom of action than they had ever enjoyed, not only with regard to their personal behavior, but also in terms of their official duties—among other things, allowing them to handle the money their jobs required, rather than holding onto the purse strings herself. This, too, was a radical and heavily criticized departure from time-honored principles of centralization of authority and enclosure. More nuns would now be exposed to the grubby realities of buying, selling, and paying wages, as they dealt more directly with tradesmen and workers.

As far as relations between the convent and the church hierarchy were concerned, it is clear that Phelipa would brook little interference in convent affairs. Although her letters to the bishop continued to be models of deference,

she was prepared to weaken, and even sever, ties to his agents and representatives in San Miguel: the vicar, sacristan, and chaplain. Her defense of the
independence of the convent, which most prominently took the form of her
war with the vicar, was, ironically, a position of which Antonia, the first abbess,
might have approved, since she, too, had bristled at the actions of the vicar and
the Count of Casa de Loja, when she saw them overstepping the bounds of
their jurisdiction. For Phelipa, responsibility for the internal government of
the convent lay squarely with the abbess, the vice-abbess, and the Definitorio;
the vicar was to advise, but not to command.

Let us begin with Manuela's response. The first three questions she answered as the others had done, with great detail on the subject of changes in
the daily distribution and strong affirmatives on the subject of the lack of
obedience and respect for the vicar: "she [Phelipa] tells her partisans that the
Vicar and the chaplain do not have to serve to the satisfaction of the bishop
but rather to that of the religiosas." Concerning the removal of the grille so
that the Franciscans could talk to the nuns and novices, she stated that she had
twice witnessed this violation of enclosure. In answer to the questions about
the disease, Manuela was very clear that Phelipa was instructing her cohorts
in the symptoms of her affliction, "telling them that they had a propensity for
it because of their temperaments (*complexiones*), and that they would probably
catch it from her, and sure enough they contracted it soon after." She concluded: "What [Phelipa's] intentions are in all this I could not say . . ."

Manuela's testimony also included a very interesting "additional comments" section. She began with the assertion that Phelipa had been elected
abbess by promising to give certain offices to her supporters, even if they were
not qualified to hold them, "telling them that if they voted for her she would
give them this or that office or job, and that the previous Preladas had done
them wrong by not giving them these positions."[34] She also criticized Phelipa's
undermining of traditional hierarchies: "she has ordered that there should be
no distinctions within the convent," so that instead of some nuns being addressed as "Reverend Mother," some as "Mother," and some as "Sister," all of
the nuns—from the novices to the *jóvenes* (the younger nuns with fewer than
8 years of profession) to the most senior nuns, from the definidoras to the
legas—should be addressed as "Mother." "With this," she wrote, "she has won
the support of the community and created a monster. . . ."[35] But there was more
scandalous behavior yet:

> None of the previous Preladas allowed the religiosas to put on theat-
> rical productions, nor to dress in the clothes of seculars; this sort of
> thing has always been very much frowned upon. But when Mother
> Phelipa became Abbess she got together her partisans and they put
> on a production and she allowed them to dress as seculars and they
> left for the "theater" dressed in skirts and wigs and other adorn-

ments; although they wore these clothes over their habits, still it did not seem right and had never been seen before in this convent. Also some dressed in capes, waistcoats, hats, cane and other adornments of men, and this did not happen for just one or two days but from Christmas Eve through the whole holy season. . . . There was also music, drums, and other loud entertainment which caused great commotion in the cloister and all of the convent. This was during the time that our Reverend Mother Vicaria [María Josepha Lina] was very sick in bed, so sick that they even came to confess her, and it was not seemly in these circumstances for them to go from cloister to cloister beating drums, playing the violin and tambourine and singing,[36] and in the cell where they had the "theater" there was also dancing, the Reverend Mother Abbess dancing with all of her partisans. During this whole period until Twelfth Night there was no prayer, no refectory, no examination of conscience, no work, all of which was against what should be . . .

Finally, Manuela complained that, in previous regimes, no one handled money except the provisora (the nun in charge of arranging the purchase of food and supplies) and the vicaria de casa (the second most important office, sort of a vice-abbess), but now Phelipa also handed out funds to the head nurse, the head sacristana (the nun in charge of keeping the sacristy in order), the head tornera (the nun in charge of the turnstile), the head gardener, and so on, so that they could pay the expenses that had to do with their particular jobs. "They are so pleased with this arrangement," she wrote, "that they deceive themselves that the convent has never been better governed . . . but the previous Preladas never permitted this because they said that it gave the nuns too much freedom and they lost the habit of submission. . . ."

The final set of responses to the interrogatory, that of Gertrudis de San José, filled 16 pages—it was the longest of the testimonies, though not by much, as prolixity was the rule rather than the exception. She began by naming the same nuns who belonged to Phelipa's faction as the others, adding that the boldest were the two vocalists (Josepha de San Luis Gonzaga and María de San Miguel), the two Urbina sisters (Augustina de la Encarnación and Josepha del Rosario), and Cayetana de las Llagas: "they are the ones that stir things up the most." Her answers to the other set questions were lengthy, but add little to the picture of what was going on in the convent during Phelipa's tenure. She had a great deal to say about the breaking of enclosure; she accused some of the nuns of talking to men without listeners nearby, among other incidents, saying that she had seen Josepha de San Luis Gonzaga talking to Manuel de Arébalo at the grille without an escucha. She also said that she had been told by one of the nurses that the doctor had been in Cayetana's cell, playing the violin while she played the guitar, and that Phelipa was there listening and even called for María Anna del Santísimo Sacramento, the second abbess and Phelipa's old nemesis, to come and listen and enjoy herself. Once, she wrote, she had seen the doctor go into the cell of the two vocalists when they were preparing their Christmas play, and he was helping them to put on their wigs. Not only were horses allowed in the convent, but the grille was also lifted so that those on the outside could see the nuns as they galloped past.

On the symptoms of the disease from which the nuns suffered, Gertrudis' testimony went into more detail than most of the others, and for this reason, she was quoted extensively in the earlier section devoted to the mal. To reiterate, she blamed the devil, but went on to describe Phelipa as the "originator of this mal" and to imply that Phelipa very consciously spread the affliction in order to win votes in the 1769 election: "in her hands it is so powerful that before the election the Urbina sisters were not part of her faction, but then she gave the mal to María Josepha and from that time on she was completely at her command."

Together, these seven testimonies describe a regime radically different from anything that had come before. Phelipa had led the convent to turn in on itself and assert its independence from outside authority. She constantly resisted the interference of the vicar and the chaplain, telling her followers that no one should govern the nuns but themselves. The assertion of conventual independence, in turn, allowed her to make many practical changes in the daily distribution and the customs of the convent—including some fairly extreme relaxations of the principle of enclosure—that made the nuns' lives easier and more enjoyable. While she had not yet attempted a point-blank assault on the vida común, the common life, she had, nonetheless, chipped away at the foundation of reform, on which the convent was built, to the point that it was nearly unrecognizable. In the process, many of the features of the vida común had fallen by the wayside, including the common kitchen, since more than half of the convent was sick and could neither eat the food prepared for the convent nor attend refectory.

The picture of convent life that emerges from these testimonies was one in which the nuns felt freer than they had ever been to recreate elements of the secular world within the cloister. Nuns galloped about on horseback in view of outsiders; friars, and even secular men, chatted with the nuns without escuchas present; nuns dressed in secular clothes (both male and female) and put on theatrical productions; nuns danced through the cloister, playing drums and tambourines; and Phelipa politicked for election behind the scenes by promising her supporters plum offices. To the obedient nuns, all of this was enough to produce a sense of great anxiety, and to the bishop, it was enough to give rise to his fear that the convent was on the edge of chaos. And as if to underscore and symbolize the extent to which the original aims of the convent had been subverted, there was the spread of a disease that periodically caused over half of the convent population utterly to lose self-control, dancing about and saying upsetting things and causing "great disturbance," even as the foundress of the reformed convent, María Josepha Lina, sank into the illness that would cause her death in August 1770.

Rich as these testimonies are, they present the views of only one of the factions in the convent; as one of the bishop's advisers, who was asked to read and comment on them, pointed out with some concern, there was no attempt to elicit the point of view of the rebellious nuns. There are a number of letters from Phelipa in the file from this period, but for the most part, they are as beautifully written and enigmatic as ever: She continued to deny everything in tones of contrition and bewilderment, pleading ignorance of her faults, begging for clarification, and pledging to obey—but only if the bishop would agree to tell her precisely what she had done wrong. In November 1770, for example, she wrote to Sánchez de Tagle, saying that she was "greatly tormented" by a letter that she had received from him. She could certainly see why he was concerned, she wrote, given the reports that he said he had received, but "I am ignorant of and cannot understand" the precise complaints, "for which reason I humbly ask you as my Father and Prelate, from the goodness of your heart to individualize, point by point, my failings, and the lapses and perturbations of peace among us, so that I can remedy them. . . ."[37] Like many of the other nuns who wrote to the bishop, Phelipa begged Sánchez de Tagle to send a visitor, especially since the Rule required a visit once a year (a sly dig, given the bishop's criticism of her for not following the Rule). Of course, the most desirable visitor would be Sánchez de Tagle himself. In this way, she could "water [his] feet with my tears" if he found her remiss, and he could forgive her. She closed by saying that, "although I am only a Woman, permit me to quote some words of San Gerónimo, and they are 'to err is human'; these words may excuse me . . . from the blame that I am sure I must bear. As your Obedient Servant I will accept any penance you give me. . . ."

There is also a defiant letter from Cayetana de las Llagas that is worth pausing over briefly for its glimpse into the icy relationship between the nuns of La Purísima and the male religious authorities of San Miguel. Here, Cayetana, more forcefully than ever before, asserts the nuns' right not to obey an unreasonable "government that treats us like animals" (she explicitly refers to the vicar's behavior, but she may also have had in mind the sacristan's administration of the "secret" interrogatory that surely could not have remained much of a secret within the convent). Dated August 17, 1770, and written in her baroque style (always including at least a full page of apologies and metaphorical flights before she got to the point), she too begged the bishop to send a visitor, one who could evaluate dispassionately the true state of things.[38] But he must be sent from Valladolid, she insisted. "He cannot be from this Villa because the priests and friars here are very antagonistic and they treat us very poorly (*nos dan a rratos un pan con unas nueses*). In their view we are all disgraced . . . they call us *cabras* (she-goats)." If someone from San Miguel were to be named the visitor, she went on:

> he might give you, my Lord, a description of our disease, but not of its particular causes. If to my great dismay you do not send us a visitor, I beg you at least to tell your subjects to whom you have given your holy kiss [i.e., the priests and friars of San Miguel] to smooth the rough edges of their government and their disagreeable manner of command, because at times this is the reason that the lowly nuns are not of a mind to obey; although it is true that we are servants and we must obey, it is one thing to be subject, and another thing, as rational creatures, to be forced to endure a government that treats us like animals. . . .

Many studies have shown that the ideas of the Enlightenment seeped into Mexico, despite (according to the old conventional wisdom) the best efforts of the Inquisition to keep them out, but no evidence of this phenomenon, perhaps, is more impressive than that a 31-year-old woman who had been "enclosed" in a convent for 14 years would use the excuse that she and her cohorts were "rational creatures . . . forced to endure a government that treats us like animals" to justify rebellion.

The Reports of the Bishop's Advisers

Sánchez de Tagle submitted the nuns' responses, along with other documents concerning the troublesome case, to three learned advisers, ostensibly for comment and suggestions as to what should be done. But his line of questioning strongly suggests that he already knew what he wanted to do: remove Phelipa, at least as abbess, if not from the convent altogether. In this, as we will see, he was not to be satisfied. Each of the consultants came to slightly different conclusions as to how serious the problems in the San Miguel convent were and what should be done to correct them. Ironically, however, their patronizing attitude and disdain for women, and presumably, their lack of commitment to the idea of the reformed convent, prevented them from taking the problems at La Purísima as seriously as did Sánchez de Tagle, who, as a reformist bishop, had more at stake in defending La Purísima's constitution. None of his advisers recommended the draconian measures for which the bishop was seeking approval.

The first of the reports was presented to Sánchez de Tagle in August 1770 by Dr. Ricardo Joseph Gutiérrez Coronel, his private secretary (*secretaría de cámara*).[39] Gutiérrez Coronel condemned what he repeatedly called Phelipa's "despotism"; however, he did not consider it to be a calculated despotism, but rather a sign of a weak leader operating in the difficult world of female pettiness and passion. Furthermore, the blame was not all Phelipa's: The vicar and chaplain should have offered firmer guidance along the way, the bishop himself failed to impose appropriate punishment when Phelipa first began to challenge the Rule in the early 1760s, and the first two abbesses were also at fault for their ill-considered zealousness. Overactive zeal and sentiment, in fact, were accusations that he flung at just about everyone, except María Josepha Lina.

Having read all of the evidence that was submitted to him (the interrogatories and relevant correspondence since 1759), he identified the convent's general problem as the "lack of a Pilot." From the declarations of the nuns, in answer to the interrogatory, and in the letters that they wrote to the bishop, one could easily detect the feminine sensibility: overzealous, overly passionate, and excitable. When these flaws are not constantly minimized, he pontificated, problems can arise, even in the strictest communities, and it is the job of the abbess, and if not the abbess, then the confessors, vicars, and chaplains, to be the "pilot" and to curb them and keep them in check, in order to prevent the "scandal and prejudice that is now attached to this Convent."

The specific problems that arose from these "defects of the female sex" and the failure of the male authorities to correct them were "lack of obedience and charity, relaxation of enclosure, disunion, discord, and disdain of constitutions and customs that threaten to bring down the beautiful edifice of Religious Perfection." Using a cancer analogy, he wondered rhetorically whether Phelipa should be removed before she poisoned the entire population, since she was the "origin of so many evils." But, answering himself, he argued that her "despotism and lack of prudence" did not seem to arise out of malice or stubbornness, since her letters demonstrated her humility, her willingness to obey, and her religiosity. "She has not only offered to obey," he reminded the bishop, "but she has put into practice many of your mandates; the problem is that what we see clearly as errors she see as gentleness or indulgence conceded to her ailing sisters, and this leads to perverse relaxations of the Rule that impede the road to perfection and scandalize the outside world." If only, he continued, the vicar had accepted Phelipa's renunciation of her right to vote before the last election, "how many evils could have been prevented?" "What an unhappy Bishopric," he lamented, "where a new convent, usually a place where zeal is especially ardent, should be so relaxed and so in danger of total destruction or at least ruinous scandal!"

What was the solution? Remove Phelipa from her office? Transfer her to her old convent of Regina Coeli? These were two possible remedies, he said, "but they are harsh ones, painful ones, that cannot be executed without taking extreme measures and without discrediting the poor Prelada, who demands our charity." For several pages, he examined the canonical arguments for both of these actions. There were only three legitimate reasons for nuns to leave the cloister, he reminded the bishop: fire, leprosy, and plague or other contagious epidemic. Canon law also allowed the transfer of an "incorrigible" nun to another convent, if there was danger of perversion of other religiosas, but this could be done only with license from the Pope. The authorities, he said, preferred to incarcerate such a nun in her own convent; this way, she could serve as an example to the other religiosas, and the scandal of a transfer would be avoided. Besides, a transfer might encourage other nuns to ask to move from convent to convent. But these measures applied only to incorrigible nuns:

> Who, in this case, is said to be incorrigible? "Incorrigible" means one who after threats, punishments, and penances remains disobedient. The usual first level of punishment is a year of fasting and penitence, next a year of incarceration. . . . To date the only punishments in this case have been paternal admonishments from Your Excellency, written to the Vicar and to [Phelipa] in the month of April of the year 1762. In that letter you tell her: "if you do not change it will be necessary to move from private to public admonishments, and also to impose appropriate punishment." But since you have not imposed any punishment so far—such as loss of the right to vote, loss of the right to hold office, removal of the veil, incarceration and reclusion—it appears that you should not proceed without trying them first, especially since she has responded with humility and sincerity that she will obey you in everything, and since her election as Abbess was permitted by the Vicar and approved by Your Excellency.

Furthermore, he said, though Phelipa's despotism was certainly to blame for the convent's problems, "all of the things of which the convent can be accused can [also] be seen as originating from the carelessness, imprudence, inattention, and lack of government of the Vicar and the Chaplain" and from the "excessive zeal" of others (presumably, the first two abbesses), which resulted in factionalism and discord. He also noted that all of the declarations he had read were written by those who voted against Phelipa, hinting that sour grapes might have fed the passion with which some of the answers were phrased. In fact, the only testimony that he found fully compelling was that of María Josepha Lina, whose "calm and moderate" testimony did not dwell on "ridiculous, trite, and childish" complaints, such as the too-grand welcome given to the Franciscan fathers (perhaps this was tactless on Gutiérrez Coronel's part, since the question about the Franciscans was one of the ones devised by the bishop himself, clearly with the aim of eliciting such complaints). The other testimonies were not necessarily wrong in their substance, he opined, but they are made untrustworthy because of their "female defects," especially their passion.

Therefore, he did not think Phelipa was "incorrigible," and for this reason, as well as for the sake of prudence, he did not think that she should, or could

legitimately, be forced to transfer to another convent. He also did not think
that she should be deposed as abbess. To remove her from office came up
squarely against the monastic Rule: "they have the right to elect her as Prelada,"
he pointed out, and for the bishop to depose her summarily, against the will
and without the participation of the other religiosas, could bring about even
greater unrest. Such a step could also invite judicial recourse, as Phelipa might
exercise her right to defend herself before a judge.[40] Furthermore, removing
her from office would require a judicial decree, and this could only be obtained
from an authority in the outside world, "from whom the defects of the Religiosas must remain even more hidden than the Religiosas themselves."

After many pages of discussion of precedents and examination of the issues from every conceivable angle, Gutiérrez Coronel finally made his way
toward a recommendation. First, he urged that, as soon as possible, the bishop
should appoint a "person of the greatest authority who enjoys the confidence
of Your Excellency" to visit the convent, delegating to him the faculty to investigate and confirm the truth of every one of the points raised in the answers
to the interrogatory. He should also be authorized to correct, admonish, rep-
rehend, and if necessary, punish any delinquencies with moderate and paternal
punishments. If this was not enough to "calm the troubled waters in which
the Religiosas find themselves submerged," the visitor should seek judicial
backing for the punishments he deemed necessary, in case there was resistance
to those punishments. But, given the "timidity of the female sex and the trac-
tability of the Religious estate," he believed that these judicial measures would
be unnecessary. He closed by recommending that the bishop approve a request
made by one of the nuns that they be allowed to take as their patron saint the
Virgin of Guadalupe, to help them in their battle against the "pernicious evil"
of the "epilepsy" epidemic. In the city of Puebla, he said, all of the convents
had sworn allegiance to this virgin, and there the illness abated completely in
many nuns, and in others, its symptoms were eased sufficiently that they could
attend choir and other communal acts. A ceremony accepting the virgin as the
patroness of the convent would be a good way to conclude the visitation that
he recommended, in the expectation that the two measures together would
"remedy not only this epidemic but all spiritual contagion and all relaxation of
religious customs, leading to the restoration and conservation of perfection."

What should we make of this report? Two things stand out. The first is the
surprising extent to which Gutiérrez Coronel was willing to treat serious
breaches of the Rule and threats to the convent's constitution and reputation
as relatively insignificant. Though he does, at one point, refer to the possibility
of the convent's "total destruction," and at another, to his fear that the crisis
would "bring down the beautiful edifice of Religious Perfection," the dominant
tone of his report is worldly-wise, unruffled, and superior. Certainly, there were
things to be lamented—he mentioned the constant and unseemly comings
and goings of the doctor, the laxity in the monitoring of the doors and turnstile,

the baskets of fruit and delectable foods that entered the convent freely—but, all things considered, he did not seem especially bothered by them. He seems not entirely to have shared the bishop's concern that at least the appearance of strict observance should be maintained in a convent that had been founded as a reformed monastery. Similarly, he was quite dismissive of the agonizing divisions within the convent, seeing them as petty and childish. These attitudes derived, it seems clear, from his contempt for women: He obviously saw that there were problems in the convent, but he did not view these problems as either worthy of grave concern or susceptible to easy correction, precisely be-cause it was a female convent. Pettiness, hurtful gossip, materialism, discord—these were bound to be present in a community of women, he believed, and one could only hope that male authorities would be able to keep them in check, which they had not done in San Miguel.

The second point that stands out is his caution regarding how to handle Phelipa. He may have viewed women, in general, as weak, but he was extremely wary of challenging her directly. The fact that he spent so much time trying to second-guess whether or not she would take judicial recourse if the bishop tried to remove her from office, or whether the other nuns would tolerate such interference on the part of the bishop, suggests that he respected both Phelipa's personal power and the power that derived from her position as abbess. Clearly, he accepted the convent's right to elect Phelipa and her right to a judicial defense if an attempt were made to remove her from office. Gutiérrez Coronel's relatively weak recommendations were driven by his perception that, to a con-siderable extent, Phelipa was untouchable, and they were underlain by a deep fear of exposing the convent's problems to the outside world. There was rela-tively little to be done, in his view, to resolve the internal situation, since to a large extent, such problems were endemic and inescapable in a female convent. What must be guarded against at all costs, however, was the broadcasting of the failure of the convent to live up to Christian ideals.

Gutiérrez Coronel's primary recommendation was that the bishop name a visitor to carry out an inspection and review of the convent. This seems unlikely to have been what Sánchez de Tagle wanted to hear, since he had been repeatedly begged by the nuns, and on at least one occasion, by the vicar, to send a visitor, or to come himself, and he had declined to do so. The reforms of the Council of Trent, in the sixteenth century, called for frequent convent visitations, preferably by the bishop in person. But for the bishop to visit, with any regularity, a town like San Miguel, over a hundred miles distant from Valladolid, was not realistic. (The bishop did not even make regular visits to the convents in Valladolid, the seat of the bishopric, in the eighteenth century.) Still, why was Sánchez de Tagle reluctant to name someone else to handle the visita? One answer is that, as we have seen, the rebellious nuns did not want a visitor from San Miguel—whom, they assumed, would be prejudiced against them—and would not approve such a visitor. A second possibility is that the bishop feared that a visitor would merely become enmeshed and would, by extension, further enmesh him in an impossible situation. Although Sánchez de Tagle seems to have been less misogynistic than Gutiérrez Coronel, at least in the sense that he took the troubles of the convent seriously, where Gutiérrez Coronel tended to dismiss them, he nonetheless shows clear signs in his letters of the church's characteristic assumption that women were weak, irrational, devious, and unpredictable, and that serious reform was almost impossible to sustain, for this reason. Those female qualities seemed to be very much on display at La Purísima, and keeping one's distance was the prudent thing to do. Better, the bishop may have thought, to let the poor vicar struggle along and, for his part, to fulminate from afar.

The second report was commissioned by the bishop from Dr. Maestro Miguel Joseph Moche, a prebend in the Michoacán cathedral, and it was submitted in January 1771.[41] Like Gutiérrez Coronel, Moche saw the problems of the convent as "descending from the top," that is, from Phelipa, though he also blamed "the Infernal Enemy" for "planting weeds in a garden that should be planted with virtue." As early as April 1762, he noted, the bishop had found it necessary to reprimand the "excesses of the present Prelada [Phelipa]." Although the Rule prohibited all collusion regarding the election of officers of the convent, Phelipa disregarded this mandate and divvied up offices before the election even took place, in exchange for votes. Once in office, she treated with contempt those who did not belong to her faction, even if they were senior to her. "When they ask her permission for small or trivial things," he complained, "she ridicules them, but in reality asking license for these matters of little consequence conserves the habit of subordination; subjecting one's will to that of another exercises humility, spiritual modesty, and obedience, which are the jewels of the Religious life." It was bad enough that the convent was divided into factions, but that one constantly spoke badly of the other and of the vicar, whom they ought to venerate, even when he did not act with complete fairness, and that those in Phelipa's faction assumed an authority of command that they did not possess, was even worse.

But also like Gutiérrez Coronel, Moche was not prepared to advise the bishop to remove Phelipa as abbess. "Despite all this," he wrote, "I cannot conceive that the Prelada does these things out of malice; it is not credible that one who left behind the outside world, her Patria, and her convent, to found a Reformed convent, should abandon these laudable goals and risk eternal happiness. It may be that she lacks the fortitude to deny the desires of her allies, or to reprimand their excesses. . . ." Moreover, while many of the changes that Phelipa introduced were wrongheaded, some were relatively minor, for example, the change in the hours during which silence must be observed, and even the practice of handing out money to her dependents (although Moche gives six reasons, expounded at length, why this was not a good idea). More important on a scale of seriousness was the breaking of cloister represented by the too-frequent entry of gardeners and doctors, especially the latter (here, he disapprovingly cites the example of the doctor listening to music in the cell of one of the sick nuns). "And who, My Lord, could fail to be filled with anguish upon seeing the carelessness with which modesty is trampled in that convent!" he wrote, mentioning the removal of the grille of the choir and the "shameful" horseback riding sheerly for the amusement of the nuns, and especially the sick nuns. Even more serious were the lapses in the duties of the escuchas. "The listeners," he wrote, "are the eyes of the Abbess" (this metaphor sounds bizarre in English translation, but in fact, the "listeners" were not really meant to "listen," but to see):

> and their absence can lead to fatal consequences and grave dangers. Your Christian modesty would be deeply offended and the chaste ears of Your Excellency scandalized if I were to relate the obscene acts that have taken place at the grilles of other convents, well distant from your bishopric, all of which could have been prevented by the presence of escuchas. All the Rules of all the monasteries command that not even the confessor should enter the cloister alone; the escuchas should stand far enough away not to hear, but close enough to see.

The most dangerous problem in the convent, however, in Moche's opinion, was the spread of Phelipa's affliction, "which appears to be the work of the Devil." Though there was some question about whether or not it was feigned, he was inclined to believe that it was, for several reasons, which he carefully presented:

> First, it is a malady from which the Prelada and her cohorts especially suffer; they and she make up a party of the sick. Second, the disease appears arbitrarily, and seemingly at the will of the sufferers; when they are among their own, it worsens, and in the presence of those who are not in their faction, it subsides. Third, it is a disease that one not so much catches as learns, as if it were a particular talent, or at least its symptoms have been taught; the evidence for this is that one nun asked another if she wanted her to show her the movements and visages that she ought to display in order to have it. Fourth, the fury and attacks of those who have the disease are directed against those who are not part of their Party. Fifth, the convent is in the middle of the Villa, but all of the contagion has remained in the cloister; this pernicious malady has not spread to the seculars outside the convent.

The nefarious impact of the disease was manifested in lapses in religious observance and disquiet in the convent, he continued; the abbess "invents scandalous ways to amuse the sick, such as bringing horses into the convent for them to ride, giving as an excuse that the disease is not curable with ordinary medicines." It was because of the disease's effects on religious observance, and on the community as a whole, "which suffers even more than the victims of the disease," that it must be called "diabolical."

What was the remedy? One possibility would be to remove the abbess from her position, on the grounds that she fomented divisions and factionalism. This was not only a drastic step, but it would also offend the many who were deeply devoted to their abbess, and "it could bring about such scandal that the remedy would be worse than the disease." Unfortunately, she still had 2 years to go to complete her term, and the convent could not wait that long. So Moche proposed an alternative that he hoped would correct the situation, or at least ease it:

> One of the principal causes of disorder is the idea which seems to
> have taken hold among those who occupy offices in the convent that
> these offices exist not so much to give them a chance to serve, as to
> exalt them personally, and to distinguish those who would otherwise
> have no preeminence. They think these positions are meant to allow
> them not to serve, but rather to command. . . . Pride, and disdain for
> the lowly donada, prevent them from performing their chores; they
> see instead only the honor and authority associated with the office.

The solution to the convent's problems, then, was to replace the nuns who had this attitude with others who were less prideful. While it would be very tricky to remove the abbess from office, Moche thought that it would not be so hard to replace her accomplices. The beauty of this plan was that most of those who had the wrong attitude toward office holding were also those who suffered from the mal:

> Is the disease real or is it feigned? If it is real, this automatically
> makes them ineligible to hold certain offices; indeed, simple charity
> requires that they be relieved of the burdens of office. If it is feigned
> (which the preponderance of the evidence suggests) this also makes
> them ineligible, and reason persuades that they be replaced by those
> who are free of this ridiculous behavior, unworthy of the most
> lapsed layperson.

The disease, then, would be the "touchstone" that would expose the religiosas of Phelipa's band: Those who were feigning its symptoms would either cease, in their desire to command and to retain their positions of importance, or they would continue to claim to be ill and lose their offices. The truly sick, meanwhile, would be relieved of duties that they should not hold. The abbess herself would be put to wonder whether the same thing might happen to her, and the result would be a return to the life of Christian perfection that they embraced upon entering the convent. The procedure of relieving sick nuns from office must be carried out with "wisdom, care, and prudence," however. The vicar must prepare a list of the afflicted nuns and the offices they hold, and then he should replace them with healthy nuns, giving those he removed the "specious explanation that he is doing this to relieve the sick nuns of their chores so that they may get well."

Would Moche's proposal have worked? Probably not, at least if the goal, as he himself stated, was to root out the disease. First, it was unrealistic to exclude all sick nuns from office. Table 3.1 shows the convent's officeholders from 1769 to 1772 and their state of health in 1766 (based on the "catalog" prepared for the 1766 visitation), and it reveals two relevant facts. One, many nuns still held multiple positions in the convent; in other words, office holding was still something of a burden, although obviously less so than in the convent's early days. Two, many of the nuns were in poor health. In fact, the state of convent health in 1770, when Moche proposed to assign offices only to healthy nuns, was worse than it appears in the table, since we know that, by this time, at least 9 of the 14 rebellious nuns were afflicted with the mal, while the 1766 catalog shows only 7 of them as being in poor health. Out of a total population of 25 nuns in 1770, then, at least 17 were sick: 7 were described in 1766 as suffering "broken" or "very broken" health, 4 had "somewhat broken" health, and 4 more were described as either "not very robust" or "middling." In addition, we know that two of the healthy nuns in 1766 contracted the mal thereafter. That left only 8 nuns at most to assume over 39 offices, if Moche's plan to exclude sick nuns from office holding was adopted. Even if the vicar could employ more "specious" reasoning to discriminate between the mal and other sicknesses, and therefore exclude only the 9 nuns afflicted with this particular illness, this was still an oppressive responsibility for the remaining 16 nuns, 1 of whom was incapacitated by paralysis (Anna María Rita de Jesús), 1 of whom was blind (Anna María de los Dolores), and 1 of whom was so ill that she died in mid-1770 (María Josepha Lina).

Second, his view of the nuns' attitude toward office holding, inspired by his disdain for women, led him to greatly overestimate their desire to hold office in the first place. There were two pieces of evidence that he no doubt drew on in making his recommendation. The first was the letter that Cayetana de las Llagas wrote to the bishop in 1769, quoted at length in the early pages of this chapter. In it, she employed a tone that could be taken as arrogant, saying approvingly that, in other convents, "the nuns who hold office tell the servants what to do, and the servants do the actual work," but her point was not that the San Miguel nuns who held office should not have to do any work, but rather that they should not have to do so much work that it interfered with their ability to perform their spiritual and religious duties. The second was the report that Phelipa had promised offices for which they were not eligible to nuns who supported her. But here, too, there is an alternative interpretation of her actions: Phelipa could make a good case that expanding the ranks of

TABLE 3.1. Officeholders 1769–1772 and Their State of Health in 1766

Rebellious faction

Phelipa de San Antonio (very broken health)	Abbess
María Anna del Santísimo Sacramento (broken health)	Definidora
	Tornera Mayor
Josepha de San Luis Gonzaga (broken health)	Definidora
	Refitolera
	Vicaria del Canto
María de San Miguel (somewhat broken health)	Obrera Mayor
	Ropera Mayor
Josepha Ygnacia de Santa Gertrudis (robust)	Secretaría
	Sacristana Mayor
Cayetana de las Llagas (good as far as can be seen)	Escucha de Primera Reja
Augustina de la Santísima Encarnación (very robust, but known to have mal by 1770)	Provisora
Xaviera de la Sangre de Christo (apparently good)	Portera Mayor
Vicenta del Corazón de Jesús (healthy)	Tornera Segunda
	Obrera
Antonia de San Joseph (not very robust)	Escucha de Segunda Reja
	Zeladora del Silencio
Josepha del Rosario (robust in 1766, but known to have mal by 1770)	Segunda Provisora
Gertrudis de San Joachín (somewhat broken health, known to have mal by 1770)	Maestra de Ninas
	Zeladora del Silencio
Ygnacia de San Juan Nepomuceno (middling)	Vicaria de Choro
	Sacristana
	Ropera
Anna María de los Dolores (apparently robust)	Sacristana

Obedient faction

María Josepha Lina de la Santísima Trinidad (very broken)	Vicaria de Casa
Anna María de los Dolores (very broken)	Definidora
	Portera mayor
Manuela de la Santísima Trinidad (very broken)	Definidora
	Maestra de Novicias
Theresa de la Luz (healthy)	Vicaria de Choro
	Segunda Sacristana
	Segunda Ropera
María de Jesús (not very robust)	Tercera Enfermera
Rita de la Santísima Trinidad (not known; had not entered convent in 1766)	Vicaria de Choro
Gertrudis de San Joseph (somewhat broken)	Segunda Enfermera

Not named as part of any faction

Anna María Rita de Jesús (habitually broken health; paralysis)	Could not hold office
María Anna del Corazón de Jesús (somewhat broken health)	Enfermera Mayor
Manuela de San Raphael (middling)	Tercera Tornera
	Obrera
Anna Rosa de Guadalupe (robust)	Enfermera

Sources: "Cathálogo de las Señoras religiosas . . . 1766," AHAM, Diocesano, Gobierno, Visitas, Informes, Caja 504 (XVIII), exp. 66; "Capítulo y elección de Prelada, y demas officios del Real Convento de la Concepción de la Villa de San Miguel el Grande," 1769, AHAM, Diocesano, Gobierno, Religiosas, Capuchinas, Caja 210 (XVIII), exp. 33.

officeholders, by making more nuns eligible for a wider range of offices, would ease the burden on all of the nuns.

In fact, a letter from Phelipa to the vicar, written in August 1770, strongly suggests that office was *not* seen by the sick nuns (or the well nuns, for that matter) as a prize, an end in and of itself. It concerned the resignation of Augustina de la Encarnación as Provisora. Augustina was one of Phelipa's partisans, and her reason for resigning her office was "the illness that God has seen fit to visit upon so many of us." Phelipa urged the vicar to approve this resignation without delay, citing her own failure to release Gertrudis de San Joachín (another of her partisans) from her office until her situation was truly painful to behold, even though Gertrudis had begged for relief. She also asked that Josepha del Rosario, who found herself "without strength to continue," be allowed to resign her position as second provisora. In all three cases, then, rebellious nuns, afflicted with the mal, were trying to resign the very sort of offices (relatively high offices, with considerable responsibility) that Moche assumed that they would cling to, at all costs.[42]

The third, and final, report was submitted in April 1771 by Licenciado Joachín de Cuevas, the chief legal adviser to the bishop (promotor fiscal).[43] Like the other two advisers, Cuevas described the state of the convent as dismal and believed that the culprit was Phelipa, but even more than the other two, he downplayed the importance of the crisis and criticized the nuns who complained about Phelipa's regime. "Though that convent does not lack for thorns, they are neither so many nor so sharp as to constitute an intractable problem, and the convent is not close to being lost, as has been publicized." He came to this conclusion, he said, after studying the responses of the nuns to Agüera's questions—nuns he pointedly calls "mal-contented," as opposed to their usual designation as the "obedient," or "well-adjusted," nuns. "Seen in the light of day," he wrote:

> and with due consideration, it appears that they exaggerate the lapses of observance in the convent that have originated with the present Abbess, and they wrap themselves in the mantle of protectors of the honor of God, by which means they hope to bring about their own elevation to command. . . . Their complaints do not have as object solely the greater glory of God, but rather are mixed with a bit of temporal convenience, or as it is often said, they stem more from jealousy than from zeal (*mas de celos que de celo*). . . . If they were all unanimous in their clamoring for enclosure, silent prayer, and the rest of the demands of their Institute it would be possible to believe that their complaints are born of their fine spiritual impulses; but to lament that the convent has become relaxed and then to cite mainly feminine delinquencies such as the favoritism shown by the Prelada to her followers, the injurious words spoken against the

vicar, and other ridiculous statements cannot be taken as pure Religious zeal. . . .

No one, he continued, claims that the Divine Office is not being sung, or that the cloister is not being maintained, or that silence is not being observed, or that work is going undone, and these are the principal tasks of the religious life. The other incidents recounted by the nuns are scarcely worthy of creating scandal: the removal of the grille when the Franciscans visited, the abuse of the donadas by Phelipa's faction, the occasional discreet retirement of the escucha when family members visit, the overly long visits of the doctor and surgeon, the horses in the convent—all these were of little consideration and not enough to judge that the convent is in a deplorable state.

Cuevas did, however, take seriously the spread of Phelipa's affliction, since "however one looks at it, whether it is real or feigned, the truth is that it is very injurious to observance of the religious life." Like the others, however, Cuevas advised the bishop to act with "prudence and not rigor." Moving against the abbess might inflame the convent and make things worse; "the female lack of common sense" might even cause some to flee the convent or try to commit suicide. The best solution would be for the bishop to bow to the pleas of the nuns on both sides and to send them a visitor. This visitor would interview all of the nuns, take account of the excesses attributed to the abbess, ascertain the extent of failure to follow the Rule, and either form a new daily distribution or command that they follow the one they had. In the meantime, Cuevas suggested merely that the bishop write a letter to the community, in which he should stress how embarrassing he found their complaints and how much time addressing those complaints had taken away from the "vast business of the bishopric." From now on, the nuns should be told to direct their complaints to the vicar, and not to the bishop. "At least by this means the Religiosas will not claim your attention with such a multitude of letters that in order to answer all of them it would be necessary to name another Bishop solely for this purpose."

Almost as an afterthought, Cuevas came up with a plan similar to Moche's to combat the feigned illness. Those afflicted with the disease should not be allowed to come to the parlor, he wrote, nor to the grilles, and they should be made to observe cloister with the greatest strictness. The excuse that they should be given is that "they cannot be allowed to be seen in these public places as long as they are using insolent words and demonstrating the unpredictable movements with which they scandalize chaste eyes." In this way, those who were feigning the disease would cease, not wanting to observe such rigorous enclosure. Also, before the next election, or a few months before, the bishop should ask the abbess to tell him how many religiosas were ill with either chronic pain, heart problems, or hysteria, in order to excuse them from office holding. Like Moche, Cuevas seemed to believe that this would have the effect of reducing the number of feigned episodes, since the nuns would not want to lose their right to hold office.

The End of the Crisis

Cuevas's modest recommendation (that the bishop write a letter to the community, whose main point would be to tell them to stop writing him) may not have been what the bishop had in mind when the whole process of soliciting outside opinions began, but by the time it was put before him in April 1771, it was probably the most realistic option. Sánchez de Tagle, almost 77 years old and ill for years, had written to King Charles III just 1 month earlier, asking for permission to name an "auxiliary bishop" to help him in his work, given his broken health. The request was denied.[44] One year later, he was dead.

Did Phelipa, then, win her battle with the bishop, or at least outlast him? The simple answer to the question is that she did not. Phelipa remained in power only a few months longer than Sánchez de Tagle. New elections for abbess were held in the fall of 1772, and her name was not even among those receiving votes. Instead, votes on the 20 ballots cast were divided among three nuns: Gertrudis de San José, with 10; Manuela de la Santísima Trinidad; with 8; and María Anna del Santísimo Sacramento, with 2. Since there was no majority, a second vote was necessary, and this time, Gertrudis received 13 votes. She would serve as abbess for three terms, until 1781. Her vicaria de casa became Manuela, the second highest vote-getter. Thus did the two nuns whose responses to the bishop's interrogatory had been the most sharply critical of Phelipa become the two most senior officers in the convent.

How did this happen, when Phelipa's faction was so much larger? There are three possible explanations, very different from each other, but not necessarily mutually exclusive. The first is that the tragic, premature death in August 1770 of María Josepha Lina, the convent's foundress and the one woman who commanded the respect of all, even those in the rebel faction, had deeply shaken the community and inspired enough self-recrimination that Phelipa and her followers began to have second thoughts about their own projects and behavior. In this scenario, Phelipa's faction—defiant, but far from impious, concerned about their immortal souls, which they had been told repeatedly, they were in danger of losing—in effect, voluntarily withdrew from convent leadership, ceding it to the reformed faction.

Lest this seem a far-fetched explanation for the failure of any of the rebellious nuns to figure in the election for abbess in 1772, let us consider the powerful role that María Josepha Lina, in life and in death, played in the convent. Our main source is, once again, her "exemplary" life story, written by Father Juan Díaz de Gamarra and based on the notes of her confessor, Father Luis Phelipe Neri de Alfaro.[45] This document must, of course, be read with great care, since its intention was hagiographical, not biographical. As with the author's treatment of María Josepha Lina's childhood (see Chapter 1), there is clearly much that is exaggerated, and perhaps even invented, in order to emphasize the qualities of her character that the author deemed most worthy of emulation. Nonetheless, there are anecdotes whose basic outlines ring true, given what we know of what went on behind the walls of the convent. Moreover, María Josepha Lina's own words, and the comments made about her by the other nuns, lend credence to Díaz de Gamarra's overblown language: Independent of the book, she comes across as an unusually gentle, forgiving, modest, and devout woman. But more important for our purposes, she was clearly a woman thoroughly dedicated to the idea of the reformed convent to which she had committed her fortune and her life. It is the way that María Josepha Lina quietly went about living the austere life of strict observance, even when those around her were agitating so vigorously for relaxation, that may have transformed her into something of a martyr upon her death and diminished Phelipa's and her followers' will to continue their defiance of the constitution that she had so carefully devised.

Like most hagiographers, Díaz de Gamarra divides María Josepha Lina's life in religion into chapters devoted to her admirable characteristics: her faith, charity, humility, obedience, and so on. In every chapter, she is depicted as a model of the reformist ideals enshrined in the convent's constitution and in the distribution and practices that Antonia, the first abbess, had imposed on the new community (and to which the other nuns so strongly objected). For example, one entire chapter is devoted to her "continual prayer," the very thing that Phelipa and her followers found so exhausting in the early years and that, more than anything else, gave rise to the first convent crisis. Nothing, Díaz de Gamarra wrote, kept María Josepha Lina from exact observance of the Rule when it came to attendance at choir, neither severe toothaches nor inflamed eyes in which she allowed insects to collect so as not to interrupt her prayers by swishing them away. She embodied submissiveness: Her "wise" confessor sometimes refused to confess her in order to test her faith; the other nuns would ask her how she could survive without this consolation, suggesting that she should send for him, or even take judicial recourse, but she would reply that she put her soul in the hands of her spiritual father, and that if he did not come to her, it was a sign that he did not judge her ready, and she accepted his decision. In what was almost certainly a reference to Phelipa, it was said that one abbess, well aware of María Josepha Lina's great modesty, during a period of recreation, commanded her to dance in front of everyone. She obeyed immediately, again placing the principle of obedience above all else. She always chose the most lowly seating or processing position in any ceremony, and if others stood to honor her high status within the community, she would immediately sit on the ground, shamed by the attention.

Her willingness to mortify her body was extraordinary: "the eye recoils merely to gaze upon the cruel instruments with which she punished her body. . . . hair shirts, iron nails in her shoes, breastplates with sharp points . . . all this she used to tame her flesh and subject it to the spirit." She fasted constantly and never ate anything that was not prepared for the community; even when she was sick in bed, she always asked if the food that she received was the same food served in the refectory. Although she had been given a cell, she chose to sleep in the common dormitory, on a narrow, hard mat. To ease the burdens on the donadas (whom Phelipa's faction treated with such great scorn), María Josepha Lina rose before they did, went to the kitchen to light the fire and put water on to boil for breakfast, and begged them to let her help them clean garbanzos, lentils, and beans. In short, where Phelipa's faction demanded less prayer, a looser interpretation of the Rule, personal servants— or, at the very least—a more servile donada class, more independence from outside authority, and more creature comforts, including better food and cells of their own, María Josepha Lina stood for the exact opposite. When she died a painful death (of what cause, we do not know; Díaz de Gamarra only reports that hundreds of legged, hairy worms came out of her nose in her final days, later metamorphosing into butterflies), it is not hard to imagine that the whole community, rebels and members of the obedient faction alike, was deeply affected. As novice mistress, María Josepha Lina had had close relationships with most of the younger nuns during their year of probation, and she seems to have been universally beloved. With her death, perhaps for many in Phelipa's faction, resistance to the reformed life in religion, which she exemplified, seemed no longer important enough to pursue in quite the same determined fashion as before.[46]

A second explanation for the failure of Phelipa or her cohorts to figure in the 1772 elections also sees the rebel faction as running out of the will to continue the fight, not just because of the death of the foundress, but because of a climate of reformism in the entire colony of New Spain, manifested in the recent "vida común reforms" in the bishopric of Puebla and the archbishopric of Mexico, which required the unreformed convents in those regions to adopt the common life. This, of course, had no direct effect on La Purísima, since by constitution, it was already a reformed convent dedicated to the common life, but since Phelipa's battle was against that constitution, after the events in Puebla and Mexico, she would have had to fight not just the local vicar and her own bishop, but (most likely) the king himself (indeed, as we will see in Chapter 4, when the vida común reforms are discussed at length, Charles III did eventually impose the reforms on the whole colony).

The third explanation is that the absence of any rebel candidates for abbess was not voluntary, but rather was imposed from outside. In this scenario, none of the rebellious nuns received a single vote because the vicar, who had to approve not only the election, but also the candidates for office, had found a way to engineer election results to his liking. Perhaps he disallowed Phelipa's candidacy, or that of any of her followers, by using some variation on the recommendations of Moche and Cuevas, to the effect that sick nuns should not be permitted to hold high office.[47] Although ordinarily, the vicar would exclude only nuns who were ineligible according to the monastic Rule (like Cayetana de las Llagas and Josepha Ygnacia de San Luis Gonzaga, who were ineligible because they were illegitimate), and not women who were sick, unless they were truly incapacitated, the situation may have been deemed serious enough to risk unrest among the rebellious faction. Or perhaps he saw this risk as lessened because of the way that Phelipa's faction had reacted to María Josepha Lina's death and because of the climate of the times. In fact, perhaps the best explanation for the election outcome is one that combines all three factors—pressure from the vicar; a diminished will to rebel, out of respect for María Josepha Lina; and a recognition that in New Spain, in general, the tide had turned in favor of conventual reform.

With these elections, Phelipa returned to her position in the Definitorio, the leading "obedient" nuns took over the leadership of the convent, and the crisis seems to have come to an end. Factionalism diminished sharply, at least to judge by the fact that complaints directed by one group of nuns against another (as opposed to one individual nun against another) disappeared in the convent correspondence. Although illness continued to plague the convent, and the implication that some nuns were not as sick as they pretended to be runs like a thread through the various visitations that were conducted in the following decades, there was no further mention of "epidemics" of epilepsy, or indeed, any mention of the salto/mal at all. The maladies from which the nuns suffered in the following decades were much more ordinary and less frightening, if no less a burden for the convent population at large. Visitations in the 1770s and 1780s, including a visit by the bishop in 1775, were generally positive with regard to the state of the convent, in terms of both its religious functions and its function as a community.

But does this mean that, with the elevation of the obedient faction to power, La Purísima returned to its roots as a bastion of reform? Ironically, no. As we will see in Chapter 4, while Phelipa may have lost her battle to govern the convent or ceded the battleground to the rival faction, efforts on the part of individual nuns to modify the strict interpretation of the Rule associated with the first three abbesses did not cease—and indeed, continued to bear fruit, although the form of protest changed significantly. As we will also see, it appears that, despite their criticism of Phelipa's regime in the bishop's interrogatory, Gertrudis de San José and Manuela, the two highest officials of the convent, proved to be less committed to the principle of rigorous reform than Antonia, María Anna, Anna María de los Dolores, or María Josepha Lina had been. So, also, were the bishops who succeeded Sánchez de Tagle. In short, in the following decades, both the convent leadership and the episcopal leadership were considerably more moderate and flexible than during the crises of 1761–

1762 and 1769–1772, when three strong personalities—Antonia de la Santísima Trinidad, Phelipa de San Antonio, and Bishop Pedro Anselmo Sánchez de Tagle—came up against each other in defense of implacable positions on broad principles involving the very nature of the religious life.

NOTES

1. Sister María Manuela de la Santísima Trinidad to Lic. Agustín de Agüera, n.d. (but included in a packet labeled "Gobierno del convento . . . 1769"), AHAM, Diocesano, Gobierno, Religiosas, Capuchinas, caja 209 (XVIII), exp. 23.

2. Sister María Cayetana Josepha de las Llagas to Bishop Pedro Anselmo Sánchez de Tagle, 7 November 1769, AHAM, Diocesano, Gobierno, Religiosas, Capuchinas, caja 209 (XVIII), exp. 23.

3. By "offices" in this context Cayetana meant positions within the convent, such as nurse, gardener, or novice mistress.

4. Bishop Pedro Anselmo Sánchez de Tagle to Lic. Agustín de Agüera, 16 February 1770, AHAM, Diocesano, Gobierno, Religiosas, Capuchinas, caja 209 (XVIII), exp. 23.

5. "Gobierno del Convento, 1769," AHAM, Diocesano, Gobierno, Religiosas, Capuchinas, caja 209 (XVIII), exp. 23. All of the responses to the interrogatory are included in this packet of materials.

6. Quoted by Dr. Maestro Miguel Joseph Moche in his report to Bishop Pedro Anselmo Sánchez de Tagle, 17 January 1771, AHAM, Diocesano, Gobierno, Religiosas, Capuchinas, caja 209, exp. 23.

7. Dr. Ricardo Joseph Gutiérrez Coronel to Bishop Pedro Anselmo Sánchez de Tagle, 18 August 1770; Dr. Maestro Miguel Joseph Moche to Bishop Pedro Anselmo Sánchez de Tagle, 17 January 1771, AHAM, Diocesano, Gobierno, Religiosas, Capuchinas, caja 209 (XVIII), exp. 23; Lic. Joachín de Cuevas to Bishop Pedro Anselmo Sánchez de Tagle, 26 April 1771, AHAM, Diocesano, Gobierno, Religiosas, Capuchinas, caja 209 (XVIII), exp. 24.

8. Mervyn J. Eadie and Peter F. Bladin, *A Disease Once Sacred: A History of the Medical Understanding of Epilepsy* (Eastleigh, England: John Libbey, 2001), 74.

9. Eadie and Bladin, 72–75. Many pharmaceutical preparations were intended to treat both hysteria and epilepsy and other nervous diseases and diseases of women: see Felix Palacios, *Palestra Pharmaceutica Chymico-Galenica*, (Madrid, 1706), Part IV, 350; Part II, 149, 215 (which specifically mention epilepsy; many others were intended to treat apoplexy, lethargy, paralysis, and other convulsive and hysterical diseases). See also Paula Susan De Vos, "The Art of Pharmacy in Seventeenth and Eighteenth-Century Mexico" (Ph.D. diss., University of California at Berkeley, 2001), chapter 5.

10. John J. Barry, "Distinguishing Nonepileptic from Epileptic Events," *Epilepsy Quarterly* 4:1 (Spring, 1996).

11. Beatriz Espejo, *En religiosos incendios* (Mexico City: Universidad Nacional Autónoma de México, 1995), 23; Kathleen A. Myers and Amanda Powell, *A Wild Country Out in the Garden: The Spiritual Journals of a Colonial Mexican Nun* (Bloomington, Ind.: University of Indiana Press, 1999), 264; Vicar Juan de Villegas to Bishop Pedro Anselmo Sánchez de Tagle, 29 August 1761, AHAM, Diocesano, Gobierno, Reli-

giosas, Capuchinas, caja. 209, exp. 23; Lavrin, "La vida femenina," 88; "Milagros de una monja," Archivo Histórico del Arzobispado de México, caja 1816, apparently a summary of a consultation commissioned by the Inquisition concerning visions of Sor María Teresa de la Santíssima Trinidad Aycinena. Thanks to William Taylor for the latter reference.

12. For more on the Puebla epidemic, see Loreto López, *Los conventos*, 298–300.

13. Pedro de Horta, *Informe Médico-Moral de la Peñosíssima y Rigorosa Enfermedad de la Epilepsia que a pedimento de la M.R.M. Alexandra Beatriz de los Dolores, dignisísima Priora del Convento de Religiosas del Glorioso y Máximo Doctor Señor San Gerónymo* (Madrid: Domingo Fernández de Arrojo, 1763).

14. Anne Fadiman, *The Spirit Catches You and You Fall Down: A Hmong Child, Her American Doctors, and the Collision of Two Cultures* (New York: Noonday Press, 1998).

15. D. P. Walker, *Unclean Spirits: Possession and Exorcism in France and England in the Late Sixteenth and Early Seventeenth Centuries* (London: Scholar Press, 1981), 11.

16. Walker, 14.

17. Among others, Fernando Cervantes has noted a diminishing presence of the devil in religious discourse, in general, in the eighteenth century, but (to summarize his argument very briefly), Cervantes thinks that there was more going on than simply the influence of rationalist thinking, that churchmen were deliberately emphasizing popular ignorance, rather than diabolical interventions, in order to avoid giving credence to a concept of the devil, advocated by the Franciscans and the Jesuits, in particular, with which they did not agree. Thus, the devil as an important actor was a victim, in a certain sense, of antimonastic, specifically, anti-Jesuit and anti-Franciscan, sentiment within the secular clergy. Fernando Cervantes, *The Devil in the New World: The Impact of Diabolism in New Spain* (New Haven, Conn.: Yale University Press, 1994), 126–136.

18. Walker, 12.

19. Walker, 14.

20. Walter Friedlander, *The History of Modern Epilepsy: The Beginning, 1865–1914* (Westport, Conn.: Greenwood Press, 2001), 81.

21. In the next several paragraphs, besides the sources cited, I have drawn on some of the interpretations of demonic possession in other parts of the world, including the excellent literature on the Salem witch accusers, a group of young girls who suffered, in a general way, from some of the same kinds of symptoms as the nuns of La Purísima and who seem also to have been influenced by group dynamics and interactions with each other. John Demos, *Entertaining Satan: Witchcraft and the Culture of Early New England* (New York: Oxford University Press, 1982), especially 117–131; Paul S. Boyer and Stephen Nissenbaum, *Salem Possessed: The Social Origin of Witchcraft* (Cambridge, Mass.: Harvard University Press, 1974); Carol F. Karlsen, *The Devil in the Shape of a Woman: Witchcraft in Colonial New England* (New York: Vintage, 1989).

22. Dr. Maestro Miguel Joseph Moche to Bishop Pedro Anselmo Sánchez de Tagle, 17 January 1771, AHAM, Diocesano, Gobierno, Religiosas, Capuchinas, caja 209 (XVIII), exp. 23.

23. Demos, 117.

24. H. Erik Midelfort, *A History of Madness in Sixteenth-Century Germany* (Stanford, Calif.: Stanford University Press, 1999), 31.

25. See Cervantes, 102–104; Midelfort, 49–79; Karlsen, 249, 339, and note 35. This sort of interpretation is also implied in Michel de Certeau, *The Possession at Loudun* (Chicago: University of Chicago Press, 2000), and Po-Chia Hsia agrees that the "most spectacular case" of the spread of disease/possession was at Loudun, although he also mentions a case in which possession by the devil spread from one convent to another, as news of an exorcism in Marseilles in the early seventeenth century led to a mass possession at Lille, in the Spanish Netherlands (149–150).

26. Po-Chia Hsia, 144.

27. Solange Alberro, "La licencia vestida de santidad: Teresa de Jesús, falsa beata del siglo XVII," in Sergio Ortega, ed., *De la santidad a la perversión* (Mexico City: Grijalbo, 1985), 234.

28. Bishop Pedro Anselmo Sánchez de Tagle to Vicar Juan de Villegas, 14 August 1761, AHAM, Diocesano, Gobierno, Religiosas, Capuchinas, caja 23 (XVIII), exp. 23.

29. For another emphasis on possession "or similar afflictions" as resulting in the victim becoming a center of attention and being able, at least partially, to resolve or counteract the psychological effects of spiritual doubt, difficult daily routines, practices, schedules, discipline, and solitude, see Ramos Medina, *Místicas y descalzas*, 243.

30. This pattern, in which the principal at first sincerely believes herself to be afflicted by a force beyond her control and then learns to manipulate her behavior, is also the interpretation given by Solange Alberro in the case of a "false beata" of the mid-seventeenth century. In this case, as with Phelipa, the beata seems to have had some imitators, although this point is not emphasized by the author. Alberro, 23–37. It seems also to be roughly similar to the story of the possession of Jeanne des Anges, the prioress of the convent at Loudun, who began to show symptoms of possession in the early seventeenth century that spread to others in the convent. See Certeau, especially 221–226. Finally, it is the explanation favored by D. P. Walker in his interpretation of half a dozen cases of possession in late sixteenth- and early seventeenth-century England and France. See Walker, 16.

31. Dr. Maestro Miguel Joseph Moche to Bishop Pedro Anselmo Sánchez de Tagle, 17 January 1771, AHAM, Diocesano, Gobierno, Religiosas, Capuchinas, caja 209 (XVIII), exp. 23.

32. Dr. Maestro Miguel Joseph Moche to Bishop Pedro Anselmo Sánchez de Tagle, 17 January 1771, AHAM, Diocesano, Gobierno, Religiosas, Capuchinas, caja 209 (XVIII), exp. 23.

33. Besides her response to the interrogatory, see also Abbess Anna María Josepha de los Dolores to Dr. D. Pedro Jaurrieta, 11 October 1770, AHAM, Diocesano, Gobierno, Religiosas, Capuchinas, caja 209 (XVIII), exp. 23.

34. McKnight, 81, mentions that politicking to win election to the post of abbess was not uncommon, and Martín describes an uncannily modern political scene in the seventeenth-century convents of Lima, in which "inmates of the nunneries employed pressure groups, propaganda campaigns, trading of votes, secret deals, promises and bribes, articulation of 'platforms,' and patronage with zest and efficiency," 259.

35. Teresa of Avila's reforms also aimed to create a more egalitarian community, in large part, by eliminating the use of family names in favor of newly adopted names in religion, a practice that was almost universally adopted in all Mexican convents and even many beaterios. But Teresa also approved of diminishing convent hierarchies by using only the title "Sister" for all nuns, except for the prioress or abbess. Perhaps significantly, Phelipa's egalitarian title of choice represented an inflation: Everyone was to be "Mother." Jodi Bilinkoff, *The Avila of St. Teresa* (Ithaca, N.Y.: Cornell University Press, 1989), 127.

36. There was a convent tradition of "processing" during fiestas, which is probably what María Manuela meant by "going from cloister to cloister," but it was a practice frowned upon by reformers, and it was, perhaps, in especially bad taste when the foundress was so ill and would soon die. Loreto López, *Los conventos*, 120.

37. Abbess Phelipa de San Antonio to Bishop Pedro Anselmo Sánchez de Tagle, 16 November 1770, AHAM, Diocesano, Gobierno, Religiosas, Capuchinas, caja 209 (XVIII), exp. 23.

38. Sister María Cayetana de las Llagas to Bishop Pedro Anselmo Sánchez de Tagle, 17 August 1770, AHAM, Diocesano, Gobierno, Religiosas, Capuchinas, caja 209 (XVIII), exp. 23.

39. Lic. Ricardo Gutiérrez Coronel to Bishop Pedro Anselmo Sánchez de Tagle, 18 August 1770, AHAM, Diocesano, Gobierno, Religiosas, Capuchinas, caja 209 (XVIII), exp. 23.

40. Manuel Ramos Medina recounts the story of a nun in Mexico City who engaged in a long battle with the archbishop, who tried to prevent her from taking office in the 1720s, imprisoned her, and removed her from the convent. She pursued the case judicially, all the way back to Spain. Ramos Medina, *Místicas y descalzas*, 169–180.

41. Dr. Maestro Miguel Joseph Moche to Bishop Pedro Anselmo Sánchez de Tagle, 17 January 1771, AHAM, Diocesano, Gobierno, Religiosas, Capuchinas, caja 209 (XVIII), exp. 23.

42. Abbess Phelipa de San Antonio to Vicar Juan de Villegas, 28 August 1770, AHAM, Diocesano, Gobierno, Correspondencia, Religiosas, caja 39 (XVIII), exp. 21.

43. Lic. Joachín de Cuevas to Bishop Pedro Anselmo Sánchez de Tagle, 26 April 1771, AHAM, Diocesano, Gobierno, Religiosas, Capuchinas, caja 209 (XVIII), exp. 24.

44. Mazín, 203–204.

45. Díaz de Gamarra, *Ejemplar de religiosa*, 35, 65, 86, 38, 78, 51, 56, 57, 72–73, 44, 95.

46. Zavala, 67, says that his interviews with elderly nuns in the early 1940s indicate that the nuns still revered "Madre Lina" and believed that she continued, "as in life," to look over them and protect them and the decorum and sanctity of the convent. My interview with Sister María Lilia of the San Miguel convent in August 2004 confirms that reverence for "la azucena de San Miguel" (the lily of San Miguel) continues today.

47. Three of the four definidoras did come from the ranks of the rebellious nuns (Phelipa herself, Josepha de San Luis Gonzaga, and María Anna del Santísimo Sacramento), but by long-standing custom, these positions were not elected, but filled according to seniority.

PART II

Struggle

4

"To live happily and in peace within . . . their enclosure"

Changing Relationships among Bishops, Abbesses, and Nuns, 1772–1792

For 20 years after the 1772 elections in which Phelipa de San Antonio and her faction were marginalized, the efforts of abbesses and bishops alike were directed toward finding a way for the nuns of La Purísima to live in calm compliance with their constitution, if not always contentment—as Bishop Luis Fernando Hoyos y Mier put it in his visit of inspection in 1775, "to live happily and in peace within the narrow confines of their enclosure."[1] In contrast to the rigidly zealous first abbesses and the unyielding Bishop Sánchez de Tagle, they believed that this required enforcing the Rule with a gentle hand, exercising flexibility where possible, involving the nuns in their own government, relaxing the strict interpretation of the vow of poverty, and if all else failed, granting special privileges to particularly nettlesome nuns in order to keep the peace.

These informal policies, designed to enforce the vida común in a less obnoxious way than previous regimes had done, were both abetted and complicated by broad changes in ecclesiastical policy toward convents that were introduced across the viceroyalty. Beginning in 1769, the same year that Phelipa was elected abbess, and culminating in 1774, on the eve of the Hoyos y Mier visitation, Catholic reformers centered in Puebla and Mexico City began seriously to insist that *all* female convents adhere to the vida común. Phelipa, in other words, had taken office determined to make La Purísima look and operate more like the other "relaxed" convents in New Spain at a time when those convents were beginning to be asked to make themselves look and operate more like La Purísima. That it was out of sync with the experience of other Mexican convents had made Phelipa's goal of attenuating the vida común more difficult. Now, after Phelipa's exit from office, pro-vida común attitudes in the higher reaches of the ecclesiastical hierarchy helped to discourage a resurgence of her movement. But the hard-line climate of reform also made it awkward for the abbesses of La Purísima and the bishops of Michoacán to put into practice the principles of flexibility, consultation, and calculated relaxation that they deemed necessary in the wake of the decade of rebellion.

This chapter will explore the ways that multiple factors—the vida común reforms as well as the policies employed within the convent and within the bishopric—combined to make it possible for the convent to avoid any recurrence of open rebellion for the remainder of the colonial period. The chapter has two parts. The first introduces the vida común reforms in the colony as a whole, and the second is devoted to the methods used by bishops and abbesses to defend the vida común while making it palatable to the majority of the convent.

The Vida Común Reforms: Background and Implications

The vida común reforms were far from the first attempt at convent reform in Mexico, and they were just one of many such attempts in the Catholic world at large over the centuries.[2] In fact, convent reform was a cyclical phenomenon that dated from well before the Council of Trent (the series of three major summits held between 1545 and 1563 called to deal with the Protestant threat to Catholicism): Various pre-Tridentine reformist movements were spearheaded by popes, bishops, church councils, and enough abbesses that the "reforming abbess" became a stock character in the hagiographical literature.[3] The battle over reform versus relaxation in the convents grew more pitched after Trent, however.[4] Protestant reformers had not only criticized the worldliness and decadence of the convents—this was nothing new, since Catholic reformers had been making some of the same points—but also challenged the convents at a more fundamental level, by denigrating the Catholic emphasis on celibacy and instead making marriage and the family central to Christian devotional values and practices.[5] This challenge to the very essence of the convent made it necessary for the Tridentine reformers to take up reform in a serious way.[6]

At Trent, the convent was re-envisioned as not just a retreat from the world, but also a renunciation of it. The nun's entrance into a convent, reformers believed, must be infused with a clear sense that she would never leave it again, that her earthly life was over, and that she was reborn into a new life as a bride of Christ.[7] The principle of enclosure was thus elevated to the highest level: Nuns were never to leave the convent, outsiders were rarely to enter, family visits would be restricted, and the doors and turnstiles that gave access to the outside world would be closely monitored at all times. Rigorously enforced enclosure would not only protect against the scandals that the Protestants had publicized to such great effect, but would also allow for more regularized and more frequent daily prayers and exercises, since the nuns would have more time to devote to the contemplation of God. Presumably, young women with a true vocation would desire the rigors of enclosure, rather than chafe under them; they would see the cloister in the light in which it was intended, as the surest path to Christian perfection. They would willingly embrace poverty and chastity, and they would be obedient to a fault.

Resistance to the Tridentine decrees enforcing the vows of enclosure and poverty was immediate and sustained, and in Europe, as well as in Mexico, these canons were ignored and watered down more often than not. But at least they remained technically in effect—and could be revived when a particularly reform-minded bishop or abbess chose to do so. In one area where convents were concerned, however, Trent did not conform to its reputation for high-minded reformism and willingness to regulate even the smallest details of Christian life: There was no canon providing for the enforcement of the mo-nastic injunction to live the common life, the vida común. Indeed, in Europe, the vida común was resisted so strenuously by so many nuns and their families that the papacy backed down on imposing it across the board, and it was never made a requirement for all convents.[8] As we have seen, Mexican convents that paid more than lip service to the vida común were few. Most convents allowed nuns to maintain their own kitchens, to build their own cells, and to keep personal servants. The convent as an extension of elite society, in Mexico, as in Catholic Europe, was seen as too necessary to family survival and prestige to allow it to become a place where the austerity associated with the vida común could be tolerated.

The eighteenth century, however, brought a new round of criticisms of the convent—this time, not just from Protestant critics, but from "enlightened" critics within the Catholic world and within the church itself. The influence of Enlightenment thought, with its enshrinement of the values of simplicity and social utility and its condemnation of aristocratic excess and ostentatious dis-plays of clerical wealth, led to a shift in the critique of the convent: To the time-honored condemnation of cloistered convents as allowing a style of life that was too worldly and too comfortable (even decadent) were added the com-plaints that they perpetuated a style of worship that was too "baroque," too full of pomp and excessive celebration, and that they were parasitical and socially useless.

Eighteenth-century ecclesiastical reformers, like the Catholic reformers at Trent 200 years earlier, sought ways to counter these criticisms. For Mexico, one response came around the middle of the century, when bishops and royal officials began to restrict new foundations to certain kinds of convents and to refuse to authorize others of which they disapproved. After 1747, the only new foundations for the remainder of the colonial period were either convents of nuns who followed a regimen of strict observance (besides the reformed Conceptionists at La Purísima, there were the Capuchins, with four new foundations; the Carmelites, with two; and the Poor Clares, with one) or convents of teaching orders, specifically, the French Company of Mary, which founded three convents after midcentury. La Purísima was, thus, by the nature of its foundation as a reformed convent, a part of the large project of eighteenth-century Catholic reform.[9] Manuel de la Canal's project to bring the Capuchin order to San Miguel in 1736 was a little premature; his daughter's proposal for a reformed convent of Conceptionists, almost 20 years later, caught the first wave of Catholic reformism and was approved rapidly.

The second response to criticism of the convent as too worldly and too supportive of baroque religiosity was to enforce not only the vow of poverty, but also the vida común, a style of life in whose simplicity and austerity Catholic reformers saw a natural answer to the critics of the convent. In 1765, the most serious project of conventual reform the colony had ever known began, under the stimulus of the Bishop of Puebla, Francisco Fabián y Fuero.[10] First, he urged upon the nuns in convents of *calzadas*—unreformed convents—closer observance of their vow of poverty and issued an edict against excessive ornamentation in the convents and sumptuousness in the liturgy. He followed this up a year later with another edict ordering the expulsion of most of the schoolgirls, or "niñas," and the separation of those who remained from the religiosas, especially in the cells and dormitories, on the grounds that the presence of the girls in their cells interrupted the nuns' meditations.[11] Then, in 1768, he circulated a pastoral praising the virtues of the vida común, which would give the nuns "more time to devote to their religious duties without having to be personally engaged in all the daily details of their existence."[12] Finally, a year later, in another edict, he required adoption of the vida común in his bishopric.

"The common life," he wrote, "is not a harsh and difficult institution, it is not a frightening and terrible Monster, whose very name should strike terror in the souls of the Religiosas. . . ." Almost as if he had taken note of the problems that the nuns of La Purísima had experienced and wished to allay fears that similar problems would accompany the imposition of the vida común in the Puebla convents, he continued: "It is not intended that the sick should be required to follow a rule of strict observance, nor that they be required to serve themselves; nor that the healthy should abandon strict observance in order to serve their offices"; therefore, the plan was to allow as many personal servants as there were religiosas and to employ additional servants to perform communal tasks.[13] Giving detailed instructions as to how to construct the kitchens, refectories, storerooms for food and clothing, infirmaries, and dormitories that would be needed to effect the change of lifestyle, he indicated his seriousness of purpose when he observed that, to create space for these rooms, most individual cells would have to be removed.[14] Thus, his vision for the convents, in many ways, resembled that of the foundress of La Purísima from almost 20 years earlier: Meals were to be prepared and eaten in common; clothing would be laundered and distributed centrally; nuns would sleep in dormitories; all personal items were to be removed from the cells that were allowed to remain; all money received by the nuns was to be incorporated into the convent's treasury; visits of relatives were to be restricted; visitors might be offered modest refreshments, but the playing of music and theatrical performances were definitely banned.[15] Furthermore, servants were to be limited to those necessary for the functioning of the convent, although the rule of thumb that there should be at least as many servants as there were religiosas was a definition of "necessary" that was considerably more liberal than at La Purísima.

Soon afterward, Fabián y Fuero's compatriot and fellow reformer, Archbishop Francisco de Lorenzana, took up the banner of conventual reform in the archbishopric of Mexico, supported by Charles III. "The female convents are full of servants and secular persons, to the extent that they resemble disorderly villages more than communities of nuns in peaceful retirement from the world," he wrote. Fabián y Fuero and Lorenzana took convent reform so seriously that the topic formed the basis of one of the most significant discussions at the important Fourth Provincial Council in 1771 and, indeed, seems to have inspired the American prelates' call for the council to be held in the first place.[16] The recommendation of the Council, opposed only by the bishops of Durango and Yucatán, was to extend the Fabián y Fuero plan—mandatory vida común and expulsion of the niñas from the convents—throughout the viceroyalty.

Resistance to the vida común reform was swift and strong. A flurry of petitions, letters, and suits was quickly generated by the nuns and their representatives to encourage Charles III to overturn the recommendations of the Fourth Provincial Council—in other words, to use royal power to subvert ecclesiastical process. In some places, requests for exemptions from various provisions of the vida común regulations amounted to resistance to the whole project. In other places, there was violent opposition to the reform, especially in Puebla, where Bishop Fabián y Fuero acted in an "authoritarian and despotic" fashion to impose the vida común. In the most notorious case, he sent in an army of workers to demolish the individual cells in the convent of Santa Inés of Puebla, causing a "rebellion" in the process.[17]

Despite this resistance, in 1774, after some delay as petitions of protest from the nunneries were mulled over by a wavering Charles III, a royal edict called for the vida común to be adopted everywhere in the viceroyalty, though it moderated the Puebla reforms in that it did not force nuns who had professed under the previous system to adopt the new way of life—only entering novices would be so required.[18] Since, according to the edict, the nuns who had already professed were allowed to decide for themselves whether or not to follow the new regimen, votes were taken throughout the viceroyalty. In the five convents of the bishopric of Puebla, 161 nuns out of 284 decided to reject the vida común lifestyle. In the archbishopric, the response was even more negative: Not one of the 601 nuns in 10 convents accepted it.[19] The recalcitrant nuns were accused of resisting the Pope, who had approved their vows of poverty; resisting the Fourth Provincial Council, which had ordered them to observe the common life; and resisting the king, "whom they offend with their insolence, almost committing the crime of lese majesty."[20]

In time, enforcement of the vida común reform began to relax, as had happened with so many previous convent reform efforts; by the early 1780s, there were already signs of diminishing official enthusiasm for the vida común, and by the late 1780s and early 1790s, it was, for all intents and purposes, abandoned, as we will see in Chapter 5. Nonetheless, in the early 1770s, while La Purísima was struggling to emerge from its decade of rebellion *against* the vida común regime of the first abbesses, in the rest of the colony, support for the reforms was at its height. In his 1775 *visita*, it is clear that Bishop Hoyos y Mier wanted to defend the vida común, both because it was a principle enshrined in the convent's constitution and also because of the contemporaneous viceregal reform in which he seems to have genuinely believed. But he also felt a strong need to address the issues raised by the rebels by softening some of the harshness of the nuns' existence. In other words, he had to reconcile local needs and ideological imperatives.

The Hoyos y Mier *Visita*

In 1775, Bishop Sánchez de Tagle's successor, Luis Fernando de Hoyos y Mier, finally carried out the visit of inspection for which the nuns of both factions during the second phase of the rebellion had been clamoring.[21] This was the first visitation since 1766, and the first by a bishop since the convent was established in 1756. It went surprisingly smoothly, considering La Purísima's roiled recent history. The ceremonies began on October 22, at 10:00 A.M., when Hoyos y Mier, in his white vestments, was met by the vicar, the chaplain, and the chief sacristan—also wearing white—outside the small convent cemetery. He entered the crowded church through its main door, a side entrance, and was conducted in procession to the main altar, where he received the monstrance (the gold or silver receptacle that held the sacred host) from the vicar and displayed it to the throng. To the accompaniment of violins, the singing of the nuns from behind the choir grille at the back of the nave, and the lingering scent of incense, he inspected the altars; the outer sacristy, with its baptismal font; the confessionals; the craticule (the small opening through which the nuns, behind their double grille, received communion); and other parts of the church proper. Although he recommended a smaller craticule and the installation of new confessional screens with tinier openings, in general, his report on this part of the visit was positive: For the most part, he wrote, everything was "decent" and well-cared-for.

He then changed his vestments from white to black, preparing to leave the domain of the public and enter the domain of the nuns. Pausing at different points in the church to intone the three customary responses—one in the front of the church, in the presbytery, for the gathered clerics; one in the central part of the nave, for the people; and the last, next to the choir grille at the rear of the church, for the nuns—while the church bells rang constantly, he finally disappeared from the view of the assembly into the interior sacristy, where he was greeted by some 20 senior choir nuns (those who had been professed at least 8 years). The eight confessionals for the nuns were situated in this inner sacristy, a room, that he approvingly noted, was bright with ample light. The confessionals he found to be entirely satisfactory, with their grille of iron on the inside and an overleaf of tin with minuscule holes on the outside. He also examined the turnstile, through which the robes and instruments of the mass were passed from the inner sacristy, where they were cared for by the nuns, to the outer one.

Next came a slow circuit around the main patio of the convent, passing through all of the cloisters, after which Hoyos y Mier entered the lower choir and then climbed the stairs to the upper choir, trailed by the vicar, the chaplain, the senior nuns, and the notary, who recorded all of the bishop's movements and comments. Then he visited the refectory, where the nuns ate together at long tables arranged in a U shape; the *noviciado*, the part of the convent where the novices lived apart from the nuns; the *jovenado*, where the younger professed nuns lived; the parlors, where the nuns were allowed to greet visitors from behind a double grille; and the workrooms, where the nuns sewed, embroidered, and performed other tasks. Last came an inspection of the rear patio, where the dormitories and cells of the senior nuns were located, and the *niñado*, the part of the convent where the schoolgirls lived and learned, with its own patio and separate offices.

Over the next several days, following these physical inspections of the church and convent, the bishop met individually with each nun, inviting her opinions and complaints on a wide range of issues regarding her sisters' observance of the Rule and respect for the customs of the convent. This "confidential and personal visit" (*visita secreta y personal*) provided the grist for an important report (to be discussed in detail later) in which the bishop mandated changes in convent practices designed to keep the nuns on the path toward Christian perfection.

The centerpiece of the *visita* came on November 1, when Hoyos y Mier presided over the election of a new abbess. Everything needed for the election was laid out on a table in front of the lower choir grille. After the chaplain celebrated the mass of the Holy Spirit, the doors of the church were closed;

the novices, legas, and jóvenes retreated; and the senior nuns who were eligible to vote entered the lower choir, seating themselves behind the grille. The scribe called out their names, in order of seniority; if present, they responded "Ave María Santísima." The chapter in the Rule on elections was read aloud, the vocalists sang the hymn "Veni Sanctus Spiritus," and the election began. The convent secretary passed around an urn to demonstrate that it was empty. Each nun then wrote the name of her choice for abbess on her ballot. The ballot of one nun who was sick in bed was sent for, and each ballot, folded in a particular way, was deposited in the urn, which was placed on the table below the craticule. There were 23 ballots cast, and Gertrudis de San José was reelected as abbess with 12 votes, the bare majority. The second highest number of votes went to Manuela de la Santísima Trinidad, who once again became vicaria de casa. Gertrudis (as was customary) resigned the position, and the bishop (as was customary) refused to accept her resignation. She was then seated by the other religiosas on a special chair, a crown was placed on her head, and the novices and legas and jóvenes were invited to return. Each religiosa, in order of seniority, knelt before the new abbess and pledged to obey and respect her.

A More Flexible Bishop

Hoyos y Mier must have been pleased at this reelection of the two leading obedient nuns, since his primary goal, especially in light of the recent royal decree requiring all nuns to follow the vida común, was to protect the core of the convent's constitution. Three years earlier, in 1772, it had been impossible to predict if the election of the two most outspoken and strong-willed "obedient" nuns (now reelected) would prove salutary or disastrous—certainly, in the past, abbesses devoted to the principles of the convent's constitution had been unable to lead effectively, and the result had been over a decade of rebellion. But Gertrudis de San José had proven to be a cautious and moderate leader, and things had been calm since 1772. This made Hoyos y Mier's mandated tasks of strengthening the vida común and expelling the niñas from the convent easier. But at the same time that he insisted on adherence to the convent's constitution, he also found ways to soften the austerity associated with the vida común; several of his provisions and recommendations clearly sought to appease the nuns, who continued to chafe under that constitution, even though the open rebellion against it had quieted. Taken as a whole, then, his *visita* reveals a politic and relatively flexible prelate—in contrast to his predecessor Sánchez de Tagle.

His report (based on his own observations and on the confidential, or "secret," visit—the individual interviews with all of the nuns) began by striking a positive note. He stated that he detected "no grave defects" of observance; in fact, he wrote, he was impressed by the nuns' "true charity and virtue, and the good example that they set for each other, and the notorious zeal with which even the sick, as well as the healthy, attend Choir . . . and other acts of community. . . ." Nevertheless, he continued, he did discern "some minor lapses," which "although they do not for now impede observance of the solemn vows, could under other circumstances and at other times come imperceptibly to compromise the will of the Religiosas to live happily and in peace within the narrow confines of their enclosure."[22] He proceeded to issue 18 commands, or *providencias*, 3 of which were centrally concerned with the vida común.

One demanded that all of the nuns who were not legitimately impeded by their health from doing so must eat together in the refectory, and must eat the meals prepared in the common kitchen. The shared meal, preceded by the nuns' highly structured entrance into the refectory and followed by an equally hierarchically determined exit, was not only at the symbolic heart of the vida común, but also, nuns who did not celebrate their community by eating together missed out on the spiritual lessons read aloud during these meals.[23] The measure came in response to insinuations on the part of some of the nuns that sickness was being used as an excuse to avoid the common meals and the common dining room.

The theme of rededication to the common life also turned up in two provisions concerning handiwork produced in the convent. At La Purísima, an hour each day was set aside for quiet labor, such as embroidery or sewing, mending their linens, for example, or sewing new underskirts or tunics, or repairing the priests' vestments and keeping the items in the sacristy in good shape. But in most Mexican convents, nuns devoted some of the time in the workroom to crafting small items that they gave away to benefactors or relatives, in return for which they received a small donation (*limosna*). Sometimes convents became renowned for certain kinds of manufacture: The nuns of La Concepción in Mexico City, for example, were known for their exquisite artificial flowers, and other convents were famous for sweet confections or medicines made from traditional recipes.[24] Hoyos y Mier intended to limit and rechannel these activities at La Purísima. Measure 6 forbade the nuns from giving presents to their confessors, unless the gifts were of token value, offered in "just and pure" gratitude for spiritual benefits received. Measure 7 prohibited an individual nun from keeping any monetary donation that the gift of her handiwork might bring—instead, this money must go directly to the abbess, and from her, to the provisioner, to be used for the common expenses of the convent.

Other reform-minded measures included a stern insistence on attendance at choir, except in cases of serious illness; strict observance of the Rule with regard to one's hair (it must be cut very short) and habit (some nuns did not use proper headgear at all times); and close supervision of the doors, parlor, and sacristy, to be sure that no one from the outside entered without license of the abbess, that no one was unaccompanied within the cloister, and that, when outsiders were admitted to any of these areas and the nuns could not avoid meeting them, their faces were covered by their veils. Here, Hoyos y Mier added that the abbess could not command a nun to raise her veil or to go to the door or grille to greet a visitor from the outside; to do so against the will of the nun, he wrote, could cause her spiritual ruin. (Presumably, an abbess might be tempted to order such a thing if the visitor in question was an important patron of the convent who had expressed a desire to meet with one of the nuns; Hoyos y Mier sought to avoid this abuse of the power by the abbess.) Finally, in a separate report, Hoyos y Mier ordered the complete reclusion of the "niñas educandas" of San Miguel—the girls who attended the convent school—mandating that, from now on, they must pray apart, eat apart, and live apart from the nuns, and he devised a new daily schedule of activities for the niñas to be sure that this goal was accomplished. The significance of this final measure requires some background to appreciate.

La Purísima, like many convents, especially in the education-conscious eighteenth century, was meant by its foundress to operate a small school, where young girls over the age of 8 would board, paying 12 pesos a month, while they were instructed by the nuns in the feminine arts and the rudiments of reading and writing. According to the foundation documents, the clean division between the secular world and the convent world was to be maintained by separating the girls' living quarters and daily activities from those of the nuns. But this ideal was hard to uphold in an environment in which the niñas were often related to one of the nuns (at least five of the schoolgirls in 1775 had sisters who were nuns or novices) or had developed a close relationship to them, an eventuality that was, in a certain sense, encouraged by the expectation that a fairly large proportion of the niñas would choose to follow in the spiritual footsteps of the nuns. As one visitor later put it, it was natural that, entering the school at an early age, the niñas would "come to love the convent and the Religiosas, and these tender first impressions would last until, perhaps, they themselves became Religiosas."[25] Indeed, at the time of the Hoyos y Mier visit, there were four novices and at least three nuns (probably more—the records regarding the niñas are incomplete) who had previously lived in the convent as niñas, and two of the niñas would eventually become religiosas.

The blurring of the line between the niñas and the religiosas was particularly notorious at unreformed convents of *calzadas*, the targets of the vida común reformers, where the proportion of the population composed of so-called niñas was often huge and licenses for other laywomen to reside in the convent on a temporary basis were relatively easy to obtain. A census of the convent of Nuestra Señora de la Salud in Pátzcuaro in the late 1780s, for example, indicated that 184 girls and women lived in the collection of houses and patios that comprised the convent, but only 30 of them were nuns: There were 51 "niñas" (14 of whom were at least 40 years old and 5 of whom were over 60), 24 other laywomen living temporarily in the convent for a variety of reasons (though mainly to provide service to the nuns), and 79 servants, including 1 slave.[26] The expulsion of the niñas from the convents of the archbishopric of Mexico and the bishopric of Puebla had already taken place. In his actions at La Purísima, then, the bishop of Michoacán was following the lead of other reform-minded authorities.

The number of niñas at La Purísima, however, was never very large (there were only 14 of them at the time of the Hoyos y Mier visit), and they seem to have been mostly school-age girls and a few young women hoping to enter the convent, but having to wait until they could amass a dowry. They did not have the relatively formal obligations to serve the nuns that many unreformed convents imposed on impoverished "girls." There is only one reference to a laywoman, other than a niña, living in the convent, and hers was a special case because she wanted to take the white veil in death (her health did not permit such a step in life); moreover, she was willing to provide double the dowry required of legas; and she was a relative (probably a sister) of the vicar.[27] The small number of lay girls and women living in the convent fits La Purísima's profile as a reformed monastery with a modest teaching function. In this sense, then, compared with other convents, La Purísima was not a major offender of the reformist principle that religiosas and niñas should be kept strictly apart and that the number of laywomen living in the convent should be limited. But this did not prevent Hoyos y Mier from ordering the niñas' complete separation from the nuns, "without allowing them from now on to mix with the Religiosas in Choir, cloister or other parts of the convent . . ." They were to live apart in their niñado until their school could be built.

This measure was not well received by either the niñas or most of the nuns (although it is true that some nuns complained about the noise that the girls made in the cloister or about the immodesty of their attire, and they may have welcomed the reform). Less than 2 years later, in 1777, the school closed altogether—according to the abbess, because the girls were so "disconsolate" at their forced reclusion that they begged their parents to remove them. It was not reopened until years later, and then not so much to fulfill the convent's teaching function or as part of a relaxation of the reformist impulse, as because the income provided by the school became necessary to help keep the convent from falling even deeper into debt.[28]

Hoyos y Mier was concerned, then, to protect the ideal of La Purísima as a reformed convent, even when (as in the case of the niñas) the abuses of the principle of reform were far from egregious. But in other ways, the bishop showed himself to be flexible and willing to listen not only to the nuns who criticized their peers for too-loose observance, but also to those who complained of too-strict practices. Most important among the "relaxed" measures that he proposed was a new and less rigorous daily distribution, or schedule of prayers, devotions, and community activities. He did this, he said, "according to the sentiments and desires that a majority of the community expressed to me" in order to "alleviate their burdens and give them more rest." The notary charged with recording the proceedings of the visit wrote:

> The Religiosas of this Convent have made manifest their strong desire for moderating changes in the distribution that they have observed up to now, since it contains a number of non-essential exercises and acts of community; and condescending to their insistent supplications, so that in relieving them of some obligations, they may guard, fulfill, and execute more faithfully those that their Holy Rule requires, [Bishop Hoyos y Mier] orders that the Religiosas observe the following [summer] schedule [the morning schedule would begin half an hour later in winter]:

4:30:	Wake-up, private prayer
5:00:	Choir for one-half hour of prayer, followed by Prime, and then by one-quarter hour of prayer
6:00:	Breakfast
6:30:	Mass, then singing of the three lesser hours of the Divine Office (Terce, Sext, None)
8:00:	Small refreshment, one-half hour in workroom with spiritual lesson, followed by convent tasks
11:00:	Examination of conscience
11:30:	Refectory, with spiritual lesson (except on days of recreation), give thanks in Choir, rest until 2:00
2:00:	Vespers, followed by the Magnificat, the Rosary of Five Mysteries with the litany, three Our Fathers and Ave Marías, then chocolate and rest until 6:00
6:00:	Complin, Matins, the Magnificat, and commemoration of San Miguel, one-quarter hour prayer
8:00:	Refectory, spiritual lessons, give thanks
9:00:	Blessing of the abbess, an Our Father and Ave María, recitation of the Creed, retire to bed[29]

This schedule was based on the modified schedule that had been adopted in 1761 to replace the too-onerous original schedule devised by the first abbess, but it was less demanding and more flexible.[30] Hoyos y Mier omitted a 15-minute examination of conscience that had followed the 6:00 P.M. prayers, stating that the nuns could perform this self-examination in their cells. One hour of scheduled time in the workroom was also eliminated. Other than this, the main innovation was to leave free the hours roughly between 9:00 A.M. and 11:00 A.M. and between 3:00 P.M. and 6:00 P.M., where before, these hours had been fairly closely scheduled. Some of the nuns no doubt went to the workroom, while others were given time to complete convent tasks; they could use their own judgment to a greater extent than in the past.

There were other signs of accommodation besides a less exacting daily schedule. For example, while he reiterated that the nuns were to eat together in the refectory, at the same time, Hoyos y Mier ordered that the food prepared in the common kitchen be "better seasoned" and that the midday and evening meals be served "without skimping," and with ample condiments. The abbess, he continued, must make sure to treat all of the nuns equally, "with love, gentleness, and prudence." She must allow all of them to take recreation at the appropriate time and on the appropriate days, although he made clear that those recreations should not "have the odor of the outside world," and he specifically prohibited "theatrical representations," especially those in which nuns used men's and women's secular costumes (which "thankfully has not been done here," he added, either ignoring or ignorant of the scandalized reports of such productions only a few years earlier). Hearing complaints from the sick that they had to sleep in their habits, he allowed them to wear only a tunic and sash at night, so that they would be more comfortable and better able to "conserve their health." While he suggested that healthy nuns should continue to sleep in the full habit, he permitted it to be a matter of conscience rather than an absolute rule. These were relatively small measures, but perhaps the most important thing was that the new bishop was not only willing to make the long journey to San Miguel, but also that he seemed to be willing to listen to the nuns' complaints and to act upon them.

A More Responsive Bishopric

Indeed, responsiveness on the part of the bishop's office to the complaints of the nuns and the needs of the convent as a whole was another of the tools by which the bishops and their representatives attempted to contain discontent and prevent the recurrence of discord in the convent for the rest of the colonial period. This responsiveness took several forms. One was more frequent visits than during the Sánchez de Tagle tenure. There was the Hoyos y Mier *visita*, which we have just surveyed; in addition, Bishop Juan Ignacio de la Rocha visited San Miguel for 6 months in 1781, during which time he devoted considerable attention to the nuns.[31] Although these were the only two bishops who visited in person after the initial visit of Bishop Martín de Elizacochea in 1756 (Fray Antonio de San Miguel "visited" from Celaya, 50 kilometers distant, in 1792), from 1772 forward, if the bishop did not make an appearance, then his representatives, usually the vicars, were consistent in carrying out a complete *visita* every 3 years. This meant that the nuns had a chance to comment on the state of the convent with much greater frequency than in the past, an opportunity that most chose to exploit fully. (In time, though, at least some of the nuns became slightly jaded by this process: In his report on the confidential interviews with the nuns in 1788, the vicar dutifully noted that some of them "wish to know the recommendations made as a result of this visit, since every three years they are asked what changes should be made, and they have never seen any of them put into effect."[32]) But even if the interviews were seen by male officials more as placating the nuns than as eliciting their opinions with the idea of following through on their suggestions, it is still possible to argue that the nuns had a voice that they lacked under Sánchez de Tagle's policy of denying them the "consolation" of regular visits.

Another form of increased responsiveness in the late colonial period was the more or less regular consultation between the abbess/Definitorio and the episcopal authorities, a dialogue shaped by guarded respect on the part of the bishop's office for the independence of the convent where its internal governance was concerned. Occasionally, an episcopal visitor or the vicar, in a letter or report to the bishop, would display a flash of the kind of arrogantly paternalistic attitude that had characterized Bishop Sánchez de Tagle's and his advisers' dealings with the nuns. It was especially frustrating for the visitor when the triennial elections did not produce a majority vote for abbess on the early ballots, and the nuns, "full of malice," persisted in "throwing away" their votes on hopeless candidates—for example, candidates of illegitimate birth or candidates who did not have the requisite number of years as a professed nun—causing the election process to go on and on, to the immense displeasure of the male authority presiding over it.[33]

But more characteristic of the convent–bishop relationship from the mid-1770s forward was the frequent solicitation of the abbess's or Definitorio's opinions and recommendations. For example, the nuns were regularly asked to recommend specific individuals to serve as their chaplains, mayordomos, sacristans, and other positions of importance to the convent. (Ironically, when asked in 1778 for the names of priests they would like to see named as chaplain, the convent nominated Father Pedro Rubí, the priest who, 15 years earlier, had been banished from San Miguel by Sánchez de Tagle because of his relationship with Phelipa. They turned to Rubí—"with whom we already have experience"—after their first candidate, a priest from Guanajuato with whom they had already communicated regarding the position and whose character and credentials they had had checked out by "disinterested persons," turned out not to possess a license to confess nuns.[34]) They were also consulted at great length about how the growing financial problems of the convent should be resolved, and they came to exercise much more control than before over which aspirants to the religious life would be allowed to join the convent. On the latter subject, Hoyos y Mier issued two mandates, one of which ordered that, in addition to the standard information about a prospective nun's family background and the interview conducted by a priest to determine whether she was acting of her own free will, there should be another "secret" report prepared by two religiosas who would be named by the Definitorio, in which the applicant's "life and habits, physical condition, docility, discretion . . . and other qualities necessary for valid profession in religion" would be addressed. The second measure required the Definitorio to vote (by casting either a white ball or a black ball) on applicants entering the novitiate and on novices who were ready to profess. In the case of professions, the novice mistress was to report to the Definitorio on the health, personality, and customs of the novice under her care so that an informed decision could be made.

None of this means that the correspondence between the abbess or Definitorio and the bishop lost its tone of humility and deference on the one side, and paternalism and authority on the other. But the relationship was, in fact, understood by all to be not nearly so unequal as these habits of language implied. The religiosas had clear spheres of power into which the bishops (even Sánchez de Tagle, as we have seen) were reluctant to intrude. The nuns were very well aware and protective of their "customs," the practices that, over the years, guided by their convent's constitution, they had developed to interpret and observe the Rule. On one occasion in 1798, for example, the vicar was perceived by the nuns as having overstepped the bounds of his authority by failing to call for a vote as to the suitability of one particularly obnoxious novice for the religious life. Both he and the Definitorio were convinced that she should not be allowed to profess, but the abbess protested to the bishop that, even though she agreed with the vicar's position, she deplored his actions, which went against the custom of the nuns' voting on questions of denying profession to a novice (*desnudez de hábito*), a right granted by the Hoyos y Mier reforms of 1775.[35] In short, there is a distinct sense that the post-crisis bishops genuinely wished to avoid interfering with the internal functioning of the convent. There is also a sense that the abbesses and higher ranking nuns understood that they enjoyed a relatively broad range of independent action, and that the "consultations" with the bishop's office were, in fact, more like statements informing the episcopal authorities of the convent's preferences and opinions.

A Looser Interpretation of "Poverty"

Another means that the abbesses seem to have employed in order to keep the peace was to follow Hoyos y Mier's recommendation that food from the common kitchen ought to be more flavorful and more plentiful. From convent account books and statements about individual rations we can infer that the dietary standard of living for the nuns of La Purísima in the post-rebellion period at least equaled, if not exceeded, that of the relaxed convents of *calzadas* in the bishopric, Santa Catarina and Nuestra Señora de la Salud, convents that were ostensibly less committed than La Purísima to the observance of the vow of poverty (tables 4.1 and 4.2). This discussion will focus on food rather than other living expenses, in part because it was by far the largest convent expense,

TABLE 4.1. Per Capita Convent Living Expenses (in Pesos)

	Food	Other Living Expenses*	Total
La Purísima 1791	133	38	171
Nuestra Señora de la Salud 1791–1793	131	35	166
Santa Catarina 1774–1778	136	33	169

La Purísima 1791: Per capita amounts based on population of 39 nuns; Nuestra Señora de la Salud October 1791 to October 1793: Per capita amounts based on population of 45 nuns; Santa Catarina: Per capita amounts based on population of 74 nuns.
* Not including clothing or maintenance of physical plant.

Sources: "Cuentas . . . 1790–1791, AHAM, Diocesano, Gobierno, Religiosas, Concepcionistas, Caja 255 (XVIII), exp. 42;" "Cuentas . . . 1791–1797," AHAM, Diocesano, Gobierno, Religiosos, Dominicas, Caja 267 (XVIII), exp. 159; "Nuevo arreglo para el govierno de sus rentas . . . ," AHAM, Diocesano, Gobierno, Religiosos, Catarinas, Caja 242 (XVIII), exp. 335.

in part because it forms the easiest basis of comparison among convents, and in part because it presents a particularly interesting and complicated case, as we will see toward the end of this section.[36]

First, the issue of the quantity of food. All convents purchased large amounts of cacao, meat (especially mutton), and bread, and so these items are the most easily compared from one convent to another.

Cacao

The all-important refreshment called "chocolate" was a frothy drink that consisted of a mixture of cacao, sugar, cinnamon, and water. Chocolate was consumed two or three times a day, including during periods of fasting (when the bread that otherwise always accompanied the chocolate was omitted), and was considered a healthful and necessary drink—so much so that when the Carmelite nuns of the convent of Santa Teresa, founded in Valladolid in 1825, tried to follow the practice of their order and abstain from chocolate, the bishop's office insisted that they drink it daily, arguing that "this nourishment (*alimento*) is commonly consumed by all the people of our land . . . and their stomachs are so habituated to its consumption that its absence is strongly felt."[37] Each choir nun at La Purísima in the early 1780s received two disks (*tablillas*) of cacao a day; there were 20 disks to a pound of cacao, so the total daily consumption was 1.6 ounces. This was exactly the same as the amount given to the nuns of Santa Catarina.[38] The accounts of the convent of Nuestra Señora de la Salud indicate that those nuns received about 2 ounces of cacao a day, although this per capita amount is inferred from the total amount of cacao

TABLE 4.2 Living Expenses at La Purísima, Nuestra Señora de la Salud, and Santa Catarina, Selected Years (in Pesos)*

La Purísima, 1791	
Food expenses	
Bread	984
Lard	288
Sugar	245
Cacao	462
Cinnamon	216
Mutton	2,082
Chickens (for the sick), eggs, tortillas, atole, chile, tomatoes, and other items requested by the Provisora	810
Salt	60
Snacks or fruit drinks given to visitors at the grille	approximately 35
TOTAL FOOD EXPENSES	5,182
Other living expenses	
Candles	264
Soap	144
Shoes	180
Charcoal	180
Errand runners	60
Phamacist's services, medicines from pharmacy, and herbs, aguardiente, pulque, charcoal, sugar, etc., used by the convent to make their own medicines	438
Doctor	approximately 150
Paper	24
Sand (for blotting ink)	33
TOTAL OTHER LIVING EXPENSES	1,473

Nuestra Señora de la Salud, Oct. 1791 to Oct. 1793 (annual average)	
Food expenses	
Chocolate (cacao, sugar, cinnamon)	1911
Lard	228
Bread	396
Flour	617
Mutton	879
Beans, corns, chiles	362
Salt	65
Fish for Lent	30
Given to the Provisora for ordinary weekly expense	1,397
TOTAL FOOD EXPENSES	5,885
Other living expenses	
Infirmary	355
Shoes	88
Candles	296
Errand runners and other miscellaneous salaries	96
Soap	146
Miscellaneous living expenses for poor nuns without pensions	600
TOTAL OTHER LIVING EXPENSES	1,581

(continued)

TABLE 4.2 Living Expenses at La Purísima, Nuestra Señora de la Salud, and Santa Catarina, Selected Years (in Pesos) *(continued)*

Santa Catarina, annual average 1774–1778	
Food	
Flour	2,218
Lard	207
Sugar, cacao, cinnamon	2,165
Beef	1,224
Mutton	3,337
Salt	151
Saffron	57
Garbanzo, lentils, rice, beans, chile	337
Fish	101
Cooking oil	15
Brown sugar	39
Special foods for fiestas, etc.	209
TOTAL FOOD EXPENSES	10,060
Other living expenses	
Candles	435
Soap	119
Medical	
Special foods, etc., for infirmary	518
Doctors' fees (2 doctors)	300
Surgeon's fee	90
Phlebotomist	51
Pharmacy	300
Shoes	94
Charcoal	198
Salaries of mayordomo, 3 errand runners, 1 mozo to slaughter the animals, 1 mozo to pasture the animals and bring them in from the fields	approximately 300
TOTAL OTHER LIVING EXPENSES	2,405

* Not including extraordinary expenses.

Sources: "Cuentas . . . 1790–1791, AHAM, Diocesano, Gobierno, Religiosas, Concepcionistas, Caja 255 (XVIII), exp. 42;" "Cuentas . . . 1791–1797," AHAM, Diocesano, Gobierno, Religiosos, Dominicas, Caja 267 (XVIII), exp. 159; "Nuevo arreglo para el govierno de sus rentas . . . ," AHAM, Diocesano, Gobierno, Religiosos, Catarinas, Caja 242 (XVIII), exp. 335.

purchased by the convent and is therefore less accurate than the stated ration that we have in the case of the other two convents.[39] Thus, we know that the nuns at La Purísima received exactly the same ration of cacao as the nuns of Santa Catarina, and they *might* have received a slightly less generous ration than the nuns of Nuestra Señora de la Salud.

Meat

La Purísima consumed 89 sheep a month (supplied by the mayordomo from his hacienda) in the early 1790s, which yielded something like 1,850 pounds of meat (using contemporary calculations from Spain), or an average of about $1^1/_2$ pounds of mutton per day per nun. If we factor in the 20 donadas, daily consumption falls to perhaps $1^1/_4$ pounds (the donadas almost certainly were given less than the nuns). Obviously, this is a very generous amount.[40] However, it is not out of line with the meat rations received by other nuns in other convents. We know that the choir nuns at Santa Catarina were given 1 pound of mutton and $^1/_2$ pound of beef each day, while at the convent of Santa Clara (Querétaro), each professed nun received $1^1/_4$ pounds of mutton a day plus several pounds of bacon.[41] According to convent accounts, the nuns at Nuestra Señora de la Salud were given just a bit over $^3/_4$ of a pound of mutton a day, and they also received a substantial ration of beef.[42] The nuns at these three convents, however, had to feed their personal servants from these amounts, which the nuns of La Purísima did not have to do. Taking into account, then, that La Purísima had no personal servants, the amount of animal protein seemingly consumed by the nuns themselves is greater than the amount consumed at the more relaxed convents.

Bread

The 2.1 pesos per nun spent on bread at La Purísima each month in 1791 is roughly in line with the amounts spent on bread and flour at Nuestra Señora de la Salud, at 1.9 pesos per nun, and the amount spent on flour at Santa Catarina, at 2.5 pesos per nun. We know that the ration for the nuns at Santa Catarina was 18 ounces of bread a day—as in the case of mutton, a large amount that must have fed the nuns' personal servants as well as the nuns themselves.[43] While it is true that La Purísima bought all of its bread (while Santa Catarina baked its own and Nuestra Señora de la Salud combined the two methods) and therefore, presumably, spent more for less product, we can still assume that the nuns of La Purísima consumed at least as much bread (we know that they were given bread six times a day) as the nuns at the other two convents, and probably more, since again, besides themselves, they were only feeding community servants, not personal servants, with their purchased loaves.

The second issue besides quantity of food is its quality. If the nuns at La Purísima were eating at least as abundantly as their counterparts at the elite convents by the 1770s and 1780s, thus addressing Hoyos y Mier's injunction that the midday and evening meals be served "without skimping," did the abbesses also follow through on the other part of his recommendation, that the food prepared in the common kitchen be "better seasoned," and served with "ample condiments"? This is not easy to determine. It does seem fairly clear that, earlier, during the period of the rebellion, the nuns' diet was blander and probably less varied than that of Santa Catarina. The minutely detailed accounts from the convent's first 10 years of existence yield a picture of a diet that included several seasonings (saffron, pepper, cloves, and chile) and also some variety: nuts (especially almonds), tomatoes, lentils, peas, beans, garbanzos, rice, eggs, fruit, raisins, fish, and chicken.[44] However, the appearance of variety is deceptive. The fish was for Lent only; the chickens and eggs were mainly for the sick; and the nuts, raisins, cloves, and fruit were mainly used for special occasion meals, not as an everyday feature of the diet. Furthermore, the amount of spices and seasonings used in cooking appears to have been much less at La Purísima in the early years than at Santa Catarina, where the choir nuns were given $1^1/_2$ ounces of saffron each week to season their meat, and where cumin was also distributed on a weekly basis, along with pepper, chiles, onions, tomatoes, and salt. By contrast, at La Purísima, there was no mention in the detailed accounts from the period of the rebellion of cumin or salt, and the $^1/_2$ pound of saffron a month, distributed among at least 20 nuns, was far less than the ration at Santa Catarina. Unfortunately, after 1770, the level of detail in recording food purchases at La Purísima diminishes, and spices, condiments, and most purchases of fruits and vegetables are lumped together under a catchall category of "other food purchases." Conclusions about the quality of the nuns' diet are also complicated by the fact that all convents had gardens and orchards, and spending on food does not take into account the vegetables and fruits that the nuns might be growing for themselves. All we really know is that La Purísima, by 1791, was spending as much on food per nun as the relaxed convents, which suggests both abundance and variety.

In sum, if we cannot state with confidence that the quality of the food at La Purísima "caught up" with the other convents after the rebellion, it does seem certain that, in terms of quantity, La Purísima was right there with the other convents of the bishopric. In fact, if anything, the nuns of La Purísima seem to have consumed more meat and bread than the nuns at Santa Catarina and Nuestra Señora de la Salud. How can we explain this, especially in light of the fact that (as we will see in more detail in Chapter 5), budget shortfalls were already making it clear that extravagance in spending could not be tolerated? It makes sense that abbesses trying to satisfy disgruntled nuns and preserve calm in the convent would want to be sure that the nuns had plenty to eat, even if this did violate the spirit of the vow of poverty; but did they need *more* than the nuns at the other two convents?

There are two explanations for the abbess's behavior in presiding over not just adequate, but intentionally excessive food purchases. One is that a traditional function of an elite convent was daily food giveaways. The poor, often friends or relations of the nuns and the donadas, gathered at the convent's main portal several times a day to receive food that was taken directly from the provisioner's storehouse for this purpose—in other words, not food left over from a meal, but food *purchased* for the purpose of *giving it away*. According to the abbess in 1782, Josefa Ygnacia de Santa Gertrudis, licenses for such extractions were granted more or less as a matter of course.[45] We may guess that the abbesses thought that it was important for the nuns to partake of the psychic rewards of charitable giving, to enjoy the feeling that one belonged to an elite group that could afford to give away food. In fact, La Purísima, increasingly, could *not* afford to give away food, and that it continued to do so shows that the abbess felt that charity served an important function in the life of the convent.

The second explanation, perhaps even more significant, is that extra food was purchased and the nuns allowed huge portions of mutton and bread so that they could use these commodities as bartering tools. This possibility is suggested by a comment by a nun whose personal story will be detailed later: She writes of giving away part of her bread allotment to a poor woman from San Miguel, who did errands for her through the turnstile, since she did not have any other way to pay her for her services.[46] Here, the convent's "excessive" food purchases, and the abbess's practice of handing out licenses to take food directly from the storehouse, become ways to compensate for the lack of personal servants. In the other elite convents, nuns would have a personal servant to run errands or perform other small tasks, but at La Purísima, other ways had to be found for nuns to "hire" help. What appears, in other words, to be an unnatural level of food consumption becomes, in this interpretation, a way that the abbesses finessed (without violating) the convent's constitutional prohibition against personal servants. Thus, as much as the abundant and well-seasoned diet that Hoyos y Mier had ordered, the privilege of offering charity to one's friends and relatives—and the implicit right to use food to barter services that nuns needed because they lacked personal servants—helped to keep the peace in the convent.

Making Exceptions

A final way that authorities—abbesses, bishops, and vicars—preempted renewed rebelliousness was by employing (reluctantly) a policy of exceptionalism, of granting special privileges to individual nuns. We have just seen that the post-rebellion abbesses granted exceptional licenses to remove food from the storehouse, more or less upon request. After the Hoyos y Mier visit, letters asking for privileges, dispensations, or other special treatment begin to appear with some frequency in the convent correspondence with the bishop as well.

Most of these pleas were for minor exemptions. However, there is one long letter that for its brazenness, as well as for the glimpses it provides into daily life in the convent, stands out as worthy of sampling at some length.

In 1783, Josepha de San Luis Gonzaga wrote to Licenciado Joachín de Cuevas, who was in charge of convent affairs under the vacant see.[47] The purposes of the letter were, first, to ask that certain privileges granted to her and to her fellow vocalist, María de San Miguel, by previous abbesses and bishops (there are several references to concessions made to them by Hoyos y Mier) be guaranteed by Cuevas, and second, to request new ones, most notably, a personal servant, or at least a donada, who would be devoted solely to their care. The criticism of the inadequacy of the service provided by the donadas and the great need for personal servants described in this letter are familiar from the times of Phelipa. The difference is that, under Phelipa, there had been an effort to convince the bishop that *all* of the nuns needed personal servants, based on the principle that, without servants, it was impossible for anyone to fulfill the obligations of both religious office (the Divine Office and other acts of community) and daily chores, and that it was thus impossible for the convent to function. Here, Josepha is making the case not for the across-the-board introduction of personal servants, but rather for a personal servant for herself and María de San Miguel based on their particular circumstances: their age, their ill health, and their long service to the convent.

> My venerable Father: for a long time I have not allowed myself to write to you because of the immense weight of the affairs that occupy your attention . . . , but you, whom God entrusted to provide aid and comfort to those who of us who have given up everything to serve Him . . . , are our only hope of remedy. . . .
>
> Sir, we two are Religiosas with music scholarships who have served in this Choir since the first days of the foundation; we assumed the obligation to play and sing as long as our health and strength endured, I as second voice and first violin, and my Mother [María de San Miguel] as first voice and second violin. For twenty years we sang at every function: the three special devotions established by the founding nuns, which are celebrated five times a year beginning at five o'clock in the morning and ending at nine o'clock at night; the weekly masses; the daily masses for the souls of our patrons; the novenas; and many others. Most of the burden of singing has fallen on my Mother and me, because although there are two other Religiosas with music scholarships, one is the organist (she is currently our abbess) and the other plays the bass-viola and has been able to sing only from time to time. She has a pretty voice but she is sickly.

Bishop Hoyos y Mier, she said, had recognized their hard work and had granted them leave to cut back on their duties:

> For twenty years we shouldered the burden of this work until God sent Sr. D. Luis Fernando de Hoyos to visit us and to console us, and he told us that we had suffered long and hard enough and that we should not worry about the fact that it was no longer possible for us to carry on in the same way as before; and with these words we began to stop doing certain things, and each day we do less (although we have not given up all of our tasks) because our health is poor, and our strength is scarcely enough even for an ordinary mass, which we can sing only with tremendous effort, and afterwards for two, or three, or even more days we cannot even kiss the Host or perform the smallest chore.

Josepha continued by complaining that she had been misled when she entered the convent, seemingly confirming the argument that the nuns who chose La Purísima made assumptions about the style of life that would be followed within the convent, based on their knowledge of other Conceptionist convents, and did not expect a reformed, austere way of life:

> My Father, when we took the holy habit they made us many promises among which was that we would be given someone to serve and help us, since the tasks of playing and singing in the choir, studying music, attending community functions, performing the chores that go along with our offices, and sweeping, cleaning, and sewing, are incompatible. That we were not to have personal servants gave me pause . . . but I was soothed with so many promises that I believed, like a child, that to promise was to comply.

The failings of the donadas as servants particularly rankled Josepha, as we may infer had been the case for all of the rebellious nuns (whom the bishop and vicar often accused of "abusing" the donadas):

> How much we have suffered is impossible to express, and on many occasions we have begged the abbesses to grant us a servant to attend to our great needs, since often we are both sick in bed and then there is no one to take care of us. It is true that sometimes they have conceded this benefit, but it has never been permanent because the ones who are principally responsible for attending and consoling the nuns are the donadas, who are quick to complain about the first thing that comes into their heads, and they go to the abbess complaining that they are not our slaves, that they are doing the community a favor by their service, and then they are exonerated

from doing anything that is against their inclination, bringing us much tribulation.

Her annoyance, however, had developed recently into grave concern about whether the special privileges that she had enjoyed to this point would be maintained. Cuevas, trying to find ways to economize in order to confront the convent's deepening budget deficit, had evidently written to Josepha to tell her, in no uncertain terms, that her constant requests for exceptions and exemptions could not be tolerated:

> But now our despair is even greater because once again having begged for some relief, there has been a response in your name, Sir, to the effect that we must take care of ourselves as best we can, that the convent is not responsible for giving us someone to serve us. Sir, what should our hearts feel upon hearing these words, when so many exceptions are made and privileges granted to those who are younger and less burdened with work? Even the donadas, after ten years of bad service, are rewarded with a reduced work load and are even allowed to take the veil. But for us, after fifty-four years of service between us, there is no retirement and no relief. . . .

At this point, and at great length, Josepha recounted every single office that she and María de San Miguel had held during their 27-year tenure at La Purísima, as well as every illness from which they had suffered over the years. She then suggested that one way to find someone to take care of them would be for Cuevas to threaten to expel the "least useful or most burdensome" of the donadas, so that another one, more willing to serve, could enter in her place. She did not really expect him to expel anyone, she conceded, but perhaps the threat of expulsion would cause the donadas to stop running to the abbess with frivolous complaints.

Josepha then moved on to other requests. "By doctor's orders," she wrote, her undergarments must be made of fine linen, not crude linen or cotton, a privilege that was granted to her many years earlier; 4 years ago, she and María de San Miguel were also given underskirts of fine linen, after having worn ones made of rough cloth for over 20 years, during which they "suffered immense torment." Both she and María de San Miguel had to have cotton stockings because they could not tolerate wool.

They had also been allowed special treatment regarding their diet since "the food that is prepared for the Community is impossible to eat." Josepha, like most of the other nuns in the convent, consumed two "tablillas" (20 to the pound) of cacao a day, but María de San Miguel received five a day (she took chocolate in the morning, again at "second breakfast," again in midafternoon, and a fourth time in the evening, when she was given two tablillas instead of just one—in other words, she consumed $1/4$ pound of cacao each day). As another special request, Josepha was given an egg and half of a chicken each day, while María de San Miguel received a quarter of a chicken. Ever since they had had a bad experience with sick chickens being slaughtered for their consumption, they had petitioned successfully to keep live chickens in their cells, but now, they were too feeble to slaughter and prepare them—another reason they needed someone dedicated to their service.

All of the nuns were given bread six times a day, but some time ago, Josepha and María had asked to combine their portions and to have the loaves left unsliced, so that they would preserve their freshness longer. Recently, however, because the bread was "heavy and made from the worst flour" and they could neither chew nor digest it easily (María de San Miguel had no teeth and also had sores in her mouth that caused her great pain if she ate too much), they had proposed to the abbess that she give them the money she spent on their bread so that they could buy biscuits (*biscochos*) or some other kind of bread instead. The abbess agreed to this plan on the condition that it not be made public in the community, but Josepha was worried that they might lose this privilege if the secret got out, so she asked Cuevas to make this a permanent dispensation.

Some time ago, Josepha and María had stopped sleeping in the dormitory or eating in the refectory, and here they sought to justify those failures to observe the common life. The refectory, Josepha wrote, was very drafty and humid, and "the experience we have had of its bad effects on us has obliged us not to attend this office. Whenever we have eaten meals there we have had to remain immobile for hours afterwards because any movement or exercise after eating does much damage to our health." The dormitory, she continued, consisted of one long room, with two windows and four doors, leading into the cloister, the refectory, and the provisioner's storehouse. Because of these many apertures and its vaulted ceiling, the dormitory, like the refectory, was very drafty, and during the rainy season, the walls and ceiling fairly dripped water because they were made of very porous stone. Those who slept there suffered so terribly that "it is a pity to see them." Clearly, neither Josepha nor María was fit to sleep in these conditions and must sleep in their cells, but this gave rise to another problem: The Rule stipulated that nuns must not sleep in the dark, so in order to comply, they needed a separate allotment of candles. "As you know, my Father," Josepha wrote, "the worst pains of the sick occur at night, and to suffer them in the dark would cause me mortal anxiety, for which reason I hope that you will make a discreet disposition to succor us in this regard."

Until the early 1770s, it had not been so important for the convent to commit to granting these expensive exceptions for the two nuns because, as Josepha noted rather proudly, they had enjoyed the benefits of regular donations from three benefactors.[48] One of them used to give Josepha and María so many rebozos that the abbess was able to supply the entire convent with ones they could not use. He also sent stockings, lengths of fine linen, semi-fine cotton, linen for underskirts, wool from Ypres for habits, serge for cloaks, sheets, quilts, thread, silk, paper, strings for their instruments: "all that we needed for our cell." In addition, this benefactor gave them anywhere from 4 reales to 2 pesos a week by way of donation. A second benefactor not only gave them clothing, money, and other items, but also supplied wine for the sacristy, and for the infirmary, cane alcohol (*aguardiente*), hams, salmon, avocados, fruit, honey, and unrefined sugar (*piloncillo*), as well as an image of San José that cost 100 pesos, a large reliquary, and many other things for the convent. But these two benefactors had ceased their support of the two nuns in the early 1770s (Josepha does not say why, but perhaps it was because of the Hoyos y Mier prohibition against donations for individual nuns), and the only outside help they now enjoyed came from Josepha's brother, a doctor with a large family of his own, who did build them a cell and continued to give them medicines, money, and goods from time to time, but he was not wealthy, and often they did not tell him when they were in need because "we do not have the courage to reveal what is happening to us . . . and we do not want to cause him pain . . . though it is not easy to hide everything."

Clearly, this letter was unusual in its length, its detail, and frankly, its arrogance, but it got the desired result. Five years later, Vicar Ignacio Antonio Palacios referred, in his report on the 1788 visit, to the "personal servant" that Josepha and María enjoyed: "all of the nuns are equal in their condition and Profession, and all have renounced worldly comforts, but some have been conceded a personal servant, while others, who have begged for this privilege based on grave necessity, have not. The two vocalists are the only ones who have such a servant, a privilege granted to them by my predecessor. . . ."[49] But while the other nuns might not have had the nerve to press their cases for exceptions with quite the same boldness as Josepha, they did ask for, and receive, smaller dispensations and privileges with some frequency. For example, out of the 39 nuns in the convent in 1786, 28 had requested, and been allowed, an exemption from fasting and abstinence from meat during Lent, on the grounds of ill health.[50] This common practice, if not policy, of exceptionalism, was another of the factors that made it possible to keep the peace and also to defend the convent's strict-observance constitution and the vida común.

Conclusion

Although they did not have a direct effect on La Purísima, the vida común reforms of the early 1770s created an atmosphere in which a resurgence of demands for more relaxation was increasingly untenable. These reforms surely steeled the determination of both the abbesses and the male authorities to

enforce the basic principles of La Purísima's constitution, and sapped the resolve of the rebellious nuns. But at the same time, while the abbesses and
bishops had no choice but to bend to the reformist spirit of the times (and we
have no evidence to suggest that the abbesses and bishops were anything but
enthusiastic about the vida común reforms, which after all, validated La Purísima's way of life), they understood that stabilizing a convent that had been
deeply riven and at an emotional fever pitch for over a decade called for a
delicate balance between adherence to the vida común and the vow of poverty
and attenuation of the austerity—indeed, harshness—of the convent under its
first zealous leaders. This was a balance that Hoyos y Mier attempted to strike
in his 18 fundamentally moderate provisions for changes in the convent, a set
of rules that abbesses and bishops continued to refer to well into the nineteenth
century. It was a balance that the bishops, in collaboration with the abbesses
and the Definitorio, aimed for when they allowed the nuns more say not only
in their internal governance, but also in the outside appointments and decisions that concerned the convent. It was also a balance that the abbesses tried
to achieve when they denied personal servants to the nuns, but allowed the
purchase of huge amounts of food so that the nuns could use the food to barter
service from the broader community, and it was a balance that making strategic
exceptions to the rules helped to maintain.

Despite the restoration of relative tranquility that these measures permitted, however, La Purísima did not thrive. Recruitment of new nuns, especially
the most desirable choir nuns, lagged well behind the optimistic expectations
of the convent's benefactors, due at least in part to a lingering aura of factionalism and turbulence in the convent. But as time went on, the convent's problems became more and more clearly financial. Between 1765 (the last year for
which available accounts indicate that La Purísima's income more or less
equaled its expenses) and 1775, the convent accumulated a deficit of almost
9,400 pesos. Seven years later, in 1782, the deficit had more than doubled,
topping 20,000 pesos. The amount that the convent owed its business manager eventually reached a staggering 43,000 pesos.[51] Thus, while the convent
leaders and episcopal officials found ways to resolve the political crisis in the
convent, the financial crisis soon took its place as a serious threat to the convent's existence. The complex causes and repercussions of the financial crisis,
including the shocking decision to abandon the vida común, are the subject
of Chapter 5.

NOTES

1. "Auto de Providencias varias sobre disciplina monástica," 16 November 1775,
AHAM, Diocesano, Gobierno, Religiosas, Capuchinas, caja 211 (XVIII), exp. 44.

2. On the vida común reforms, see Lavrin, "Ecclesiastical Reform"; Nuria Sala-

zar de Garza, *La vida común en los conventos de monjas de la ciudad de Puebla* (Puebla: Gobierno del Estado, 1990); Bernard Bobb, *The Vice Regency of Antonio María Bucareli in New Spain, 1771–1779* (Austin, Tex.: University of Texas Press, 1962), chapter 3; Zahino Peñafort, *Iglesia*, 154–164; Gonzalbo Aizpuru, *Las mujeres*, 244–251; Brading, *Church and State*, 82–88; and Margaret Chowning, "Convent Reform, Catholic Reform, and Bourbon Reform: The View from the Nunnery," *Hispanic American Historical Review* 85:1 (Feb., 2005).

3. Sperling, 124; Merry E. Wiesner, *Women and Gender in Early Modern Europe* (Cambridge, England: Cambridge University Press, 1993), 182, 195; Bilinkoff, *Avila of St. Teresa*, 36. Sampson, xiii, 62–64, describes the hagiographic trope of the heroic reforming nun, who sees evil in a convent and tries to remedy it.

4. On the Council of Trent and the project of Catholic reform that preceded it, I have found most useful Po-Chia Hsia; John O'Malley, *Trent and All That: Renaming Catholicism in the Early Modern Era* (Cambridge, Mass.: Harvard University Press, 2000), especially chapter 1; Robert Birely, *The Refashioning of Catholicism, 1450–1700* (New York: St. Martin's Press, 1999); Elizabeth G. Gleason, "Catholic Reformation, Counterreformation and Papal Reform in the Sixteenth Century," in *Handbook of European History, 1400–1600*, ed. Thomas A. Brady et al. (Leiden, New York: E. J. Brill, 1994).

5. There is a significant body of literature, dating from the 1970s and 1980s, on the subject of the impact on women of the Protestant reformation. See Wiesner; Natalie Zemon Davis, "City Women and Religious Change," in *Society and Culture in Early Modern France* (Stanford, Calif.: Stanford University Press, 1975); Thomas Head, "The Religion of the Femmelettes: Ideals and Experience Among Women in Fifteenth- and Sixteenth-Century France," in *That Gentle Strength: Historical Perspectives on Women in Christianity*, ed. Lynda L. Coon, Katherine J. Haldane, and Elisabeth W. Sommer (Charlottesville, Va.: University of Virginia Press, 1990); Steven E. Ozment, *When Fathers Ruled: Family Life in Reformation Europe* (Cambridge, Mass.: Harvard University Press, 1983); Lyndal Roper, *The Holy Household: Women and Morals in Reformation Augsburg* (Oxford: Clarendon Press, 1989).

6. In Spain, this project of conventual reform was given shape and moral force by St. Teresa of Avila's reform of the Carmelite order in the late sixteenth century. In New Spain, the Carmelites quickly became the most prestigious of the reformed female convents, and the personal example set by St. Teresa was deeply influential not only among the Carmelites, but also among other nuns. See Bilinikoff, *Avila*; Arenal and Schlau, 9–12.

7. On the actions taken at Trent with regard to female convents and the effects of Catholic reformism on convent life, see Sperling, chapter 3; Loreto López, *Los conventos*; Elizabeth Rapley, *The Dévotes: Women and Church in Seventeenth-Century France* (Montreal: McGill-Queen's University Press, 1990); Gabriella Zarri, "From Prophecy to Discipline, 1450–1650," and Marina Caffiero, "From the Late Baroque Mystical Explosion to the Social Apostolate, 1650–1850," in *Women and Faith: Catholic Religious Life in Italy from Late Antiquity to the Present*, ed. Lucetta Scaraffia and Gabriella Zarri (Cambridge, Mass., and London, Harvard University Press, 1999); A. D. Wright, *Catholicism and Spanish Society Under the Reign of Philip II, 1555–1598, and Philip III, 1598–1621* (Lewiston, N.Y.: Edwin Mellen Press, 1991); Caroline Walker Bynum, *Holy*

Feast and Holy Fast: The Religious Significance of Food to Medieval Women (Berkeley, Calif.: University of California Press, 1987); Elizabeth Rhodes, "Y Yo Dije, 'Sí Señor': Ana Domenge and the Barcelona Inquisition," in *Women in the Inquisition: Spain and the New World,* ed. Mary E. Giles (Baltimore, Md.: Johns Hopkins Press, 1999).

   8. Sperling, 129–130.

   9. For more on how the vida común reforms fit into this larger project of Catholic reform, see Chowning, "Convent Reform."

   10. A few authors (especially Mario Góngora, *Studies in the Colonial History of Spanish America* [Cambridge, England: Cambridge University Press, 1974], 201, and Francisco Morales, "Procesos internos de reforma en las órdenes religiosas, propuestas y obstáculos," in *Memoria del Primer Coloquio Historia de la Iglesia en el siglo XIX,* ed. Manuel Ramos Medina [Mexico City: Condumex, 1998], 155) see Charles III as having instigated the reforms, but the scholars who have studied the matter closely seem to agree that, while the king certainly played a role in generating a climate conducive to reform of the regular orders, both male and female, nonetheless, the impetus for the vida común reforms in New Spain came from Fabián y Fuero and Archbishop Francisco Lorenzana. The best account of the origins of the reform is in Zahino Peñafort, *Iglesia,* 118–119, 154.

   11. For a detailed examination of the expulsion of the niñas from convents in the archbishopric, see Gonzalbo Aizpuru, *Las mujeres,* 239–252.

   12. Lavrin, "Ecclesiastical Reform," 185.

   13. Francisco Fabián y Fuero, *Colección de providencias dadas a fin de establecer la santa Vida Común . . . en los cinco numerosos conventos . . . de Puebla de los Angeles* (1769), 2–3, 5–7.

   14. Salazar de Garza, 16–30.

   15. Lavrin, "Ecclesiastical Reform," 186.

   16. On the Fourth Provincial Council and convent reform, see Chowning, "Convent Reform," and *El Cardenal Lorenzana y el Concilio Provincial Mexicano,* ed. Luisa Zahino Peñafort (Mexico City: Universidad Nacional Autónoma de México/Porrúa, 1999), which is a transcription of the proceedings and commentary on the Council.

   17. Lavrin, "Ecclesiastical Reform," 193. Gonzalbo Aizpuru, *Las mujeres,* 247, says that the bishop called in the "army," but nothing about the army being involved was mentioned by Lavrin, Salazar y Garza, or Brading, who also write about the rebellion.

   18. "Nos el Dr. D. Alonso Núñez de Haro, y Peralta, por la Gracia de Dios, y de la Santa Sede Apostólica . . . a nuestras mui amadas Hijas en el Señor las RRMM Abadesas . . . y demas Religiosas de los diez sagrados Conventos de Calzadas . . . ," 22 August 1774; María Justina Sarabia Viejo, "Controversias sobre la 'vida común' ante la reforma monacal femenina en México," in *El monacato femenino en el imperio español: Monasterios, beaterios, recogimientos y colegios,* ed. Manuel Ramos Medina (Mexico City: Condumex, 1995), 586; Zahino Peñafort, *Iglesia,* 156–157.

   19. Brading, 83–84; Salazar y Garza, 33; Lavrin, "Ecclesiastical Reform," 196.

   20. Zahino Peñafort, *Iglesia,* 159.

   21. "Visita a el Convento de las Monjas Concepcionistas de la Villa de San Miguel el Grande: Elección de Prelada, y de Oficialas hecha con autorización y aprobación de el Ylmo. Sr. Obispo Dr. D. Luis Fernando de Hoyos Mier . . . Año de 1775,"

AHAM, Diocesano, Gobierno, Religiosas, Capuchinas, caja 211 (XVIII), exp. 44. Most of the details come from this visit, but a few gaps or confusing descriptions have been filled or clarified with information from other visits in 1766 and 1782: "Autos de la visita que personalmente hizo el Sr. Visitador Dr. y Mtro. D. Gerónimo López Llergo en la Yglesia, Sachristia, y Convento Real de Religiosas de Na. Sa. de la Concepción," AHAM, Diocesano, Gobierno, Visitas, Informes, caja 504 (XVIII), exp. 66; and "Autos sobre la Visita, y Elección de Vicaria Abadesa, y nombramiento de Oficialas de el Convento Año de 1782," AHAM, Diocesano, Gobierno, Religiosas, Concepcionistas, caja 255 (XVIII), exp. 19.

22. "Auto de Providencias varias sobre disciplina monástica," 16 November 1775, AHAM, Diocesano, Gobierno, Religiosas, Capuchinas, caja 211 (XVIII), exp. 44.

23. Loreto López, *Los conventos*, 130.

24. Gonzalbo Aizpuru, *Las mujeres*, 217–218.

25. Vicar Ignacio Antonio Palacios to Bishop Fray Antonio de San Miguel, 27 August 1788, AHAM, Diocesano, Gobierno, Religiosas, Concepcionistas, caja 255 (XVIII), exp. 35.

26. "Nomina de las ceculares que viven en este Comvento de Nra Sra de la Salud de esta Ciudad de Pascuaro," AHAM, Diocesano, Gobierno, Religiosas, Dominicas, caja 265 (XVIII), exp. 132.

27. "Información . . . limpieza de Da. María Josefa Palacios . . . ," 1787, AHAM, Diocesano, Gobierno, Religiosas, Concepcionistas, caja 255 (XVIII), exp. 33.

28. Abbess Josepha Ygnacia de Santa Gertrudis to Dr. D. José Francisco Casillas y Cavrera, 7 August 1782, AHAM, Diocesano, Gobierno, Religiosas, Concepcionistas, caja 255 (XVIII), exp. 17.

29. "Nueva distribución . . . 1775," AHAM, Diocesano, Gobierno, Visitas, Informes, caja 505 (XVIII), exp. 75.

30. Brading, *Church and State*, 89.

31. Germán Cardozo Galué, *Michoacán en el siglo de las luces* (Mexico City: Colegio de México, 1973), 13. He was in San Miguel for such a long time because the Oratorians were resisting his authority and he was trying to reduce them to obedience.

32. Vicar Ignacio Antonio Palacios to Bishop Fray Antonio de San Miguel, 27 August 1788, AHAM, Diocesano, Gobierno, Religiosas, Concepcionistas, caja 255 (XVIII), exp. 35.

33. Vicar Ignacio Antonio Palacios to Bishop Fray Antonio de San Miguel, 27 August 1788, AHAM, Diocesano, Gobierno, Religiosas, Concepcionistas, caja 255 (XVIII), exp. 35.

34. Abbess María Gertrudis de San José to Bishop Juan Ygnacio de la Rocha, 6 May 1778 and November [illegible date] 1778, AHAM, Diocesano, Gobierno, Correspondencia, Religiosas, caja 39 (XVIII), exp. 32.

35. "Expediente promovido por la R. M. Abadesa de S. Miguel sobre que se le conceda licencia para despojar el Abito por las razones que expone a la Novicia María Juliana de Sr. S. José," AHAM, Diocesano, Gobierno, Religiosas, Concepcionistas, caja 256 (XVIII), exp. 53; Abbess María Manuela de la Santísima Trinidad to Bishop Fray Antonio de San Miguel, 31 August 1798, AHAM, Diocesano, Gobierno, Religiosas, Concepcionistas, caja 256 (XVIII), exp. 53.

36. Clothing was the largest single living expense besides food, followed closely by medicines and medical care. These expenses will be discussed in Chapter 5.

37. Lic. Antonio Camacho to the nuns of Santa Teresa, Valladolid, 4 January 1825, AHAM, Diocesano, Gobierno, Religiosas, Teresianas, caja 395 (XIX), exp. 1.

38. Sister Josefa María Anna de Sr. S. Luis Gonzaga to Sr. Prov. D. Joachín de Cuevas, 11 January 1783, AHAM, Diocesano, Gobierno, Religiosos, Concepcionistas, caja 255 (XVIII), exp. 25; "Libro en que se asientan los autos de visita de las que se han de hazer de el convento de Religiosas de Sta. Catharina de Sena de esta Ciudad que se comenzó este año de 1721," AHAM, Diocesano, Gobierno, Religiosas, Catarinas, caja 217 (XVIII), exp. 30. This expediente contains a number of *visita* records, and in the 1732 *visita*, the amounts of various commodities allotted to the nuns are spelled out clearly.

39. "Cuentas . . . 1751," AHAM, Diocesano, Gobierno, Religiosas, Dominicas, caja 267 (XVIII), exp. 152; "Cuentas . . . 1791–1797," AHAM, Diocesano, Gobierno, Religiosos, Dominicas, caja 267 (XVIII), exp. 159.

40. David Ringrose, *Madrid and the Spanish Economy*. [Online] Available: http://libro.uca.edu/ringroseshAppendixd.htm. Table D.4, "Salable Meat from Livestock Slaughtered in Madrid, Early Nineteenth Century." Figures for 1801 and 1807 show yields of meat per sheep as 22 pounds and 21.3 pounds, respectively. In the text, Ringrose indicates that "in the conversion from animals slaughtered to pounds of meat, we assume that a sheep yielded 21 pounds of mutton" (Section C.1).

41. "Libro en que se asientan . . . ," AHAM, Diocesano, Gobierno, Religiosas, Catarinas, caja 217 (XVIII), exp. 30; Ibsen, 7.

42. "Cuentas . . . 1751," AHAM, Diocesano, Gobierno, Religiosas, Dominicas, caja 267 (XVIII), exp. 152; "Cuentas . . . 1791–1797," AHAM, Diocesano, Gobierno, Religiosos, Dominicas, caja 267 (XVIII), exp. 159.

43. "Libro en que se asientan . . . ," AHAM, Diocesano, Gobierno, Religiosas, Catarinas, caja 217 (XVIII), exp. 30.

44. "Cuentas de Cargo y Data, dadas por el Sr. Conde de Casa de Loja . . . desde el año de 1756 en que fue fundado el Combento Real de la Purísima Concepción . . . asta este prezente año de 1766 . . . ," AHAM, Diocesano, Gobierno, Religiosas, Capuchinas, caja 209 (XVIII), exp. 28.

45. Abbess Josefa Ygnacia de Santa Gertrudis to Lic. Joachín de Cuevas, 26 June 1782, AHAM, Diocesano, Gobierno, Religiosas, Concepcionistas, caja 255 (XVIII), exp. 19.

46. Sister Josefa de San Luis Gonzaga to Sr. Prov. D. Joachín de Cuevas, 11 January 1783, AHAM, Diocesano, Gobierno, Religiosos, Concepcionistas, caja 255 (XVIII), exp. 25.

47. Sister Josefa de San Luis Gonzaga to Sr. Prov. D. Joachín de Cuevas, 11 January 1783, AHAM, Diocesano, Gobierno, Religiosos, Concepcionistas, caja 255 (XVIII), exp. 25.

48. Ibsen, 9, explains that some nuns earned spending money "through the system of devociones, whereby friendly and sometimes amorous male sponsors provided gifts and money in exchange for periodic visits and prayers on their behalf," a practice that was "strongly opposed by the authorities."

49. Vicar Ignacio Antonio Palacios to Bishop Fray Antonio de San Miguel, 27

August 1788, AHAM, Diocesano, Gobierno, Religiosas, Concepcionistas, caja 255 (XVIII), exp. 35.

50. "Lista de las Religiosas, Donadas y Niñas que existen en estos claustros . . . ," August 1786, AHAM, Diocesano, Gobierno, Religiosas, Concepcionistas, caja 255 (XVIII), exp. 32.

51. "Cuentas de Cargo y Data, dadas por el Sr. Conde de Casa de Loja . . . desde el año de 1756 en que fue fundado el Combento Real de la Purísima Concepción . . . asta este prezente año de 1766 . . . ," AHAM, Diocesano, Gobierno, Religiosas, Capuchinas, caja 209 (XVIII), exp. 28; "Visita a el Convento de las Monjas Concepcionistas de la Villa de San Miguel el Grande," 1775, AHAM, Diocesano, Gobierno, Religiosas, Capuchinas, caja 211 (XVIII), exp. 44; "Cuentas presentadas . . . Josef Mariano Loreto de la Canal, May 1782," AHAM, Diocesano, Gobierno, Religiosas, Concepcionistas, caja 255 (XVIII), exp. 17; Abbess María Manuela de Sr. San Rafael to Bishop Fray Antonio de San Miguel, 28 July 1797, AHAM, Diocesano, Gobierno, Religiosas, Concepcionistas, caja 255 (XVIII), exp. 42.

5

Phelipa's Vision Triumphant

The Abolition of the Vida Común

As relations between the convent and the bishop settled into a more
benign pattern in the mid-1770s, and as bitter factionalism gave way
to smaller disagreements and jealousies, La Purísima seemed poised
to enter a phase of healthy growth for the first time since the early
1760s. But a spurt of entrances of novices in the mid-1770s was short-
lived, and by 1780, a new crisis began to exert an effect on recruitment that proved to be as discouraging as the rebellions had been: a
soaring budget deficit. The worried vicar and the bishop's office
blamed the nuns themselves—and increasingly, the inefficiencies of
the vida común—for the convent's financial problems, and they
were not entirely wrong: The practice of purchasing food for the entire convent could lead to abuse or waste, and supporting a large
number of community servants was also an expensive proposition.
But in fact, the causes of the crisis went well beyond those associated with the vida común. Some of them had to do with the
church's investment and loan policies; some with lending patterns
in this particular convent; some with overspending at the time of
the foundation and construction of the convent; some with the Tridentine reform that called for a local businessman to be placed in
charge of the convent's financial affairs; some with rising prices for
food, medicines, and clothing; and some, as we saw in Chapter 4,
with the need to maintain a high standard of living and defuse the
kind of discontent that had brought the convent to the brink of disaster in the 1760s.

   Whatever its causes, however, the financial crisis had one dramatic ramification: the shocking decision made by Bishop Antonio

de San Miguel in 1792 to put an end to the vida común at La Purísima and to impose in its place the *vida particular* (the individual life), a system of individual monthly allowances in which the nuns would purchase their own food and most other necessities and support their own personal servants. In the late 1760s, at the time of the imposition of the vida común throughout the colony, the nuns of the convent of Santa Inés in Puebla had complained to the high court that, in requiring them to live the vida común, "the Bishop sought to transform their rule, converting them into *recoletas* like the Carmelites and Capuchins."[1] In San Miguel in the 1790s, the same could be said to be true, but in reverse. When the bishop imposed the vida particular on the nuns of La Purísima, he was fundamentally altering the way of life to which they had professed. The individual life was opposed to both the spirit and the letter of La Purísima's constitution, a constitution that three decades of abbesses, bishops, and vicars had risked disorder and rebellion to defend. The financial crisis, then, in a magnificently ironic turn of events, led to the triumph of Phelipa de San Antonio, from her grave.

This chapter is divided into five parts: first, the problem of lagging recruitment; second, the dimensions and causes of the financial crisis and its connection to the recruitment crisis; third, the convent's and the bishopric's attempts to set finances right, including the vida particular reform; fourth, the decision to impose the vida particular in the changing context of Catholic reformism; and fifth, the reaction in the convent to the new style of life.

The Recruitment Crisis

In its first 4 years of existence (1756–1759), 17 novices were admitted to La Purísima, an average of over 4 a year. All but 1 aspired to become choir nuns, and all of them eventually professed. During the decade of rebellion in the 1760s, however, that rate of entrance was cut in half, as only 20 girls sought admission (2 a year), most of them early in the decade, before the second phase of the rebellion. Worse, 6 of these 20 new recruits left the convent without professing, and of the 14 remaining, 4 were legas (white veil nuns). This meant that the population of choir nuns, the most prestigious nuns and the ones who paid full dowry, increased disappointingly slowly, at an average rate of just one a year. Even for the established convents, which primarily aimed to maintain existing numbers, this was a low rate of recruitment, and it was well below expectations for a new convent that was still trying to build a community.

While the 1770s did not bring a dramatic turnaround, the outlook was more positive: 16 novices entered the convent, and 14 of them (all but 1, a choir nun) professed. In fact, in 1778, the abbess, in a plea to the bishop's office for more confessors, justified her request by pointing to the much-increased size of the community.[2] Soon thereafter, however, the convent's growth once again stalled: in the entire decade of the 1780s, only 4 choir nuns professed (4 legas also entered).[3] Toward the end of that decade, the abbess worried, in a letter to the vicar, that the convent was having trouble attracting postulants: "already there have been no new novices for three years."[4]

But the convent's disappointments went beyond stagnation in the size of the population. On close examination, La Purísima never drew as many women from the upper echelons of society as the other elite, dowry-requiring convents for which we have detailed information, and tellingly, it also failed to attract a significant number of girls from the villa of San Miguel itself, an important goal of those who had originally supported the foundation of the convent in the mid-1750s. Only 11 of the 78 novices who entered La Purísima from 1756 to 1810 were born in San Miguel: the 4 Canal sisters (two of whom did not profess), 3 girls from poor families who were given one of the dowries set up by benefactors (for which one criterion was to have been born in San Miguel), two donadas who took the white veil after their 10 years of service, and two sisters from a family about which little is known. There were no nuns from the great creole families of San Miguel besides the Canal family: no Landetas, no Lanzagortas, no Teráns, no Unzagas (although these families provided financial support to the convent), no Allendes, no Sauttos.[5] By contrast, half of the choir nuns who professed in the convent of Santa Clara in Querétaro from 1775 to 1810 came from the city itself; at Santa Catarina, 57% of the nuns came from Valladolid or its surrounding towns and haciendas; and at Nuestra Señora de la Salud in Pátzcuaro, the figure was about 70%.[6]

As table 5.1 shows, of the 78 novices, relatively few were very clearly among the top social and economic elite. There were only the four Canal daughters; two girls from the Septién y Montero clan, a wealthy mining family from Guanajuato; two daughters of Captain Fernando Antonio de Miera, another

TABLE 5.1. Social and Economic Status of Novices Entering La Purísima, 1756–1810

	Choir Nuns	Legas	Total Entrances	Total Professions
Obviously high social and/or economic status	19 (14 professed)	2	21 (27%)	16 (23%)
Poor (had to seek scholarship or other outside support), or former donada	19 (17 professed)	7	26 (33%)	24 (35%)
Parents' status unknown	27 (26 professed)	4 (3 professed)	31 (40%)	29 (42%)
Total entrances	65	13	78	
Total professions	57	12		69

Guanajuato miner; the daughter of Antonio Jacinto Díez Madroñero, yet another Guanajuato miner; and the daughter of Francisco Victorino de Jaso, a very wealthy merchant/landowner in Zamora (she did not profess). Even if we stretch the criteria for "elite" to include not only the great families, but also those who had relatives who were priests or friars or nuns in other convents, those whose fathers were councilmen of minor towns in the province, and those whose fathers had a military commission (positions that certainly carried social status and at least a middling degree of wealth), we can vouch for the high social and/or economic status of only 16 of the professed nuns (23% of the total number who professed during this period).

By contrast, at least 35% of the professed nuns were poor: Either they were former donadas, their dowries had to be patched together from donations by various benefactors, or they had to be offered a scholarship. Antonia de las Llagas, for example, was 32 before she was finally able to pursue her religious vocation. Born in the small town of Yuririapúndaro, she and her sister had lived in a beaterio (a religious community and school for girls) for many years, at the expense of a benefactor. When he stopped supporting them, she came to San Miguel to look for another benefactor. Her pleas to various potential patrons bore no fruit, however. Then she learned that the convent was prepared to offer a scholarship to someone who could keep its accounts, and so she dedicated herself to the study of the "five rules of Arithmetic" and other necessary skills, and entered the convent as an accountant (a título de contadora).[7]

Admittedly, over 40% of the girls' families provided information that simply does not allow us to make judgments about their social backgrounds. On the one hand, it is tempting to assume that these families had considerable economic wherewithal, simply because they were able to amass a dowry. On the other hand, dowries provided by benefactors outside the family were not uncommon and were not always acknowledged as such; furthermore, the information on family background that the nuns and their families submitted was designed to showcase their social luster, and so the absence of titles and position may be significant. In any event, it is clear that 90% of the population of the convent was *not* "at least moderately rich," as was the case at Santa Clara in Querétaro.[8] The large proportion of nuns from non-elite families (at least 35%, and at a guess, closer to 50%), a population that included several of the convent's former servants who had served for 10 years as a donada and had then been allowed to profess, could not help but diminish the social prestige of the convent. And the less prestigious the convent was perceived to be, the more elite families from San Miguel and other towns that were the natural constituency for La Purísima stayed away.

What were the causes of this failure to recruit as many or as socially prominent girls as the convent's backers had hoped? Did La Purísima's turbulent past continue to affect its reputation—and therefore its ability to attract novices from well-to-do families, who would be willing and able to come up with the dowry necessary to become a choir nun—even beyond the end of the crisis? It seems intuitively likely that this was the case, but given the convent's enduring recruitment problems, it is useful to ask whether there were other factors besides the convent's reputation at work.

The first step is to ascertain whether La Purísima's experience was unusual among other late eighteenth-century convents, or if the rate of entrance/profession elsewhere after midcentury also slowed. Although all convents for which we have detailed information experienced decades in which they failed to admit as many novices as in others, there does not appear to be any significant long-term trend: As table 5.2 shows, three of the four convents for which we have data beginning early in the eighteenth century drew just as many or more girls in the last half of the century as in the first. The variations from decade to decade seem to have had mainly to do with rhythms of mortality. That is, convents that were already at capacity and were merely trying to maintain their size would choose to accept fewer novices in some decades than in others, depending on the number of deaths among the convent population. This meant that the patterns of profession do not show any consistent trend, instead varying from decade to decade and convent to convent, even among convents in the same city. There is one exception to this rule: In the 1770s, the vida común reforms may have discouraged entrance into some of the convents of calzadas, such as Santa Clara of Querétaro, where professions fell from 32 in the 1760s to 10 in the 1770s (although this is, by far, the most striking case). As a result of low rates of recruitment in the 1770s, some convents had to admit more novices than usual in the 1780s and 1790s in order to maintain their populations (see table 5.2). But the very fact that these convents rebounded in the 1780s and 1790s suggests that the problems were not internal, but rather related to crown and church policy. La Purísima's problems, by

TABLE 5.2. Number of Professions as Choir Nuns

	La Purísima Concepción	Santa Catarina de Sena (Valladolid)	La Concepción (Puebla)	Santa Catalina (Puebla)	Santa Clara (Querétaro)	Nuestra Señora de la Salud (Pátzcuaro)
1720s		12	30*	10*	32	
1730s		5	30	10	27	
1740s		18	10	9	13	10 (1747–1749)
1750s	15 (1756–1759)	9	0	17	23	19
1760s	10	18	9	4	32	11
1770s	13	14	13	4	10	8
1780s	4	8	18	16	24	13
1790s	12	7	19	19	38	13
1800–1810	7	15	7	5	11	14

* Annual average for the 20-year period 1720–1740.

Source: For Puebla convents, Loreto López, Los conventos; for Santa Clara, Gallagher; for others, AHAM.

contrast, appear to have been more serious, more enduring, and more structural.

Besides its history of internal conflict and rebellion, there are three other possible explanations for La Purísima's inability to reach its target population and to attract as many choir nuns as its constitution provided for: competition from other communities of religious women, regional economic woes that made convents too expensive for most families to afford, and financial problems within this particular convent.

Competition from Beaterios

We can hypothesize that La Purísima was forced to compete for highly motivated and deeply pious girls—girls with vocations sufficiently serious to find the idea of a reformed convent appealing—with a number of new female religious communities that were founded in the second half of the eighteenth century and the first decade of the nineteenth century in the bishopric of Michoacán. These communities were not convents (the two new convents established in Michoacán after La Purísima arrived too late to be much of a factor), but rather beaterios.[9] Beaterios were communities of women that were, in some ways, quite similar to convent communities. Like nuns, the residents, known as beatas, lived apart from the world, striving to adhere to the principle of enclosure.[10] They wore distinctive clothing, took names in religion, were associated with a particular church, and had a similar system of internal self-governance and outside supervision by the local priest. In one important way, they were quite different, however. Beatas took simple—as opposed to solemn—vows, and they could be released from these vows if they chose no longer to live in religion. Because the community was made up of women who chose almost on a daily basis to be there, some beaterios had a reputation as particularly pious communities, a reputation reinforced by their institutionalized poverty: Since beaterios required no dowry, they typically had very small endowments, and they supported themselves by running schools. Hypothetically, such institutions might attract girls or women with strong vocations who were not convinced that the convents were as good a place to serve God as the less prestigious, but also less materialistic, beaterios. Thus, to pursue the hypothesis, the girls who might be drawn to La Purísima because of its rigor and its reformed way of life might be the same girls who would also be drawn to the proliferating beaterios.

Between 1750 and 1795, there were at least seven beaterios formally established in the bishopric of Michoacán. The new beaterios, combined with the two that already existed at midcentury, provided space for around 250 women, about twice the number accommodated by the three established convents for Spanish girls (La Purísima, Santa Catarina of Valladolid, and Nuestra Señora de la Salud of Pátzcuaro).[11] Were the women who entered these new institutions those who in the past might have entered one of the established convents? Or were they women who would not or could not have become a nun in one of these convents?

It appears that, for the most part, the beaterios did not draw from the same population as the established convents. While all of the established convents admitted some women from families too poor to provide a dowry, such postulants were in the minority, probably even at La Purísima. But middle-class and poor women constituted the majority of the population of the beaterios. The lists of officeholders in the Colegio de Santa Rosa in Valladolid during the second half of the eighteenth century, for example, did not include a single daughter of a wealthy—or even socially prestigious—family. (Beaterios were interchangeably called "colegios," a word that emphasized their teaching function.) Furthermore, while most beatas submitted evidence of their "pure blood" before they entered the house, the seriousness with which those proofs were presented and preserved in the archives of the institution differed significantly from the obsessiveness with which the established convents guarded their racial purity. It seems likely that the population of most beaterios included more women with a mixed racial background than was true in the convents. Because the beatas did not sing the hours of the Divine Office and therefore, in theory, did not need to read, at least not as well as nuns, they tended not to be as well educated. The "catalogs" of the population of three beaterios in the late eighteenth century—San Nicolás de Obispo in San Luis Potosí, Jesús Nazareno in Celaya, and Santa Anna in San Miguel—suggest that reading and writing were not skills possessed by many beatas (at San Nicolás de Obispo, 15 of the 24 beatas could at least read a little, but fewer could write; at Santa Anna, only 8 of the 40 beatas could read and/or write; and at Jesús Nazareno, reading was not a skill or aptitude listed for a single beata).[12] These catalogs also contained assessments of the beatas' personalities that tended to be less generous than those of the nuns in the established convents, suggesting either that the women in these institutions did not possess the kind of manners and demeanor that marked a "well-educated" woman, or that the priest who compiled the catalog and collected these assessments had preconceived ideas about the levels of civility that he would find there—in either case, the point that the beaterios and the convents were perceived as quite different places is upheld. At the Colegio de Santa Anna in San Miguel, for example, 6 of the 40 women were called "violent" (an adjective not applied to any of the nuns at La Purísima, despite the fact that its catalog was composed during the decade of rebellion).[13] Thus, the beatas were significantly poorer, probably somewhat less European in appearance, less literate, and less polished than the nuns in the established convents.

These differences between beatas and nuns meant that, while the beaterios provided important new outlets for the religious energies of poor and middle-class women, they do not seem likely to have cut significantly into the number of women attracted to the traditional convents. For the most part, the two types of institution did not draw from the same pool of potential applicants. Thus, in the case of La Purísima, the fact that a new beaterio, the Beaterio de Santa Anna, was established in San Miguel at roughly the same time as the convent (1754) does not seem sufficient to explain the convent's failure to thrive. Indeed, the fact that the bishop authorized the foundation of both a beaterio and a convent within 2 years of each other strongly suggests that he did not see the two institutions as serving the same population.

Economic Factors

A second possible explanation for La Purísima's recruitment woes is regional or local economic decline. In the late eighteenth century, the royal government introduced a number of liberalizing reforms designed to promote freer trade within the empire, thus increasing the availability and decreasing the cost of imported manufactures. San Miguel was an industrial city: Could "free" trade (trade was still confined to the Spanish Empire, and direct trade with other powers was not permitted), making for cheaper imported cloth and other man-ufactures than those produced at home, have affected the local economy so much that well-to-do families could no longer afford to place their daughters in nunneries? Alternatively, did a well-documented drop-off in silver produc-tion in the late eighteenth century dry up markets in the mining districts for the goods that the city and the area around San Miguel produced, squeezing entrepreneurial profits and the local elite? Was there a Bajío-wide economic stagnation that affected decisions such as whether or not to shoulder the fi-nancial burden of paying a daughter's convent dowry?

Probably not. The fall in silver production did not occur until around the turn of the century, so it cannot help us explain trends in professions to con-vents in the 1770s, 1780s, and 1790s. And the free trade reforms did not come into full effect in Mexico until the 1790s (although Salvucci argues that, even before the limited opening of the economy to foreign imports in 1789, there was something of a shakeout among the locally owned obrajes, caused by too much competition). Moreover, even if some elite families did feel an economic pinch, their response would not necessarily have been to deny the convent to their daughters. In fact, such families might actually have been more, rather than less, likely to seize this option. First, placing a daughter in a nunnery reduced the number of heirs among whom a shrinking parental estate had to be divided, since nuns did not inherit, while daughters were forcible heirs under Spanish law. Second, at 3,000 pesos, the dowry required to become a nun might be less than the dowry necessary for an acceptable marriage, since the average amount brought by elite women to marriages (in the form of either a dowry proper or an expected inheritance) in the neighboring province of Michoacán between 1770 and 1810 was almost 10,000 pesos; in the province of Guanajuato, where San Miguel was located, it is likely that marriage dowries would be at least as high, if not higher.[14] Third, the nun's dowry did not have to be paid in cash: It could be taken as a lien on family-owned real estate (residence, obraje, rancho, or hacienda) so that her parents only had to pay interest on the amount of the dowry at 5% a year. Even if the regional economy had been sluggish (which it does not seem to have been during the most relevant decades), it would probably have had a relatively mild effect on the numbers of women entering the convents.

Financial Problems

The third, and most compelling, explanation for La Purísima's continuing problems in recruiting suitable entrants is neither competition from the beaterios nor the regional or local economic conditions of the late eighteenth century. Instead, it is the convent's deteriorating financial situation, a crisis that was both a cause and an effect of the convent's recruitment woes. When unexpectedly small numbers of dowry-paying choir nuns professed in the 1760s, during the rebellion, the endowment—dependent on the dowries that they brought—could not expand fast enough to cover early cost overruns in the construction of the convent and other expenses. Beginning in the mid-1770s, La Purísima began to "borrow" every year from its business manager, José Mariano Loreto de la Canal, the brother of María Josepha Lina, the foundress. Canal was extremely wealthy and no doubt saw it as a pious act and a way to honor his sister never to force the convent to pay off any of the deficit or even to cut spending (although he was not so pious as to cancel the debt altogether). In the short run, it was fortunate that the nuns did not have to stick to a belt-tightening budget at a time when the abbesses felt that they needed to spend relatively freely in order to guard against another outbreak of rebellion. In the long run, of course, this leniency on the part of the mayordomo allowed the deficits to get out of hand. Connected at first to the rebellions of the 1760s, which were the original cause of the recruitment drought, by 1780, the financial crisis had taken on a life of its own and was an independent cause of the new wave of recruitment problems in the 1780s.

The Financial Crisis

All of the convents in the bishopric experienced financial setbacks in the second half of the eighteenth century, but La Purísima's problems were especially acute. The causes are several, but in general terms, this was like most budget deficits: It resulted from a combination of insufficient income and excessive expenditures.

Income

When convents took in funds (say, for a dowry), their policy, logically enough, was not to expend them right away, but rather, to invest them immediately so that they would begin to produce an income.[15] (In this discussion, I refer to the lending policies and problems of convents, but most of what I have to say about convents applies to all ecclesiastical lenders.) The investments took the form of either real estate that the convents could rent out or loans to borrowers who would agree to pay 5% interest. In the bishopric of Michoacán, some convents owned a few houses and perhaps a small hacienda or rancho (Santa Catarina owned a flour mill), but most conventual wealth was invested with private borrowers, and La Purísima owned no property at all.[16] In other words, the convent's entire endowment was tied up in mortgages on private property.

As long as borrowers paid interest regularly, it was much more desirable, from a convent's point of view, that they continue to do so, rather than pay off principal. Redemptions of principal were a headache: The convent had to find a new borrower who would be as reliable as the old one and then complete the onerous paperwork and appraisals necessary to extend a loan, all in order to receive exactly the same interest rate as before, the standard, non-usurious 5%. The problem was that this system bred interest payment delinquency. With confidence that the convent would be forgiving, over time, even fairly responsible borrowers might renege, at least partially, on interest payments that would otherwise consume a large part of their disposable income. Instead of servicing the debt on their church loans, they frequently chose to meet other obligations, or when the economy was expanding (as it was through much of the eighteenth century), to make other, more attractive investments that were likely to earn a higher return than 5%. There were no good legal recourses for ecclesiastical creditors when borrowers would not or could not pay.[17] Taking recalcitrant borrowers to court typically meant losing all hope of a resumption in interest payments for a number of years, as the case made its way slowly through the legal system, and frequently resulted in the forced sale of the property and the loss of principal as well as income. Thus, most convents were inclined to tolerate many years of nonpayment rather than try to force the issue.

While all ecclesiastical lenders carried a number of debtors who had not paid interest for years, the female convents found it especially difficult to enforce loan agreements. From their cloisters, the nuns could not, of course, put face-to-face pressure on their debtors, although one of the jobs of the abbess or the secretary was to write to creditors to try to shame them into compliance. And to make matters worse, their mayordomos often had conflicts of interest that undermined timely collection of interest payments. Since the Council of Trent, control over their own treasury was removed from the nuns and granted to mayordomos, who had been chosen by the bishop. These men were selected because of their prominence as merchants, landowners, miners, and industrialists because it was thought that the convents needed a well-connected businessman to protect their economic interests and cover shortfalls, if necessary. But this meant that when they acted as the convents' agents and loaned out convent funds, the mayordomos interacted mainly with their peers and business associates, whom they were reluctant to alienate with what might be perceived as overly aggressive demands. Typically, dozens—even hundreds—of letters were exchanged yearly between the mayordomos and the convents' debtors, with the former delicately requesting payment of interest and the latter often calling on their long association with the mayordomo to ask for an extension or otherwise plead their cases for noncompliance. In 1795 alone, for example, some 445 letters were exchanged between the mayordomo and borrowers of funds from the convent of Santa Catarina, most of them concerning debt payment and extension.[18]

La Purísima did not actually begin to encounter serious interest payment delinquency until the mid-1770s. As late as 1774, the convent's borrowers were still fairly scrupulous about servicing their debts—the total interest owed to the convent in that year, for example, was 5,725 pesos (on an endowment of 114,500 pesos), and the amount actually received was 5,200 pesos, only 525 pesos less. This was probably due to the fact that most of the endowment consisted of liens (*censos redimibles*) taken when a daughter, sister, or niece entered the convent—a circumstance that made for a fairly high rate of compliance while the nun herself was alive. But as the convent population aged and liens were redeemed, inherited, or transferred to other borrowers, some of whom lacked the moral incentive to keep up regular interest payments, debt service became more irregular. In 1782, on owed interest of 5,790 pesos, the convent received only about 3,400 pesos, and in 1791, on owed interest of 7,425 pesos, the convent was paid only 5,846 pesos.[19]

Borrower resistance to prompt payment of interest was a problem shared by all of the convents, but La Purísima had special problems in this regard. Because few of the nuns who entered the convent during the colonial period were from local families (compared, as we have seen, with the nuns in other elite convents, whose families tended to live in or very near the convent towns), whenever their dowries were taken as a lien on their family's or benefactor's hacienda or residence (and liens were overwhelmingly more common than cash payments), the great likelihood was that these properties were located some distance from San Miguel. This made collection of interest, never an easy task, even more problematic. Although the information on the properties that secured these liens is frustratingly imprecise in the convent's records, we can draw some inferences about the difficulties of pressing for interest service, based on the nuns' birthplaces. Of 49 dowry-paying nuns who entered La Purísima during the period before 1810 (that is, not including nuns who came on scholarships or legas who were ex-donadas), 21 nuns came from beyond a radius of 100 miles: 4 from Mexico City, 6 from Aguascalientes, 1 from San

Luis Potosí, 4 from San Juan de los Lagos in the bishopric of Guadalajara, and 6 more from other parts of that bishopric.[20] Thus, a substantial proportion of the convent's debtors lived far enough away that, if they reneged on interest payments in a bad year or a series of bad years, the mayordomo could do little but write them entreating letters.

Another weakness on the income side that was especially acute at La Purísima was the relatively small size of its endowment, a problem directly related to the failure, in the first decade or so after the foundation, to attract large numbers of the wealthiest nuns, the choir nuns, whose 3,000-peso dowries were the backbone of convent finances. In the convent's first 4 years in existence (1756–1759), an average of almost 10,000 pesos a year in dowries was added to the endowment, but in the 1760s, this average plunged to only 2,850 pesos a year because four nuns received scholarships (one as an accountant and three as beneficiaries of patron scholarships), so they brought in no new funds; three took the white veil and thus paid dowries of only 1,500 pesos; and three more became legas without having to pay any dowry at all, because they were former donadas with 10 years' service. From 1770 to 1810, the average was even less, at some 2,300 pesos a year. Thirty-five years after its foundation, La Purísima still had an endowment that was only about a third of Santa Catarina's and a little more than half of that of Nuestra Señora de la Salud, a convent founded only a few years earlier than La Purísima (in 1747).[21]

La Purísima had another problem related to the size of the endowment and the income that derived from it. In many new convents, benefactors chose to endow specialized funds, for example, a fund to pay the salary of the convent's chaplain, a fund to cover medical or pharmaceutical expenses, or a fund from which to purchase oil for the lamps or wine for the mass. In fact, over 25,000 pesos had been intended by the early benefactors and the foundress to serve those purposes. But the construction costs for La Purísima's church and convent turned out to be much higher than expected, and at least 13,000 pesos in donations intended for upkeep were diverted to the building fund.[22] This meant that the convent had to pay, out of its general fund, some expenses that were covered in other convents by special endowed accounts. Although in time, more donations did come in, and eventually, the convent was able to finance around half of the costs of wine, wax, the chaplain's and sacristan's stipends, the fees paid to errand runners and the doctor, and the celebrations of Holy Week, Christmas, and New Year's from its special funds, this was still less than was covered in other convents.

To sum up the discussion of the financial crisis so far, a large part of the explanation for La Purísima's growing budget deficits had to do with income shortfalls. First, the endowment was disappointingly small: Some of it had been expended in construction cost overruns, but even more important was the effect that the rebellion in the convent had on the recruitment of dowry-paying nuns; later, of course, the mounting financial problems frightened away prospective nuns as effectively as the rebellions had done. Second, income from the endowment was not collected efficiently. In part, this was a church-wide problem, having to do with usury laws and fixed interest rates that gave little incentive for ecclesiastical lenders to demand repayment of loans—a situation that led inevitably to borrower complaisance and foot-dragging where debt service was concerned. In part, it was a problem that was felt especially acutely by female convents, because they were forced to depend on mayordomos, whose commission on collected interest formed a minuscule part of their personal income, giving them relatively little incentive to jeopardize close relationships with borrowers of convent funds (who were often their business partners and associates) by pressing, with unseemly insistence, for prompt compliance. Finally, in part, it was a problem that was especially serious at this particular convent because many borrowers lived relatively far away from San Miguel, complicating the logistics of collecting debts and pressuring borrowers to pay.[23]

Expenditures

Beyond these problems on the income side, La Purísima had unique expenses that proved very burdensome. Some of them were related to the fact that this was a vida común convent. First, the general fund at vida común convents had to cover some of the expenses that, in convents of calzadas, were covered by pensions or *peculios* that were set up by a nun's family at the time of her profession. The peculios were often provided for in the last wills and testaments that nuns made before they professed, signaling their "death" to the secular world, and they was known euphemistically as the fund for "chocolates." They evaded strictures against nuns' owning personal property because the fund did not "belong" to the nun—rather, she "used" income from it until her death, at which point it reverted to the convent itself (another way that endowments in unreformed convents could grow).

Just because La Purísima was a reformed convent does not mean that the nuns lacked all access to outside funds. We have already seen that they sometimes received gifts of food, money, or clothes from benefactors: Josepha Ygnacia's letter to the vicar general (Chapter 4), for example, referred to three different patrons who supplied her, and indeed, the whole convent, with money and goods. But nuns in reformed convents, like La Purísima, were not allowed to set up formal accounts with a predictable income; donations from benefactors were inherently unstable and could very well dry up, as indeed had happened to Josepha Ygnacia. Moreover, the practice of accepting gifts was mildly discouraged, as we saw in the Hoyos y Mier regulations, although it is worth pointing out that he did not forbid the practice, but rather insisted that any gifts or funds must revert to the convent as a whole and could not be kept by individuals. Thus, a range of expenses that might, in other convents, be covered

by the shadow income from the nuns' pensions had to be covered at La Purísima—and other reformed convents that adhered strictly to the vida común—
either haphazardly (from benefactors) or by the general fund.

A second problem relating to the vida común was that the convent depended, for a range of tasks, on community servants, the donadas, who were
supported entirely out of the general endowment. While the number of donadas was never considered by the nuns to be sufficient for their needs, church
authorities (the vicar, abbess, and bishop), struggling with the growing financial crisis, recognized that they were a significant burden on the convent budg-
ets, especially when they exercised their right, after 10 years of service, to take
the white veil, a practice that as we have seen was apparently unique to La
Purísima. At this point, their duties were usually reduced (sometimes neces-
sitating allowing a new donada to enter the convent), while their cost to the
convent stayed the same or, more likely, rose, since as they aged, they required
more medical care and expensive medicines. By the 1780s, there were 18 to
20 donadas in the convent. Certainly, the donadas did not eat as well or dress
as well or receive as good medical care as the nuns, but even if we guess that
they cost the convent only half as much to support as the choir nuns (perhaps
75 pesos a year versus 150 pesos for the choir nuns), this still amounted to a
considerable sum, around 1,500 pesos a year. If we add to this the amount that
the six or seven ex-donadas (now legas) cost the convent in living expenses,
the amount expended on the donadas and ex-donadas, who had contributed
nothing to the endowment, came to around 2,000 pesos a year. Then, if we
factor in the nine choir nuns in the 1780s who held one of the benefactor
dowries (having brought none of their own) or were admitted without having
to pay a dowry because of a talent or skill, we add another 1,350 pesos that was
spent annually on nuns who had not brought a dowry. It was because of this
drain on convent resources—the total of 3,350 pesos a year in expenses on
non-dowry-paying residents represented well over half of the convent's annual
income—that episcopal authorities, in 1782, put a moratorium on the entrance
of any more donadas or legas into the convent, since even though legas brought
a dowry, they cost the convent more than their dowries produced (75 pesos a
year).

There were other expenses besides the donada system that were condemned as excessive at La Purísima and were also blamed on the vida común,
particularly food costs, which amounted to 60% to 70% of the convent's total
expenses. Was this a fair criticism? Convents with a common kitchen probably
did have trouble estimating how much food to purchase for a large community.
To some extent, the abbesses made a charitable virtue of the inevitable waste,
giving unused food away to the poor. But, as argued in Chapter 4, at La Purísima they also tolerated intentional over-purchases of food not only in order
to have food to give away, but also to allow the nuns to use it to barter services
from the townswomen, in the absence of personal servants. Thus, expenses

on food *were* excessive, and the vida común *did* have something to do with the pattern of overspending, both because of its inherent inefficiencies and because the lack of personal servants was compensated for by purchasing too much food.

Authorities also criticized the convent's spending on clothing, with somewhat less justification. Clothing was a huge expense: It cost between 2,000 and 3,000 pesos to buy new habits for all of the nuns. Instead of buying new habits all at the same time, then, which it could rarely afford to do, the convent allowed nuns to request clothing as needed, but this made for a rather chaotic, hard-to-control system. As the abbess described it, at any time during the year, one nun might ask for an item of clothing, another might ask for something else, and a third might ask for something different, and the result was "disorder and great expense."[24] But while the system may have been haphazard, it does not appear to have been abused, at least to judge by the heartfelt pleas for new clothing and the many comments about the frayed and threadbare clothes that the nuns were forced to wear. In 1792, the abbess begged Bishop San Miguel to authorize 3,000 pesos for the purchase of new habits for all of the nuns, saying that they had received not a single item of clothing for the last 5 years, but he refused.[25] In general, it appears that clothing was economized on early and often, and the suggestion on the part of male authorities that the nuns were profligate in this area was only half right: It is true that they did not have a good system to replace worn clothing, but it is not true that they were spending an inordinate amount on clothes.

Medicines and medical care were different. As with food, beyond a certain point, it was extremely awkward to impose economies on sick nuns. In some years, the cost of medicines alone came to over 500 pesos, although the convent prepared at least some of its own remedies, as demonstrated by the 1791 accounts, which contain a breakdown of how much was spent on herbs; solvents, such as aguardiente and pulque; and sugar and charcoal to make syrups. Abusively excessive consumption of medicines may well have been a problem (it is impossible to judge from the records available), but large expenditures on medicines were also related to high prices in the second half of the eighteenth century. These increases occurred for two reasons: first, an expansion in the variety of drugs and medicines available due to improved, but expensive, techniques and equipment, and second, a weakening of the pious impulse that had previously led many pharmacists to donate or discount medicines that they provided to the convents.[26]

In sum, there does not seem to be any question that La Purísima's financial problems had partly to do with excessive spending. Some excesses were related to the vida común (the prohibition against a personal *peculio*, the need to support donadas entirely out of convent funds, the swelling of food expenditures because of inefficiencies in ordering for a large community and because of the practice of allowing nuns to use food as barter), and some were not (the fact that many liturgical and medical expenses had to come out of the general fund, and the high cost of medicines and clothing). But as we have seen, a large part of La Purísima's financial trouble was the result of its inadequate income base and the difficulty of collecting the income that it was owed. The problems on the income side, however, were rarely acknowledged in the many discussions of the convent's financial tribulations. Instead, the nuns themselves, and the lifestyle enshrined in their constitution, were increasingly blamed.

Dealing with the Financial Crisis

Occasional worried references to growing deficits appear in the convent's correspondence before 1782, but that was the first year that the abbess and the episcopal authorities in Valladolid began to display real concern and to take measures to resolve the problem. The new abbess, Josefa Ygnacia de Santa Gertrudis, wrote a letter proposing various "reforms" to Licenciado Joachín de Cuevas, who was in charge of the convents under the vacant see following the recent death of Bishop Juan Ignacio de la Rocha.[27] Like most of the male authorities who weighed in on the subject of the convent's dismal financial situation, she attributed its problems to excessive spending rather than to revenue shortages. All of her ideas for cutting costs involved a stricter interpretation of the principle of the vida común. From now on, she proposed, the nuns must spend "only what is absolutely required for life itself, ridding ourselves of all that is superfluous and not necessary for our health, which will allow for better observance of the vow of poverty and thus improve the wellbeing of this poor Convent, and insure that it does not continue in its present decadence. . . ."

Clothing, she recommended, should be distributed to the nuns only as needed, and only once every 3 years. Chocolate and all other food should be handled the same way: It should be divided equally among all of the nuns at designated times of the day, since although "we professed to live the common life," over the years, many dietary exceptions had been made. The practice of taking food from the provisioner's storehouse and giving it away must end; instead, only food left over from meals served in the refectory should be given away—and then only to the genuinely poor—at 3:00 in the afternoon and at no other time. The sick should eat the same meals as everyone else, and should eat in the refectory, even if they have to sit at a separate table (unless they are under specific orders from a doctor). Josepha Ygnacia concluded with a condemnation of the exceptionalism that had begun to prevail in the convent: "It is well known that in all communities there is a diversity of personalities . . . and in this one some Religiosas are so accustomed to their comforts that they ask for everything, and everything has been given to them, and sometimes even more than they ask for, although they cannot use it all."

Cuevas agreed to most of the reforms suggested by the abbess and added some of his own, although he was pessimistic that anything but "Divine Providence" could rescue the convent from the "imminent risk of total and lamentable ruin."[28] In addition to supporting her recommendations regarding closer adherence to the vida común, including the limits on food giveaways and the distribution of clothing at designated times every 3 years, Cuevas imposed some other economies. First, the convent had a practice of purchasing medicines that were not necessarily ordered by the doctor, but from now on, only written prescriptions from a physician would be honored. Second, everyone was to sleep in the dormitories, except the extremely ill, and they must sleep in the infirmary—in this way, there would be savings on candles.

But Cuevas also ordered some more fundamental reforms. He decreed that there were to be no more donadas or legas admitted to the convent without special license from Valladolid. "Neither the Vicar nor the officers of the convent shall be permitted to accept [donadas and legas] without license from this office, as this practice has resulted in a multitude of Individuals whose maintenance causes the convent enormous cost. . . ." Despite frequent complaints from the nuns that the donadas had no time to provide any personal assistance (they were all employed in community tasks, such as clothes-washing, tortilla-making, bell-ringing, bath-drawing, chocolate-grinding, errand-running, atole-making, cooking, sweeping, caring for the sick in the infirmary, and manning the turnstile), Cuevas wrote that "the number of legas and donadas that now exists I judge to be ample for the needs of the convent." Cuevas also ordered that the donadas were no longer to have the right to profess as white veil nuns after 10 years of service. This was in direct opposition to the convent's constitution. Finally, he instructed that the convent school should be reopened (it had been closed since shortly after the vida común reforms and the expulsion of the niñas from the convent), because the room and board paid by the schoolgirls could help to offset expenses.

Although these measures had no positive effect on convent finances—in 1785, the deficit reached over 33,000 pesos—they may have had an effect on convent politics, since Josepha Ygnacia de Santa Gertrudis, whose efforts to cut costs had revolved around austerity and stricter enforcement of the principal of the common life, was not reelected as abbess. Instead, in 1785, the nuns elected Augustina de la Encarnación, whose solution to the financial catastrophe could not have been more different from Josepha Ygnacia's. Almost certainly aware of the precedent offered by the convent of La Encarnación in Mexico City, which had abandoned the vida común in favor of a system of individual allowances in 1781, and probably aware of proposals at Santa Catarina to shift to a similar system, the new abbess urged the convent to take the steps that Phelipa and her faction had been pressing for since the early 1760s: dismissing the donadas and replacing them with personal servants, and abolishing the common kitchen. In short, she recommended dispensing with the most central tenets of the vida común, as it had been practiced at La Purísima since the days of the first two abbesses.

Further economizing will not work, she wrote to the vicar: The nuns were already pushed to the limits of their endurance.[29] The previous year's expenses did not contain "a single *real*" for clothing for the 40 religiosas and 20 donadas, and in fact, no money had been spent on clothing for some time, "and this is not the only necessity that the nuns have had to do without, as you have witnessed from the continual clamoring directed your way." Living the common life had simply proved unworkable: "This Convent is a Babylon of confusion . . . some ask for Licenses to admit servants because the donadas cannot attend them; others look to their relatives to feed them because the food from the common kitchen is poorly seasoned and their illnesses do not permit them to eat it . . . ," and through all of this, the convent's deficit just kept going up. Because the nuns and donadas believed that they had a right to take food from the provisioner's stores and give it away to relatives outside, there was much waste: "it causes me the greatest pain that our vow of poverty is broken by this dissipation." Meanwhile, the unmet needs of the religiosas were so numerous that "I cannot with justice demand that they attend choir; they are all so sick and lacking the comforts they require that only five or six attend each [recitation of the Divine] Office." She concluded, "this way of life [the vida común] unquiets our Souls and does not allow us to pursue our vocation . . . ; we must remember the words of Santa Teresa: 'where there is not abundance, there is not observance.'"

The solution, she wrote, lay in dismissing all of the donadas so that "only those [servants] whom the Religiosas voluntarily choose to support with their own funds" would remain. Having personal servants, instead of community servants, would save the convent a significant amount of money, because the endowment fund would no longer have to be used to feed, clothe, and care for the donadas until death. Each nun would be given the amount of interest on her dowry, and she would pay her expenses out of that amount. In this way, the convent would save money because the provisioner's office would disappear, and with it, presumably, the waste caused by spoilage and over-purchase. The new system would also cut down on the "great disgust" that was caused if one person was denied something that someone else had. Alternatively, if things were to continue as before, "the disorder will grow, and word of the state of the convent will get around and no one will want to enter." In fact, she threatened, her own health was so precarious that she could not continue as abbess unless the convent's financial problems were resolved, and she believed that "the only remedy for these problems was the vida particular" (*ponernos de particular*). Her letter to the vicar was followed by a note from the Definitorio, confirming the situation and writing of their fear that, when José Mariano Loreto de la Canal, the brother of the founder and the convent's mayordomo, died, no one would want to take his place because the burden of covering the convent's annual deficits was so great.[30]

The vicar, Ignacio Antonio Palacios, fully supported Augustina's position, as he wrote in an emotional letter to Bishop Antonio de San Miguel in 1787, in which he pointed out that the financial crisis had already delayed necessary repairs to the convent, endangering the nuns' spiritual calm and even, he implied, their virginity:

> These poor nuns are reduced to such poverty that . . . they must live
> in a convent where they are constantly exposed to insolent People
> who climb the crumbling walls and even have the audacity to sleep
> in the Cloister; this is too much to bear for these timid women of
> such delicate spirit, who live in vivid fear of a sudden Accident in
> the silence of the Night, for which they would need both temporal
> and spiritual succor. How can they even gather enough courage to
> open their doors, knowing that outside Wolves are lurking?[31]

He went on, rather circuitously, to blame the vida común for this situation. The fact that the convent's walls were falling down (having been built only half as high as they should have been in the first place because of lack of funds) not only made a mockery of enclosure, but also meant that the patios and many of the rooms in the convent were exposed to the elements. The north-facing door of the choir let in an especially unhealthy wind, with the result that "all of the nuns suffer from head colds and rheumatism and various other aches and pains, and if there are six nuns who attend Choir it is considered to be a full complement." This much sickness, in turn, put pressure on the already inadequate funds of the convent:

> The nuns adhere to the vida común, or as it is said in the vulgar,
> they all have to eat from the same pot [haver de comer de un caldero].
> But how is it possible for a single diet to accommodate both the well
> and the sick? With so many nuns ill with such diverse maladies,
> how can everyone be expected to eat the same food? If they did so
> they would continue to suffer. So it has been necessary to prepare
> separate meals for each ailing nun [se le ponga un brazero aparte],
> and this is the primary cause of the excessive expenses in this con-
> vent.

In sum, the vicar posited a vicious cycle in which the high costs of accommodating sick nuns under the vida común meant that spending consistently exceeded income, which in turn, made it impossible to repair the convent, which then caused more illness, more costs, and so on. "The only option that presents itself to set right conventual finances and avoid ruin is that which the abbess suggests . . . , that is, for a short time to minister to each nun a portion in *reales*,"—in other words, to adopt the individual life, the vida particular.

In 1792, then, responding to these pleas from both the abbess and the vicar, Bishop Antonio de San Miguel abruptly acknowledged that none of the economies were working. "Temporarily," he said, the nuns of La Purísima must adopt the vida particular in place of the vida común. They were, ideally, to continue eating and living in common, but the convent would no longer purchase or cook food for them or supply them with community servants; instead, they were to be given a personal allowance on which they would have to learn to survive. In justifying the reform, he spoke of the positive experience, in a financial sense, of the nuns of Santa Catarina of Valladolid after the "imposition" of the vida particular in 1787. But the comparison to Santa Catarina was more than a little spurious. Like most Mexican nuns, the Catarinas had always lived a version of the vida particular: separate apartments and cells, separate kitchens, and personal servants. These nuns had chosen to adhere to the common life in 1774, in accordance with the royal edict of that year, and later had "clamored"—with the full support of the bishop—to return to their more private and individualized lives.[32] The vida particular was not so much imposed on them as voted back in after a short absence.

At La Purísima, the vida particular meant that the choir nuns would receive an allowance of 20 reales a week, which amounted to 130 pesos a year, less than the 150-peso yield on their 3,000-peso dowries. Legas would receive 16 reales a week, or 104 pesos a year—more than the 75 pesos produced by their 1,500-peso dowries (if, in fact, they had brought a dowry at all). The donadas with permanent status in the community (those who had served their 10 years before the abolition of that benefit in 1782) would receive 10 reales a week. The convent would still be responsible for the clothing and medical care of the nuns and donadas, as well as for liturgical expenses and the general maintenance of the convent and church, including the stipends of the chaplain and sacristan. The money for these expenses would come from the dowries of the 11 nuns who had died, which totaled 28,000 pesos, plus 26,300 pesos in donations over the years that were earmarked for various expenses. At 20 reales a week, the allowance given to the choir nuns was significantly less than that of the nuns of Santa Catarina, who received 26 reales a week, and that of the nuns of Nuestra Señora de la Salud (on whom the vida particular was also "imposed" in 1793), who received 24 reales a week, an amount that was increased to 26 reales in 1797.[33] The much smaller allowance given to the nuns at La Purísima obviously represented an attempt to cut costs, but it had significant implications, since (as we will see) it virtually forced the nuns to find other ways to raise money for their subsistence.

In 1792, the nuns were questioned by a *visitador*, Licenciado Manuel Abad y Queipo, as to their opinions about the proposed new system.[34] The questions concerned whether the nuns understood that the convent was in serious financial trouble because spending was consistently greater than income. How would the nuns feel, Abad asked:

> if the bishop deemed it necessary to take the same action that he has taken in the case of the convent of Santa Catarina, that is, giving money weekly to each Religiosa as the funds of the Convent permit, which is also the system used in many other convents in the Kingdom.... [This system] would be imposed only until the convent's finances are repaired sufficiently to support the greater cost of the rigorously communal life, which would still be practiced insofar as possible, with all the nuns eating together, the only difference being that each would prepare her own food....

Abad y Queipo was obviously using this manner of questioning to prepare the nuns to accept what was, by that time, a decision that the bishop had already made. It worked: Most of the 32 nuns were acquiescent. They responded that they understood the convent's financial problems and that they would adopt whatever system the bishop ordered. Five were openly positive about the prospect of switching to the vida particular, including Josepha de San Luis Gonzaga, who had been agitating for this change since Phelipa's era, but also including Manuela de la Santísima Trinidad, who was one of those who had most vigorously opposed Phelipa. Five others were negative, including Vicenta del Corazón de Jesús, who had been one of Phelipa's partisans. But only one of the five who preferred the vida común objected that the new system went against the vows that she had taken upon profession, and even she said that she would reluctantly accept the bishop's decision. The others merely stated that they would obey the bishop.

The Vida Particular, Catholic Reformism, and Early Liberalism

Why did Bishop San Miguel find it necessary, or expedient, or beneficial, to impose the vida particular on La Purísima, especially since the convent's constitution and customs (unlike those of the other convents in the bishopric) clearly demanded strict observance and the vida común? The primary official justification, of course, was that it would solve the convent's debt problem. But while the reform could be seen as a way to rationalize the financial system by slowing down the increase in the rate of indebtedness—since it would shift the burden for some expenses to the nuns themselves and, if they could afford to help, their families—there was little chance that it would actually "solve" the problem (despite repeated insistence from the bishop's office that it would). Even under the most favorable circumstances, it would have taken decades before any meaningful reduction in the amount that La Purísima owed the mayordomo could be expected, since the allowances that the nuns received under the vida particular and the common expenses to which the convent was committed consumed all of the product of the endowment. A campaign to attract new dowry-paying nuns, even if it could be made to succeed, would not help for many years because the income from their dowries would be dedicated to their own allowances during their lifetimes. Only after the deaths of a significant number of nuns might enough of the interest on the endowment be released that it would be possible to devote some of it to amortization. For the short and medium terms, the best that could be hoped for was that the vida particular would hold the amount of debt steady, and even this, it does not seem to have accomplished unequivocally. There were some years of debt reductions (for example, the amount owed to the mayordomo in 1794 fell from 38,810 pesos to 36,220 pesos), but 3 years later, the debt was as high as it had ever been, at 42,181 pesos.

It is worth noting, in this regard, that there were better ways than the vida particular to reduce the debt (as opposed to simply holding it steady), and these were well known to ecclesiastical officials. They were spelled out in 1794 by the mayordomo, Narciso María Loreto de la Canal, the nephew of María Josepha Lina. He had been able to retire some of the convent's debt this year, he wrote, "solely" because he had collected some long-overdue delinquent interest.[35] A major push to get borrowers to make payments on overdue interest was awkward: The mayordomo would have to put pressure on his own business associates and friends, to whom he had made the loans in the first place because of his close connections with them. It did not happen very often. Canal implied that the back interest that he had managed to collect had been turned over more or less voluntarily; that is, he did not have to go to extraordinary lengths for it, and there is no indication that he was willing to do so. But he did make some revealing recommendations for strategies to assure relatively high debt service compliance in the future: He urged that the collateral offered to secure debts be examined rigorously (often properties that were already heavily mortgaged were offered as collateral), that a cosigner always be required (this was not always demanded of prominent borrowers), and that residents of San Miguel who sought loans be favored, since collection of interest locally would be much easier than insisting on debt service from borrowers who lived in, say, Aguascalientes. These measures might have made a huge difference for the convent's accounts had they been taken to heart: In most years for which there are surviving accounts, as little as 80% compliance with debt service would have allowed the convent to cover its expenses, even without economizing. If both economies in spending and greater emphasis on collection of interest had been put into place, it probably would have been enough to allow La Purísima slowly to resolve its financial problems—certainly to address them as effectively as the change from the common life to the individual life.

Even if its potential to effect dramatic change was exaggerated, the financial justification for imposing the vida particular at La Purísima seems reasonable: There is no question that *some* kind of resolution of the budgetary quagmire was needed. But the extent to which fixing the convent's finances was the bishop's sole motivation is called into question by a comparison with other convents in the bishopric. Rescuing the convent from imminent financial ruin was also the excuse given for imposing the vida particular on Nuestra Señora de la Salud in Pátzcuaro—but the fact is that the convent was in very acceptable financial shape and regularly ran *surpluses*. Furthermore, for 9 years *after* the imposition of the vida particular in 1793, spending was actually higher, on average (with the same number of nuns or fewer), than in the 3 years before the reform went into effect.[36] Financial reasons were also given for ordering the abandonment of the vida común at Santa Catarina in 1787, but the "decadence" of its finances, which the vida particular was ostensibly meant to correct, was purely concocted, as shown in a report that misrepresented both the convent's income and its expenditures.[37] The fact that the same justification for the imposition of the vida particular was offered at all three convents raises questions about whether rationalization of finances was the only motive of the bishop and his advisers, or perhaps more precisely, whether in the enthusiasm for rationalizing finances, very much attention was paid to the particular circumstances at each convent.

A second justification for the vida particular was also ubiquitous: that this way of life would allow nuns more effectively to adhere to their vow of poverty. The reasoning was that the vida común led to the purchase and preparation of too much food, which was then wasted when it was given or bartered away. Nuns living on a modest budget, it was implied, would follow a more austere and simple style of life than they did when the convent bought food and other items for them in bulk, as was the case under the vida común. It is clear that this potential benefit of the vida particular reform was emphasized in discussions with the nuns, since many of them echoed the wording of the official statements on this subject. But in light of the colony's recent experience with the vida común reforms, the idea that the vida particular would lead to more austerity and dignity was almost bizarre. Just 20 years earlier, Bishop Fabián y Fuero and Archbishop Lorenzana had given essentially the same reason for insisting on the change from the *individual* to the *common* life: The common life, they had argued, was a way to reinvigorate the vow of poverty, broken so often under the vida particular. Given the centuries of evidence that the vida particular increased, rather than decreased, the showiness and luxury on display in the convents, the best explanation for this convoluted argument on the part of Abad y Queipo and Bishop San Miguel is that it was intended to persuade nuns to go along with the reform who would have resisted doing away with the common life for purely financial reasons, as well as to provide cover for the reform in the eyes of the general public—and perhaps even to convince themselves that what they were doing was acceptable. That they either felt a little squeamish about the reform or were under moral pressure to allow the convent to return to its original mission is suggested by the fact that they continued, for many years, to call it a "temporary" measure (even though it was never reversed).

Obviously, though, they did not feel *too* squeamish, or they would have found other solutions to the debt crisis at La Purísima, perhaps along the lines suggested by the mayordomo. Are there any additional explanations that help us to understand this abrupt change of direction on the part of churchmen who, like the architects of the vida común reform, Bishop Fabián y Fuero and Archbishop Lorenzana, were considered "reformers"?

The place to begin is with the changing nature of Catholic reform efforts in the second half of the eighteenth century. In the 1760s and early 1770s, the reformist priorities of church activists included the need to force the regular orders to bend to royal and diocesan will; the need to impose greater discipline—through better laws, education, and training—on priests, nuns, and friars; and the need to encourage more simple, dignified, and moderate devotional practices. The vida común reforms, which church and state reformers had cooperated to bring about, had fit neatly with these shared ideas about reforms that were thought necessary to meet the implicit challenge of enlightened secularism.[38]

By the mid-1780s, however, the church had begun to reevaluate its relationship to the crown, growing more critical of it and its social policies (as well as its increasingly anticlerical policies), and progressive Catholics began to develop priorities for reform that differed from those of the state. The press for internal reform that had dominated Catholic reformism in the 1760s and 1770s did not end; indeed, efforts to halt showy burials, elaborate processions, exuberant fiestas, and other popular practices were intensified, and attempts to redefine the curriculum of the universities and colleges were also particularly notable.[39] But these changes were joined by a broader, and more socially oriented, agenda that one historian calls "proto-liberal," borrowing a term that Horst Pietschmann has applied to the Bourbon reforms as a whole.[40] In this stage, priests were instrumental in organizing the new economic societies throughout New Spain—organizations dedicated to applying "modern" principles to social and economic problems—and the church itself expanded its socioeconomic role and began to use its public platform and the mechanism of the "representation," or open petition, to offer pointed advice to the crown on social and economic matters.

What changed? What accounted for the new posture of church reformers? The most important of many factors was that the crown itself had entered into a new phase of activism aimed at restricting the power not just of the regular clergy, but of the secular church, in the temporal realm. Legislation that was designed to control and circumscribe the power of the parish priests, the enforcement of that legislation by sometimes arbitrary and pugnacious district governors, the problems that these conflicts created for the upper clergy (which had to put out fires in the provinces), and the increasingly anticlerical tone of official pronouncements had already led to reduced enthusiasm on the part of bishops and other high ecclesiastical officials for cooperation with the royal government.[41] But the crown's moves to do away with ecclesiastical immunity from prosecution in royal courts between 1784 and 1795 led one anonymous cleric to assert that royal ministers "had deliberately deceived the . . . bishops, holding out the promise of greater episcopal power as a lure for their cooperation, while at the same time intending to destroy that power completely."[42] Now there was no question about the intentions of the crown to limit, severely and unacceptably, the authority of the church.

Some members of the upper clergy reacted as conservatives (especially after the French Revolution, which had a predictably polarizing effect), arguing that it was modernizing reforms within the church that had gotten it into trouble in the first place. Changes in the curriculum of the seminaries, changes in the relationship between bishops and parish priests, and attempts to change the nature of popular piety—these were dangerously disruptive. Other church officials, however, were influenced by the increasingly "liberal" (in the sense of putting the individual at the center of the plans for economic growth and modernization) direction of royal reformers, even as they deplored the state's actions toward the church. The intendancy system may have been objectionable in its attempt to take over the administration of the tithe from the church, but some church reformers could agree with its goal of obtaining a freer rural commerce by ending the monopoly over that commerce by local officials, and by guaranteeing a degree of personal freedom and mobility for Indians and castas.[43] The attack on ecclesiastical privilege may have been abhorrent to the church, but the idea of abolishing special status for other groups (e.g., Indians) had considerable appeal as a way to improve the lives of the poorest members of society. In short, progressive reformers within the church, like reformers within the royal administration, were, in one sense, moving in similar directions, even as they became more antagonistic toward each other.

Bishop San Miguel and Abad y Queipo, who imposed the vida particular reform on the convents, were key figures in this new phase of Catholic reformism. Abad, especially, exemplified the new tendency among progressive Catholic reformers not only to criticize the state, but also to criticize the society that the crown had allowed to develop in New Spain.[44] His trenchant analysis of Mexican society included his famous condemnation of social inequality ("in America there is no gradation or middle ground: everyone is either rich or poverty-stricken, noble or infamous") and a special concern for the restrictive, illiberal conditions under which indigenous peoples lived. Following Campomanes, the influential minister to Charles III, he advocated the "absolute civil equality of the class of Indians with the class of Spaniards," and as Brading summarizes his thinking on the subject, "the only way to do this was to abolish the tribute or capitation tax, allow them [Indians] to incur such debt as they could obtain and free them from all restrictions on the sale of their produce."[45] For Abad, some of the crown legislation aiming to increase personal freedom and mobility did not, in fact, go far enough: Indians were still prohibited from making contracts, and they could not sell their products directly without permission from royal authorities.[46] He also strongly advocated division of Indian communal lands among individual members of the communities (another proposal made around midcentury by Campomanes) and argued that residence in Indian towns should not be restricted in any way. He proposed an agrarian reform based on opening up uncultivated lands to settlement by those without access to land, similar to a reform that had already been carried out in Spain.[47] In other words, following "the profound [Adam] Smith," he had faith in the individual, believed that "every individual, no matter what his race or history, would respond to economic incentives," and saw individual ownership of property and freedom of economic action as the cornerstones of successful social reform.[48]

Abad's analysis of Mexico's social problems, then, invoked certain liberal concepts, especially the idea of the primacy of the individual. If Abad could see individual freedom of action as the key to ending the misery of the Indian population of Mexico, perhaps it should not surprise us that he favored a solution to the real (in the case of La Purísima) and not-so-real (in the case of the convents of Santa Catarina and Nuestra Señora de la Salud) financial problems of the convents of his diocese that emphasized individual effort and reliance on competition and participation in the market. The prospect of nuns becoming mini-entrepreneurs and profit maximizers (the predictable result of giving nuns an allowance on which they could scarcely subsist) would have been a deeply unattractive vision for the vida común reformers, Fabián y Fuero and Lorenzana, but it was seen by the new generation of reformers, Abad and Bishop San Miguel, as another case in which economic incentives for the individual to act rationally were properly applied to an inefficient and antiquated system. If Indians were capable of making economic decisions and participating in the market, why shouldn't nuns be given the income from their own dowries and allowed to make individual choices about how to spend it? Why shouldn't they be allowed to work as hard as they wanted and enjoy the fruits of their labor? The vida particular reform, then, was undergirded not only by a late eighteenth-century emphasis on rational organization of finances and attention to the bottom line, but also by another late eighteenth-century idea: individualism. At La Purísima, these two values trumped the spiritual and symbolic virtues of the vida común.

La Purísima and the Vida Particular Reform

In 1793, about a year after La Purísima been converted to the vida particular, the nuns were asked whether the "new method of temporarily individual life" had caused any relaxation or lack of observance of the Rule and constitution or had brought any spiritual or temporal benefit to the convent.[49] As might be expected from a convent that had been divided over the issue of the vida común since its foundation, 13 nuns approved of the new system, 10 disliked it intensely, and 3 saw some positive, but also some negative, aspects of the change. (Fifteen expressed no opinion; most of them were the younger nuns and legas.) The nuns who found the new system "convenient" observed that there was less bickering and more "calm and peace" because (unlike before) everyone at the same level of the convent hierarchy received exactly the same allowance. Almost all of those who favored the change also noted that the new system allowed closer adherence to their vow of poverty, since there was less waste from food giveaways. One nun stated that she thought that attendance at choir was better under the new system; most, however, merely observed that religious observance was about the same as before.

The nuns who found the new system "inconvenient" were more vocal and gave more detailed answers than the nuns who approved. María Anna del Corazón de Jesús, for example, in a few words, painted a striking picture of a convent that was suddenly a hive of business activity: "[A]ttendance at Refectory and Choir, and observance of silence during the designated hours," she stated, "is much worse than before because everyone is constantly occupied making things to sell, the allowance they receive each month not sufficing for their subsistence." Manuela de San Raphael echoed this observation: Some nuns, she said, "on the pretext that they do not have enough to live on, are engaged in the disgraceful search for profits . . . since they have to support themselves, they think of nothing but how to buy at the lowest possible cost, and how to solicit the money with which to make their purchases." Vicenta del Corazón de Jesús agreed, adding that the nuns were too busy "lamenting that they do not have enough for their urgent needs" to attend properly to spiritual matters. Others complained that, because of the large numbers of servants suddenly present in the convent, there was much more noise and disorder. One blamed a lack of charity toward the sick on the novel perception that healthy nuns need not do anything to help ailing nuns because they now had their own servants to take care of them. Catarina de la Santísima Trinidad noted that the vow of poverty was broken by many nuns, who had taken to using "silver utensils and exquisite china plates."[50]

Over the next few years, opinion against the vida particular strengthened. In 1797, Vicar Ignacio Antonio Palacios complained that, despite the fact that the bishop had ordered the nuns to follow the individual life:

several Religiosas, in a spirit of pure sedition and capriciousness, have refused to accommodate themselves to this way of life, and they talk constantly against it, not only among the other nuns, whom they have scandalized with their disobedience, but also with Persons from the outside world, and so I ask that Your Excellency order them to obey and be quiet.[51]

Palacios noted that the abbess herself, Manuela de San Raphael, was one of those unhappy under the new regime. She had recently written to the bishop, painting a falsely rosy picture of convent finances. Although the debt to the mayordomo had reached 42,181 pesos, she argued, 28,900 pesos of this was back interest, "all entirely collectable and very secure," so that "soon" the convent's obligations would be reduced to under 14,000 pesos. "Taking into consideration the small size of that amount," she wrote, "Your Excellency will tell us if we must continue in the vida particular which in your mature and prudent judgment you imposed on us, for the good of the convent, or if we may return to the vida común, which since the foundation of this convent we have professed."[52] The bishop responded that the collection of these debts was not without its difficulties, and therefore, the time was not yet right for such a change. The nuns, he wrote, should be reassured that the vida particular did not contradict in any way the vows that they had taken.

The complaints continued over the next decade. The principle of enclosure, some religiosas reported, was repeatedly violated by workers, who entered the convent to build kitchens, ovens, and other things that the nuns ordered to equip their individual cells and enable their little manufacturing enterprises. The much increased number of personal servants put greater demands on the convent's single chaplain and meant that many nuns, especially sick nuns, were not able to hear mass, and there was no provision for burial of these personal servants when they died. Nuns who did not have outside income from families or benefactors found themselves in the "dire necessity of manufacturing things to sell, such as sweets, biscochos, cajetas, artificial flowers, and the like."[53] This was bad enough, but the servants:

who have no such needs, follow their example, with the result that there is little silence in the convent, and the *madres torneras* [the nuns who monitored the turnstile] are so busy doing the bidding of the nuns and servants with items to market, either selling them or giving them to an outside person to sell, that it prejudices the prompt service that the torneras ought to give the community.[54]

Those who have studied convents in Spanish America and elsewhere will recognize the general outlines of this picture. Nuns have always made small items as gifts to visitors, confessors, and patrons, or somewhat more rarely, for sale. A recent four-volume series on viceregal cuisine in Mexico includes three volumes on convent cooking, recognizing that, over the years, many convents had developed special recipes, especially for sweets, which they sold or distributed in small quantities.⁵⁵ Nuns might be singled out during the triennial visitation for their talents for manufacture: "knows how to make artificial flowers," for example, or "good with jellies and preserves," or "knows how to distill for medicines." So, in a sense, the scene described by the nuns of La Purísima after the imposition of the vida particular is not unusual.

But there are two significant differences. The first difference is one of degree. Most of the manufactures in other convents were not meant to be the nuns' main support, so the frantic nature of the work at La Purísima—hiring extra servants to help in quasi-business operations, a stream of workers entering the building to construct private kitchens or ovens—is on a scale beyond that of most other convents, where the manufactures were meant as gifts for confessors or benefactors, or for modest, restricted sale, at most.⁵⁶ As Jean Descola observed of the convents of Lima in the eighteenth century, "the convents monopolize the manufacture of sweets, cakes, and fancy desserts, which are served at dances, parties, and weddings; they stop at nothing to satisfy the public and increase their clientele, *not for love of profit* but for the pleasure of besting another convent" (emphasis mine).⁵⁷ At La Purísima, by contrast, the monthly allowance was so low (20 reales a week, compared with 26 for both Santa Catarina and Nuestra Señora de la Salud) that nuns were virtually forced to seek profit, and on a fairly extensive scale.

The second difference, of course, was the radical nature of the change; other convents had evolved these practices over the years, but La Purísima was forcibly converted from a strict vida común convent, with few community servants and no personal servants, to a convent of calzadas, with all that that implied, virtually overnight. Profit-minded business activities were considered inappropriate and unbecoming for all nuns, but they were particularly shocking and disruptive in a convent where those activities were previously absent. The vida particular reform created a new universe of problems that were not addressed in the rules and customs that the convent had developed during 40 years of the vida común.

This point was made in 1806 by a new vicar, Francisco de Uraga, who was much more critical of life under the vida particular than his predecessor. Although he did not see any need to correct the nuns' general adherence to the monastic estate, he did see a deeply troubling lack of order and a failure to follow the rules and dispositions set down by church authorities. This, he observed, resulted largely because these rules and dispositions were enmeshed with the life in common and so oriented to the more perfect preservation of it. When it was abolished, these rules became irrelevant, but they were not replaced by new provisions. Thus, the convent bordered on the chaotic. The nuns' allowance was so paltry, he lamented, that they were virtually forced not only to beg for charity or to undertake profit-making endeavors (*granjerías*), but also to put their servants to work. With their small weekly allowance, the nuns had to "eat, maintain a servant, provide their own clothing, and pay for medicines and the services of a doctor, since although the convent has a doctor on retainer it is impossible for him to attend to all the sick, and they have to seek the help of another." (It is unclear when the nuns were made responsible for their own clothing since, according to the 1792 edict, clothing was to be provided by the convent.) The noise and constant commotion caused by the much-increased number of servants was distracting, and the prescribed periods of silence were impossible to observe. There were multiple irregularities in the management of the turnstile and the main door, which stayed open well past the hour stipulated in the Rule, in order to give the nuns a chance to buy provisions and other necessities. Life in the convent had been totally transformed, he wrote, and "all the nuns long for the common life in all its rigor" ("la vida común en todo su rigor por la que suspiran todas las Monjas").[58]

The bishop's office continued to insist that the nuns should not use the fact that they bought their own food, cooked for themselves, worked on their own account, and maintained personal servants (who were, in some ways, more like employees in small manufacturing enterprises) as an excuse for abandoning the central tenets of the common life: eating, sleeping, working, and praying in common. But Uraga was right—it was impossible for the two lifestyles to coexist easily. Fewer than half of the nuns regularly engaged in the activities that were central to the vida común, and even attendance at choir was, by all accounts, abysmal. Simply put, efforts to maintain themselves consumed the nuns' time and energy. But despite Uraga's powerful critique, the nuns' own laments, and church authorities' continued reference to the individual life as "temporary," the colonial period came to an end with no movement in the direction of restoring the vida común at La Purísima. Just as the complaints of the rebellious nuns in the first three decades of the convent's existence had failed to move the bishop to change his position, the complaints of the nuns and their vicar, who wished to see the convent return to its constitutional roots, were ignored.

Conclusion

In Chapter 4, we examined the efforts made by the bishops, abbesses, and vicars to pull the convent together as a community—efforts that succeeded in preventing a new outbreak of rebellion. But in this chapter, we saw that the relative calm that prevailed in the convent masked a number of serious problems. The convent was not attracting enough women or enough of the "right kind" of women (that is, dowry-paying choir nuns) to assure healthy growth. In the beginning, the rebellions of the 1760s were no doubt a major reason for the lag in recruitment. But as time went on, the financial problems that resulted from a combination of the sluggish growth of the endowment, the generous spending that had been deemed necessary in order to preserve the peace, and problems in collecting the interest owed on debts (endemic in church institutions), among other things, came to constitute an independent drag on recruitment. The convent that had been meant for 72 choir nuns and 6 legas never topped 41, fewer than half of whom, in any given year, were likely to have paid the full 3,000-peso dowry of a choir nun.

The financial crisis eventually served as a pretext for Bishop San Miguel and his closest adviser, later bishop-elect Manuel Abad y Queipo, to impose a more rational and modern style of life on La Purísima—a style of life to which they were led philosophically as well as pragmatically: the vida particular. A wrenching and ultimately unpopular decision in a convent that had made its peace with its own version of the vida común, the vida particular did manage to slow down the rate of increase in the debt. But in 1810, when the wars for independence broke out, the convent was still as heavily in debt as it had been at the time of the vida particular reform. The steep depression that began in 1810, then, meant genuine financial catastrophe for La Purísima, which had no cushion on which to fall back when the economy collapsed. Once again, the continued existence of the convent was in considerable doubt. The painful adjustments that the nuns and the convent had to make to the changed situation, and the surprising success that they enjoyed (at least by some measures), is the story of Chapter 6.

NOTES

1. Brading, *Church and State*, 83.

2. Abbess María Gertrudis de San José to Provisor Dr. D. Miguel de Contreras, 10 January 1778, AHAM, Diocesano, Gobierno, Religiosas, Catarinas, Clarisas, Concepcionistas, caja 254 (XVIII), exp. 12.

3. "Autos sobre la Visita, y Elección de Vicaria Abadesa, y nombramiento de Oficialas del Convento . . . 1782," AHAM, Diocesano, Gobierno, Religiosas, Concepcionistas, caja 255 (XVIII), exp. 19.

4. Abbess María Augustina de la Santísima Encarnación to Vicar Ignacio Antonio Palacios, 1787, AHAM, Diocesano, Gobierno, Religiosas, Concepcionistas, caja 255 (XVIII), exp. 32.

5. The Sautto family was involved in a protracted feud with the Landeta-Canal-Lanzagorta families and had even tried to prevent the new convent from being built because it required closing off one entrance to the city that was close to the Sautto obraje (Salvucci, 426), but interestingly, a descendant of this family, José Luis Sautto, became one of the most successful mayordomos of the convent in the 1840s.

6. For Santa Clara, Gallagher, 109; for Santa Catarina and Nuestra Señora de la Salud, documents concerning entrances and professions.

7. "Entrada . . . Doña María Antonia Peres Gonsalo . . . 1768," AHAM, Diocesano, Gobierno, Religiosas, Capuchinas, caja 210 (XVIII), exp. 36.

8. Gallagher, 139. She also states that *all* of the 99 choir nuns who professed at

Santa Clara from 1775 to 1810 belonged to the social elite (their families were among the titled nobility or came from the higher reaches of the ecclesiastical, military, or civil hierarchies). In contrast to Gallagher, Ellen Gunnarsdóttir, "The Convent of Santa Clara, the Elite and Social Change in Eighteenth Century Querétaro," *Journal of Latin American Studies* 33:2 (May 2001), argues that, by around 1770, the convent of Santa Clara was no longer drawing the daughters of the wealthiest and most prominent Querétaro families. Her method, however, was to work from the lists of municipal council members and residents of the homes around the central plaza—that is, to start with the socioeconomic elite—and to look for relationships to nuns, whereas Gallagher started with the nuns and compiled lists of offices held by members of their families, sometimes dating back two generations. Thus, Gallagher, by defining social status to include a much broader range of offices and other indicators, used a method that will always yield a "higher" social profile. Both methods have their advantages, but since my main point here is to distinguish between the poor and the well-off nuns, Gallagher's more precise tabulations (in an appendix, she lists every girl who professed, including the names of her parents and her birthplace) better suit my purposes.

9. A convent of Capuchinas was founded in Salvatierra in 1798, after a delay of 32 years; the convent known as La Enseñanza was founded in Irapuato in 1804 by the French teaching order, the Company of Mary, after a delay of 38 years. Efforts to found a Carmelite convent in Valladolid began in 1808, but the convent was not established until 1824.

10. Particularly saintly women who did not live in a beaterio might also be known as beatas.

11. Beaterio de Jesús Nazareno in Celaya, established 1734; Colegio de Santa Rosa in Valladolid, 1743; Beaterio de Santa Anna, San Miguel el Grande, 1754; Beaterio de San Nicolás Obispo, San Luis Potosí, by 1765; Beaterio de Carmelitas, Salvatierra, 1750; Beaterio de Carmelitas, also known as Beaterio de Santa Teresa, Valladolid, 1774; Beaterio de Nuestra Señora de Guadalupe de Teresas Dominicas, by 1788; Beaterio de Santo Domingo, San Miguel el Grande, by 1791; Beaterio de Niñas Educandas, Pátzcuaro, 1795. References from miscellaneous cajas in AHAM.

12. "Catálogo de las Señoras, y Niñas, que actualmente se hallan en el Colegio de S. S. Nicolas Obispo de esta Ciudad de S. Luis Potosí," AHAM, Diocesano, Gobierno, Visitas, Informes, caja 501 (XVIII), exp. 55; "Señoras y Niñas del Colegio de S. Sta. Anna," AHAM, Diocesano, Gobierno, Visitas, Informes, caja 504 (XVIII), exp. 66; "Cathálogo de las Señoras de Hábito, y Niñas Recogidas del Beaterio de Jesús Nazareno de esta Ciudad de la Puríssima Concepción de Celaya," AHAM, Diocesano, Gobierno, Visitas, Informes, caja 502 (XVIII), exp. 65. All catalogs are from 1765 or 1766. In fact, it is unlikely that not a single one of the beatas at Jesús Nazareno could read or write, since four niñas were listed as "learning" to read. But the fact that the visitor chose not to list reading and writing as skills, but did provide detailed lists of the "feminine arts" in which the beatas excelled, says something about the differences between the ways that beatas and nuns were perceived.

13. "Señoras y Niñas del Colegio de S. Sta. Anna," AHAM, Diocesano, Gobierno, Visitas, Informes, caja 504 (XVIII), exp. 66.

14. Based on 57 marriages in which the amounts brought to the marriage by

both partners are known. Source: Notary records and estate inventories found in AHAM, Archivo de Notarías de Morelia, Archivo Judicial del Estado de Michoacán, Archivo del Ayuntamiento de Pátzcuaro.

15. Lavrin, "The Role of the Nunneries"; Lavrin, "Problems."

16. In Mexico City, female convents were major property owners and provided a significant amount of rental housing in the city.

17. Mercantile lenders, by contrast, could refuse to do business with noncompliant borrowers, a relatively effective way to ensure prompt debt service. The same threat on the part of the church would not carry the same weight, since the church rarely did day-to-day, or even year-to-year, business with its borrowers. Moreover, while merchants were theoretically bound by usury laws, they found a number of ways to get around them that were not available, or less available, to church lenders; mercantile loans were thus more costly and, therefore, were likely to be redeemed and serviced more diligently.

18. "Correspondencia de monjas . . . 1795," AHAM, Diocesano, Gobierno, Religiosas, Catarinas, caja 249 (XVIII), exp. 450.

19. "Cuentas presentadas por D. Josef Mariano Loreto de la Canal . . . 1770 al presente año de 1775," AHAM, Diocesano, Gobierno, Religiosas, Capuchinas, caja 211, exp. 44; "Cuentas presentadas por Josef Mariano Loreto de la Canal . . . 1782," AHAM, Diocesano, Gobierno, Religiosas, Concepcionistas, caja 255 (XVIII), exp. 17; "Cuentas . . . 1791," AHAM, Diocesano, Gobierno, Religiosas, Concepcionistas, caja 255 (XVIII), exp. 42.

20. Eighteen came from towns and cities that were about 50 miles away (5 from Querétaro, 2 from Celaya, and 11 from Guanajuato). Four others came from towns that were within the intendancy (later, state) of Guanajuato, but distant or difficult to reach from San Miguel: one from Salamanca, one from Villa de San Felipe, and two from León.

21. In 1781, Santa Catarina's endowment was 381,454 pesos, including 85,000 in litigation, and it added approximately 25,000 pesos in endowment over the next decade; Nuestra Señora de la Salud's endowment was 254,897 pesos in 1791, and in the same year, La Purísima's endowment was 148,500 pesos. "Cuentas (Santa Catarina) . . . 1781," AHAM, Diocesano, Gobierno, Religiosas, Catarinas, caja 242, exp. 335; "Renovación del mayordomía (de Nuestra Señora de la Salud) de D. Ignacio Barandiarán . . . 1791," AHAM, Diocesano, Gobierno, Religiosas, Dominicas, caja 265, exp. 136; "Cuentas (La Purísima Concepción) . . . 1792," AHAM, Diocesano, Gobierno, Religiosas, Concepcionistas, caja 255 (XVIII), exp. 42.

22. Vicar Ignacio Antonio Palacios to Bishop Fray Antonio de San Miguel, 22 August 1787 (included in the accounts for 1786), AHAM, Diocesano, Gobierno, Religiosas, Concepcionistas, caja 255 (XVIII), exp. 32.

23. Ecclesiastical authorities concerned about La Purísima's financial state gave some consideration to increasing the amount of the dowry in order to make up for income shortages. At the convent of Santa Catarina, for example, it had been decided to raise the dowry from 3,000 to 4,000 pesos in the late 1770s. But at least one contemporary attributed the decline in the number of professions to that convent in the 1780s to the increase in the dowry, and this reasoning led authorities to reject a similar move for La Purísima until the very end of the colonial period, when price infla-

tion made it absolutely necessary. It was felt that since the San Miguel convent was not as well established as Santa Catarina, an increase in the dowry would be especially disastrous there. Bishop Fray Antonio de San Miguel to Vicar Ignacio Antonio Palacios, 19 February 1786 (included in the accounts for 1786), AHAM, Diocesano, Gobierno, Religiosas, Concepcionistas, caja 255 (XVIII), exp. 32.

24. Abbess Josefa Ygnacia de Santa Gertrudis to Lic. D. Joachín de Cuevas, 26 June 1782, AHAM, Diocesano, Gobierno, Religiosas, Concepcionistas, caja 255 (XVIII), exp. 19.

25. Abbess María Augustina de la Encarnación to Bishop Fray Antonio de San Miguel, 1792, AHAM, Diocesano, Gobierno, Religiosas, Concepcionistas, caja 255 (XVIII), exp. 40.

26. De Vos, "The Art of Pharmacy."

27. Abbess Josefa Ygnacia de Santa Gertrudis to Lic. D. Joachín de Cuevas, 26 June 1782, AHAM, Diocesano, Gobierno, Religiosas, Concepcionistas, caja 255 (XVIII), exp. 19.

28. "Auto de varias providencias . . . [por] Lic. Joachín de Cuevas," 14 August 1782, AHAM, Diocesano, Gobierno, Religiosas, Concepcionistas, caja 255 (XVIII), exp. 19.

29. Abbess María Augustina de la Santísima Encarnación to Vicar Ignacio Antonio Palacios, 1787, AHAM, Diocesano, Gobierno, Religiosas, Concepcionistas, caja 255 (XVIII), exp. 32.

30. Definitorio to Vicar Ignacio Antonio Palacios, 16 February 1787, AHAM, Diocesano, Gobierno, Religiosas, Concepcionistas, caja 255 (XVIII), exp. 32.

31. Vicar Ignacio Antonio Palacios to Bishop Fray Antonio de San Miguel, 18 July 1787, AHAM, Diocesano, Gobierno, Religiosas, Concepcionistas, caja 255 (XVIII), exp. 32.

32. "Estado actual . . . del Convento de Santa Catharina de Sena . . . 1787," AHAM, Diocesano, Gobierno, Religiosas, Catarinas, caja 246 (XVIII), exp. 398.

33. "Valladolid, 1793. Sobre Nuevo arreglo, y assistencias pecuniarias a las Religiosas Dominicas del convento de Ntra Sra de la Salud de Pazquaro, entre tanto se restablecen sus fondos en estado de sufrir los precisos gastos de la vida rigurosamente común," AHAM, Diocesano, Gobierno, Religiosas, Dominicas, caja 266 (XVIII), exp. 145.

34. "Visita suspendiendo por ahora e interin se desempeña el Convento la Vida común en quanto a las asistencias de las Religiosas, y no en mas," 1792, AHAM, Diocesano, Gobierno, Religiosas, Concepcionistas, caja 255 (XVIII), exp. 42.

35. Sr. D. Narciso María Loreto de la Canal to Vicar Ignacio Antonio Palacios, 23 July 1794, AHAM, Diocesano, Gobierno, Religiosas. Concepcionistas, caja 255 (XVIII), exp. 42.

36. "Cuentas de monjas del Sagrado convento de Religiosas . . . 1791–1797," AHAM, Diocesano, Gobierno, Religiosas, Dominicas, caja 267, exp. 159; "Cuentas . . . 1797–1804," AHAM, Diocesano, Gobierno, Religiosas, Dominicas, caja 267, exp. 161.

37. For a more detailed examination of this report, see Chowning, "Convent Reform."

38. For a discussion of internal contradictions and inconsistencies in these reform efforts, see Chowning, "Convent Reform."

39. On the continuation of cooperative efforts in these regards, see Voekel.

40. Juvenal Jaramillo Magaña, *Hacia una iglesia beligerante: La gestión episcopal de Fray Antonio de San Miguel en Michoacán (1784–1804): Los proyectos ilustrados y las defensas canónicas* (Zamora: Colegio de Michoacán, 1996), 27; Horst Pietschmann, "Consideraciones en torno al protoliberalismo, reformas borbónicas y revolución. La Nueva España en el último tercio del siglo XVIII," *Historia mexicana* 41:2 (Oct.–Dec. 1991).

41. William B. Taylor, *Magistrates of the Sacred: Priests and Parishioners in Eighteenth-Century Mexico* (Stanford, Calif.: Stanford University Press, 1996), 16–17.

42. This important legislation receives a full treatment in Nancy Farriss, *Crown and Clergy in Colonial Mexico, 1759–1821: The Crisis of Ecclesiastical Privilege* (London: Athlone, 1968), especially chapter 7. The quotation appears on p. 103. See also Brian Connaughton, *Ideología y sociedad en Guadalajara (1788–1853)* (Mexico City: Consejo Nacional para la Cultura y las Artes, 1992), 84.

43. Pietschmann, 175.

44. Francisco Morales, *Clero y política en México (1767–1834): Algunas ideas sobre la autoridad, la independencia y la reforma eclesiástica* (Mexico City: Sep Setentas, 1975), 51; Carlos Herrejón Peredo, "México: Las luces de Hidalgo y Abad y Queipo," *Caravelle: Cahiers du monde hispanique et luso-bresilien*, 54 (1990), 115. Abad's essays are collected in Manuel Abad y Queipo, *Colección de los escritos más importantes que en diferentes épocas dirigió al govierno* (Mexico City: Mariano Ontiveros, 1813).

45. Quoted in Brading, *Church and State*, 230, 232.

46. Lillian Estelle Fisher, *Champion of Reform: Manuel Abad y Queipo* (New York: Library Publishers, 1955), 72–73.

47. Jaramillo, 161.

48. Brading, *Church and State*, 232; Jaramillo, 176, 180.

49. "Visita . . . 1793," AHAM, Diocesano, Gobierno, Religiosas, Concepcionistas, caja 255 (XVIII), exp. 42.

50. "Visita . . . 1793," AHAM, Diocesano, Gobierno, Religiosas, Concepcionistas, caja 255 (XVIII), exp. 42.

51. "Visita . . . 1797," AHAM, Diocesano, Gobierno, Religiosas, Concepcionistas, caja 255 (XVIII), exp. 50.

52. Abbess María Manuela de San Raphael to Bishop Fray Antonio de San Miguel, 28 July 1797, AHAM, Diocesano, Gobierno, Religiosas, Concepcionistas, caja 255 (XVIII), exp. 42.

53. "Visita . . . 1797," AHAM, Diocesano, Gobierno, Religiosas, Concepcionistas, caja 255 (XVIII), exp. 50.

54. "Visita . . . 1800," AHAM, Diocesano, Gobierno, Religiosas, Concepcionistas, caja 374 (XIX), exp. 1.

55. Mónica Lavín, *Dulces hábitos: Golosinas del convento* (Mexico City: Clío, 2000); Mónica Lavín, *Sor Juana en la cocina* (Mexico City: Clío, 2000); Rosalva Loreto López, *Un bocado para los ángeles: La cocina conventual novohispana* (Mexico City: Clío, 2000).

56. Kathryn Burns does describe the financially pressed nuns of some Cuzco convents as relying on sales of small items they manufactured in order to survive, but this was in the aftermath of the Great Rebellion. The same frustrations on the part of officials were expressed there as at La Purísima: "Their rules and conduct manuals

warned sternly against making and selling large quantities of anything," Burns writes, "yet the nuns had little choice but to look beyond their locutorios in search of a living" (182).

57. Quoted in Antonio Ignacio Laserna Gaitán, "El último de reforma de los monasterios femeninos en el Perú colonial: El auto del arzobispado Parada de 1775," *Anuario de Estudios Americanos* 52:2 (1995), 277.

58. "Visita y Capítulo del convento de Religiosas de Purísima Concepción de la Villa de San Miguel el Grande," 1806, AHAM, Diocesano, Gobierno, Religiosas, Concepcionistas, caja 374, exp. 1. In the same expediente is the formal recommendation prepared by Lic. Ignacio Alvarez Gato, the vicar general for monasteries under the vacant see. Alvarez Gato based his report on Uraga's, accepting his view that the nuns themselves preferred the common life and acknowledging the problems caused by the vida particular. The most he could do, however, was to warn the nuns in stern language that they must observe decorum, remind them that preservation of enclosure was of paramount importance, and urge them to follow the Rule and not to let their personal goals stand in the way of this commitment. The only specific recommendation he made was to prescribe uniform clothing for the niñas and the servants.

6

La Purísima after Independence

Toward Extinction

One of the most moving documents in the convent correspondence of the late colonial period is a letter written by Manuela de la Santísima Trinidad to Bishop Antonio de San Miguel in June 1793, asking for permission to accompany the nuns of "La Enseñanza" (the French Company of Mary) to found a new convent. In her distraught letter, Manuela explained that she had been working for many years toward the foundation of a Conceptionist convent dedicated to Our Lady of Guadalupe, an "advocation that my heart has always adored," in the northern city of Aguascalientes, the birthplace of an increasing number of girls and women in the San Miguel convent. The new foundation would be an extension of La Purísima; she and three or four others from San Miguel would go out as founding nuns, just as Antonia del Santísimo Sacramento, María Anna del Santísimo Sacramento, Phelipa de San Antonio, and Gertrudis de San Raphael had done 37 years earlier.

She explained that she had lined up patrons and benefactors, collected letters and documents from the city council and the citizenry in favor of the foundation, and made sure that there were funds pledged to acquire appropriately elegant instruments of mass for the sacristy and to stock the infirmary. When all of this had been completed to her satisfaction, she had sent the documents to Viceroy Revillagigedo, asking him to help her obtain a royal license. He was favorably inclined, especially after he received a positive report from the three officials he sent to Aguascalientes to investigate the possibility of a successful foundation. But then things started to go wrong. The viceregal fiscal, a high-level official with the ear of Revillagigedo, began to press for the convent to be founded by nuns of the Company of Mary, a teaching order, instead of nuns from La Purísima, and he prevailed. If she wanted to remain part of the new convent at all, Manuela had no recourse but to beg, "with tormenting pain in my heart," to be allowed to join the Marian nuns (with whose Rule she was not even familiar, she said) in the foundation that she had worked so hard to bring to fruition.[1]

Manuela de la Santísima Trinidad's eagerness, at age 59, to leave the convent where she had spent 37 years of her life, to found a new convent that would surely experience many of the growing pains that La Purísima had suffered, and that she had suffered along with her sisters, is a powerful testament to her belief that the traditional convent still had a central role to play in Mexican Catholicism. By the 1790s, however, as we have seen, that belief had already begun to fade in the highest reaches of the diocesan hierarchy. Manuel Abad y Queipo and Bishop Antonio de San Miguel's willingness to tolerate a convent that was as much attuned to the virtues espoused by Adam Smith as to those of St. Teresa was an early indication that they no longer saw the female convent in the same way as earlier Catholic reformers had done. Increasingly, church authorities leaned toward the idea that, if there was a place for the convent in the modern world, it was as an institution that served a positive social good, not (or at least, not primarily) as an expensive and financially inefficient institution devoted to prayer alone, and available to only a tiny minority of the female devout. Although it was the viceroy, and not the bishop, who had the final say in choosing a teaching order over a contemplative order for the new foundation in Aguascalientes, the bishop acquiesced in the decision, and indeed, in the nineteenth century, the Mexican church, as the church in many parts of Europe had done earlier, began to allow, and even encourage, new roles for women in religion, de-emphasizing the enclosed, contemplative convent, and supporting instead the foundation of teaching, charitable, and later, nursing orders, and the establishment of lay organizations of women.

Given the precedent among the European churches, it is almost certain that this shift would have taken place in Mexico eventually. But the wars for independence at once speeded up and delayed the transition, by dramatically altering the social, economic, and political context in which the convents operated. Events hastened the demise of the old convent, but also made it difficult for a new kind of convent to emerge, as it did in most of Catholic Europe. There was no burgeoning of the number of female religious in nineteenth-century Mexico, as there was, for example, in France, Italy, Ireland, and Germany.[2] Instead, the number of female religious slowly shrank until, in 1863, they were forced out of the convents. The literature on the Mexican convent in the nineteenth century is quite weak, so the context in which we should place La Purísima's history is poorly established, but it appears that, in a story of general decline, La Purísima was among the convents that suffered the most.

La Purísima on the Eve of Independence

In 1810, just before the wars for independence began, it might have seemed that La Purísima was about to turn a corner in its long struggle for institutional success. In his report on the 1809 visitation, Vicar Francisco de Uraga produced an uncharacteristically optimistic report. First, during the tenure of Abbess Augustina de la Encarnación (one of the notorious Urbina sisters from the days of the rebellion), the convent had begun to resolve some long-standing problems with its physical structure. Taking office in 1800, Augustina had initiated a process that culminated, 4 years later, in a lawsuit against the five heirs of the Count of Casa de Loja to force them to pay for repairs to the convent, parts of which were described as "threatening imponderable ruin."[3] The grounds for the lawsuit were that the count had taken responsibility, in numerous documents, for finishing the convent and its church, but had never done so. Besides the half-finished walls that threatened the very chastity of the nuns, the suit pointed out that the church was supposed to be a "perfect Cross," but only the foot of the cross had been completed, while the altar was built against a "temporary" adobe wall that was likely to come crashing down at any moment. At the time that the nuns moved into their new convent in 1765, the supporting documents for the suit alleged, it was "common knowledge" that there was still much work that remained to be done. Since that time, however, the count's estate had paid for no work at all, except for a second-story cloister built in 1797. Necessary repairs and construction costs had been borne either by the convent or by the bishop.[4]

The count's heirs fought back against the lawsuit, arguing that, if there was unfinished work, it was because the funds with which he had been entrusted to complete the convent—specifically, the foundress's 58,000-peso inheritance—had run out; indeed, they produced documents to demonstrate that he had, in fact, spent 11,345 pesos more than this amount, out of his own pocket.[5] Furthermore, they pointed out, much of the work that the nuns wanted done fell into the category of maintenance, for which they had no responsibility. The convent claimed, for example, that the cracked dome over the main door entrance had never been properly finished, but the count's son pointed out that one of the abbesses had planted peach trees on top of the roof; the damage, he said, came from the weight of the trees and water, not from poor or unfinished construction. In light of this evidence, the bishop's office backed off and declined to support the lawsuit. But although the convent was foiled in its attempt to get the count's estate to help the convent make needed repairs, it did succeed in calling sufficient attention to the problem that the intendant, as representative of the king (who was, in turn, patron of the convent), appears to have stepped in and helped with some of the more urgent projects.[6] In any event, by the 1809 inspection, Vicar Uraga could point to significant improvements.

Second, the 1809 report also noted, in this positive vein, that the convent's accounts were in the competent hands of a new mayordomo, the first manager who was not a member of the Canal family. Many defects (unspecified) in the collection of interest income had been remedied, Uraga wrote. Before this new mayordomo had taken over, expenses had consistently exceeded the amounts collected, even though spending had been cut to a minimum, with the institution of the vida particular. Thus, the overall debt had continued to mount yearly. But a grateful Uraga observed, "this has ceased with the new Mayordomo who has been appointed, and thanks to his energy and exactitude this branch [the collection of interest income] is proceeding nicely."[7]

But Uraga also identified an ominous problem: The convent population was top-heavy with elderly nuns. During the previous 15 years (since 1794), only seven nuns had entered the convent (three more entered a year later, in 1810, in what was perhaps a too-hasty burst of recruitment, since one of the novices who entered the convent that year turned out to be as obnoxious as she was long-lived). There were fewer nuns in 1809 (38) than in 1797 (41), well below the 78 envisioned by María Josepha Lina de la Canal when she wrote the convent's constitution in 1754.[8] Making matters worse, Uraga wrote, among the older nuns, there were few with good leadership abilities. Of the 28 nuns who met the criteria for high office—they were choir nuns of legitimate birth who had been professed for at least 8 years—5 were too sick to serve, and others, he said, were disqualified either because of their advanced age or because they lacked "those qualities that are required in order to maintain good order in the Community." Thus, the recruitment woes that had afflicted the convent almost from the beginning continued. As we will see, they were to grow much worse after independence, but it is worth emphasizing the extent to which La Purísima entered the post-1810 period with a population that was already aging and experiencing a shortage of good leaders.

Insurgency and Independence, 1810–1821

The wars for independence that broke out in and around San Miguel in 1810, and lasted for almost a decade, gave the city a heroic reputation and a change of name (from San Miguel el Grande to San Miguel de Allende, in honor of its most famous independence hero, Ignacio Allende), but they were catastrophic for the local society and economy.[9] As one of the original centers of the insurgency, San Miguel was occupied by the troops of the Spanish commander Manuel Flon in October 1810 (his arrival having been preceded by an announcement that nothing would be left standing of the city), and the houses of the Canal, Allende, Aldama, Lanzagorta, Malo, and other families implicated in the revolution were sacked.[10] After Flon's departure, as De la Maza tells it, the city

> regained in part its former calm, but its . . . tranquility was an illu-
> sion. It was left abandoned, since the Spaniards, lifeblood of com-
> merce, had fled; the creoles, boisterous and rebellious, who with the
> former had formed the upper crust of society, had joined the war;
> the workers and farmers filled the ranks of the insurgent armies;
> and the local regiment of soldiers fought in distant provinces. In-
> dustry was paralyzed; commerce scarcely existed and poverty took
> hold of the city for the first time in its history.[11]

For the next 7 years, San Miguel was transformed into a wary, nervous city of the overnight poor. Its citizens—those who did not flee to Mexico City or Spain—walked the streets armed against the numerous bandit and/or insur-gent armies that threatened it always and succeeded in occupying it on several occasions. (One of the more infamous leaders of these bands, or "gavillas," was apprehended just as he was preparing to break down the main door of the convent of La Purísima in order to remove the riches that important citizens had supposedly hidden with the nuns.)[12]

If the town, as a whole, suffered, the cloistered nuns of La Purísima were hit especially hard, since they had no option of flight, no possibility of seeking new sources of revenue, and no ability (beyond appeals to his conscience) to command that their mayordomo devote more of his own energies to their business affairs. In this, they were not alone: The decade of insurgency was disastrous for all five of the female convents in the bishopric, since their in-come depended on the willingness of borrowers to service their debts, on time and in full. As we have seen, debt collection was not easy—even in good times—and in these horrendous times, it became almost impossible. Else-where in Mexico, the female convents did not suffer as much because more of their wealth was in urban property, whose rents remained relatively high. This was particularly true of Mexico City, where approximately 80% of con-ventual wealth was propertied wealth. Outside of the capital city, in other bish-oprics besides Michoacán, about half of the assets of the female convents' wealth was in mortgages on large rural estates and half in rents on property. This was compared with a ratio of propertied wealth to liens and loans in Michoacán of about 1:8.[13]

In 1811, disruption was the order of the day, but outright destruction was not yet widespread. La Purísima's income fell from an average collection, in recent years, of slightly under 6,000 pesos (about 2,000 pesos short of what the outstanding capital should have produced in interest), to around 4,500 pesos.[14] In 1812, interest income dropped sharply again, to 3,433 pesos, but it was in 1813 that the real disaster began: For 6 years, from 1813 to 1818, the convent was able to collect only an average of around 1,800 pesos a year, and in several years, the collection barely topped 1,000 pesos—this was less than a fifth of the amount that the convent needed to pay the nuns' allowances under the vida particular; to pay the salaries of their doctors, pharmacists, sacristans, and errand runners; and to purchase enough wine, oil, and candles to preserve some semblance of religious observance.[15] Even the Canal family reneged on debt service, beginning in 1813. This turned out not to be a bad thing in the long term, since the new mayordomo arranged for the debt that the convent had accumulated in favor of the previous mayordomo, Narciso María Loreto de la Canal, to be reduced by the amount that the Canal family owed, so some of the convent's huge debt, dating from the 1770s, finally began to disappear. But in the meantime, the nuns were deprived of 1,200 pesos a year that the Canals had regularly paid in interest until now.[16]

As we have seen, one of the complaints at La Purísima about the vida particular was that the allowance of 12 pesos a month (increased from 10 pesos because of the significant inflation in food and other costs around the turn of the century) for each choir nun did not cover their most basic needs—hence, the need for them to enter the market as small producers.[17] Now, however, they were forced to accept a reduction in this already insufficient portion. In 1818, the choir nuns agreed to try to live on 10 pesos a month instead of 12 (with two exceptions), while the legas took between 5 and 7 pesos instead of 8, and the donadas, 4 pesos instead of 5.[18] This reduction in their allowances, however, did not even come close to aligning the convent's income with its expenditures, and the vicar, Francisco de Uraga, had to try to make up the difference using a combination of parish surpluses, loans that he arranged from local creditors, and his own personal wealth—mainly the latter.[19] The situation grew so dire that, in 1819, in a letter to the cathedral chapter of the bishopric (which was in charge of convent affairs under the vacant see), he sadly proposed the unthinkable—to extinguish the San Miguel convent and transfer the nuns to another monastery:

> . . . the economic state of this Monastery of Religiosas is more infe-
> licitous than Your Excellencies can imagine, and it demands more
> funds than those to which I have access. In the beginning I believed
> that the new Mayordomo would collect its rents more effectively
> [than the previous mayordomo] and would be capable of alleviating
> my burden in part, given his activity and industrious determination.
> In fact, he has done the best that he can: he has given powers of
> attorney to commissioned agents, he has pursued judicial settle-
> ments, and he has taken legal recourse against distant debtors; but
> after much expense and many delays, nothing has been achieved,
> and my monthly expenditure has continued. It is true that last year I
> had a brief respite, with the dowry of a nun [which we spent instead
> of invested], and that lasted until November; but since then there

has only been one month [in which I have not had to support the convent from my own funds]. I have personally invested around 24,000 pesos, an amount that would seem incredible if there were not receipts to show for it . . .

Uraga went on to hint at a lack of responsiveness and understanding of the situation on the part of episcopal authorities:

I am beginning to realize that if I were to die, the nuns would perish; and even while I live, I fear I will have to watch them die of hunger without being able to do anything about it. I have consulted with Your Excellencies various times; once you told me to sell the silver of the Church but there is such a small amount that [the proceeds from its sale] would scarcely last for a month; on another occasion you told me to borrow at interest from wealthy citizens; but there are none [in San Miguel]. Thus it seems to me that there is only one option: it is hard, but there is no other, and it is that these Religiosas be transferred from here to other Convents of their Rule, taking with them the lien documents for their dowries, as the late Abbess suggested to me, a thing which seemed to me strange at the time, and impracticable; but I now realize that we must contemplate this solution, because surely much time will pass before even current interest can be collected, not to mention back interest, that is, unless God works a miracle, as it seems He has done until now. Perhaps, Your Excellencies, the oppression of my spirit has made me think so darkly but it is good to prepare for the worst: I beg you to forgive me, and to apply all the grace and serenity of your great learning and advise me what measures would be most effective, in order not to arrive at such an extreme course of action.[20]

San Miguel and La Purísima in the Postindependence World

Two years after Uraga wrote this despairing letter, after over a decade of warfare and disruption, Mexico finally achieved its independence from Spain. But despite widespread euphoria over the successful revolution, building a new nation and rebuilding its economy proved to be extremely difficult. The magnitude of the economic task was especially great in those parts of the country (like the region around San Miguel) that had been powerfully dependent on the silver economy. The mines had been abandoned or destroyed during the wars, and putting them back into production was such a costly enterprise that only well-capitalized foreign (mainly British) companies could entertain the possibility of doing so. In the end, even these companies were frustrated by the expense of transporting new equipment to the geographical center of the country, across long stretches of mountainous terrain, in order to try to drain the mine shafts that had flooded with disuse or destruction. Thus, the silver mines did not begin to come back into anything approaching full production (by pre-1810 standards) until the 1840s.

But even then, San Miguel did not regain its former status as a thriving small town connected to the silver economy. The mining centers that had once been the main markets for San Miguel's textiles, leather goods, and tools now had other options for these supplies: Foreign imports were both cheaper and of higher quality than could be produced in San Miguel or by any other do-mestic manufacturer. The city's days as an industrial center were over. The textile factories disappeared, although cottage weaving industries continued to exist, helping to preserve the reputation of the town's citizens as industrious and hardworking. After 1835 or so, the city did resume some of its commercial functions, but with independence, the abandonment of many mines, and the opening of new western ports, the most important route became not the old colonial route between Mexico City and the silver mining north, but rather the route between Mexico City and Guadalajara, and it bypassed San Miguel to the south. Instead of stopping in San Miguel, most travelers and merchandise instead went through Celaya, Salamanca, and Irapuato on their way from Mex-ico City to either Guadalajara or Guanajuato.[21] By the time the railroad came to San Miguel, toward the end of the nineteenth century, it was such a sleepy town that, when the trains arrived, between 2:00 A.M. and 4:00 A.M., porters and drivers did not even bother to meet them.[22] As late as 1941, one traveler wrote that, although San Miguel was not that far from the cities of Celaya and Querétaro, "the roads are not good for motoring, and in the wet season they are virtually impassable"; the 1938 *Motorist Guide to Mexico* did not even men-tion the town.[23] Ironically, the relative lack of economic opportunity meant that San Miguel did not suffer nearly as many of the physical transformations that more prosperous Mexican cities experienced; thus, in the late 1930s, when North American artists, who transformed the Canal summer home into an art school, the Instituto Allende, and later, tourists, discovered San Miguel, its colonial charm was very much intact—its disadvantages turned into opportu-nity. But the ancestors of those who have benefited from the tourism boom paid a high price for it.

The Deepening Recruitment Crisis

The painfully slow recovery of the economy of the region in the postindepen-dence period goes far to explain one of the central themes in La Purísima's nineteenth-century history: its failure to replace its aging population. From the 38 professed nuns (choir nuns and legas) that the vicar, in 1809, had already considered inadequate, the number fell to 24 in 1823 and to 17 in 1844. By

1857, the number of choir nuns and legas was only 14, despite a recruitment bubble in 1854.[24] Other convents in Mexico also shrank after 1810, but few as dramatically as this one. No doubt the reduced economic prospects of many of the prominent families of the region caused them to think twice about taking on new debt in order to pay for a daughter to enter a convent—the 3,000-peso dowry that had seemed a reasonable price to pay for a girl's safety and honor before 1810 now appeared to be quite a high price indeed. And even if the parents of prospective nuns had been willing to take a new lien on their property to pay a dowry, in many cases—at least through the 1830s and into the 1840s—they had insufficient collateral to do so, since both urban and rural property (though especially the latter) had lost much of its value in the wars for independence and was slow to recover to pre-1810 levels.

Worse, the convent dowry, fixed at 3,000 pesos, could not adjust to changed circumstances in the way that marriage dowries could. The marriage dowry, as a custom and institution, was on the decline anyway in late eighteenth- and early nineteenth-century Mexico, and after 1810, it virtually disappeared. Furthermore, the average amount that a young woman brought to her marriage by way of expected inheritance (at least in the southern part of the bishopric, in what is now the state of Michoacán) was less than half of what it had been in the three previous decades.[25] Thus, if we can imagine a world in which decisions about how best to place one's daughter in a socially acceptable situation were made strictly on the basis of cost, marriage became more of a bargain than the convent. Of course, this was never such a world— entrance into the convent was at least as often a spiritual decision as it was a social decision, and almost never lacked a strong spiritual component. Nonetheless, comparing the fixed dowry needed to enter a convent and the diminishing prospects of inheritance required to make a good marriage allows us to see clearly that economics worked against the recruitment of new nuns in the post-1810 period.

But there were other factors, besides the weak economy, that discouraged entrance into the convent. Most obvious was the heated and unstable political climate, in which some of the most inflated rhetoric and passionate controversy revolved around the question of the role of the church in Mexican society.[26] There were three aspects of political posturing and policy-making that had a direct effect on the convents and their ability to attract new postulants.

First, the convents suffered, in a material sense, as a result of government policy. After independence, the wealth of the church was no longer considered untouchable by any government, no matter its ideological leanings.[27] All of the postindependence governments were impecunious, and all cast an invidious eye on the vast assets of the church, including the female convents—no matter that much of this wealth existed on paper only, in the form of mortgages on the homes and rural estates of the propertied classes. Both liberals (self-righteously) and conservatives (apologetically) tapped the church for loans that everyone knew would never be repaid, demanded that the church guarantee loans made to the government by private lenders, and used property tax policies to skim off a portion of the church's income. The property taxes hurt the convents directly, to the extent that they were owners of real property, and indirectly, since private borrowers frequently announced that they were reducing their interest payments in the amount of the new taxes.[28] The government's demands for loans from the church hurt even more. These demands were directed initially to the bishops, who, in turn, looked (among other places) to the convents, and imposed a quota for each convent to contribute, based on the size of its endowment.[29] The bishop implicitly justified the assignment of these quotas by pointing to the diminished size of convent populations—convents with fewer nuns than before no longer needed such a large endowment income in order to survive. Thus, the ecclesiastical policy of requiring the convents to help the church meet its forced loan obligations contributed to the very thing that could be used to justify it: reduced interest in entering a daughter in a convent.

Second, and probably more important, the convents suffered because of the *threat* of material loss. Despite the hated quotas, La Purísima and the other convents did not actually suffer major financial reverses because of government policy or episcopal policy in response to government demands (until, of course, the final blow that nationalized their wealth and closed the convents down altogether in 1863). But the threat of imminent attacks on the church's assets was ever-present. Several times, proposals to nationalize church wealth were introduced at the national level, only to be beaten back furiously by the church and its conservative allies. Evidence that this threat was perceived as very real is that, on more than one occasion, the abbess of La Purísima asked permission to sell the convent's silver, since (as Josepha del Espiritu Santo put it in 1829, repeating an unfounded rumor) "it is well-known that they are seizing the silver from the temples."[30] The same panicked reactions occurred at other convents (although at the convent of Nuestra Señora de la Salud in Pátzcuaro, it was the mayordomo who had heard the rumor and wanted to sell the silver before it could be confiscated, and the abbess who resisted).[31] The fear of what might happen, in other words, was as damaging to the convents' reputations and prospects as what actually did occur.

Third, there was the ideological antagonism of the so-called liberal purists (*puros*) to the male and female convents. Liberal journalists and politicians used antimonastic diatribes as partisan tools to galvanize opinion against the church, which was the bulwark of the conservative opposition to their policies. Although many liberals articulated a broadly anticlerical agenda, the monasteries came in for early, and particularly vicious, attack, since while the secular church was seen by more moderate liberals (some of whom were personally quite devout) as serving important social purposes, the monastic orders were not.[32] Male religious were condemned (often in witty rhymes and broadsides) as drunkards, womanizers, and social parasites—while nuns were seen as victims of the convent system, which imprisoned them against their will.

José Joaquín Fernández de Lizardi set the tone for writing about the female convents in his 1819 novel *La quijotita y su prima*, in which a father obliged his daughter to enter a convent because she was in love with someone of whom he disapproved. This was a rather mild version of the convent-as-prison trope that was common in the late eighteenth century in France and in the early nineteenth century in Mexico and the United States (both the French and the U.S. critiques of the convent were influential among Mexican liberals). In the early 1830s, a strongly anticlerical government in Mexico was supported by authors like "Tremebundo," whose 1833 tract, "Ridding Ourselves of Nuns and Friars" ("Quitada de Monjas y Frailes"), depicted female convents as places where young girls were warehoused by their families against their will, and spent their days hoping to be liberated from their prisons or looking for a moment when they could escape.[33] This author, like many others, was especially obsessed with the idea that girls who entered convents had no real option to say "no," and once professed, could not change their minds; if girls with a true vocation sincerely wanted to spend their whole lives locked away in a convent, he wrote, so be it, but "let us not deny the door to she who repents of her decision, who wants to use the freedom that God has granted her."

Criticism of the monasteries had, of course, always featured as a distinct theme within anticlerical rhetoric, but in the nineteenth century, the calls for the suppression of the monasteries, liberation of the cloistered nuns, removal of education from the hands of the regulars, and privatization of property owned by the orders were much more openly and widely expressed than before, in the new postindependence context of freedom of the press, elevation of the values of individualism over community, and improved communications with the outside world, including highly vocal anti-Catholic groups in the United States.[34] It is not hard to imagine that the concerted attack on the principles upon which the convents were based (community, enclosure, self-denial) gave rise to fears about the future of the institution on the part of parents, and that hearing and reading about nuns as victims or prisoners had an effect on the girls themselves—who, without necessarily becoming less devout, might very well have chosen another outlet for their religiosity, perhaps as a member of the growing number of female-dominated pious associations.

Even though the convents may have been an easy target for liberal politicians, there was clearly deep ambivalence as to how far one could go in an attack upon the orders. For example, a liberal Spanish parliament, in 1820, had prohibited the admission of novices of either sex to the convents, but the new Mexican nation was not prepared to go that far, and it refused to adopt this law.[35] Some antimonastic legislation was proposed but, until the definitive liberal Reform in the mid-1850s, never passed (for example, nationalization of monastic wealth and forced submission of the convents to civil authority); other laws were passed, but never enforced (laws insisting that public schools replace church schools) or only partially enforced (laws preventing church institutions from selling their property without government permission), or framed in a passive manner (laws giving the full protection of the state to friars and nuns *if* they chose to leave their convents).[36] Still, the fact that many of the liberal proposals did not become effective law was ultimately not very reassuring. In sum, this was a new world, in which both the wealth and the very existence of the convents were fair game in the political arena, and surely these factors dampened enthusiasm for the convent on the part of girls and families who would have considered the religious life as not only an honorable, but also a secure estate just a generation earlier.

The Bishop and the Convent: Changing Episcopal Attitudes toward La Purísima

Besides the weak economy and the antagonistic political climate, however, another more subtle factor played a role in the recruitment drought at La Purísima: the insensitivity of the bishop's office to the needs of this particular convent, one that had never risen to the levels of prestige, wealth, and institutional success of the longer established female convents in the bishopric. In the decade or so after 1810, diocesan inattention derived from the confusion of war and economic collapse and also from the fact that there was no bishop between the death of Marcos Moriana y Zafrilla soon after he arrived in the bishopric in 1809 and the appointment of Juan Cayetano de Portugal in 1831.[37] Convent affairs were handled from 1809 until 1831 by the cathedral chapter and the vicar general for convents, a position that existed officially before 1809, but was not active until after Moriana y Zafrilla's death. But instead of the relationship between the bishopric and the convent improving after the long-delayed arrival of the new bishop, the case for episcopal apathy after 1831 is even more compelling than before. There are two kinds of evidence to suggest that Bishop Juan Cayetano de Portugal (1831–1850), a progressive bishop in the mold of Manuel Abad y Queipo and Bishop Antonio de San Miguel, and the great Reform-era Bishop Clemente de Jesús Munguía (1852–1868) were, at best, of two minds about how to handle the recruitment crisis at La Purísima and, at worst, indifferent to the convent's internal needs, as long as its finances remained stable.

Limiting Admissions

The first body of evidence comprises documents concerning entrances into the convent, which reveal a very strange rhythm of admissions after independence. Between 1832, the first year of Portugal's administration, and 1863, when the convents were closed down by the government, there were only 2 single years when nuns entered La Purísima: 1844, when three novices were admitted, and 1854, when six novices entered.[38] Even if we accept that the economy and the political situation had combined to produce an overall reduction in the number of girls who wished to enter the convent, we would still expect to see a fairly even pattern of entry, perhaps two or three scattered over the course of a decade, as opposed to the four, five, or six we might have seen in better times. We would not expect to see a sudden burst of demand in a short space of time, and then long gaps, with no interest at all. Thus, this unusual pattern seems most unlikely to have reflected the demand for admission to the convent on the part of devout women, and instead to have resulted from a restriction of the supply of spaces in the convent by the bishop, who had to authorize all admissions.

Why would the bishop resist authorizing entrances into the convent? First, we should ask if this was a general phenomenon throughout the bishopric, or one peculiar to La Purísima. Entrance documents from other convents show that none of them displayed such a bizarre spacing of admissions. Although Santa Catarina (Morelia) did slowly lose about half of its population over the course of the first half of the nineteenth century, there was nothing irregular about the rhythm of entries into the convent, while Nuestra Señora de la Salud in Pátzcuaro did not lose much population, and maintained a very steady rate of entrance, admitting between 7 and 10 new nuns a decade, just as in the colonial period. Even the beleaguered nuns of the Capuchin convent of Sal-vatierra (founded in 1798), who—at one point—despaired of being able to mend multiple internal rifts and asked the bishop to extinguish the institution and disperse the nuns among three other convents, managed to grow via a regular rate of entrance.[39] It is true that the other two late-founded convents— La Enseñanza of Irapuato (1804) and the Carmelites of Morelia (1824)—never reached their target populations, and it is also true that the prioress of the Irapuato convent wrote a letter begging the bishop to authorize more entrances in 1849, implying that he was dragging his feet; but in both cases, admissions were fairly evenly spaced and were numerous enough that they did allow the convents to grow slightly during the postindependence period.[40] (For populations of the six convents in the bishopric at different points in the nineteenth century, see table 6.1.)

The best explanation for the bishops' failure to allow regular admissions at La Purísima is that they were trying to protect the convent's endowment, although why refusing to admit new nuns accomplished this goal requires some elaboration. After independence, the bishops' motivations for protecting any convent's endowments became more complicated than the paternalism and financial rationalism that characterized the colonial period. The interests of the church, as a whole, had changed. It was now important that the bishop be able to tap the convent's endowment or demand a share of the endowment

TABLE 6.1 Number of Choir and White Veil Nuns
in Six Convents in the Bishopric of Michoacán,
1800–1860*

Date	Population

La Purísima Concepción, San Miguel Allende (Conceptionists)

Date	Population
1797	41
1809	38
1823	24
1830	16
1839	17
1844	17
1848	17
1851	15
1857	14

Santa Catarina de Sena Morelia (Dominicans)

Date	Population
1794	64
1800	54
1809	50
1815	38
1818	33
1821	34
1824	34
1833	23
1839	27
1843	28
1851	26
1857	32
1860	25

Nuestra Señora de la Salud, Pátzcuaro (Dominicans)

Date	Population
1806	41
1810	37
1816	33
1828	33
1834	38
1838	37
1842	36
1851	32
1858	27
1863	23

La Purísima Concepción, Salvatierra (Capuchins)

Date	Population
1798	14
1808	22
1817	22
1818	20
1825	21
1829	20
1831	21

TABLE 6.1 (continued)

Date	Population
La Purísima Conceptión (continued)	
1832	22
1837	19
1843	26
1850	22
1856	28
1858	30
La Enseñanza, Irapuato (Company of Mary)	
1804	7
1809	14
1810	16
1833	18
1854	16
Convento de Jesús María, Morelia (Carmelites)	
1824	7
1826	16
1839	16
1845	15
1852	15

* Does not include the Capuchin Convent for daughters of Indian caciques in Morelia.

income, in case of a forced loan by the government. That the convents did not squander their endowment funds was, thus, a matter of broad and pressing institutional concern. Not only might the nuns need these funds, but so also might the church as a whole.

Why did limiting admissions protect the endowment? The fact that a smaller number of nuns would register fewer expenses and constitute less of a drain on the endowment was not the answer, since if new nuns brought in fresh capital, as happened in the other convents of the bishopric (albeit at a slower rate than before independence), interest income from the increased endowment compensated for the higher level of expenses, while the general fund was enlarged—a good thing. The problem at La Purísima was that the kind of postulants who actually wanted to enter were not those who brought new capital and added to the endowment. Instead, they were almost exclusively women from poor families, who could not afford a dowry. These women *would* constitute a drain on the endowment, since they would have to be supported by scholarships. The bishop consistently demonstrated his reluctance to use extant scholarship funds by failing to authorize timely competitions to fill the vacancies created by the deaths of holders of the benefices that had been established at the time of the convent's foundation. Women who would have liked to compete for one of these scholarships languished in the niñado or waited patiently in their parents' homes until the opportunity arose, often when they were in their 30s or even 40s. As long as the scholarship-dowries were not assigned to an individual nun, they remained a part of the endowment that the church could tap if it needed to do so.

If there had been girls from elite families who desired entrance to La Purísima and brought a dowry, the bishop would, presumably, have authorized their admission without delay, as he did for the other convents. In fact, the bishop's office did show a ready willingness to admit the few dowried women who presented themselves, even when these women were not as well suited for the religious life as some of the women who could not afford a dowry. Two of the three women admitted with dowries between 1820 and 1863 probably would not have been accepted in the colonial period. Atilana de la Luz Ortiz, for example, became a choir nun despite the fact that she could not read and therefore could not pray the Divine Office (the bishop's office had to make an exception for her, allowing her to pay the dowry of a choir nun, but to pray only the office of the white veil nuns), and Antonia Cuéllar's age—she was 46 years old when she entered—would surely have been a strong impediment in the colonial period.[41]

The (unrealistic) desire to admit only paying nuns helps not only to explain episcopal reluctance to authorize admissions, but it also helps us understand why the admissions, when they occurred, came in clusters. Twice, the bishop overcame his aversion to admitting women without dowries, even agreeing to use the endowment to support non-elite women, who could not afford a dowry. Why? Because of an even more pressing threat to the endowment: legislation aimed at consolidating the smaller convents and closing some of them down. The bishop's response, when these threats from liberal governments arose, was to authorize a spate of admissions designed to quickly boost population size. The first of these laws was proposed in 1834 (it was passed by the senate, although not by the chamber of deputies), and it called for all convents with fewer than 19 nuns to be closed. The nuns would then be moved to another convent, and the government would take over the vacated convents and their property. They would bring their own dowries with them to the new convent, but the rest of the endowment (mainly the dowries of deceased nuns and the unassigned scholarship funds) would revert to the state.[42] Soon after this law was approved by the senate, the strongly anticlerical government that had framed it was toppled and replaced by a government more friendly to the church, so the bishop did not act in response to it at this time, but in 1844 (when the conservative government was replaced by a liberal government) and 1854 (the year of the liberal revolt that brought to power the government that, within a decade, would close down the convents altogether), the admissions clusters can be seen as corresponding to a potential threat to the small convents. In the first of these years, 1844, the bishop specifically decreed that convents with fewer than 19 nuns should use their endowment funds to provide dowries for enough nuns to bring the number up to that minimum.[43] In 1854, the fact that the dowries of five of the six new nuns also came from the endowment (and the sixth was paid by a sister of the mayordomo) suggests a similar decree, although I have not found concrete evidence of it, and it is possible that there was no formal order, but rather that the new bishop, Munguía, simply put out the word that if the convents asked to be allowed to create new scholarships from endowment funds (*dotes de gracia*), he would approve the request.

All three of the nuns who were admitted to La Purísima in 1844 had obviously been ready and willing to enter the convent long before they were allowed to do so, having lived many years in the niñado, hoping to secure a dowry from a benefactor. Teresa de Alcantara was 40, Guadalupe Montero de Espinosa was 36, and Ygnacia García was 32 when, in 1844, they became the fortunate beneficiaries of the bishop's recent decree, two of them receiving dowries from the general endowment and the third being assigned a dowry from one of the benefices established at the time of the convent's foundation. All were described as "girls with long-standing aspirations to the religious estate," who were admitted "as far as possible, to sustain our Convent in the future." Ygnacia, for her part, wrote that "it has been many years, as you [the members of the Definitorio] know, since I decided to consecrate myself to God, embracing the religious estate in this holy convent, but my complete poverty was the great obstacle that I had to surmount before I could realize those desires that burned ardently and vividly inside of me, and consumed my heart. . . ."[44]

In sum, from the pattern of admissions, we can infer that the bishop was more interested in protecting and, he hoped (in vain), expanding the convent's endowment than he was in preserving its vitality and spiritual relevance in the city of San Miguel, for both of which purposes it clearly needed a larger population. He would bend to the fervent wishes of the nuns and their vicar to increase their number only when it became a political necessity to do so. Thus, Bishop Portugal seems, like Abad y Queipo in the 1790s, to have been willing to sacrifice the effective internal functioning of the convent, and its image and role in the larger community, to the goal of preservation of its financial health. To be fair, in a story that is beyond the scope of this narrative, Portugal encouraged, or at least tolerated, the emergence of many other opportunities for women in the church during his long tenure as bishop—for example, the Vela Perpetua, a lay organization that was committed by its charter to female leadership (men could join, but could not be officers), made its first appearance in the bishopric during his administration, and a shift of church resources into schools for girls and teacher training can also be detected in its early stages during the 1830s and 1840s—but it seems clear that he was not willing to expend the same energy and financial resources on propping up the convents.

Refusing to Negotiate

This harsh characterization of the bishop's attitude and behavior is supported by another body of evidence that also suggests a certain indifference to the convent's communal and spiritual well-being. On numerous occasions, the members of the Definitorio begged the bishop to allow them to revise certain customary practices or to make an exception to one of the provisions of their constitution, and he declined to do so, although both they and the local vicars deemed these changes crucial for the convent to continue to function. In some cases, the bishop may have been on firm legal ground in his denials, but the manner of his dealings with the nuns was perfunctory and unimaginative—a far cry from the deep involvement of Bishop Pedro Anselmo Sánchez de Tagle in the affairs of the convent during the rebellions of the 1760s, or even the careful consultations carried out by Bishop Antonio de San Miguel during the vida particular reform of the 1790s.

Over time, as the death of the older nuns relentlessly depleted La Purísima's population and new nuns were not admitted on a regular basis, a governance vacuum arose that made the problem of finding nuns who were suitable for office holding that had been described by Vicar Uraga in 1809 seem minuscule by comparison. By 1851, a deaf nun was serving in the turnstile and a blind nun was monitoring the front door (positions that were almost perversely ill-suited to women with these particular infirmities); and the four-member Definitorio was composed of three women over age 75 and a fourth who was so objectionable that the community had been trying for over a decade to find a way to exclude her from any position of power, if they could not force her transfer to another convent.[45]

Several of the exceptions that the nuns requested concerned this desperately unhappy nun, Concepción de San Felipe Neri. Concepción had entered the convent in 1810, perhaps in a rush to admit new novices after the vicar's 1809 report had pointed out the dangerous generational imbalance in the convent. Such a thorn in the community as she quickly proved to be would have been a cause for concern, even before 1810, but at least, at that time, she would have been one among 35 to 40 nuns. In a convent composed of only 15 to 17 women, however, she was an overwhelmingly malevolent presence. "This religiosa, ever since she became a nun, has given all of us much cause for suffering, with her restless and intemperate disposition; her behavior that is very far from that of a modest subordinate . . . and every day the situation grows worse," the Definitorio wrote in 1842. She terrorized the convent to the extent that even the abbess was afraid of her and could not correct her misbehavior.

She gossiped viciously and attended community functions only when it suited her; "she makes fun of everything and everyone and fears no one, for which reason she is incorrigible. She calls everyone names . . . and to her servants she is a tyrant. . . . She eavesdrops on everyone and shows up everywhere when we least expect it, to see whom we are with and what we are doing. She leaves us no freedom of action, and she does not even allow us to confess in peace, hiding behind walls to listen to us." So cruel and upsetting were the things she said to Father Remigio Gonzales, one of the vicars of the convent, that he, "being in broken health, scarcely finished his visitation when the havoc that she created caused his death."

Said by the vicar to be disconsolate in her chosen estate, Concepción had hinted that she wished to leave the convent altogether, an almost unheard-of stance (a few unhappy nuns did ask to change convents, but hers was the only case in this diocese in which a nun suggested that she might do what the liberals would have liked to see happen more often: break her vows and for-swear her life in religion). Indeed, according to the vicar, she should never have become a nun, and would have been better off as a "señora de familia," a wife and mother; but her "judgment is so poor," he added, that he was not sure that she was suited to this role either. She spent much of her time at the grille, hungry for news of the outside. "While God has protected the rest of this community from the tempting and distracting contagion of the world," the vicar wrote, "[she] has become almost completely secularized by her constant contact with people outside the convent." She had multiple ongoing relation-ships with outsiders, including men, with whom she discussed La Purísima's internal affairs "without fear of the escucha" (listener), and when she served as the convent's secretary, she broadcast much of the business of the convent to the outside.[46]

Evidently, she had revealed her true personality soon after professing in 1811, and it is clear that she had been widely despised and feared since that time, but in 1839, a more serious problem arose: She was due, by virtue of the custom that seniority dictated the composition of the Definitorio, to join that advisory body upon the death of the next nun older than she. The vicar, con-cerned about a possible crisis in convent governance, agreed with the nuns that this was an intolerable prospect. "There is not a single nun in the convent who believes her capable of filling this position," he wrote. The Definitorio confirmed this view: "With great pain we hear the younger religiosas say, 'if I had known this Religiosa I would not have professed in this convent; if things are this bad now . . . when the time comes for her to serve [in the Definitorio], woe to us. We would rather die than have our Convent in her power.' "

To try to avert the catastrophe of Concepción's taking her place on the council, the vicar asked the bishop to allow the members of Definitorio to be elected, rather than elevated on the basis of seniority alone, pointing out that the Rule prescribed only the manner of choosing the abbess, not the way that the advisory body was chosen. In fact, some convents did elect a Definitorio. Thus, what they were asking for was not against the Rule. The bishop, however, denied the request in a short statement, saying that it was dangerous to change the customs of a convent.[47] In 1842, the Definitorio tried a different tack, writing to the bishop to beg him to remove Concepción from the convent and place her in a different one. Their case was based on a promise that a visitor had made during the last inspection: He agreed that Concepción had done great harm to the convent, and he told the abbess that, if she did not reform her ways, to let him know and he would send her to another convent. In their petition, the Definitorio adduced many examples of her bad habits, behavior, and character (summarized earlier), in support of their case that, far from mending her ways, she was more "incorrigible" than ever, but the bishop denied this request as well.[48]

In 1845, the abbess and the members of the Definitorio asked once again to be allowed to change the manner in which the advisory body was chosen. A different, recently appointed vicar agreed that it was time to replace the Definitorio, since, at present, the council was composed of "one nun who is completely deaf, another one who is blind and lame, and one who is demented (although with frequent lucid intervals)." He approved of a system in which, every third year, the two oldest members of the four-member Definitorio would be rotated out and an election held to fill their spots, although the older nuns would be eligible for reelection and could thus retain their positions. But he cautioned that, although this plan had great merit and did not contradict the Rule, he feared that its inspiration came from a desire to keep Sister Concepción out of office. This, he said primly, would deprive her of representation and isolate her. He suggested that the bishop force the religiosas' motivations out into the open by insisting that they accuse her of some transgression. If they could not name a punishable act that she had committed, then it would be clear that their actions were inspired by "ignoble reasons and unjust sentiments." The vicar general for convents, Pelagio Antonio de Labastida (later, archbishop of Mexico), agreed with the vicar's assessment—he, too, was suspicious of the nuns' motives and was not inclined to go along with their request. He added that electing an abbess was hard enough among communities of women, since they rarely achieved unanimity or even a clear majority, and to add elections for other posts would be to invite trouble. In general, he concluded (echoing Bishop Portugal, in his earlier decision) that it was never a good idea to change established practices.

The desperate nuns wrote back to point out that they had already held the election, that it had been approved, and that elections to fill the Definitorio were common in other convents. In response, the bishop rescinded the election that they had just held and ordered a new one, making it clear in stern language that, if they wanted to exclude Sister Concepción, they had to give the reasons why. In response, the nuns once again submitted evidence that she was indiscreet and imprudent, that her religious conduct was not appropriate, that she caused disturbances that made the abbesses cry bitter tears, that her conduct toward her sisters was not sisterly, that she had a strong and meddlesome temperament and did not bother to hide it from those on the outside, and that she caused the disgust and mortification of the whole community. But Vicar General Labastida replied that none of this constituted a physical or moral impediment to holding office, and therefore, he concluded that the nuns were simply trying to exclude one member of the community. The request was turned down, and by 1848, despite the best efforts of the other nuns, Concepción had entered the Definitorio.[49]

There may have been good legal reasons for the bishop to ignore the pleas of the Definitorio and the advice of three of the four vicars who served the convent during the period that poor Concepción, so miserable in her religious estate, took out her frustrations on the convent as a whole, although the system of election proposed by the Definitorio seems to have fallen within the boundaries established by the Rule, and even the nuns' motives, which the bishop was determined to take into account in evaluating a request for a change in customary practice, seem to have been justifiable—after all, there is no question that Concepción's presence had a strong, destructive impact on the convent community. On the other hand, as we saw in the case of Phelipa de San Antonio in the 1760s and early 1770s, removing a nun from office was extremely tricky and required careful canonical consideration (even if the authorities were unanimously convinced of her unsuitability), and while Concepción's was not a case of removal from office, but rather a case in which the Definitorio was trying to prevent her from taking office in the first place, the issues may have been seen as similar. With Phelipa, the bishop was concerned lest she take legal action to protect her position, and it is certainly possible that this bishop feared that Concepción might also retaliate legally. That would have been consistent with her character. But, in a way, it does not matter if he was in the legal right or not—the point that needs making is that he did not provide any juridical or other considered justification for his decisions, did not try to convince the nuns of the rightness of his position, did not try to conciliate them, and did not commiserate with them about the difficulties of community life. Frankly, he and his vicars general just did not seem to take their problems and petitions very seriously.

This attitude represented a significant departure from the complex historical relationship between the bishops and the abbesses of La Purísima. From Pedro Anselmo Sánchez de Tagle through Antonio de San Miguel, the bishops had run the gamut from highly confrontational to highly conciliatory, but all had been deeply involved in the convent's governance, often erring on the side of patriarchal meddlesomeness in order to be sure that the convent's officers governed in a way that preserved peace and avoided scandal. We need only remember the long, passionate letters that Sánchez de Tagle penned to all of the actors in the rebellions of the 1760s, not to mention the interrogatory he insisted on and the reports he commissioned, all designed—of course—to exert as much control over the nuns as possible, but also designed to assure the nuns that their needs, their foibles, their failures, and their problems were being closely scrutinized. Similarly, Antonio de San Miguel was careful to send his most senior adviser, Abad y Queipo, to San Miguel in 1792 to prepare the groundwork for the imposition of the vida particular reform before he actually carried it out, and then he authorized another special visitation a year later to see how the reform was working and to allow the nuns to articulate their objections to it. Although he was clearly not prepared to allow a reversion to the vida común, no matter what the nuns said about it, it was deemed important to appear to consult with them. And even if they were not involved in a crisis or a major challenge, the other colonial bishops not only wrote to the nuns collectively with some frequency, but also wrote individual letters to the nuns (mainly, of course, the abbess, but by no means exclusively), in which they often displayed an impressive knowledge of the different personalities, quirks, ailments, and talents of the nuns in each convent. This kind of close relationship was what animated the vow of obedience—to blindly obey a distant and uncaring or uninvolved authority would not have been easy to tolerate.

In contrast to the colonial bishops, there were no post-1810 bishops and only one vicar general, Basilio Peralta y Quesada (who served in the early 1830s), who came close to filling this role. Peralta y Quesada must have spent virtually his entire day in correspondence with the dozens of nuns in all of the convents of the bishopric who wrote to their "padrecito" with great frequency and affection, an affection that he clearly returned. The thick packets of letters to and from him provide example after example of paternalism in its most benign guise. But after he moved on to another post in the ecclesiastical hierarchy a few years later, there was no one in the bishop's office who took this kind of personal interest in the nuns. The reports of Sister Concepción sharing the problems of the convent with the outside world, gossiping about the nuns with people from the outside, listening in on others' confessions, and avoiding community activities would have caused the colonial bishops to pay special attention to the convent. But Portugal and the vicars general after the mid-1830s did not comment on them, and in fact, their responses do not even give the impression that they read them very carefully.

This view of episcopal indifference and inattention is confirmed by a testy exchange in 1851 between the convent's last vicar before the extinction of the convent, a virtuous, committed priest named Maximiano Moncada, and ecclesiastical authorities. Moncada articulated (insofar as it was at all prudent to do so) his and the nuns' frustrations with the apparent failure of the bishop to see what was happening to the convent and to appreciate the problems that it faced merely in order to continue to function at a minimal level. Immediately after he took over as vicar, he was called upon to preside over the triennial election, but to his dismay, as he wrote to the bishop in June 1851, out of just 15 nuns in the convent, 8 were ineligible to serve as abbess:[50]

> Balvina de San Luis Gonzaga because she is almost blind and ill
> with Shingles (*Erpis*)
> Josefa de San Francisco de Sales because she is completely blind
> Loreto de la Sangre de Cristo because she is not of legitimate birth
> and is almost deaf
> Rosalía de San Francisco de Paula because she is not of legitimate
> birth and is losing her vision
> Manuela del Dulce Nombre de Jesús because she is not of legitimate
> birth and is very sick
> Ygnacia del Corazón de María because she is not of legitimate birth
> and cannot vote for abbess because she has only been professed
> for six years
> Guadalupe del Sagrado Corazón because she has only been pro-
> fessed for seven years
> Teresa de Nuestra Madre Purísima because she has only been pro-
> fessed for six years

Given this situation, he requested permission to dispense with the remainder of the 8 years in the probationary period of the three nuns who had entered the convent in 1844, and he also asked that the four illegitimate nuns be "habilitated" to serve as abbess. These measures would at least provide some semblance of choice and critical mass in the election. Moncada's request, however, like all of the previous ones, was denied in a short sentence appended to his letter and returned to him.

Shocked at this insensitivity to what he saw as a desperate situation, Moncada fired back another letter in July.[51] In his earlier letter, he wrote, he must not have done a very good job of informing the vicar general of the sad state of the convent—otherwise, he would not have dismissed his request so lightly. He restated his argument, more forcefully this time, pointing out that there were only six religiosas who were technically eligible to serve as abbess. This number, he wrote:

> is already much reduced; but it should be added that of these six it
> is certain that three are unelectable: Sister Concepción by virtue of
> her past behavior will not have a single vote, Sister Atilana scarcely
> knows how to read and requires a companion help her recite the
> prayers, and Sister Rafaela, with her head bowed by illness and great
> age, will not enter into the election. There remain, then, only three
> for whom votes can be cast, and this leaves the nuns little choice
> (*libertad*) in the election. I am given to understand that this lack of
> choice has produced unquiet and turbulence in the consciences of

some of the nuns, and for this reason I beg Your Grace to give me prudent direction in conducting this election.

He then repeated his request—that the four illegitimate nuns and the three nuns who had entered in 1844 be allowed, on a one-time-only basis, to enter the election for abbess. This time, the new bishop-elect, Clemente de Jesús Munguía, agreed to the request: The illegitimate nuns and the three who were recently professed were approved for office. One of the nuns whose probationary period was shortened was elected in the 1851 vote, and in 1857, as we will see, although the habilitation of the illegitimate nuns was supposed to be only temporary, for the first time in the convent's history, an illegitimate nun became abbess. Thus, on the eve of the extinction of the convents, the bishop's office, which had so stubbornly resisted change, was finally forced to come to terms with the transformation of this particular convent's population since independence.

Convent Life after Independence

Finances and Lifestyle

The dysfunctionally small population of the convent, the impoverished and/or irregular social background of many of the nuns, and the fact that nuns were admitted in bunches, rather than in a more or less evenly spaced pattern, all had effects on interpersonal relationships and daily life in the convent, and we will turn to them soon enough, but the most striking aspect of the nuns' postindependence lives—the thing that leaps, unexpected, out of the documentary record—was the distinct improvement in the convent's financial situation and standard of living. Although the decade of insurgency was horrendous, things began to improve rapidly in the 1820s. The 20 surviving account books for the postindependence period show that, in stark contrast to most of the colonial period, surpluses were the rule rather than the exception. Every year from 1828 to 1831, for example, the convent collected between 500 and 1,500 pesos more than it spent, and the surpluses accumulated, so that, by the end of 1831, the convent had a 3,146-peso credit with the mayordomo. By 1835, the credit had grown to 4,775 pesos. In 1839 and 1840 alone, the mayordomo collected almost 5,000 pesos more than the convent spent. In 8 of the 20 years, the convent took in more than it spent, and in only 4 years did the convent spend more than it had on account with the mayordomo (1822 and 1846–1848). In the other 8 years, the convent spent more than it took in that particular year, but did not spend beyond what it had on account with the mayordomo.[52]

The most astonishing thing is that the surpluses occurred despite an unprecedented level of spending. In 1830, new habits (*vestuario*) were purchased for all of the nuns, yet there was money left over to repair their organ. Both of these were expenses that, in earlier years, might well have been deferred. The next year, the convent spent 654 pesos on painting and repair of the church. In 1836, full of confidence, it not only spent 440 pesos on a new set of clothing for each nun, but also spent 905 pesos on a new cloister in the patio of the sacristy, as well as unspecified amounts for whitewashing and painting the three patios of the convent and their cloisters; building a fountain in each of the four corners of the principal patio on the second floor; paving the patio of the niñado; whitewashing the kitchen and building new ovens and braziers; installing full-length glass windows in the workroom, the room where they stored and manufactured medicines, and the upstairs dormitory; and reroofing parts of the cloister of the niñado. Over the next 4 years, they spent 185 pesos for a new bell, 210 pesos to build a kitchen in one of the cells, 260 pesos for a piano, and at least 1,400 pesos on clothing. But even after this spurt of spending, they still had a significant surplus, and so in 1841, they began work on the bell tower that is, today, one of the distinguishing features of the church. The 1841 accounts showed that, in that year, they spent 2,814 pesos on the tower and the cemetery, and in 1843, they finished the tower, at an additional cost of 1,373 pesos. This still left enough for 1,080 pesos to be spent on clothing in 1843.

There were substantial clothing expenses virtually every year—a startling contrast to the last two decades of the colonial period, when the nuns went without new habits until the old ones were in threads. One of the complaints registered in the 1851 visitation was that, even though some of the nuns had as many as three good habits, nonetheless, they were given 50 pesos a year for new ones, an increase over the 40-peso clothing allowance of the previous decade. Each nun still received only a small pension of 12 pesos a month for food and personal needs, unchanged from the late colonial period, but they benefited significantly from increased communal spending, not only for cloth-ing, but also for medicine, doctor's visits, construction costs (such as kitchens in private cells), and incidentals, such as paper, cooking implements, brooms, and buckets. The convent also supported a larger number of servants per nun than at any time in its history. In 1851, the vicar complained that there were 15 nuns and 35 servants; even, he said, if we assume that each nun needs one personal servant and the community at large needs 13 servants, that was still 7 too many. Thirty-five servants was almost double the number of donadas that the colonial convent employed, with many fewer nuns to serve.[53]

The unaccustomed amount of disposable income seems to have created an almost giddy climate of spending, by the historical standards of this convent, producing unprecedented violations of the vow of poverty. It became the cus-tom to celebrate the birthdays of the abbess and the nun who supervised the niñas, as well as the feast day of the Virgin of Guadalupe and Twelfth Night, with plays that they put on in the cell of the abbess, for which the nuns dressed in outfits and valuable jewels that they borrowed from secular women. The triennial visitations provided another occasion to justify large expenditures; the vicar wrote disapprovingly that "each senior nun spends more than she should to decorate her cell in luxurious fashion, borrowing crystal, mirrors, silver services, etc., and the Abbess serves a very fine meal, on the convent's account, to the persons who enter for the visitation." The custom of processing through the convent on important religious days, bearing the holy images of the saints, took on a new twist when the processions began to stop in each nun's cell so that she might "receive" the image; this, in turn, inspired the nuns to spend money to decorate their cells and purchase refreshments.[54] It is unclear from the vicar's report and the interviews with the nuns which of these expenditures (other than those associated with the visitation) were borne by the convent and which by the individual nuns, but the account books show an increasing amount spent on religious observances, which suggests that a way was found for at least some of these expenses to be absorbed by the convent. Moreover, the generous 40- to 50-peso clothing allowance each year could also be seen as a way that the convent supported these extra individual expenditures, since some of that allowance could be diverted to other uses.

The building of the bell tower from 1841 to 1843 brought the displeased intervention of the bishop's office. With a substantial credit of 6,653 pesos in the 1840 accounting, the nuns decided to initiate work on the tower the next year, without prior authorization from Morelia.[55] Too late, the vicar general rebuked them for the lack of consultation and insisted that, in the future, the convent must submit a detailed budget and secure a license from the bishopric for any work that it planned, "whether large or small." The vicar general also ordered the mayordomo to turn in each year a copy of the accounts, along with the original receipts. The nuns and their mayordomo bridled at what they saw as excessively strict oversight. The Definitorio was willing, the nuns wrote, to obtain a license for large construction works or other big expenses, but it defended its ancient right to spend small amounts at its own discretion. The letter included a long disquisition on the meaning of the word "works." For his part, the mayordomo was entirely willing to send copies of the yearly accounts, but not the original receipts, which, he said, it was important that he keep in his possession for his own protection.[56]

The convent did suffer shortfalls during the war with the United States, spending more than it collected in all 3 years of the war—1846, 1847, and 1848. Anticipating reduced income and increased demands by the government for loans and contributions, the bishop's office told the convent and the mayordomo, in 1846, that they must cut spending, to which the mayordomo responded, somewhat disingenuously, that reducing expenses was quite impossible. The nuns, he said, received only a modest monthly pension, and it was simply unthinkable to reduce this amount, while cutting back on liturgical costs and salaries was also impossible. Threatening to resign in favor of someone "with more intelligence and better means," the mayordomo flatly refused to make any cuts.[57] As a result, by 1848, the convent owed him 2,212 pesos—a far cry from the over 40,000 pesos that the late colonial convent owed Narciso María de la Canal, but still enough to concern the nuns and the vicar. It was decided that they must indeed introduce some economies, and they settled on reducing the 40 pesos a year that each nun had been given for clothing, to 30 or, perhaps, even 20 pesos (an amount for which the colonial nuns would have been pathetically grateful). The issue blew over by 1849, when income again exceeded expenses by almost 1,800 pesos. For the rest of the period up to 1856, there were consistent surpluses.

How did the convent achieve this amazing financial turnaround? The smaller number of nuns who had to be fed, clothed, and cared for from the endowment funds was, of course, an important factor. The drop in the convent's population—from a high of 41 in 1797 to 16 to 17 in the 1830s, 1840s, and 1850s—meant that living expenses, always the largest part of the budget expenditures, fell in equal proportion: To pay 41 nuns their 10-peso monthly pension cost almost 5,000 pesos a year; to pay 16 nuns 12 pesos a month cost 2,300 pesos. Even if revenues stayed the same, the reduced number of nuns to support would make a significant difference in the financial situation of the convent—and would go a long way toward explaining how the nuns could afford to pay for improved maintenance, new construction, better clothing, more servants, increased communal purchases, more frequent medical care, and numerous celebrations.

But this is not the whole story. While we might expect that, given the region's economic problems after independence, the convent's yield on investments and ability to collect debts in a timely manner would be less than in the late colonial period, that was clearly not the case.[58] Not only were expenses less than in the colonial period, but revenues were also greater. On average, over 90% of the interest income that was owed to the convent was actually collected in the postindependence period, compared with under 70% in the colonial period, and this meant that revenues from 1829 to 1849, at almost 7,300 pesos a year, were almost 50% *higher* than in the colonial period from 1770 to 1790, at a little under 5,000 pesos (table 6.2).

Given the uncertainty of the economic environment, it is very impressive that the postindependence mayordomos were able consistently to pressure borrowers to service their debts on time and in full. How did they do it? How did they manage to collect more interest income than the colonial mayordomos, in a less propitious economic environment? The obvious answer is that they worked harder on behalf of the convent than their predecessors. Several accounts show expenses incurred by the mayordomo for travel to various towns and haciendas to personally collect debts; for example, in 1822, Vicente de Umarán spent 100 pesos on a trip to Celaya to collect interest from the convent of San Agustín, to Valle de Santiago to collect from the Balbuena family, and

TABLE 6.2 Convent Income, Selected Years*

Year	Income (Pesos)	Year	Income (Pesos)
1756	2,333	1821	4,659
1757	2,943	1822	4,718
1759	4,152	1828	4,798
1761	4,837	1829	6,568
1763	5,001	1830	8,723
1764	4,510	1836	5,855
1765	5,264	1837	5,308
1770–1775	4,870 (annual average)	1838	7,214
1782	3,446	1839	7,743
1786	5,892	1840	11,807
1790	5,846	1841	10,327
1811	4,292	1842	6,945
1812	3,433	1843	8,452
1813	1,902	1844	4,349
1814	1,181	1845	5,408
1815	1,401	1846	6,445
1816	1,262	1847	5,142
1820	5,758 (includes 1,500 pesos donated by Vicar Uraga and 3,000 in a dowry, which was spent instead of invested)	1848	7,185
		1849	8,870

* Accounting procedure was to carry over surpluses or deficits from the previous year, but here I have included just the amounts actually collected in each year, not the carry-over. Does not include amounts paid to board niñas in the school, since recording of this income is inconsistent and there were years when the school itself did not exist.

to Irapuato to collect from Francisco Gamino.[59] In 1847, one of the few times when the convent ran a deficit for 2 consecutive years, the mayordomo apologized abjectly to the nuns, writing that he was very upset and that he feared he had not tried hard enough to collect the interest and rents. He explained that the problem was the "circumstances in which we find ourselves today," a clear reference to the war with the United States.[60] They responded that they were entirely satisfied with his efforts, as indeed, they should have been: For many years, they had paid him a 5% commission on what he took in, only 1% more than the colonial mayordomos received (although eventually, they increased the commission to the 8% that other convents had paid, starting in the early postindependence period).[61] Indeed, the nuns were so pleased with the work of their mayordomo that, several times, they gave him a "gratuity" (500 pesos in 1838, 200 pesos in 1839, and 400 pesos in 1840) on top of his commission.

Why did these postindependence mayordomos work harder than the colonial mayordomos? One of the characteristics of the colonial mayordomos was that they were prominent, extremely well-connected businessmen, who were chosen precisely for those qualities. Well into the postindependence period, such a businessman was still considered to be the ideal mayordomo. Vicar Francisco Uraga, for example, in an 1828 letter to the vicar general, wrote that the current mayordomo had recently died, and that the nuns had been looking for a replacement. The matter, he said, was "very delicate, because . . . the nuns do not have a reserve fund and they need a subject who can supplement their income from time to time, and they also need someone who can deal with distinguished property owners, someone of a certain substance himself." "There have been various applicants," he lamented, "but none in whom all of these characteristics are united."[62] As we have seen, however, a mayordomo with both excellent social credentials and great wealth was a double-edged sword—Uraga, like others, had always assumed that someone "of a certain substance" was the only sort of debt collector that "distinguished property owners" would heed. But the problem was that it was often hard for these men to put pressure on borrowers who were their friends, relatives, and business associates; it was ungentlemanly to badger them or take them to court over an unpaid or partially paid debt. And since a wealthy mayordomo's own livelihood did not depend on his commission from the convent, it was often easier to let the debts slide year after year.

In the end, it was fortunate for the convent that it was not able to find someone who was both socially well connected and wealthy. The convent's choice was José Luis Sautto—ironically, a descendant of a family of textile mill owners who had battled to prevent the convent from being built and who had been aligned against the Canal family in San Miguel politics. The Sautto family was socially prominent, but José Luis does not appear to have been a wealthy man. It is impossible to prove, because the notary archives for San Miguel have been lost or destroyed, and so we have no details about family wealth or the men who dominated the local economy in the nineteenth century, but if we are to believe Uraga that the convent had been unable to come up with someone who was both "distinguished" (which Sautto was) and wealthy, then we can infer that Sautto was not especially well-to-do. Sautto himself commented, in 1846, that the bishop should look for someone of "better means" to replace him. If he was indeed fairly dependent on his commission from the convent, that is the best explanation for his considerable energy in collecting debts. Sautto served the convent until at least 1857, and while the previous mayordomo, Vicente de Umarán, had already resurrected convent finances from the dark days of the decade of insurgency, Sautto presided over a period of even better collections; beginning the year after he took over, in 1829, revenues jumped from the mid-4,000-peso range of the 1820s to an average of well over 7,000 pesos for the rest of the period (see table 6.2). In sum, the economic doldrums of the postindependence period (as opposed to the economic catastrophe of 1810–1825) worked to the advantage of the convent, since under these circumstances, the steady income that might be achieved via the commission from the convent was sufficient to inspire hard work and hard-headedness from their mayordomo.[63]

The postindependence mayordomos appear to have been not only more energetic than the colonial mayordomos, but also shrewder about investing and managing the limited funds of the nuns. Almost certainly because they were willing to challenge delinquent borrowers in court and press for settlements, sometimes in cash and sometimes in ceded property, the mayordomos acquired, on behalf of the convent, a small body of urban property that it had never had before: In 1841, this property (which consisted of an inn, a two-story house, four other sizable houses, three small houses, 10 outbuildings, and an orchard) produced in rents about 1,120 pesos a year. All of the properties were located in San Miguel, which made collection of the rents much easier than collecting debts on property in faraway places. Later, in the early 1840s, as the political situation worsened and talk of privatizing property owned by the convents gained steam, Sautto appears to have sold the inn, which was worth about 10,000 pesos, probably funding some of the cost of the bell tower.[64]

Factions and Factionalism

If the lifestyle of the nuns after 1830 or so was, in a material sense, almost certainly more comfortable and more luxurious than the lives of the colonial nuns, what of other aspects of the convent experience? We have already seen that there was considerable tension generated by the mere presence of Sister Concepción, but should we picture a convent that was unified by its dislike of a single nun, and undivided on other issues? Clearly, that was not the case; virtually every triennial election for abbess was hotly contested, and multiple ballots were regularly required in order for a majority to form. On at least three occasions (1821, 1836, and 1857), the vicar had to step in and appoint an abbess because the factions were too fixed for compromise.[65] But identifying the nature and causes of these fault lines and divisions is necessarily a matter requiring speculation.

One possibility is that the factions in the convent revolved around the perennial issue of reform versus relaxation. The material comfort that made the nuns' lives easier in the postindependence period was not necessarily something that would have made their lives more satisfying; indeed, for the more Rule-conscious nuns, it was definitely not an unqualified positive. Small luxuries and laxities contravened the solemn vows that all nuns took, and historically, of course, they had been especially frowned upon at this convent and had been at the root of the convent's troubles since its foundation. It is reasonable to hypothesize that the split in the convent revolved around this old issue, as some nuns condemned their sisters, who were seen as self-indulgent and too-worldly. Does the slim evidence from the convent records support this hypothesis?

After the horrific decade of insurgency, there does, indeed, seem to have been a subtle shift of attitude away from a fairly strong pro-reform position in the late colonial period, when nuns were increasingly dissatisfied with the spiritual quality of their lives under the vida particular, and in the direction of relaxation. After enduring the decade of the insurgency—one in which the vicar feared that he might have to watch them die of hunger—perhaps the nuns felt that they deserved to spend a little on themselves and enjoy small pleasures. We can certainly infer a creeping sense of entitlement, manifested in their spending habits and the increasing number and elaborateness of their fiestas and celebrations. It also appears to have been the attitude of the male authorities (the vicars, vicars general, and bishops) that it was not really worth trying to enforce the Rule strictly under the trying circumstances of the times, with the very future of the convent in Mexico being called into question. Until the late 1840s, there was no more than a perfunctory mention in the documentary record of the need to return to the simplicity and austerity of the colonial convent that existed before the vida particular reform. None of the vicars or abbesses spoke out about excessive relaxation of the Rule; and as we have already seen, on the rare occasions when the bishop and his vicars general weighed in on the convent's internal affairs, it was not in order to correct the nuns' too-worldly behavior or deviations from the path of strict observance, but rather to supervise their finances or reject a plea for a change of customs.

Beginning (coincidentally?) after the war with the United States, however, a campaign by Vicar Moncada to restore monastic discipline and return the convent to its reformist roots struck a chord with at least some of the nuns.[66] According to his own account, around half of the convent was uncomfortable with the extent to which the Rule had been relaxed, a rough proportion that is confirmed by the interviews with each of the nuns during the 1857 visitation. A majority of them complained that the abbess, María de San Juan Sacramentado, was too lenient and insufficiently attuned to enforcement of the solemn vows of poverty and enclosure. She was accused of giving away expensive gifts, such as lengths of chambray cloth; delegating the task of presiding over the common meal to a member of the Definitorio; allowing far too many recreation days, so that some weeks, the nuns had only 2 days of regular attendance at choir; denying nuns the confessional if they had not performed their convent tasks; inviting the recently professed nuns to her cell at night for meetings that did not end until 11:00 P.M. or 12:00 A.M., ostensibly to instruct them, but instead, only teaching them "to ignore the rule of silence"; and failing to provide the recently professed nuns with the woolen underwear that the Rule required.

Moncada himself did not blame the abbess so much as he blamed (im-

plicitly) the action taken by Bishop Antonio de San Miguel in 1792: the abolition of the vida común. The spirit of community had weakened to such an
extent, he wrote, that the abbess could no longer govern effectively:

> As a result of not having lived the life in common for many years,
> during which time each nun has managed her food, servants, and
> cell with a certain independence, something has happened which in
> similar cases will always happen, and that is that their spirit of cor-
> poration—that unity of ideas, actions, and interests that is the very
> soul of the religious community, the thing that makes easy the diffi-
> cult observance of their solemn vows—is greatly weakened, if not
> lacking altogether. The nuns do not behave with that blind and
> ready obedience that conserves in them unity and peace, nor can the
> Abbess use the tools of government effectively, because she first has
> to make subtle inquiries as to whether or not she will be obeyed and
> by whom, or she must make frequent concessions, in order not to
> depreciate her authority completely. In sum [most of] the nuns fol-
> low their own paths, adhering to their own ideas and excusing
> themselves because of their age and infirmities.

He offered a number of specific suggestions to remedy the situation, but significantly, he revealed that he had also proposed to the nuns the reinstitution
of the vida común in the convent. As in the entire history of the convent, the
nuns split down the middle: Five of them said that they desired to return to
this way of life, while four opposed any change. Moncada reluctantly concluded
that the "terrain was not yet prepared" for the return to the common life. Thus,
on the surface, at least, it appears that by midcentury, the old split between
spiritually serious, reform-minded nuns and those whose motivations to enter
the convent and preferences, once they were there, were somewhat more
worldly, had reemerged.

But if we dig a little deeper, it turns out that it is not so easy to ascertain
the intensity of feeling behind this split over whether or not to bring back the
vida común. While there is no question that the issue of reform versus relaxation was the central issue in the rebellions and factionalism of the 1760s and
1770s, it is less clear that this was the case in the 1850s. The nuns' 1857 complaints about excessive relaxation were expressed under circumstances and in
ways that suggest that they may have been inspired as much by a desire to
please the vicar as by sincere commitment to the idea of restoring the rigors
of the vida común. The criticisms of the abbess and her insufficiently strict
ways were given in answer to questions put to them by a vicar whose reformist
energy had been on display for years. Since 1851, Moncada had been writing
the bishop about the lack of monastic discipline in the convent (to little effect),
drawing up new and stricter daily distributions, and formulating detailed recommendations for reform, all *preceding* the interviews with the nuns during

the 1857 visitation. Thus, most of the complaints articulated by the nuns concerned problems that Moncada had already identified in writing and probably in sermons. There is clearly room to question whether or not he had planted the idea, for example, that the abbess permitted too many recreations, an accusation repeated with suspicious frequency by the nuns. One can easily imagine Moncada asking the question in a way that was designed to elicit a particular response. It is possible, then, that some of the nuns in the 1850s were simply seizing on the issue of relaxation in order to please their demanding (but attentive) vicar. A bonus was that they could use condemnation of relaxation among their sisters to criticize those they did not like, using a weapon that put themselves, of course, above reproach.

What other fissures, besides differences of opinion over adherence to the Rule, might go farther in helping us to understand the daily tensions of life in this convent? Here is where some of the patterns of admission (discussed earlier) offer alternative ways to imagine how the community might have become divided in the postindependence period, encouraging the formation of factions that could then adopt the language of reform that Moncada provided in order to express their differences. One possibility is that the factions might have developed along lines of class, wealth, and/or social background. The likelihood that the community would suffer from this kind of division was, of course, increased by the admissions policies and realities of the postindependence era: More women were admitted without wealth, social standing, or even legitimacy than ever before in the convent's history. Thus, the last generation and a half of women admitted during the colonial period (1792–1810) might have seen themselves as fundamentally different from the younger women admitted in the late 1820s and early 1830s, who were, as a group, considerably less prominent and less wealthy than they were. It is certainly possible that arrogance based on sentiments of superior rank emboldened Sister Concepción, a dowried nun and a member of the last colonial generation, and made her so difficult.

However, while class and wealth may have been major causes of resentment and factionalism through the late 1830s and into the 1840s, they seem likely to have faded over time as root causes for intraconventual tensions, for the simple reason that, by midcentury, virtually no one came from a wealthy or prominent family. The possibility of resentment on the part of the illegitimate women (since they were denied access to high office until the bishop finally made an exception for them in 1851), and of snobbish behavior toward them on the part of the legitimate nuns, seems somewhat more likely to have endured. One small hint of this is that, in 1854, when the vicar wrote to the bishop to report on the recent election, he commented that, although the four illegitimate women had been habilitated for office during the previous (1851) election on a one-time-only basis, they now believed that they had been granted this right in perpetuity. The vicar's tone was more resigned than outraged, and there is no indication that he disqualified them.[67] All the same, it does not seem likely that this was a major basis of rifts in the convent. In the 1857 election (in which the balloting for abbess reflected rock-hard alliances and factions that the vicar stubbornly hoped to overcome with repeated balloting, and that the nuns equally stubbornly refused to abandon), Moncada was eventually forced (after 20 ballots) to give up on the election and appoint an abbess. The woman he named, Rosalía de San Francisco de Paula, was of illegitimate birth. Although Moncada acknowledged that this appointment might be "interpreted in a sinister manner and censored with acrimony," he obviously felt that this was a choice that stood at least some chance of smoothing the tensions, rather than stirring them up.[68] In sum, while the admissions patterns did have the potential to exacerbate tensions and feed factionalism along lines of class, wealth, and social background, these factors probably faded in importance over time, and by midcentury, when factionalism seems to have reached its height, they do not appear to have great explanatory power.

There is another factor, however, that loomed larger over time, rather than diminished in its ability to divide the convent: generational splits. The reduced number of nuns and, especially, the fact that the new nuns since 1810 had been admitted in clusters, could not help but make for sharper generational conflicts than would be the case in a convent with a mature and normal age structure. Ironically, then, the generational conflict that was a major source of friction in the convent's early years now resurfaced in its waning years. Vicar Moncada, lamenting the failed election and the fact that he had had to appoint an abbess in 1857, indicated that he had not chosen the nun with the largest plurality of votes, but rather a woman who, to him, represented a "middle ground" (*medio término*) between an older group of nuns and a younger group.[69] Some of the nuns, in the 1857 interviews, referred to the abbess's special relationship with the "jóvenes," the six recently professed (1855) nuns whom she "instructed" in her cell in late-night meetings. There had been another large cohort of eight nuns who had entered the convent in the late 1820s and early 1830s, now aging, but mostly still living, in the mid-1850s, and it appears to have been this group who clashed with the 1854 group, who were in loose alliance with the two nuns of the three admitted in 1844 who were still living.

Thus, while issues of reform and relaxation and issues of class, wealth, and social background should not be discounted at any time during the post-independence period as causes of friction, my sense is that they were secondary in importance to the split along generational lines. Like all of the factors that stood to divide the convent, generational differences were heightened by the pitifully small numbers of nuns who were recruited, and as we have seen, broader economic and political factors, beyond the control of the convent or the bishop, were largely responsible for this phenomenon. But they were also fostered by the erratic admissions policies of the bishops. Thus, there is a connection between the attitude of the bishops and the factionalism that made the last years of the convent so trying, and it may even have figured in the failure of the convent to survive the Reform.

Dissolution

Vicar Moncada had expressed the hope that his choice of abbess in 1857, Rosalía de San Francisco de Paula, would calm the convent, but she did not really have much of a chance. These were years of trauma for the convent not only because of its internal divisions, but also because of events external to La Purísima. In 1854, a barracks revolt in southern Mexico brought to an end the last dictatorship of Antonio López de Santa Anna and installed a liberal regime that soon demonstrated that it would make good on the calls for radical reform, especially anticlerical reforms, that had grown louder and more steady since the end of the disastrous war with the United States. The so-called Reform laws were passed in 1855 and 1856, and although they had far-reaching implications for other corporate entities, particularly the indigenous communities, they were squarely directed at disempowering the church in the economic, political, and social realms. They called for an end to church courts' jurisdiction in civil cases (the Ley Juárez), the immediate sale of all church-owned property that was not used for strictly religious purposes (the Ley Lerdo), and the creation of a civil registry of births, marriages, and deaths (significant because the church had always been the legal keeper of these records), along with state regulation of the fees, or stipends, that priests could exact for performance of their spiritual functions at baptisms, marriages, and burials (the Ley Iglesias). Following up on the Reform laws, in 1857, a new liberal constitution was adopted that declined to make Roman Catholicism the national religion and pointedly refused to recognize monastic orders: "the State cannot allow any contract, pact, or agreement to go into effect that has for its object the impairment, loss, or irrevocable sacrifice of individual liberty, no matter whether the cause is work, education, or religious vows. Consequently, the law does not recognize monastic orders, nor can it permit their establishment."[70]

The uproar caused by this legislation and the new constitution led to a war to overthrow the liberals and restore the privileges of the church. The War of the Reform, also known as the Three Years' War, lasted from 1858 until 1861. The violent resistance of the church and the conservatives to the laws of the Reform, and their success at mobilizing large segments of the population for war, infuriated the liberals, who passed a much more radical wartime law in July 1859. This law (among other things) nationalized church wealth (as opposed to the Lerdo law, which had merely forced the church to sell its property); suppressed all male religious orders (reducing the religious to the status of secular clergy); closed the novitiate for female convents; and prohibited novices from professing. For the time being, the female convents were spared, and although the liberals were victorious over the conservatives in 1861, the intervention of the French in Mexico—by invitation of the conservatives—the very next year led to brief optimism that they might survive in the long term.[71] But in late February 1863, from his roving seat of government, President Benito Juárez ordered the suppression of the female convents. In the areas that were not under French control, federal troops moved in to be sure that the convents complied with the order.

The nuns of La Purísima had a little over a month to prepare for their removal from the convent, time enough to arrange which nuns were to be housed with which families and to send out for safekeeping the few valuables that the convent possessed. Still, there was hope that a divine intervention would prevent this calamity, and so it was something of a shock when it was learned that the troops were nearing San Miguel. Father Vicente de J. Campa describes the day they arrived:

> Almost as soon as we became aware that a force was on its way to carry out the announced exclaustration of the Religiosas . . . [Commander] D. Ygnacio Echegaray arrived on the tenth of April, at two o'clock in the afternoon, with something like one thousand five hundred men, and the provincial governor (*gefe político*) [of the department of Allende], in a very precipitous and abrupt manner, ordered the exclaustration to take place immediately, and sent various communications regarding the matter, of which because of his unseemly urgency only one could be answered.[72]

These communications sent by the provincial governor concerned the creation of exact inventories of the contents of the church and convent, the manner in which these should be turned over to the parish priest or other authorized persons, and (most galling) an insistence that the exclaustration must take place that very night "without excuse or pretext for delay." Furthermore, the nuns must be accommodated in the houses on a list provided by his office, houses of "persons whose good conduct and probity are notorious in this population." The assurance that he had ordered that the nuns be treated with "all the decorum and civility that their situation demands" was scarcely enough to compensate for the arrogance of the idea that the government had a right to identify the citizens with whom the nuns should be housed.[73]

Abbess Teresa de Nuestra Madre Purísima responded to this latter point in a letter written on the same night, which Campa reproduced:

> It is a quarter to seven in the evening, and I have just received the message announcing the execution of the decree of exclaustration, along with the list of houses that the governor's office has offered us . . . With respect to the hour in which we will make our departure, if

God disposes, it will be between nine o'clock and eleven o'clock to-
night. We believe that you will understand if we do not choose to
occupy the houses that [the government] has made available to us,
since we have already accepted the offers of the persons on the list
that we append and we expect that it will meet with your approval.
God be with you.[74]

Campa continues his account of the day's events:

From nine o'clock to eleven o'clock that night the nuns, their servants and the niñas took their departure from the convent, fortu-
nately without incident or disorder of any sort, settling two by two in
the houses that had been offered to them beforehand, ignoring the
list of houses provided by the government, and the other ladies and
girls were collected by their relatives and those that had no relations
were placed for the time being in private houses . . .

By refusing to abide by the arrangements made by the provincial governor,
the nuns managed to preserve their dignity, even as they were forced out of
the convent. All the same, the image of some 14 nuns, several of them elderly,
half-blind, or infirm, leaving the convent in the dark of night, with 1,500 federal
troops as their witnesses, makes a sad contrast to the day, almost 100 years
earlier, in 1765, when 25 mostly young women took possession of their new
convent in the midst of a joyful celebration, with the whole population of the
villa crowding the streets and filling the rooftops of the heavily adorned houses,
watching in wonder and respect as they processed. In the larger scheme of
things, the convent had never been a great success and would not, perhaps, be
greatly missed in the town. But for the women that Campa called the "poor
Señoras," who had no other usefulness, no other identity, than being a nun,
exclaustration was a tragedy.

NOTES

1. Sister Manuela de la Santísima Trinidad to Bishop Fray Antonio de San Miguel, 19 June 1793, AHAM, Diocesano, Gobierno, Correspondencia, Religiosas, caja
39, exp. 44. See also Amerlinck de Corsi and Ramos Medina, 261, on the Aguascalientes foundation.

2. For a broad treatment, Jo Ann Kay McNamara, *Sisters in Arms: Catholic Nuns
through Two Millennia* (Cambridge, Mass.: Harvard University Press, 1996), especially
chapters 17, 18, and 19. For France, see Rapley, *The Dévotes*, and Ralph Gibson, *A Social History of French Catholicism, 1789–1914* (London, New York: Routledge, 1989),
105–107; for Ireland, see Mary Peckham Magray, *The Transforming Power of the Nuns:
Women, Religion, and Cultural Change in Ireland, 1750–1900* (New York: Oxford University Press, 1998), 8–11; for Italy, see Caffiero; for Germany, see Margaret Lavinia
Anderson, "The Limits of Secularization: On the Problem of the Catholic Revival in

19th Century Germany," *Historical Journal*, 38:3 (1995); and Manuel Borutta, "Enemies at the Gate: The Moabit Klostersturm and the Kulturkampf: Germany," in Christopher Clark and Wolfram Kaiser, eds., *Culture Wars: Secular-Catholic Conflict in
Nineteenth-Century Europe* (New York: Cambridge University Press, 2003), 237.

3. Francisco Veyra y Pardo to Indendant Juan Antonio de Riaño, 4 April 1800,
AGN, Templos y Conventos, vol. 6, exp. 1. "In particular," the local official wrote, "it is
to be feared that the adobe wall that forms the cross section of the church, the very
wall on which stands the altar at which the mass is celebrated, from one day to the
next will come crashing to the floor."

4. Vicar Ignacio Antonio de Palacios to Bishop Fray Antonio de San Miguel, 8
July 1801, AGN, Templos y Conventos, vol. 6, exp. 1.

5. "Cuenta de los gastos erogados en la fábrica material del Real Convento de la
Purísima Concepción de la Villa de S. Miguel el Grande . . . ," Valladolid, 1805, AGN,
Templos y Conventos, vol 26, exp. 2.

6. Amerlinck de Corsi and Ramos Medina, 229.

7. "Visita . . . 1809," AHAM, Diocesano, Gobierno, Religiosas, Concepcionistas,
caja 374 (XIX), exp. 10.

8. "Visita, y Elección de Vicaria Abadesa, y nombramiento de Oficialas del Convento . . . 1797," AHAM, Diocesano, Gobierno, Religiosas, Concepcionistas, caja 256
(XVIII), exp. 50; "Visita . . . 1809," AHAM, Diocesano, Gobierno, Religiosas, Concepcionistas, caja 374 (XIX), exp. 10.

9. The famous "grito de Dolores," reenacted every September 16 to celebrate
Mexican independence from Spain, refers to the town just to the north and west of
San Miguel, where several of the San Miguel elite had their sheep ranches. Hidalgo
took the banner of the Virgin of Guadalupe, which came to symbolize his campaign,
from the nearby sanctuary of Atotonilco, the baroque gem built by Father Luis Phelipe Neri de Alfaro, the confessor of the foundress of La Purísima.

10. De la Maza tells the story that the two sisters of Hidalgo and the wife of
Aldama, along with about 15 to 20 other women, had taken refuge in the convent of
La Purísima; allegedly, they were brought to Flon, on his orders, and told that they
must try to influence their sons, brothers, and husbands to put down their arms. De
la Maza, *San Miguel*, 158–161.

11. De la Maza, *San Miguel*, 161.

12. De la Maza, *San Miguel*, 167.

13. Anne F. Staples, "La cola del diablo en la vida conventual (Los conventos de
monjas del arzobispado de Mexico, 1823–1835)," Ph.D. diss., El Colegio de México,
1970, chapters 2 and 3; Lavrin, "Mexican Nunneries," 304–305.

14. The accounts for 1811 are given from April 1811 to April 1812; then the mayordomo changed his method of reporting and covered from January to January for the
following years. Thus, we are missing the accounts from January to April 1811, and
we have double reporting of the months from January to April 1812. The 1811 figure,
then, is approximate.

15. "Quaderno que contiene las cuentas pertenecienes al Sagrado Real Convento
. . . 1811–1816," AHAM, Diocesano, Gobierno, Religiosas, Concepcionistas, caja 374
(XIX), exp. 11; "Cuentas . . . 1817 . . . 1818," AHAM, Diocesano, Gobierno, Religiosas,
Concepcionistas, caja 374 (XIX), exp. 13 and 14.

16. Letters from mayordomo Vicente Umarán, AHAM, Diocesano, Gobierno,

Religiosas, Concepcionistas, caja 374 (XIX), exp. 15; "El Real Convento de Señoras Religiosas de la Purísima Concepción de esta Villa, debe al Caudal libre de los Señores Canales, hasta el 13 de Abril de 1808 que entregó el Sr. Coronel D. Narciso María Loreto de la Canal," AHAM, Diocesano, Gobierno, Religiosas, Concepcionistas, caja 374 (XIX), exp. 19.

17. In 1800 the allowances of the nuns in the other convents of the bishopric were also increased because of inflation.

18. "Cuentas . . . 1818," AHAM, Diocesano, Gobierno, Religiosas, Concepcionistas, caja 374 (XIX), exp. 13.

19. Letters from mayordomo Vicente Umarán, AHAM, Diocesano, Gobierno, Religiosas, Concepcionistas, caja 374 (XIX), exp. 15.

20. Vicar Francisco de Uraga to Sres. Governadores [of the vacant see], 2 September 1819, AHAM, Diocesano, Gobierno, Religiosas, Capuchinas, caja 359 (XIX), exp. 11. The cathedral chapter members to whom this letter was addressed asked Uraga for a list of the convent's debtors, saying that they would try to get the viceroy to issue the highest executive orders against the wealthiest borrowers on the list, without admitting any excuse or moratorium. This certainly produced no solution, since independence was less than 2 years away, at which time the viceroy's orders would be meaningless.

21. A sampling of travelers' accounts in the nineteenth century turns up very few people who went through San Miguel; instead, all took the southern route. See, for example, John Lewis Geiger, *A Peep at Mexico: Narrative of a Journey Across the Republic from the Pacific to the Gulf in December 1873 and January 1874* (London: Trubner and Co., 1974); Albert M. Gilliam, *Travels Over the Table Lands and Cordilleras of Mexico During the Years 1843 and 44* (Philadelphia: J. W. Moore, 1846); Albert S. Evans, *Our Sister Republic: A Gala Trip through Tropical Mexico in 1869–70* (Hartford, Conn.: Columbian Book Company, 1870), 212–220. Evans also mentions a textile factory in Celaya that, he said, "supports half the town" (215), another indication of San Miguel's eclipse.

22. Hudson Strode, *Now in Mexico* (New York: Harcourt, Brace, 1941), 304.

23. Strode, 304, 313.

24. "Cuentas . . . 1823, AHAM, Diocesano, Gobierno, Religiosas, Concepcionistas, caja 374 (XIX), exp. 20; "Cuentas . . . 1844," AHAM, Diocesano, Gobierno, Religiosas, Concepcionistas, caja 374 (XIX), exp. 43; "Puntos que han visitado las monjas de la Concepción en los escrutinios para el capítulo de octubre 1857," AHAM, Diocesano, Gobierno, Religiosas, Concepcionistas, caja 376 (XIX), exp. 52.

25. The average amount brought by women to elite marriages from 1770 to 1810 in Michoacán was about 10,000 pesos; from 1810 to 1850, it was about 4,500 pesos (based on 57 and 104 marriages, respectively). Source: Notary records and estate inventories found in AHAM, Archivo de Notarías de Morelia, Archivo Judicial del Estado de Michoacán, Archivo del Ayuntamiento de Pátzcuaro.

26. There is a large body of literature on "culture wars" in Europe over the issue of the role of the church in nineteenth-century society, but there is much less information on Mexico, although the issues would appear to be comparable. Clark and Kaiser have recently edited a good compilation of essays that lay out the issues, survey the battles in a number of European countries, and provide good bibliography.

27. On the Mexican government's demands for forced loans, see Lavrin, "Problems and Policies," and "Mexican Nunneries," and Michael P. Costeloe, *The Central*

Republic in Mexico, 1835–1846: Hombres de Bien in the Age of Santa Anna (Cambridge: Cambridge University Press, 1993), especially 11, 127–130.

28. Lavrin, "Mexican Nunneries," 294.

29. Lavrin, "Mexican Nunneries," 289–301; and for Michoacán, José Luis de Sautto to Alejandro Quesada, 2 March 1842, AHAM, Diocesano, Gobierno, Religiosas, Concepcionistas, caja 375 (XIX), exp. 39.

30. Sister María Josefa del Espiritu Santo to Vicar General, 7 May 1829, AHAM, Diocesano, Gobierno, Religiosas, Concepcionistas, caja 374 (XIX), exp. 25; untitled note from the local vicar dated 23 July 1829, appended to a letter from Sister María Josefa del Espíritu Santo to Vicar General, AHAM, Diocesano, Gobierno, Religiosas, Concepcionistas, caja 374 (XIX), exp. 25.

31. Abbess María Josefa Mónica de San Antonio to Dr. D. Jose Felipe Basques, 19 February 1837, AHAM, Diocesano, Gobierno, Religiosas, Dominicas, caja 380 (XIX), exp. 60.

32. On the question of liberal piety, see Voekel.

33. Tremebundo, "Quitada de las Monjas y Frailes," October 29, 1833. North American "convent narratives" include, most famously, María Monk, *The Awful Disclosures of Maria Monk, as Exhibited in a Narrative of Her Sufferings During a Residence of Five Years as a Novice and Two Years as a Black Nun, in the Hotel Dieu Nunnery in Montreal* (New York: Howe & Bates, 1836); Rebecca Reed, *Six Months in a Convent, or, The Narrative of Rebecca Theresa Reed, Who was Under the Influence of the Roman Catholics About Two Years, and an Inmate of the Ursuline Convent on Mount Benedict, Charlestown, Mass., Nearly Six Months, in the Years 1831–2* (Boston: Russell, Odiorne & Metcalf, 1835); and Josephine Bunkley, *The Testimony of an Escaped Novice from the Sisterhood of St. Joseph* (New York: Harper & Brothers, 1855).

34. Francisco Morales points out that "the first ideological attacks against the religious orders came not only from liberal circles but also from the friars themselves," who took advantage of freedom of the press to air internal disputes and shed an unflattering light on the convent from the inside. Francisco Morales, "Mexican Society and the Franciscan Order in a Period of Transition, 1749–1859," *The Americas* 54:3 (1998), 342.

35. Mariano Cuevas, *Historia de la iglesia en México*, vol. 5 (Mexico City: Editorial Patria, 1947), 129.

36. Costeloe, 128–129; Staples, 37–38; Francisco Santa Cruz, *La piqueta de la Reforma* (Mexico City: Editorial Jus, 1958), 7–9.

37. Between 1809 and 1821, the impediment to the appointment of a new bishop was that the bishop-elect, Manuel Abad y Queipo, was alleged to be illegitimate and therefore was never confirmed; after 1821, the delay in naming a new bishop was because of a dispute between the papacy and the new Mexican nation over who had the right to make clerical appointments (patronage). Spain had been granted patronage in the sixteenth century, and Mexico now claimed the same right, but the papacy refused to recognize it. Not until compromise was reached in 1831 were new bishops or cathedral chapter members named, which meant that Michoacán was not the only diocese that had been without a bishop for many years.

38. During the period of the vacant see, between 1810 and 1832, there were 14 nuns admitted, 11 in the 3 years from 1829 to 1831. One girl who entered in 1816 died soon after professing, and three others did not profess because of ill health or for

unstated reasons. At most, four provided a dowry (for two of them, documents that would confirm payment of a dowry are missing). The others received a dowry either from the Landeta benefice, established at the time of the foundation, or from the 12,000-peso Uraga donation, a gift from the beloved vicar, who had already supported the convent out of his own pocket during the dark days of the insurgency.

39. Father Francisco Ygnacio Castaneda to the bishop's office, 2 July 1816, AHAM, Diocesano, Gobierno, Religiosas, Capuchinas, caja 212 (XIX), exp. 73; anonymous letter to the bishop's office, 1828, AHAM, Diocesano, Gobierno, Religiosas, Capuchinas, caja 359 (XIX), exp. 19.

40. María de la Luz del Río to Vicar General of Monasteries, 2 January 1849, AHAM, Diocesano, Gobierno, Religiosas, De la Enseñanza, caja 386 (XIX), exp. 35.

41. Entrance of María Antonia Cuéllar, November 1829, AHAM, Diocesano, Gobierno, Religiosas, Concepcionistas, caja 375 (XIX), exp. 29; Entrance of María Atilana de la Luz Ortiz, December 1830, AHAM, Diocesano, Gobierno, Religiosas, Concepcionistas, caja 375 (XIX), exp. 29.

42. Staples, 37.

43. Vicar Maximiano Moncada to Vicar General, 6 August 1851, AHAM, Diocesano, Gobierno, Religiosas, Concepcionistas, caja 376 (XIX), exp. 52. This decree would have applied to La Purísima, La Enseñanza, and the Carmelites of Morelia.

44. Abbess and Definitorio to Vicar General, 26 August 1844, AHAM, Diocesano, Gobierno, Religiosas, Concepcionistas, caja 375 (XIX), exp. 39.

45. Vicar Maximiano Moncada to Vicar General, 6 August 1851, AHAM, Diocesano, Gobierno, Religiosas, Concepcionistas, caja 376 (XIX), exp. 52.

46. Abbess and Definitorio to Vicar General, 5 September 1842, AHAM, Diocesano, Gobierno, Religiosas, Capuchinas, caja 361, exp. 39; Lic. José Manuel Fernández to Bishop Juan Cayetano de Portugal, 16 September 1839, AHAM, Diocesano, Gobierno, Religiosas, Concepcionistas, caja 375 (XIX), exp. 28.

47. Lic. José Manuel Fernández to Bishop Juan Cayetano de Portugal, 16 September 1839, AHAM, Diocesano, Gobierno, Religiosas, Concepcionistas, caja 375 (XIX), exp. 28; Abbess and Definitorio to Vicar General, 5 September 1842, AHAM, Diocesano, Gobierno, Religiosas, Capuchinas, caja 361, exp. 38.

48. Abbess and Definitorio to Vicar General, 5 September 1842, AHAM, Diocesano, Gobierno, Religiosas, Capuchinas, caja 361 (XIX), exp. 38; Vicar General to Definitorio, 19 September 1842, AHAM, Diocesano, Gobierno, Religiosas, Capuchinas, caja 361 (XIX), exp. 38.

49. Vicar José Alejandro Quesada to Lic. José María García, 1845, AHAM, Diocesano, Gobierno, Religiosas, Concepcionistas, caja 376 (XIX), exp. 50.

50. Vicar Maximiano Moncada to Vicar General, 17 July 1851, AHAM, Diocesano, Gobierno, Religiosas, Concepcionistas, caja 376 (XIX), exp. 52. In the text of his letter, Moncada refers repeatedly to nine who were ineligible, but he only names eight, and it appears likely that he counted Ygnacia del Corazón de María twice, once as too recently professed and once as illegitimate.

51. Vicar Maximiano Moncada to Vicar General, 17 July 1851, AHAM, Diocesano, Gobierno, Religiosas, Concepcionistas, caja 376 (XIX), exp. 52.

52. The same pattern of high income and expenses running below income is noted by Lavrin, "Mexican Nunneries," 307.

53. Vicar Maximiano Moncada to Vicar General, 6 August 1851, AHAM, Diocese-

sano, Gobierno, Religiosas, Concepcionistas, caja 376 (XIX), exp. 52; Vicar Maximiano Moncada to Dr. Luis G. Sierra, 14 November 1857, AHAM, Diocesano, Gobierno, Religiosas, Concepcionistas, caja 376 (XIX), exp. 52.

54. Vicar Maximiano Moncada to Vicar General, 6 August 1851, AHAM, Diocesano, Gobierno, Religiosas, Concepcionistas, caja 376 (XIX), exp. 52.

55. Mayordomo José Luis de Sautto to Vicar Alejandro Quesada, 2 March 1842, AHAM, Diocesano, Gobierno, Religiosas, Concepcionistas, caja 375 (XIX), exp. 39.

56. Abbess María Josefa de Señor San Juan Evangelista to Vicar José Alejandro Quesada, 4 July 1842, AHAM, Diocesano, Gobierno, Religiosas, Dominicas, caja 382 (XIX), exp. 87.

57. Mayordomo José Luis de Sautto to Vicar General, 23 October 1846, AHAM, Diocesano, Gobierno, Religiosas, Dominicas, caja 383, exp. 97.

58. This conventional wisdom holds that the Mexican economy was in a downward spiral from 1810 to 1880. All notary and other economic documents for San Miguel have been lost, so it is impossible to make more than the most general statements about the local economy, but for an argument that in the Bajío region, in general, the post-1810 depression had begun to lift by the 1830s, see Margaret Chowning, "The Contours of the Post-1810 Depression in Mexico: A Reappraisal from a Regional Perspective," *Latin American Research Review* 27:2 (Spring, 1992).

59. "Año de 1821 a 1822. Cuenta que presenta el mayordomo . . . ," AHAM, Diocesano, Gobierno, Religiosas, Concepcionistas, caja 374 (XIX), exp. 20.

60. "Cuentas . . . 1847," AHAM, Diocesano, Gobierno, Religiosas, Concepcionistas, caja 376 (XIX), exp. 46.

61. "Cuenta que el Mayordomo Administrador de los propios y rentas del Convento de Religiosas Dominicas . . . forma por fin del mes de Dez. de 1838, de los réditos cobrados, y gastos erogados desde 1 de Mayo del mismo año," AHAM, Diocesano, Gobierno, Religiosas, Dominicas, caja 381 (XIX), exp. 76.

62. Vicar Francisco Uraga to Vicar General, 24 January 1828, AHAM, Diocesano, Gobierno, Religiosas, Teresianas, caja 395 (XIX), exp. 4.

63. "Cuentas . . . 1841," AHAM, Diocesano, Gobierno, Religiosas, Concepcionistas, caja 374 (XIX), exp. 38.

64. "Cuentas . . . 1841," AHAM, Diocesano, Gobierno, Religiosas, Concepcionistas, caja 375 (XIX), exp. 38; "Cuentas . . . 1846," AHAM, Diocesano, Gobierno, Religiosas, Concepcionistas, caja 376 (XIX), exp. 44. In 1841, the inn was listed as producing an income of 700 pesos a year, and by 1846, it was no longer among the properties owned by the convent.

65. "Capítulo y elección . . . 1821," AHAM, Diocesano, Gobierno, Religiosas, Concepcionistas, caja 374 (XIX), exp. 18; "Capítulo y elección . . . 1836," AHAM, Diocesano, Gobierno, Religiosas, Concepcionistas, caja 375 (XIX), exp. 28; Vicar Maximiano Moncada to Vicar General, 11 November 1857, AHAM, Diocesano, Gobierno, Religiosas, Concepcionistas, caja 376 (XIX), exp. 52.

66. It is commonly accepted that after the war with the United States, reformist impulses among the liberals intensified, in part as a reaction to the disaster of the war—it seemed obvious to them that major social, economic, and cultural reforms, not piecemeal or half-hearted political reforms, were necessary to prevent future disasters. What is much less explored in the literature is the question of whether there

was a Catholic reformist movement as well, perhaps also in response to the war. If that argument were to be made, Moncada would be a good example of a nineteenth-century Catholic reformer.

67. "Capítulo y elección . . . 1854," AHAM, Diocesano, Gobierno, Religiosas, Concepcionistas, caja 376 (XIX), exp. 55.

68. Vicar Maximiano Moncada to Vicar General, 11 November 1857, AHAM, Diocesano, Gobierno, Religiosas, Concepcionistas, caja 376 (XIX), exp. 52.

69. Moncada's rectitude and desire to adhere to the Rule are apparent everywhere, but the fact that he endured 20 identical ballots, when his predecessors tended to give up at 3 (1821) or 4 (1836) is an excellent example of his character. "Capítulo y elección . . . 1821," AHAM, Diocesano, Gobierno, Religiosas, Concepcionistas, caja 374 (XIX), exp. 18; "Capítulo y elección . . . 1836," AHAM, Diocesano, Gobierno, Religiosas, Concepcionistas, caja 375 (XIX), exp. 28.

70. This translation is adapted from *The Catholic Encyclopedia*'s entry on Mexico.

71. Although the intentions of the liberal government with regard to the female convents were signaled in 1861, when in Mexico City, nuns in the 21 female convents were relocated so as to reduce the total number of convents to 9—some of the choices made in terms of which nuns moved in with which other nuns were a bit perverse; for example, recollected nuns were placed in relaxed convents. Antonio García Cubas, *El libro de mis recuerdos* (Mexico City: Editorial Porrúa, 1986 [1905]), 37–38; Muriel, *Los conventos*, 512.

72. Report of Father Vicente de J. Campa to Lic. Luis Macouzet, 13 April 1863, AHAM, Diocesano, Gobierno, Religiosas, Concepcionistas, caja 376 (XIX), exp. 57.

73. Gefatura de policía del Departamento de Allende to Father Vicente de J. Campa, 10 April 1863, AHAM, Diocesano, Gobierno, Religiosas, Concepcionistas, caja 376 (XIX), exp. 57.

74. Abbess María Teresa de Nuestra Madre Purísima to Father Vicente de J. Campa, 10 April 1863, AHAM, Diocesano, Gobierno, Religiosas, Concepcionistas, caja 376 (XIX), exp. 57.

Epilogue

The Convent of La Purísima Concepción in Post-Reform Mexico

After the nuns of Mexico were expelled from the convents in 1863, they could now—according to civil law—live as they pleased.[1] The liberals had set the nuns free. But the energies of most of these women now turned to finding a way to undo their liberation, to stay together and recreate the cloister in the homes to which they had been sent, or in the shared residences that most of them acquired, in the faithful expectation that, eventually, they would be allowed to resume their lives in community.[2] It was the official position of the ecclesiastical hierarchy that in their new, private lives, the former nuns should continue to live by their solemn vows of poverty, chastity, obedience, and (as far as possible) enclosure, but church officials felt that they could not sanction, or at least could not be seen as sanctioning, any efforts to rebuild the communities themselves, after two defeats at the hands of the liberals (in 1861, in the War of the Reform, and in 1867, with the victory of Juárez and the republicans over the French). Thus, the bishops refused to authorize new admissions or professions until late in the nineteenth century, when Porfirio Díaz's conciliatory policies toward the church finally made it safe for the convents to emerge from the shadows. In the meantime, contact between the nuns and the bishop's office, and even between the nuns and the local priests who served as their vicars, was much reduced. The extent to which the nuns were able to stay together, then, was largely a function of their own energy and determination; they were only minimally supported by the church establishment.

Recreating the cloistered state and convent routines when there was no cloister, however, was not an easy task, especially since any kind of meeting or community activity had to be kept secret from the government. In 1870, the archbishop[3] of Michoacán, at the request of the beatas of the Beaterio de Jesús Nazareno in Celaya, provided guidelines for maintaining their religious estate as far as possible without arousing the ire of government officials, and these instructions give some indication of the awkwardness of the situation that both the beatas and the nuns faced.[4] The women were to leave their houses only with permission of the vicar or rectora (more or less, the beaterio equivalent of the abbess), and then only to attend mass, take communion, carry a message to the house of the rectora, visit a sick sister, or attend community functions, and in all cases, they were to be accompanied by another woman, preferably, another beata. Sundays they were to spend in the church, following a schedule created by the vicar. They were to dress in their habits while inside their homes and wear dark and modest clothing outside the house. They were allowed to engage in work appropriate to their sex and to charge a just price for their labor, and they could invest their earnings in their own necessities and those of their sisters in religion, but they were not to turn these earnings over to their family or hosts. Every month, they were to give a part of their earnings to their rectora. These instructions seem to have been generally similar to those followed by the nuns, although the nuns were encouraged to add fasting to their routines, had to observe a regimen of silence at certain times of the day, and were encouraged to live together in houses that were close by the church, so that they could maximize their observance of the vow of enclosure. Adhering to these restrictive measures without the solace and support of a larger community must have been a challenge, and the anxiety caused by the loss of their way of life and their physical surroundings and the inexorable diminution of their numbers continually put the survival of the communities in doubt.

How did the nuns of the former convents of the archbishopric fare in the post-Reform period? Most of them struggled, but managed to preserve at least some semblance of community. The Dominican nuns of Santa Catarina in Morelia, for example, found a house into which they could move, as a community, fairly soon after 1863, and they worked hard to maintain enclosure and otherwise live according to their vows. It appears that none of the Catharine nuns lived outside of this common dwelling, a remarkable achievement in holding the community together. But still, their path was not easy. In 1874, they were reduced to 18 nuns (from 25 in 1860), and by 1879, their numbers had fallen to 7, in what must have been a devastating half-decade marked by the deaths of 11 sisters. This disaster prompted the prioress to write two urgent letters to the bishop's office, begging him to allow the women in the novitiate to profess (it is unclear whether these were women who had been admitted to the novitiate before 1863, or if the bishop had authorized recent entrances, but was reluctant to allow professions, in light of the inflamed political circumstances). "Our situation," she wrote, "is worsening at an extraordinary rate, and the great effort that the Religiosas have made to sustain strict observance is carrying them rapidly to the grave. . . ." She asked for permission to allow seven choir nuns and one white veil nun to profess. Even though none of them could bring a dowry, she wrote, they were "abundant in virtue." She promised to carry out these professions with "great prudence in order to avoid the dangers of the civil authorities." When, 2 months later, she had not heard from the bishop's office, she wrote again, even more desperately:

> The many preoccupations of your office have not permitted you the
> time to respond to my letter of late May; after all, on your shoulders
> rests the weight of an extensive Archdiocese. But I am witnessing
> the violent destruction of this community that soon will disappear,
> as well as the painful uncertainty of the young women whom it ap-
> pears that God has chosen specially because of their fervor and apti-
> tude, who desire to form a new community. . . .

The bishop did respond to this second letter, but his answer was not the one that the prioress desired. He did not feel that the time was yet propitious to allow new professions.[5]

Finally, in 1888, the first post-Reform profession was permitted, and the nuns of Santa Catarina began slowly to rebuild. Over the next 8 years, nine novices were admitted. Although only six of them professed, the powerful next wave of admissions in the first decade of the twentieth century made it clear that the convent would survive. By 1904, there were 13 nuns, and by 1914 (the last date for which I have found records), 17 new nuns had joined 80-year-old Sister María de Jesús de Nuestra Señora de Guadalupe, the only nun who remained of those who had professed before 1863.[6] To judge by the reports of the visitations in both 1901 and 1904, the nuns had managed almost completely to recreate their previous lifestyle. Although they complained about the porosity of the grille, abuses of the main door and turnstile, the absence of silence at the appropriate times of day, and the inequality among the beds provided for the nuns in their cells (here, the visitor professed to be quite puzzled, since the beds all appeared to him to be exactly the same), these complaints indicate that the physical conditions of the cloister had been largely reproduced. Perhaps even more significant, they suggest that the psychic status quo had been restored to the extent that the nuns could devote emotional energy to the relatively petty complaints that, from time immemorial, had been a part of their triennial interviews.[7]

The Dominican nuns of Nuestra Señora de la Salud in Pátzcuaro also faced obstacles in their early efforts to hold the community together, and also overcame them, although not until late in the nineteenth century. In 1874, their numbers were reduced to 12 (from 23 in 1863), and by 1882, they were down to 9. They did not hold an election between 1865 and 1874, because of the "calamitous circumstances of the times" and because they felt that there was no place they could meet that would not attract the attention of the authorities. Like the Catharines, however, they had found a house to live in together, which they had modified in order to observe enclosure as far as it was possible to do so, and even though they were few in number, there are references to servants and young girls whom they were educating.[8] It is unclear exactly when they began to admit new novices in the post-Reform era, but by 1900, there were 17 nuns, and in the period from 1900 to 1914, the convent rebounded more quickly than any other in the archdiocese: During those years, there were 28 admissions, and 26 of these women professed, bringing the number of nuns to around 40 to 45 by 1914, close to an all-time high.[9] Many of these girls brought dowries, although an innovation was a sort of floating dowry scale, seemingly adjusted according to the ability of the novice to pay. The names of many of the new recruits indicate that, as always, they came from families who figured among the Pátzcuaro elite.

Like the other nuns, the Teresas of Morelia, a late-established (1824) Carmelite convent, agonized early about how to stay together. In 1873, there were still 12 nuns (compared with 15 in 1852), but by 1885, their numbers had fallen to 7. Although they had a suitable house to share, not all of the nuns lived in it, and they were finding it hard to maintain the same level of strict observance as before their exclaustration. Their vicar chastised them for "allowing your religious spirit, which animated you with such fervor in the cloister, to decay"; he noted disunion, laxity, and communication with laypeople, "in a word, lack of observance of the Rule and the essential obligations of your estate." He acknowledged that exclaustration had inevitably made observance more difficult, but he urged the Teresas to pray and attend mass even more often than before, to fast for 9 days every 3 months, to live together in their house where at all possible, not to leave the house or entertain visitors without the permission of their superiors, to eat in common, and to observe silence.[10] But by 1914, this convent, too, had rebuilt. There were now 19 nuns: 14 choir nuns, 1 novice, and 4 lay sisters—like the Pátzcuaro convent, an all-time high.[11]

Letters and election records indicate that the Capuchin nuns of Salvatierra somehow held together as a community after 1863, although they did not have a common residence, and in 1882, only 10 of the 20 nuns actually lived in Salvatierra—7 lived in Celaya, 1 in San Miguel Allende, and 2 in Acámbaro.[12] This prompted one of the nuns to petition to be transferred to the Capuchin convent in the Villa de Guadalupe because she had heard that "they have the good fortune to be able to live in common." Indeed, it appears that, as late as 1897, they still had found no adequate residence in which they could live together, since a young woman who had been living with some of the nuns in a ruin of a house for 8 months was told by the abbess that, because they had no proper living quarters, she should apply to the Capuchin convent in Morelia instead, even though she had been admitted to Salvatierra by unanimous vote of the aging sisters.[13] By 1913, however, the Capuchins of Salvatierra had not only acquired a house, but also had recently completed a fairly extensive construction project that gave each of the nuns her own cell, and they had also outfitted a room to serve as the novitiate. There were at least 13 nuns at that time.

Thus did most of the nuns in the archdiocese battle, more or less successfully, to hold their communities together, until around the turn of the century, when—as they had always had faith would happen—the Díaz regime's policy of conciliation toward the church finally emboldened the hierarchy to allow large numbers of new admissions. The rejuvenated orders were still not allowed to occupy their old sites (most of the convent buildings had been sold or converted to other uses by the state, which took them over during the Reform—schools, barracks, jails), but they did begin to grow again. They adjusted to the times by enlarging their teaching or other service functions, in part in order to support themselves, and in part in order to blend in with the new teaching and charitable orders that were in great vogue, having been invited by the hierarchy to come to Mexico from Europe, or having been founded by activist bishops or other churchmen in the full flush of renewed religious enthusiasm after *Rerum Novarum* (1891), the encyclical that promoted "social Catholicism," a church committed to helping the poor.[14] It was less controversial to set up or invite in a new order (they were now called "congregations" in order to avoid the use of the word "convent") than to restore one of the old, suppressed orders; and hence, the prudent thing was for the old orders to make themselves over in the image of the new ones.

What about La Purísima? What happened to the convent buildings is fairly clear. The church continued to function, probably with the assistance of some of the former nuns, who continued to mend the linens, clean the sacristy, and support the priest. Late in the century, it received a new dome, which—with the bell tower that the nuns added in the 1840s—completed the look of the church as we see it today. The cloisters were converted, first, into a barracks during the war with the French (which ended in 1867, when Archduke Maximilian, styled Emperor of Mexico, was executed in nearby Querétaro), and then they became a primary school. During the 1910 Revolution, the convent, once again, was used as a barracks, reverting to use as a school after 1920, and then, in 1938, becoming an art school founded by North Americans (and later supported by the Mexican government). Finally, after a restoration that began in 1962, it became the lovely Centro Cultural El Nigromante, named after Ignacio Ramírez, a native son of San Miguel and, ironically, one of the most vehement anticlericals of his generation of Reform-era liberals.

Of the nuns themselves, however, there is a complete dearth of archival information. While the other convents in the bishopric that stayed together generated a fairly substantial paper trail, as we have seen, there is no record of elections, visitations, petitions, or correspondence concerning the nuns or convent of La Purísima in the documents filed under "Concepcionistas," misfiled along with any of the other convents' records, in the correspondence of the vicar general or the bishop, in the records of episcopal visitations and parish business, or in the documents concerning pious associations and schools, all of which I have combed systematically.[15] Of course, it is possible that the convent's records after 1863 were simply lost, but the record-keeping before that date was so extraordinarily complete that that seems unlikely. At the very least, one would expect there to be a passing mention of the nuns of La Purísima in documents concerning other convents or other business of the archbishopric, if they had clung with any success at all to that identity. But there is none. In short, there is no indication in the archival record that the nuns were able to stay together after their expulsion or that they made any serious attempt to do so. We must assume that the perennial problems of the convent—inadequate numbers, poor leadership, tension over reform versus relaxation, generational divides, and lack of connection to the city in which the convent was located (only 3 of the 14 nuns in 1863 were from San Miguel)—came together to make it impossible to overcome the inherent difficulties of sustaining the community in the face of civil disapprobation and ecclesiastical caution.

But while the archival trail runs out in 1863, the story does not end here. Today, visitors to the church of La Concepción and the Centro Cultural can purchase rosaries, medals, prayer cards, scapulars, missals, crucifixes, and other religious items from a little shop to one side of the church, run by Conceptionist nuns. Unlike most Mexican nuns, who occupy houses physically apart from their churches, the modern-day Conceptionists of San Miguel are fortunate enough to live in a house adjacent to the church—actually, a part of the former convent—and they still use the old choir built for the nuns in the eighteenth century. Their version of the convent's history was told to me by Sister María Lilia in August 2004. According to her, in 1912, four of the nuns from the old convent—who would have been between 75 and 80 years old by then, assuming that they were the four youngest of those who had professed in 1855—returned to the convent (from where she did not know) and took up residence in quarters that form part of the nuns' house today.

Ten years later, in 1922, with only one of these original nuns still alive (was she María Soledad del Señor Ecce Homo, the youngest of the six nuns to profess in 1855?), the parish priest of San Miguel undertook a project to renew the convent, no doubt as part of the broader campaign by the church in the 1920s to strengthen itself against the renewed anticlericalism of the victorious revolutionaries. He recruited four young women from his hometown of Pueblo Nuevo (Guanajuato) as novices. But clearly, María Soledad, now age 85, could not instruct the young girls by herself, and so the priest approached the Conceptionist convent of San José de Gracia in Mexico City, to see if they were willing to send four nuns to San Miguel. I suggested to Sister María Lilia that they were like "founders" (seeking a neat parallel between these women and the four original founding nuns, who had come from Mexico City in 1756), but she corrected me, calling them instead "restorers" (*restauradoras*). With the four nuns from Mexico City, the four novices, and the old nun from the original convent, the house began to take new shape, just in time for the religious persecution of the Calles regime to force them, once again, to leave their house in 1926. Two of the jóvenes gave up and returned home; the others took refuge in private residences, just as in 1863. Not an auspicious beginning for the newly restored convent.

But when the nuns returned, in 1930 or 1931, to their small house next to the convent church, their whole long history began to turn around. In a word, they flourished, as never before. By 1964, there were over 60 nuns in the convent, finally approaching the population that María Josepha Lina had envisioned 200 years earlier. Today, there are about 40 women, their numbers depleted not by a failure to thrive but by the number of nuns whom they have sent out to undertake new foundations since 1958 in the states of Morelos, Guerrero, and Querétaro: in the towns of Tlalnepantla, Taxco, Iguala, Chilapa, Pedro Escobedo. In 2004 and 2005, Sister María Lilia expected that there would be two more new foundations.

One way to bookend this story is with the nuns' joyous entrance into their convent in 1765, on one end, and their sad exit in 1863, on the other. But another way is with the hopeful enthusiasm of the four original founding nuns, who braved the difficult journey from Mexico City to San Miguel in 1756, on one end, and the pride and faithful certitude of the modern-day nuns, sending out their own sisters to new foundations, on the other. The latter is not only a happier ending for the vision of the young foundress, María Josepha Lina de la Canal, but also a better metaphor for the resilience of Mexican Catholicism.

NOTES

1. In theory, the nuns' dowries were returned to them so that they would have the same financial support that they had had in the convent. In practice, the chaos of the Reform period (when the church was trying to conceal its assets and record-keeping was a nightmare) and the absence of a mayordomo to collect interest on their behalf meant that the luckiest nuns reached a settlement with their debtors, in which they received a small cash payment in exchange for canceling the debt, and the unluckiest nuns never saw a cent.

2. This generalization is true for the bishopric of Michoacán, as this epilogue demonstrates, and based on anecdotal evidence, it is probably true for the rest of Mexico, but studies of convents in other bishoprics for this period have not been made.

3. The bishopric of Michoacán was elevated to an archbishopric in 1863, and the bishoprics of Zamora and León were created at the same time.

4. Decree of Archbishop José Ignacio Arciga, 17 March 1870, AHAM, Diocesano, Gobierno, Colegios, Varios, caja 10 (XIX), exp. 18.

5. "Elección capitular . . . 1874," and "Capítulo . . . 1880," AHAM, Diocesano, Go-

bierno, Religiosas, Catarinas, caja 373 (XIX), exp. 176; María Petra de S. S. José Priora Santa Catarina de Sena to Governador de la Mitra, late May 1879 and 24 July 1879, AHAM, Diocesano, Gobierno, Religiosas, Dominicas, caja 384 (XIX), exp. 138.

6. "Lista de las Religiosas Dominicas del Convento de Santa Catarina de Sena, 1914," AHAM, Diocesano, Gobierno, Religiosas, Dominicas, caja 384 (XIX), exp. 139.

7. "Informes secretos sobre el convento de Catarinas, 15 August 1901, exp. 2; Visita secreta . . . August 1904," AHAM, Diocesano, Gobierno, Religiosas, Varios, caja 81 (XX), exp. 1 (Catarinas).

8. "Elección capitular . . . 1874," and "Elección capitular . . . 1882," AHAM, Diocesano, Gobierno, Religiosas, Dominicas, caja 384 (XIX), exp. 133.

9. Various expedientes concerning entrances and professions, AHAM, Diocesano, Gobierno, Religiosas, Dominicas, caja 384 (XIX); various expedientes concerning entrances and professions, AHAM, Diocesano, Gobierno, Religiosas, Varios, caja 82 (XX); and for the figure for 1900, Arsenio Robledo to Mitra, 11 February 1900, AHAM, Diocesano, Gobierno, Religiosas, Varios, caja 82 (XX), exp. 1.

10. "Año de 1873. Expediente sobre capítulo verificado . . . 1 March 1873," AHAM, Diocesano, Gobierno, Religiosas, Teresianas, caja 396 (XIX), exp. 26.

11. "Visita secreta del convento de Religiosas Teresas de esta ciudad, practicada por el Ilmo Sr. Arzobispo . . . 13 January 1914, AHAM, Diocesano, Gobierno, Religiosas, Teresianas, caja 396 (XIX), exp. 26.

12. Sister María Josefa Jesús to Archbishop, 1882, AHAM, Diocesano, Gobierno, Religiosas, Capuchinas, caja 361 (XIX), exp. 79.

13. Sister Antonia Josefa to Archbishop, n.d. 1882, AHAM, Diocesano, Gobierno, Religiosas, Capuchinas, caja 361 (XIX), exp. 80; entrance María Redentora Monreal, 31 August 1897, AHAM, Diocesano, Gobierno, Religiosas, Capuchinas, caja 361 (XIX), exp. 82.

14. For example, in the archbishopric of Michoacán, the new late nineteenth- and early twentieth-century congregations included the Congregación de Hijas de María Inmaculada de Guadalupe, founded by José Antonio Plancarte y Labastida in Zamora, and the Congregación de Hermanas de los Pobres, Siervas del Sagrado Corazón, also founded in Zamora by Bishop José María Cázares. Among the foreign orders that made their first appearance in Mexico were the Hermanas Salesianas de María Auxiliadora.

15. The convent of La Enseñanza in Irapuato also seems to have fallen apart after the Reform.

Appendix

Bishops and Abbesses, 1756–1863

BISHOPS

Martín de Elizacochea	1745–1756
Pedro Anselmo Sánchez de Tagle	1757–1772
Luis Fernando Hoyos y Mier	1772–1776
Juan Ignacio de la Rocha	1777–1782
Antonio de San Miguel	1783–1804
Marcos Moriana y Zafrilla	1809
Juan Cayetano Gómez de Portugal	1831–1850
Clemente de Jesús Munguía	1852–1868

ABBESSES

Antonia del Santísimo Sacramento	1756–1761
María Anna del Santísimo Sacramento	1761–1762
Anna María de los Dolores	1762–1769
Phelipa de San Antonio	1769–1772
Gertudis de San José	1772–1782
Josepha Ygnacia de Santa Gertrudis	1782–1785
Augustina de la Encarnación	1785–1794
Manuela de San Raphael	1794–1800
Augustina de la Encarnación	1800–1812
[gap in records]	
Francisca de la Purificación	1821–1827
Josepha del Espiritu Santo	1827–1834
Josepha de San Juan Evangelista	1834–1848?

Matilde de San Juan Nepomuceno	1848–1851
María de San Juan de Jesús Sacramentado	1851–1857
Rosalía de San Francisco de Paula	1857–1861
Teresa de Nuestra Madre Purísima	1861–?

Bibliography

ARCHIVES USED

Archivo del Cabildo Catedral de Morelia (ACCM)
Archivo General de la Nación (AGN)
Archivo Histórico del Arzobispado de Michoacán (AHAM)
Archvio de Notarías de Morelia (ANM)
Archivo Histórico Municipal de Morelia (AHMM)
Archivo Judicial del Estado de Michoacán (AJEM)
Archivo del Ayuntamiento de Pátzcuaro (AAP)
Archivo Histórico del Arzobispado de México

PUBLISHED SOURCES

Abad y Queipo, Manuel. *Colección de los escritos más importantes que en diferentes épocas dirigió al gobierno.* Mexico City: Mariano Ontiveros, 1813.
Ajofrín, Francisco de. *Diario del viaje que hicimos a México fray Francisco de Ajofrín y fray Fermín de Olite, capuchinos.* Mexico City: Secretaría de Educación Pública, 1986 [1936].
Alberro, Solange. "La licencia vestida de santidad: Teresa de Jesús, falsa beata del siglo XVII." In *De la santidad a la perversión,* ed. Sergio Ortega. Mexico City: Grijalbo, 1985.
Amerlinck de Corsi, María Concepción, and Manuel Ramos Medina. *Conventos de monjas: Fundaciones en el México virreinal.* Mexico City: Condumex, 1995.
Anderson, Margaret Lavinia. "The Limits of Secularization: On the Problem of the Catholic Revival in 19th Century Germany." *Historical Journal* 38: 3 (1995).

Arenal, Electa, and Stacy Schlau. *Untold Sisters: Hispanic Nuns in their Own Words.* Albuquerque: University of New Mexico Press, 1989.

Baernstein, P. Renée. *A Convent Tale: A Century of Sisterhood in Spanish Milan.* New York and London: Routledge, 2002.

Barry, John J. "Distinguishing Nonepileptic from Epileptic Events." *Epilepsy Quarterly* 4:1 (Spring, 1996).

Benitez, Fernando. *Los demonios en el convento: Sexo y religión en la Nueva España.* Mexico City: Editorial Era, 1985.

Bilinkoff, Jodi. *The Avila of St. Teresa.* Ithaca, N.Y.: Cornell University Press, 1989.

———. "Confessors, Penitents, and the Construction of Identities in Early Modern Avila." In *Culture and Identity in Early Modern Europe, 1500–1800,* ed. Barbara B. Diefendorf and Carla Hesse. Ann Arbor, Mich.: University of Michigan Press, 1993.

Birely, Robert. *The Refashioning of Catholicism, 1450–1700.* New York: St. Martin's Press, 1999.

Bobb, Bernard. *The Vice Regency of Antonio María Bucareli in New Spain, 1771–1779.* Austin, Tex: University of Texas Press, 1962.

Borutta, Manuel. "Enemies at the Gate: The Moabit Klostersturm and the Kulturkampf: Germany." In *Culture Wars: Secular-Catholic Conflict in Nineteenth-Century Europe,* ed. Christopher Clark and Wolfram Kaiser. New York: Cambridge University Press, 2003.

Boyer, Paul S., and Stephen Nissenbaum. *Salem Possessed: The Social Origin of Witchcraft.* Cambridge, Mass.: Harvard University Press, 1974.

Brading, David. *Church and State in Bourbon Mexico: The Diocese of Michoacán, 1749–1810.* Cambridge, England: Cambridge University Press, 1994.

Bravo Ugarte, José. *Luis Phelipe Neri de Alfaro: Vida, escritos, fundaciones, favores divinos.* Mexico City: Editorial Jus, 1966.

Brown, Judith C. *Immodest Acts: The Life of a Lesbian Nun in Renaissance Italy.* New York: Oxford University Press, 1986.

Bunkley, Josephine. *The Testimony of an Escaped Novice from the Sisterhood of St. Joseph.* New York: Harper & Brothers, 1855.

Burns, Kathyrn. *Colonial Habits: Convents and the Spiritual Economy of Cuzco, Peru.* Durham, N.C.: Duke University Press, 1999.

Burr, Claudia, Claudia Canales, and Rosalía Aguilar. *Perfil de una villa criolla: San Miguel el Grande, 1555–1810.* Mexico City: Instituto Nacional de Antropología e Historia, 1986.

Bynum, Caroline Walker. *Holy Feast and Holy Fast: The Religious Significance of Food to Medieval Women.* Berkeley, Calif.: University of California Press, 1987.

Caffiero, Marina. "From the Late Baroque Mystical Explosion to the Social Apostolate, 1650–1850." In *Women and Faith: Catholic Religious Life in Italy from Late Antiquity to the Present,* ed. Lucetta Scaraffia and Gabriella Zarri. Cambridge, Mass., and London: Harvard University Press, 1999.

Cardozo Galué, Germán. *Michoacán en el siglo de las luces.* Mexico City: Colegio de México, 1973.

The Catholic Encyclopedia: An International Work of Reference on the Constitution, Doctrine, Discipline and History of the Catholic Church. New York: Appleton, 1907–1912. Online edition, published by New Advent.

Certeau, Michel de. *The Possession at Loudun.* Chicago: University of Chicago Press, 2000.

Cervantes, Fernando. *The Devil in the New World: The Impact of Diabolism in New Spain.* New Haven, Conn.: Yale University Press, 1994.

Chowning, Margaret. "The Contours of the Post-1810 Depression in Mexico: A Reappraisal from a Regional Perspective." *Latin American Research Review* 27:2 (Spring, 1992).

———. "Convent Reform, Catholic Reform, and Bourbon Reform: The View from the Nunnery," *Hispanic American Historical Review,* 85: 1 (Feb., 2005).

Clark, Christopher, and Wolfram Kaiser, eds. *Culture Wars: Secular-Catholic Conflict in Nineteenth-Century Europe.* New York: Cambridge University Press, 2003.

Connaughton, Brian. *Ideología y sociedad en Guadalajara (1788–1853).* Mexico City: Consejo Nacional para la Cultura y las Artes, 1992.

Costeloe, Michael P. *The Central Republic in Mexico, 1835–1846: Hombres de Bien in the Age of Santa Anna.* Cambridge, England: Cambridge University Press, 1993.

Cuevas, Mariano. *Historia de la iglesia en México.* Volume Five. Mexico City: Editorial Patria, 1947.

Dávila y Garibi, José Ignacio Paulino. *Diligencias generalmente observadas en la Nueva Galicia para la fundación de conventos de monjas de vida contemplativa.* Mexico City: Editorial Cultura, 1959.

Davis, Natalie Zemon. "City Women and Religious Change." In *Society and Culture in Early Modern France,* ed. Natalie Zemon Davis. Stanford: Stanford University Press, 1975.

De la Maza, Francisco. *Arquitectura de los coros de monjas en México.* Mexico City: Instituto de Investigaciones Estéticas, Universidad Nacional Autónoma de México, 1973.

———. *Arquitectura de los coros de monjas en Puebla.* Puebla: Gobierno del Estado, 1990.

———. *San Miguel de Allende.* Mexico City: Instituto de Investigaciones Estéticas, Universidad Nacional Autónoma de México, 1939.

Demos, John. *Entertaining Satan: Witchcraft and the Culture of Early New England.* New York: Oxford University Press, 1982.

De Vos, Paula Susan. "The Art of Pharmacy in Seventeenth and Eighteenth-Century Mexico." Ph.D. diss., University of California at Berkeley, 2001.

Díaz de Gamarra y Dávalos, Juan Benito. *El sacerdote fiel, y según el Corazón de Dios. Elogio Funebre . . . a P. D. Luis Phelipe Neri de Alfaro.* Mexico City: Imprenta de la Biblioteca del Lic. D. Joseph de Jauregui, 1776.

———. *Ejemplar de Religiosas, Vida de la muy reverenda madre Sor María Josefa Lino* [sic] *de la Santísima Trinidad, fundadora del convento de la Purísima Concepción, en la ciudad de San Miguel de Allende, Obispado de Michoacán.* Mexico City: Imprenta Alejandro Valdés, 1831.

Eadie, Mervyn J. and Peter F. Bladin, *A Disease Once Sacred: A History of the Medical Understanding of Epilepsy.* Eastleigh, England: John Libbey, 2001.

Espejo, Beatriz. *En religiosos incendios.* Mexico City: Universidad Nacional Autónoma de México, 1995.

Evans, Albert S. *Our Sister Republic: A Gala Trip through Tropical Mexico in 1869–70.* Hartford, Conn.: Columbian Book Company, 1870.

Fabián y Fuero, Francisco. *Colección de providencias dadas a fin de establecer la santa Vida Común . . . en los cinco numerosos conventos . . . de Puebla de los Angeles.* 1769.

Fadiman, Anne. *The Spirit Catches You and You Fall Down: A Hmong Child, Her American Doctors, and the Collision of Two Cultures.* New York: Noonday Press, 1998.

Farriss, Nancy. *Crown and Clergy in Colonial Mexico, 1759–1821: The Crisis of Ecclesiastical Privilege.* London: Athlone, 1968.

Fisher, Lillian Estelle. *Champion of Reform: Manuel Abad y Queipo.* New York: Library Publishers, 1955.

Franco, Jean. *Plotting Women: Gender and Representation in Mexico.* New York: Columbia University Press, 1989.

Friedlander, Walter. *The History of Modern Epilepsy: The Beginning, 1865–1914.* Westport, Conn.: Greenwood Press, 2001.

Gallagher, Ann Miriam. "The Family Background of the Nuns of Two Monasterios in Colonial Mexico: Santa Clara, Querétaro, and Corpus Christi, Mexico City (1724–1822)." Ph.D. diss., The Catholic University of America, 1972.

García Cubas, Antonio. *El libro de mis recuerdos.* Mexico City: Editorial Porrúa, 1986 [1905].

García Ugarte, Marta Eugenia. *Breve historia de Querétaro.* Mexico City: Colegio de México, 1999.

Geiger, John Lewis. *A Peep at Mexico: Narrative of a Journey Across the Republic from the Pacific to the Gulf in December 1873 and January 1874.* London: Trubner and Co., 1974.

Gerhard, Peter. *México en 1742.* Mexico City: Porrúa, 1962.

Gibson, Ralph. *A Social History of French Catholicism, 1789–1914.* London, New York: Routledge, 1989.

Gilliam, Albert M. *Travels Over the Table Lands and Cordilleras of Mexico During the Years 1843 and 44.* Philadelphia: J. W. Moore, 1846.

Giraud, Francois. "Mujeres y familia en Nueva España." In *Presencia y transparencia: La mujer en la historia de México,* ed. Carmen Ramos Escandón et al. Mexico City: Colegio de México, 1987.

Gleason, Elizabeth G. "Catholic Reformation, Counterreformation and Papal Reform in the Sixteenth Century." In *Handbook of European History, 1400–1600,* ed. Thomas A. Brady et al. Leiden, New York: E. J. Brill, 1994.

Góngora, Mario. *Studies in the Colonial History of Spanish America.* Cambridge, England: Cambridge University Press, 1974.

Gonzalbo Aizpuru, Pilar, ed. *Familias novohispanas, siglos XVI al XIX.* Mexico City: Colegio de México, 1991.

———. *Las mujeres en la Nueva España: Educación y vida cotidiana.* Mexico City: Colegio de México, 1987.

González Sánchez, Isabel. *El Obispado de Michoacán en 1765.* Morelia: Gobierno del Estado, 1985.

Gunnarsdóttir, Ellen. "The Convent of Santa Clara, the Elite and Social Change in Eighteenth-Century Querétaro." *Journal of Latin American Studies* 33:2 (May, 2001).

Hansen, Ron. *Mariette in Ecstasy.* New York: Edward Burlingame Books, 1991.

Harline, Craig. *The Burdens of Sister Margaret: Private Lives in a Seventeenth-Century Convent.* New York: Doubleday, 1994.

Head, Thomas. "The Religion of the Femmelettes: Ideals and Experience Among Women in Fifteenth- and Sixteenth-Century France." In *That Gentle Strength: Historical Perspectives on Women in Christianity,* ed. Lynda L. Coon, Katherine J. Haldane, and Elisabeth W. Sommer. Charlottesville, Va.: University of Virginia Press, 1990.

Hernández, Jorge F. *La soledad del silencio: Microhistoria del Santuario de Atotonilco.* Mexico City: Fondo de Cultura Económica, 1991.

Herrejón Peredo, Carlos. "México: Las luces de Hidalgo y Abad y Queipo." *Caravelle: Cahiers du monde hispanique et luso-bresilien* 54 (1990).

Holler, Jacqueline. *Escogidas Plantas: Nuns and Beatas in Mexico City, 1531–1601.* Columbia University Press, electronic book, 2002.

Horta, Pedro de. *Informe Médico-Moral de la Peñosíssima y Rigorosa Enfermedad de la Epilepsia que a pedimento de la M.R.M. Alexandra Beatriz de los Dolores, dignisísima Priora del Convento de Religiosas del Glorioso y Máximo Doctor Señor San Gerónymo.* Madrid: Domingo Fernández de Arrojo, 1763.

Ibsen, Kristine. *Women's Spiritual Autobiography in Colonial Spanish America.* Gainesville, Fla.: University Press of Florida, 1999.

Jaramillo Magaña, Juvenal. *Hacia una iglesia beligerante: La gestión episcopal de Fray Antonio de San Miguel en Michoacán (1784–1804). Los proyectos ilustrados y las defensas canónicas.* Zamora: Colegio de Michoacán, 1996.

Kagan, Richard. *Urban Images of the Hispanic World.* New Haven, Ct.: Yale University Press, 2000.

Karlsen, Carol F. *The Devil in the Shape of a Woman: Witchcraft in Colonial New England.* New York: Vintage, 1989.

Landa Fonseca, Cecilia, ed. *Querétaro: Textos de su historia.* Querétaro: Instituto Mora, 1988.

Laserna Gaitán, Antonio Ignacio. "El último de reforma de los monasterios femeninos en el Perú colonial: El auto del arzobispado Parada de 1775." *Anuario de Estudios Americanos* 52:2 (1995).

Laven, Mary. *Virgins of Venice: Enclosed Lives and Broken Vows in the Renaissance Convent.* London: Viking, 2002.

Lavín, Mónica. *Dulces hábitos: Golosinas del convento.* Mexico City: Clío, 2000.

———. *Sor Juana en la cocina.* Mexico City: Clío, 2000.

Lavrin, Asunción. "El capital eclesiástico y las élites sociales en Nueva España a fines del siglo XVIII." *Mexican Studies/Estudios mexicanos* 1 (Winter, 1985).

———. "De su puño y letra: Epístolas conventuales." In *El monacato femenino en el imperio espanol: Monasterios, beaterios, recogimientos y colegios. Homenaje a Josefina Muriel,* ed. Manuel Ramos Medina. Mexico City: Condumex, 1995.

———. "Ecclesiastical Reform of Nunneries in New Spain in the Eighteenth Century." *The Americas* 22:2 (October, 1965).

———. "Espiritualidad en el claustro novohispano del siglo XVII." *Colonial Latin American Review* 4:2 (1995).

———. "Mexican Nunneries from 1835 to 1860: Their Administrative Policies and Relations with the State." *The Americas* 28:3 (1972).

————. "Problems and Policies in the Administration of Nunneries in Mexico, 1800–1835." *The Americas* 28:1 (1971).

————. "The Role of the Nunneries in the Economy of New Spain." *Hispanic American Historical Review* 46:4 (November, 1966).

————. "Unlike Sor Juana? The Model Nun in the Religious Literature of Colonial Mexico." *University of Dayton Review* 16:2 (Spring, 1983).

————. "Values and Meaning of Monastic Life for Nuns in Colonial Mexico." *Catholic Historical Review* 58:3 (October, 1972).

————. "La vida femenina como experiencia religiosa: Biografía y hagiografía en Hispanoamérica colonial." *Colonial Latin American Review* 2: 1–2 (1993).

————. "Women in Convents: Their Economic and Social Role in Mexico." In *Liberating Women's History*, ed. Bernice A. Carroll. Urbana, Ill.: University of Illinois Press, 1976.

Loreto López, Rosalva. *Un bocado para los ángeles: La cocina conventual novohispana.* Mexico City: Clío, 2000.

————. *Los conventos femeninos y el mundo urbano de la Puebla de los Angeles del siglo XVIII.* Mexico City: Colegio de México, 2000.

————. "La fundación del convento de la Concepción: Identidad y familias en la sociedad poblana, 1593–1643." In *Familias novohispanas, siglos XVI al XIX,* ed. Pilar Gonzalbo Aizpuru. Mexico City, Colegio de México, 1991.

Magray, Mary Peckham. *The Transforming Power of the Nuns: Women, Religion, and Cultural Change in Ireland, 1750–1900.* New York: Oxford University Press, 1998.

Malo, Miguel J., and F. León de Vivero. *Guía del turista en San Miguel de Allende, GTO.* Mexico City: N.d., n.p.

Martín, Luis. *Daughters of the Conquistadores: Women of the Viceroyalty of Peru.* Albuquerque, N.M.: University of New Mexico Press, 1983.

Mazín, Oscar. *Entre dos majestades.* Zamora, Mexico: Colegio de Michoacán, 1987.

McKnight, Kathryn Joy. *The Mystic of Tunja: The Writings of Madre Castillo, 1671–1742.* Amherst, Mass.: University of Massachusetts Press, 1997.

McNamara, Jo Ann Kay. *Sisters in Arms: Catholic Nuns through Two Millennia.* Cambridge, Mass.: Harvard University Press, 1996.

Mercadillo Miranda, José. *La pintura mural del Santuario de Atotonilco.* Mexico City: Editorial Jus, 1950.

Midelfort, H. Erik. *A History of Madness in Sixteenth-Century Germany.* Stanford, Calif.: Stanford University Press, 1999.

Monk, María. *The Awful Disclosures of Maria Monk, as Exhibited in a Narrative of Her Sufferings During a Residence of Five Years as a Novice and Two Years as a Black Nun, in the Hotel Dieu Nunnery in Montreal.* New York: Howe & Bates, 1836.

Morales, Francisco. *Clero y política en México (1767–1834): Algunas ideas sobre la autoridad, la independencia y la reforma eclesiástica.* Mexico City: Sep Setentas, 1975.

————. "Procesos internos de reforma en las órdenes religiosas, propuestas y obstáculos." In *Memoria del Primer Coloquio Historia de la Iglesia en el siglo XIX,* ed. Manuel Ramos Medina. Mexico City: Condumex, 1998.

————. "Mexican Society and the Franciscan Order in a Period of Transition, 1749–1859." *The Americas* 54:3 (1998).

Muriel, Josefina. *Conventos de monjas en la Nueva España.* Mexico City: Editorial Santiago, 1946.

Myers, Kathleen A. "A Glimpse of Family Life in Colonial Mexico: A Nun's Account." *Latin American Research Review* 28:2 (1993).

———, ed. *Neither Saints Nor Sinners: Writing the Lives of Women in Spanish America.* New York: Oxford University Press, 2003.

Myers, Kathleen A., and Amanda Powell. *A Wild Country Out in the Garden: The Spiritual Journals of a Colonial Mexican Nun.* Bloomington, Ind.: University of Indiana Press, 1999.

Núñez de Haro y Peralta, Alonso. "Nos el Dr. D. Alonso Núñez de Haro, y Peralta, por la Gracia de Dios, y de la Santa Sede Apostólica . . . a nuestras mui amadas Hijas en el Señor las RRMM Abadesas . . . y demas Religiosas de los diez sagrados Conventos de Calzadas . . ." 1774.

O'Malley, John. *Trent and All That: Renaming Catholicism in the Early Modern Era.* Cambridge, Mass.: Harvard University Press, 2000.

Ozment, Steven E. *When Fathers Ruled: Family Life in Reformation Europe.* Cambridge, Mass.: Harvard University Press, 1983.

Palacios, Felix. *Palestra Pharmaceutica Chymico-Galenica.* Madrid, 1706.

Paz, Octavio. *Sor Juana Inés de la Cruz, or The Traps of Faith.* Cambridge, Mass.: Harvard University Press, 1988.

El Pensador Mexicano, ed. José Joaquín Fernández de Lizardi (1812–1815).

Pietschmann, Horst. "Consideraciones en torno al protoliberalismo, reformas borbónicas y revolución. La Nueva España en el último tercio del siglo XVIII." *Historia mexicana* 41:2 (Oct.–Dec. 1991).

Po-Chia Hsia, R. *The World of Catholic Renewal, 1540–1770.* Cambridge, England: Cambridge University Press, 1998.

Ramos Medina, Manuel, ed. *Memoria del Primer Coloquio Historia de la Iglesia en el siglo XIX.* Mexico City: Condumex, 1998.

———. *Místicas y descalzas: Fundaciones femeninas carmelitas en la Nueva España.* Mexico City: Condumex, 1997.

———, ed. *El monacato femenino en el imperio espanol: Monasterios, beaterios, recogimientos y colegios. Homenaje a Josefina Muriel.* Mexico City: Condumex, 1995.

Rapley, Elizabeth. *The Dévotes: Women and Church in Seventeenth-Century France.* Montreal: McGill-Queen's University Press, 1990).

Reed, Rebecca. *Six Months in a Convent, or, The Narrative of Rebecca Theresa Reed, Who was Under the Influence of the Roman Catholics About Two Years, and an Inmate of the Ursuline Convent on Mount Benedict, Charlestown, Mass., Nearly Six Months, in the Years 1831–2.* Boston: Russell, Odiorne & Metcalf, 1835.

Relación del siglo XVIII relativa a San Miguel el Grande. Mexico City: Vargas Rea, 1950.

Reza Díaz, Julio. *Atotonilco.* Zamora, Michoacán: Impresiones Laser del Valle de Zamora, 2002.

Rhodes, Elizabeth. "Y Yo Dije, 'Sí Señor': Ana Domenge and the Barcelona Inquisition." In *Women in the Inquisition: Spain and the New World,* ed. Mary E. Giles. Baltimore, Md: Johns Hopkins Press, 1999.

Ringrose, David. *Madrid and the Spanish Economy.* [Online] Available: *http://libro.uca.edu/ringrose/Appendixd.htm.*

Romero, José Guadalupe. *Noticias para formar la historia y la estadística del Obispado de Michoacán.* Guanajuato: Gobierno del Estado de Guanajuato, 1992 [1860].

Roper, Lyndal. *The Holy Household: Women and Morals in Reformation Augsburg.* Oxford: Clarendon Press, 1989.

Salazar de Garza, Nuria. *La vida común en los conventos de monjas de la ciudad de Puebla.* Puebla: Gobierno del Estado, 1990.

Salvucci, Richard. "Aspectos de un conflicto empresarial: El obraje de Balthasar de Sauto y la historia social de San Miguel el Grande, 1756–1771." *Anuario de Estudios Americanos* 36 (1979).

Salzman, Mark. *Lying Awake.* New York: Knopf, 2000.

Sampson Vera Tudela, Elisa. *Colonial Angels: Narratives of Gender and Spirituality in Mexico, 1580–1750.* Austin, Tex.: University of Texas Press, 2000.

Sánchez de Tagle, Esteban. *Por un regimiento, el regimen: Política y sociedad. La formación del Regimiento de Dragones de la Reina en San Miguel el Grande, 1774.* Mexico City: Instituto Nacional de Antropología e Historia, 1982.

Santa Cruz, Francisco. *La piqueta de la Reforma.* Mexico City: Editorial Jus, 1958.

Sarabia Viejo, María Justina. "Controversias sobre la 'vida común' ante la reforma monacal femenina en Mexico." In *El monacato femenino en el imperio español: Monasterios, beaterios, recogimientos y colegios,* ed. Manuel Ramos Medina. Mexico City: Condumex, 1995

Scaraffia, Lucetta, and Gabriella Zarri, eds. *Women and Faith: Catholic Religious Life in Italy from Late Antiquity to the Present.* Cambridge, Mass., and London, Harvard University Press, 1999.

Soeiro, Susan. "The Social and Economic Role of the Convent: Women and Nuns in Colonial Bahia, 1677–1800." *Hispanic American Historical Review* 54:2 (May, 1974).

Sperling, Jutta Gisela. *Convents and the Body Politic in Late Renaissance Venice.* Chicago: University of Chicago Press, 1999.

Staples, Anne F. "La cola del diablo en la vida conventual: Los conventos de monjas del arzobispado de Mexico, 1823–1835." Ph.D. diss., Colegio de México, 1970.

Strode, Hudson. *Now in Mexico.* New York: Harcourt, Brace, 1941.

Super, John C. *La vida en Querétaro durante la colonia, 1531–1810.* Mexico City: Fondo de Cultura Económica, 1983.

Swain, Diana Romero. "One Thousand Sisters: Religious Sensibility and Motivation in a Spanish American Convent, Santa María de Gracia, 1588–1863." Ph.D diss., University of California, San Diego, 1993.

Taylor, William B. *Magistrates of the Sacred: Priests and Parishioners in Eighteenth-Century Mexico.* Stanford, Calif.: Stanford University. Press, 1996.

Tremebundo, "Quitada de Monjas y Frailes," October 29, 1833.

Tutino, John. *From Insurrection to Revolution: Social Bases of Agrarian Violence, 1750–1940.* Princeton, N.J.: Princeton University Press, 1986.

Voekel, Pamela. *Alone Before God: The Religious Origins of Modernity in Mexico.* Durham, N.C.: Duke University Press, 2003.

Von Germeten, Nicole. "Corporate salvation in a colonial society: Confraternities and social mobility for Africans and their descendants in New Spain." Ph.D. diss., University of California at Berkeley, 2003.

Walker, D. P. *Unclean Spirits: Possession and Exorcism in France and England in the Late Sixteenth and Early Seventeenth Centuries.* London: Scolar Press, 1981.

Wiesner, Merry E. *Women and Gender in Early Modern Europe*. Cambridge, England: Cambridge University Press, 1993.

Wright, A. D. *Catholicism and Spanish Society Under the Reign of Philip II, 1555–1598, and Philip III, 1598–1621*. Lewiston, N.Y.: Edwin Mellen Press, 1991.

Zahino Peñafort, Luisa. *Iglesia y sociedad en México, 1765–1800: Tradición, reforma y reacciones*. Mexico City: Universidad Nacional Autónoma de México, 1996.

―――, ed. *El Cardenal Lorenzana y el Concilio Provincial Mexicano*. Mexico City: Universidad Nacional Autónoma de México/Porrúa, 1999.

Zarri, Gabriella. "From Prophecy to Discipline, 1450–1650." In *Women and Faith: Catholic Religious Life in Italy from Late Antiquity to the Present*, ed. Lucetta Scaraffia and Gabriella Zarri. Cambridge, Mass., and London, Harvard University Press, 1999.

Zavala, Leobino. *Tradiciones y leyendas sanmiguelenses*. Mexico City: M.E. Zavalo de Campos, 1990.

Index

Page numbers followed by n *indicate Notes. Page numbers annotated with* t *denote tables.*

Note: The nuns' religious names have been entered alphabetically by the first name. See p. 62 for an explanation of the inclusion or, in some cases, omission in this text of the name María as the first part of a name in religion. Alternate versions of these names appear in the documentation and have been included parenthetically.

vida particular (the individual life), 184,
200, 202, 203–6
antipathy toward, 209, 210, 224, 249
imposition of, 184
justifications for, 205
in La Purísima, 209–12, 218n.58, 224,
236, 240, 249
Villegas, Vicar Juan de, 15
advice from the bishop for, 87–88, 90–
91
on Antonia del Santísimo
Sacramento, 67–68, 79
as intermediary, 61–62, 70
and Phelipa de San Antonio, 101, 102,
104, 119
and the rebellion in La Purísima, 81–
91, 127
Virgin of Guadalupe, 110, 131
Virgin of Loreto chapel. *See* Nuestra
Señora de Loreto chapel
Virgin Mary, as abbess, 30
visitation (*visita*)
documentation prepared for, 41–42
to La Purísima, 151, 156–58, 240, 244
private interviews with nuns during,
202–3, 250–51, 252
requests for, 87, 127–28
as solution to dissent in La Purísima,
87, 131, 132–33, 139, 143, 163–64
vocation
and cloister, 153
examination for, 22–23, 54n.6, 65–66

Voekel, Pamela, 7–8
vows, breaking, 229, 237

war
of independence (*see* independence)
with the United States, 244–45, 246
War of the Reform (Three Years War),
253, 263
Willis, Thomas, 106
witches, as possessed, 112, 145n.21
women
Catholic ideal of, 8
convents as necessary for, 9, 13, 28–
29, 44
18th-century perceptions of illness
among, 106
lay organizations for, 8–9, 220, 235
male clergy's disdain for, 62, 84, 85,
88, 90–91, 115, 128, 129, 133,
136
motivations among, for entering
convents, 64–66
obedience in, 26

Xaviera de la Sangre de Christo, 47*t*, 121,
137*t*

Ygnacia de San Juan Nepomuceno
(Ygnacia de Señor San Juan
Nepomuceno), 48*t*, 121, 137*t*
Yucatán, convent reform in, 155